"Jesus is Victor!"

Princeton Theological Monograph Series

K. C. Hanson, Charles M. Collier, and D. Christopher Spinks,
Series Editors

Recent volumes in the series:

Linda Hogan
Religion and the Politics of Peace and Conflict

David C. Mahan
*An Unexpected Light: Theology and Witness in the Poetry and Thought
of Charles Williams, Micheal O'Siadhail, and Geoffrey Hill*

Jeanne M. Hoeft
*Agency, Culture, and Human Personhood: Pastoral Thelogy
and Intimate Partner Violence*

Jerry Root
*C. S. Lewis and a Problem of Evil: An Investigation
of a Pervasive Theme*

Michael S. Hogue
*The Tangled Bank: Toward an Ecotheological Ethics
of Responsible Participation*

Philip Ruge-Jones
*Cross in Tensions: Luther's Theology of the Cross
as Theolgico-social Critique*

Charles Bellinger
The Trinitarian Self: The Key to the Puzzle of Violence

Gale Heide
System and Story: Narrative Critique and Construction in Theology

Kevin Twain Lowery
*Salvaging Wesley's Agenda: A New Paradigm
for Wesleyan Virtue Ethics*

"Jesus is Victor!"

The Significance of the Blumhardts for the Theology of Karl Barth

CHRISTIAN T. COLLINS WINN

PICKWICK *Publications* · Eugene, Oregon

"JESUS IS VICTOR!"
The Significance of the Blumhardts for the Theology of Karl Barth

Princeton Theological Monograph Series 93

Pickwick Publications
A Division of Wipf and Stock Publishers
199 W. 8th Ave., Suite 3
Eugene, OR 97401

www.wipfandstock.com

ISBN 13: 978-1-55635-180-8

Cataloging-in-Publication data:

Collins Winn, Christian T.

"Jesus is victor!": the significance of the Blumhardts for the theology of Karl Barth / Christian T. Collins Winn.

xxvi + 306 p. ; 23 cm. —Includes bibliographical references and index.

Princeton Theological Monograph Series 93

ISBN 13: 978-1-55635-180-8

1. Barth, Karl, 1886–1968. 2. Blumhardt, Johann Christoph, 1805–1880. 3. Blumhardt, Christoph, 1842–1919. I. Title. II. Series.

BX4827.B3 C56 2009

Manufactured in the U.S.A.

For Julie

Caritas sine fine est

Contents

Acknowledgments

THIS PROJECT WOULD NOT HAVE BEEN POSSIBLE WITHOUT THE GENER-ous assistance, patience, love, and prayer of many people. Dieter Ising, Gerhard Sauter, Jürgen Moltmann, and Bruce McCormack gave of their time and expertise in varied and crucial ways. I would also like to thank Hans-Anton Drewes and Amy Marga at the Karl Barth Archive in Basel, Switzerland, for assistance with questions about Barth's personal collection of Blumhardt writings.

Thomas Buchan, Peter Heltzel, Joel Scandrett, and Erik Panikian read drafts, gave encouragement, and provoked my thinking on a whole range of issues and topics while researching and writing. Their friendship often sustained me. I was also fortunate to receive helpful suggestions on the form and content of the Blumhardt chapters from Simeon Zahl.

A special word of thanks goes to Sister Ruth Rhenius, Trudy Zimmermann, and Charles Moore and the Brüderhof community without whose assistance with the many German sources consulted, the project would have been almost impossible. Sister Ruth's help was particularly invaluable as was her spiritual advice and counsel and her never-flagging hope. In many ways, she embodies the Blumhardts' conviction that "Jesus ist Sieger!" Charles Moore and the Brüderhof also deserve a special word of thanks for the generous gift that they contributed to the project in the form of the many pages of translated Blumhardt materials. I am grateful for their support and interest in this project and inspired by their example of universal hope, communal love, and the longing for justice.

I would like to thank the communities of the New Providence Presbyterian Church of New Providence, NJ, and the Eden Prairie Presbyterian Church of Eden Prairie, MN, for their financial and spiritual support during my doctoral studies. Their prayer and personal encouragement were always timely and cheerful.

I am also grateful to the members of my dissertation committee for their support, friendship, and guidance during my research and writing: Chris Boesel, Morris Davis, Frank Macchia, and Donald Dayton. Thanks especially to Chris Boesel for his guidance, friendship, and support as the committee chair. I would be remiss if I did not acknowledge the profound contribution of Donald Dayton. While I was still a seminary student, it was Dr. Dayton who initially suggested that I investigate the influence and significance of the Blumhardts for Barth's theology. His constant support, friendship, prodding, and genuine care for this project and its author were of such quality that I do not think it unfair to claim that I know what it means to have a *Doktorvater*. Thank you for the faith, hope, love, and time that you put into me; I will be forever grateful.

This project would never have begun, nor would it have reached completion without the constant love, warmth, laughter, patience, and compassion of my family. I would like to thank Tom, Jeanne, Christine, and Justin Winn, Geneva Guthrie, and John, Deb, Mimi, Geoff, and Paula Crumrine, for their emotional, spiritual, intellectual, and financial support through the many twists and turns taken during my doctoral work. Though I will try, I will never be able to repay your love.

Those with whom you live know you best. To my two boys, Jonah and Elijah, your love, joy, and laughter were always an inspiration. I look forward to being able to spend more time loving, learning, and laughing with you. For Julie, my constant companion to whom this work is dedicated, words simply cannot express what I owe to you. My life turned on our meeting, and in every turn since then your love and compassion have been like a lodestar. I hope you will accept this humble token of my love.

Finally, I give thanks to the living and risen Jesus Christ. My only hope is that in all my labors I will have been made to point to you whose love overcomes all things. Lord, have mercy upon us! Even so, come, Lord Jesus!

Introduction

The Problem and Thesis of this Study

KARL BARTH (1886–1968) IS WIDELY REGARDED AS ONE OF THE MOST important theologians of the twentieth century. His influence continues to reverberate out of the last century into our own context. Yet, to date no full-scale theological biography of Barth has been attempted. This is due, among other reasons, to the massive amount of literature that Barth himself produced, as well as to the extensive secondary literature that has been produced in response to him. Over both of these issues, however, there hovers the common conviction among interpreters that the meaning of Barth's theology for the modern (let alone the postmodern!) world has yet to be fully understood. This is due, in some part, to the complex dynamics and historical circumstances regarding the origins of what one recent interpreter called "The Barthian Revolt in Modern Theology."[1]

This uncertainty about the real importance of Barth's theology is also rooted in the thing itself, for it was of the nature of Barth to be always on the move. Thus many who had been caught up in the energy and power of Barth's earliest publications, the two editions of the *Römerbrief*,[2] were dismayed when they turned to Barth's later dogmatic works. A similar reaction can be detected among those who prefer Barth's *magnum opus*, the *Church Dogmatics*.[3] Among the latter, the response was often to dismiss Barth's early work as an aberration. Thankfully, these attitudes are now being cleared away by the work

1. This is the title of Gary Dorrien's fine study of Barth's theology published by Westminster John Knox in 2000.

2. The first edition appeared in December 1918, and the second, substantially revised edition appeared in 1922. The second edition was translated into English by Sir Edwyn Hoskins in 1932.

3. 14 volumes, translated by G. W. Bromiley; German original, *Kirchliche Dogmatik*.

of Bruce McCormack and others,[4] who have shown that the Barth of
the two editions of the *Römerbrief* is in substantial continuity with the
Barth of the monumental *Church Dogmatics*.

There are, however, major lacunae that still remain in our understanding of Barth's theology, and these in large measure have to do
with the question of Barth's many theological interlocutors. Over the
last sixty years, Barth's theology has been compared, in keeping with
established academic tradition, to the theological giants who preceded,
accompanied, and followed him. This method has proven both helpful and enlightening for understanding and highlighting many of the
distinct dynamics and innovations in Barth's theology. At least in the
Anglo-American context, however, this approach has not often been
balanced with concern for many of the actual theological interlocutors—
especially those of the nineteenth century—whom Barth engaged over
his long career. This is due in part to the fact that some of those whom
Barth chose to follow or to count as his theological forefathers are not
well known in the English speaking world, and, even if they were, many
of them would be the source of considerable embarrassment in academic circles. When one considers the nineteenth-century theologians
that Barth listed in 1927 as important for his theological journey, only
one could be considered well known: Søren Kierkegaard.[5] The others
are footnotes, at best, in many histories of theology in the nineteenth
century. However, there are two figures mentioned in the list who can
be shown to have influenced Barth in such a decisive fashion that it
would be hard to imagine Barth's early development without them. We
are speaking, of course, of the two Blumhardts, father and son, with
whose influence on Barth we will be occupied in this study.

The basic thesis and burden of this work is to demonstrate that
the life and thought of both Johann Christoph Blumhardt (1805–1880)
and Christoph Friedrich Blumhardt (1842–1919)—two Pietist pastors

---

4. See McCormack, *Karl Barth's Critically Realistic Dialectical Theology*.
McCormack's work is particularly indebted to Michael Beintker, *Die Dialektik in der
»dialektischen Theologie« Karl Barths*; and Ingrid Spiekermann, *Gotteserkenntnis*.

5. This list can be found in the foreword to Barth's *Die christliche Dogmatik im
Entwurf*, on page vi. Among his theological forefathers Barth includes, other than
Kierkegaard, the elder and younger Blumhardts, Isaak Dorner, Hermann Kohlbrügge,
Hermann Kutter, Julius Müller, Franz Overbeck, and August Vilmar. In most circles,
only Dorner, Overbeck, and to some extent Müller would be considered as "theologi-
cally important" figures worthy of study in their own right.

from the Württemberg region of southern Germany—were of decisive importance for Barth's theology. It will be argued that the many disparate themes and dynamics that are found within the theology of the two Blumhardts find their crystallization in their eschatology and that Barth's appropriation of this "Blumhardtian eschatological deposit" was fundamental to the development of his own theology. Furthermore, and contrary to much current scholarship on Barth, their theology and theological concerns, as seen above all in their eschatology, though critically reconstructed by Barth and thereby transformed, was not merely an episodic influence on him. Rather, the Blumhardts had a lasting, even life-long effect on Barth, such that their imprint can be detected in his mature theology.

"Who are These Blumhardt Characters Anyhow?"[6]

Though still largely unknown to modern theological scholarship, the Blumhardts have exerted substantial influence on the development of German theology in the twentieth century. Johann Christoph Blumhardt, often referred to as the elder Blumhardt, became famous in certain circles both within Germany and beyond because of events that unfolded in the small village of Möttlingen where he was the local pastor. According to church documents as well as eyewitnesses, for almost a two-year period from 1842 to 1843 Blumhardt found himself dealing with a purported case of demonic possession. One of his parishioners, Gottliebin Dittus, had approached him complaining of strange events happening in the night. Initially Blumhardt was repelled by the woman, but as he involved himself more and more deeply in her life and struggles he was confronted by troubling theological and spiritual realities for which he was ill-equipped. After two years of prayer and fasting, Bible reading and counseling, the struggle came to an end with the shriek of the alleged demonic power, who through the mouth of Dittus's sister confessed that "Jesus is the Victor!" This phrase would become the watchword and theological thematic for both Blumhardts in their respective ministries.

In light of what he had experienced in Möttlingen, Blumhardt would be led to rediscover certain themes in Scripture that he believed

---

6. This is the title of Vernard Eller's 1969 *Christian Century* essay in which he introduced the unknown Blumhardts to *Century* readers.

had long been suppressed. In effect, the Möttlingen conflict came to represent for Blumhardt a new "Word from the Lord" given for the larger church. It was not a discovery that Blumhardt had asked for or produced, but rather was forced upon him through his experience with Gottliebin Dittus. At the same time, this "new Word" was nothing other than that which the prophets and apostles had originally proclaimed: i.e., the present and active power of Christ Jesus the victor who overcomes the powers and principalities. He would interpret this new encounter with the gospel through the idiom with which he was most familiar, Württemberg Pietism. What he surmised was that God's work of transformation, or the sowing of "new birth" in humanity, was not simply a spiritual reality, but quite literally physical. That is, spiritual "new birth" was to be accompanied by God's healing work of transformation through "the miraculous" as signs of hope for the final transformation of all things. The presence of Jesus as the victor represented the ongoing struggle of the Lord to bring the new world of the kingdom of God visibly into history.

In light of these reflections, the phrase "Jesus is Victor" became shorthand for the inbreaking power of the kingdom of God to liberate humanity from spiritual *and* physical bondage. Blumhardt would develop these insights within the pronounced eschatological context of Württemberg Pietism. Drawing on the chiliastic hope for the kingdom of God, he argued that the healing powers experienced at Möttlingen were meant for the whole cosmos. The physically concrete events at Möttlingen were anticipations of the world transformation that the kingdom of God would historically instantiate. By linking the experience of healing and exorcism with a general or universal outpouring of the Spirit, Blumhardt gave the personal dimensions of Christian spirituality and piety a cosmic and eschatological horizon. In his counseling ministry, Blumhardt would constantly emphasize that one seeks healing not for immediate relief from suffering, but that one might become a sign of hope that God's final restoration of all things was approaching.

Though the elder Blumhardt would increasingly emphasize the social dimensions of the kingdom, it was his son Christoph who would develop this aspect fully. After his father's death in 1880, Christoph would carry on his father's ministry without much change. But by 1894, he had become so alienated from the churchly and pietistic culture of his environs that he chose to no longer be identified as a pastor. He ex-

pressed great dissatisfaction that the message of hope for the kingdom
that his father had developed had been turned into an excuse for people
to seek a blessed life with no concern for the groaning of humanity.
Rather, like his father, Christoph believed that the true goal of the kingdom was the transformation of the whole world: "We do not first want
to save ourselves and be satisfied with this, but we want to take to heart
the sighing of all creation, the lamenting and groaning of countless
human beings who are certainly not helped by our salvation, but who
are helped a great deal if we cry out and pray: 'Thy Kingdom come!'"[7]
Following the cosmic orientation of his father, Christoph began to turn
away from the church and churchly circles, and towards the needs he
discerned in society and the world.

Accompanying this turn was a reconsideration and re-contextualization of his father's message and experience.[8] In brief, Christoph
came to the conviction that though his father had recovered a hope for
the kingdom of God as made concrete in real physical transformation,
he had not seen that the full extension of this hope must include a vision of the transformation of the social conditions of humanity. While
for the elder Blumhardt, "Jesus is Victor" had implied the *healing of the
body*, for Christoph it implied the *healing of the body politic*, for at the
core of the gospel of Jesus Christ was a new vision of society: "if we
were to bring together all the words of Jesus and the apostles dealing
with the final purpose of human history, we would soon discover that,
in spirit, Jesus concerns himself with the political and social situation,
that his kingdom could not come or even be conceived apart from the
overthrow of the established order."[9] In contradistinction to his father,
Christoph began to envision the struggle with the powers and principalities in explicitly social and political terms. The powers against
which Jesus struggled, and over which he would triumph, were now the
structures that oppressed humanity and curtailed human flourishing.[10]

---

7. C. Blumhardt, *Eine Auswahl aus seinen Predigten*, II:89.

8. See Meier, *Christoph Blumhardt: Christ*, 35–44.

9. Eller, *Thy Kingdom Come*, 23–24.

10. "Christoph created a much more intimate relationship between God's miraculous deeds and those human efforts that God wills to use as signs and manifestations
of the coming kingdom. The direct enemy of humankind, according to Christoph,
represented, not an otherworldly demonic force, but those forces that attempted to
dehumanize humankind through social oppression. The miraculous in our midst was

Equally important was Christoph's more explicit identification of the kingdom of God with the person of Jesus Christ. In Jesus the kingdom had entered the world as a seed that was now growing. In Christ, God had begun to penetrate the whole universe, making his presence immanent, and extending an invitation to all to participate in his dynamic and liberative action in history and society. Jesus himself (i.e., the narrative shape of his life as seen especially in the Synoptics), became the objective basis and criteria for identifying where the kingdom was present in the world, struggling with the powers and principalities. Through this, the Pietistic and Evangelical emphasis on a "personal relationship with Jesus" was reconfigured to refer to one's participation with God in the struggle against injustice. In fact, for Christoph, the primary place where Jesus could be found was among the poor, the oppressed, and those struggling for justice.

When combined with his growing agitation with churchly circles, these insights would lead Blumhardt to publicly identify himself with the Social Democratic Party (SPD) in 1899, eventually serving as a representative of the party in the Württemberg *Landtag* from 1900 to 1906. In Socialism, Blumhardt believed that he discerned a hope for a transformed world that was remarkably similar to the hope that the kingdom of God represented, and because the established church had consistently aligned itself with the status quo, Blumhardt argued that the atheist Socialists were more Christian than the Christians. Naturally, Blumhardt's identification with the SPD and his public rebukes of Christendom would make him a pariah in most churchly circles, and he would even be defrocked, losing his pension.[11] But he would interpret his loss of ecclesiastical privileges as a gift from God, freeing him for work among the poor, whom he identified as the true locus of God's work in the world. He expressed this new relationship between the poor and God in a way that presages the later constructions of Liberation Theology:

> Do we want to follow Jesus on this way? Then we must accept
> him in this company. Then the call comes to us to set to work

---

the authentically human, not a participation in supernatural activity. Christoph never totally forsook an openness to supernatural occurrences. But neither did he restrict the divine activity to the realm of the supernatural and the unexplained." Macchia, *Spirituality and Social Liberation*, 166.

11. See Bentley, *Between Marx and Christ*, 29–31.

wholeheartedly, for *here* is Jesus. He himself, speaking about the time of his absence, does not say, "I was rich and you respected me." He says, "I was poor, I was hungry, I was thirsty, I was imprisoned, and you came to me, to the poor Savior. You came to me, who sat as a guest at the table of the lowest men. There you came to me." Here must be your whole heart; here you must do the deeds of faith; for it is from here that the power comes which will overthrow the world, the wretched, *unhappy world.*[12]

While in the *Landtag*, Blumhardt engaged in political debates on wage reform, tariffs, and transportation for the working poor. However, after only two years of work he began to have serious doubts, not about the ideals of Socialism, but rather about the practical platform and turbulent party politics he experienced during the violent debates over Eduard Bernstein's Marxist revisionism. Though he continued to stress that Socialism was a "sign" of God's kingdom, he would no longer be able to call it *the* "sign." Rather, it was a parable of the kingdom; limited in its correspondence to God's kingdom, but nonetheless a true *gnomon* or "pointer" to the coming kingdom of God, in which all things would be restored. Though he would remain committed to Socialism until his death in 1919, even remaining a member of the party and continuing to consult leading figures in Swiss Socialist circles, Blumhardt expressed what might be called a more realistic assessment of human attempts to bring the kingdom into the world: though they were an imperative, they were nonetheless flawed, awaiting the coming of Jesus to bring their hopes to fulfillment.

Though neither Johann Christoph nor Christoph Blumhardt understood or saw themselves as theologians, their own highly occasional and idiosyncratic ruminations on the nature of the kingdom of God, its relationship to Jesus, the Holy Spirit and history, as well as the recovery of the public and social dimension of Christian hope would spur and inspire many theologians in the twentieth century. This was most certainly the case with Karl Barth.

---

12. Blumhardt, *Auswahl*, III:342.

A Well-Known, but Not Well-Understood Relationship

The question of "theological influence" is a notoriously difficult relation to pin down. What does one mean by "influence"? Clearly it implies two terms and a relationship, but what is the nature of the relationship? Does "influence" mean a direct personal relationship, or a shared context or ethos, or perhaps a thematic dependence, or is it simply, for want of a better description, a shared theological orientation? Can theological influence only be detected at the outset of a theological program, like the flowing of a tributary into a river, or can it be discerned and located all along the way? Can the theological influence of one person on another be said to change not in terms of dissipation or increase, but in the terms of transformation, such that the one receiving the influence re-interprets, or re-constructs, that which they have already inherited? Can theological influence begin under the aegis of one thematic but later be found to have blossomed in a different locale? This rather pedestrian list of questions indicates that an analysis of the influence of the Blumhardts on Barth is no simple affair.

It is generally acknowledged that Barth was influenced by the Blumhardts in his break with theological Liberalism. Almost all of the interpreters of Barth's theology see the meeting between Barth and Christoph Blumhardt, which happened in April 1915,[13] as the decisive moment in his break with the Liberal theology that he had learned during his student years. Most interpreters recognize in the Blumhardts a particular kind of theological objectivism, which would form the basis on which Barth would be able to escape the anthropocentric theology of German Liberalism. There is also widespread agreement that Barth was influenced by the Blumhardts in his dialectical relationship to Swiss Religious Socialism. These acknowledgements, however, constitute the extent of engagement with the question of the Blumhardts' influence on Barth. This is problematic for Barth studies for at least two reasons.

First, it skews our understanding of Barth's *theological development*. Many of the most important interpretations of Barth concentrate solely on the early influence of the Blumhardts. They tend to see the Blumhardts influence primarily in the area of Barth's complicated relationship to Religious Socialism. Because Barth left Religious Socialism

---

13. See Busch, *Karl Barth: His Life*, 84–86 for a description of this encounter.

behind, many (perhaps unconsciously) surmise that the Blumhardts must also have been left behind, and were therefore a merely episodic influence on him. Unfortunately this line of inquiry ignores the persistent presence of the Blumhardts even up to the closing volumes of the *Church Dogmatics*.[14] Thus the theological significance of the Blumhardts for Barth is lost sight of, and a well-rounded picture of Barth's theological development is hampered.

Second, and related to our first point, ignoring Barth's discussion of certain Blumhardtian themes in the later volumes leads to a skewed understanding of some of Barth's *deepest theological intentions*. Though Barth discusses and engages the Blumhardts significantly during the formative stage of his theological development, it is in the later volumes of the *Church Dogmatics* where he engages most constructively and systematically the central themes of the Blumhardts. What is more, Barth does not slavishly repeat the Blumhardts' thoughts, but he makes their theological concerns his own, reconstructing and reconstituting them anew in ways central for his own theology. The presence of this late material gives weight to the thesis that the themes of the Blumhardts provided Barth with some of the most important elements of his theology. Their persistent presence as theological interlocutors makes plausible the presupposition that the Blumhardts' life and thought influenced Barth both in the deeper structures of his thought as well as in some of its thematics.

The Contributions of this Study

There are two major and two minor contributions that this study hopes to make. The first major contribution is that it seeks to introduce the Blumhardts' witness and the attendant theological categories produced by the same into Barth studies so that a deeper appreciation and fuller picture of Barth's theology can come into focus. All acknowledge that the Blumhardts were central characters in the development of Barth's theology; therefore a fuller exposure to their thought and its dynamics will only help to enhance and further illumine our understanding of Barth's own theology.

---

14. *Church Dogmatics* IV/3, 165–274, esp. 168–171. Hereafter abbreviated as *CD*; *The Christian Life: Church Dogmatics IV.4, Lecture Fragments*, 233–60, esp. 256–60. Hereafter abbreviated as *CL*.

The second major contribution is to clarify the extent of the Blumhardts' significance for Barth both in his early development and in his mature theology. Our study will show that the Blumhardts' watchwords "Jesus is Victor" and "Thy kingdom come"—which could be described as a pair of unsystematic, though inter-penetrating, summations of a dense and rich complex of dynamic theological thought and action—were central to Barth's rethinking of his theology in the early 1910s, and that the basic orientation developed during this period remained up into the late volumes of the *Church Dogmatics*. Barth's appropriation of Blumhardtian themes as well as his appeal to them as models for theological thinking and biblical interpretation shows that they were of great significance for his thought.

Our minor contributions are not addressed directly, but indirectly. The first minor contribution of this study is that if further confirms the basic thesis developed by Bruce McCormack. McCormack's work, *Karl Barth's Critically Realistic Dialectical Theology* successfully challenged the work of Hans Urs von Balthasar, who had argued that Barth's theology should be seen in two phases that are fundamentally at odds with one another. Von Balthasar posited a two-stage theory in which a "dialectical Barth" was placed over against a "dogmatic Barth." McCormack, following the work of other scholars, has successfully shown that this thesis is misguided, resting on a misunderstanding of Barth's doctrine of revelation. Though our study does not engage the doctrine of revelation or even dialectical methodology directly, by showing that the early influence of the Blumhardts did not wane, but was incorporated into the new context of the *Church Dogmatics*, further confirmation of the continuity between Barth's early and late theology is revealed.

The second minor contribution of this study is that it opens the question of the importance and influence of Pietism on Barth's theology. The Blumhardts' primary context and theological tradition was Württemberg Pietism. Though they were involved in a largely unselfconscious but complex negotiation with that tradition, they were still shaped by the dynamics, themes, and concerns of Pietism. The depth and extent of their influence on Barth thus inevitably raises the question of the influence of Pietism on Barth's theology. Of the two minor contributions, this one is rife with future possibilities for Barth studies.

The Challenge and Limitation Confronting this Study

There is a significant challenge and limitation that confronts our study.

The Challenge of Representing the Blumhardts' Theology

In his study of Christoph Blumhardt, Martin Stober notes that the younger Blumhardt was the source of inspiration for a variety of theological and ecclesial movements both within and without the church: "Frequently, completely different and opposite movements of theology and church took single aspects of his faith and thinking for themselves. Religious socialists or Pentecostals, Pietists or dialectical theologians— for all of them the Württemberg pastor and spiritual counselor had something captivating."[15] I highlight this observation, which is applicable to the elder Blumhardt as well, to illustrate obliquely some of the key challenges that confront an interpretation of the Blumhardts.

That the Blumhardts, both father and son, have proven to be such compelling figures to such a wide diversity of movements and theological perspectives is one of the results of the profound integration of life and thought, and of theology and ethics, in their thought. At the same time, interpreters of their thought are faced with a number of difficulties. For instance, many of their key theological motifs and themes are in dialectical tension with their opposites, giving their theology a dynamic tension but also causing problems when too much weight is given to one pole of the dialectic over against the other. Also problematic is the clearly detectible theological development within both Blumhardts and especially between them. Such issues can prove particularly challenging when trying to give an ordered presentation of their thought. However, there are three key areas where convergence must be noted: 1) the integration of life and thought; 2) the integration of theology and ethics; and 3) the continuity of the message of the father and the son. Here, we will discuss the first two in association with what might be called their "kerygmatic theology," while the latter will be mentioned briefly in isolation.

There are many challenges associated with attempting to give a coherent and systematic portrayal and analysis of the Blumhardts' theology. Perhaps the most important is doing justice to the peculiar form of

15. Stober, *Christoph Friedrich Blumhardt*, 7.

their theology. Their thought is best described as a form of "kerygmatic theology." That is, theirs is a theology developed and presented overwhelmingly in the form of proclamation and spiritual counsel. Whether in sermons, letters, songs, or even reflections on difficult questions or themes, though the reader is confronted with provocative theological themes and ideas, the same cannot be described as exclusively theoretical or abstract reflections. Rather, the theology of the Blumhardts exhibits the quality of a "witness" that must be experienced or narrated to be understood. This quality is, at least in part, the result of the integration of life and thought and theology and ethics.

Many commentators have noted that the kerygmatic quality flows from the profound integration of life and thought that can be seen in the Blumhardts' message. As Friedrich Zündel, the elder Blumhardt's biographer, notes, "Blumhardt's preaching was based on his experiences and hopes."[16] That is, both Blumhardts saw their *kerygma* as determined by an overwhelming sense that they had simply been commissioned as witnesses of the kingdom of God, quite apart from their control. At the base of both of their theologies was the Möttlingen "Kampf" and subsequent awakening movement, which we will discuss at length below. Both Johann Christoph and Christoph Friedrich saw these two episodes as objective events that had not been manufactured. As such both understood themselves as persons who had been commandeered and commissioned as "witnesses." They saw themselves always as messengers and actors, not as persons who had come to their insights about the kingdom of God through theological study, but rather as those who were compelled to serve as witnesses to the in-breaking kingdom that was coming to transform the world.[17] Though later the younger Blumhardt would emphasize the need to plead with God for further revelation,[18] the primary emphasis for both was always on the divine initiative that shaped the experiences associated with the Möttlingen "Kampf." Though their message bears the unmistakable stamp of the many disparate struggles and events that each passed through, the act-

---

16. Zündel, *Johann Christoph Blumhardt*, 256.

17. See Ising, *Johann Christoph Blumhardt*, 355. In reference to Christoph Blumhardt, see Groth, "Chiliasmus und Apokatastasishoffnung," 97–98.

18. This can especially be seen during the period of Christoph's reconsideration of his father's message (roughly 1890–1896), as portrayed in his *Damit Gott Kommt*.

ing, living God is always the primary subject and object to whom they attempt to point.

Aside from the integration of life and thought, another key aspect of their kerygmatic theology to note is the integration of theology and ethics. As we will show, the key themes of the Blumhardts' theology are crystallized in the watchwords: "Jesus is Victor!" and "Thy kingdom come!"

The first "watchword," intimately linked with the events at Möttlingen, referred to the reality of the in-breaking kingdom whose coming portended a new outpouring of the Holy Spirit and the transformation of all things that would find proleptic instantiations in the form of miraculous personal, physical and social transformation. Though not without precedent, the Blumhardts' proclamation of these and other themes always evidenced a profound integration of theology and ethics. The theological claims associated with the slogan "Jesus is Victor!" were always-already ethical claims where praxis was demanded in the form of prayer and action, waiting and hastening towards the coming of the kingdom.

Dieter Ising has argued in reference to the elder Blumhardt that the key themes were worked out in a "kerygmatic" form: "Blumhardt's further thoughts on 'Jesus is Victor' progress not towards a theological system, but are concerned about individual questions, which he is confronted with in his sermons and spiritual counsel."[19] The initial kernel insights expressed in the thematic slogan "Jesus is Victor" became for both the father and the son a new light by which to re-read Scripture, world history, and the cosmos. In the Blumhardts' writings and sermons, this re-reading of Scripture and reality is always accompanied by exhortation and practical guidance, through which their themes can meet a penultimate *telos*.

Here, the second watchword "Thy kingdom come!" becomes important, for the reality that Scripture points to, and which the Blumhardts believed they had experienced afresh in the events at Möttlingen, was not a static reality but living, active, and on the move. The risen Jesus is present as one who issues a summons and seeks faithful human parables. The basic form of faithful human action is the sigh for the kingdom: "Thy kingdom come!" At the base of many of their themes is

19. Ising, *Johann Christoph Blumhardt*, 348.

a dialectical tension between divine initiative and human response that can be highly suggestive and productive for theological reflection and ethical action.

The occasional nature of the Blumhardts' proclamation also requires sensitivity to development if one is to avoid the temptation to flatten out their highly original thought by simply deducing key principles. When this sensitivity is exercised, a developmental tension becomes evident in their thought. In fact, the obvious development found in the son over against his father raises the question of whether continuity or discontinuity should be the primary way to describe the thought of the son vis-à-vis his father. It is the conviction of this author that though there is significant discontinuity between the message of the father and the son, it is to be found within a far greater continuity. Thus, there is a challenge of how to bring often disparate or even conflicting themes into tension such that the productive energy in the Blumhardts' common *kerygma* can be retained and their theology grasped as a whole. Nonetheless, within the limitations of our project, the goal will be to faithfully render the original intentions and dynamism of the Blumhardts' thought by giving a coherent historical and thematic presentation that accounts for the developmental differences and dialectical tensions, while at the same time emphasizing the continuity in the theology of the Blumhardts.

The Limitation of Our Investigation

In what follows we will take as our guiding conviction that the Blumhardts were indeed significant theological interlocutors for Barth throughout his theological development. This conviction casts a wide net, since it assumes that the whole of Barth's theology has been affected in differing ways by his engagement with the Blumhardts. Though our study will explore and give good reason for accepting this conviction, it will not attempt to offer an exhaustive account of Barth's theological development in the light of the Blumhardts. Rather, our focus will be on illustrative examples that bear the imprint of the Blumhardts' deep influence on Barth.

To accomplish our goal we will limit our investigation to Barth's early engagement with the Blumhardts' thought from 1916 to 1919 and then turn our attention to the materials from the later volumes of the *Church Dogmatics*. By so doing, it will become clear that Barth found the impulse he had received from the Blumhardts early in his theological journey to be of continuing relevance and importance even as his long career came to a close.

The Outline of This Study

The outline of our study will proceed along the following course: In chapter 1, we engage many of the most significant and relevant interpreters of Barth's theology with our central presupposition in mind, expecting certain common themes to emerge that will guide our own investigation of the Blumhardts significance for Barth. The approach of the chapter is primarily analytical and it functions as an archeological investigation of the major interpreters of Barth with the goal of revealing the nature of the lacuna that our study seeks to address. As will be seen, the majority of Barth's interpreters are aware of the Blumhardts influence on Barth, but their awareness of this influence doesn't shape their interpretation of Barth, nor is it illuminating as to the Blumhardts' real significance for Barth's beginnings, development, and mature theological vision. At the same time, however, their initial thoughts, however perfunctory, can give some guidance about a direction of inquiry, as much because of what they don't say as what they do.

Chapters 2 and 3 constitute an outline of the life and thought of the Blumhardts. Both chapters contain an expository and a synthetic element. In the expository sections, the narrative histories of the two Blumhardts are developed and recounted in what might be described as a straightforward, even naïve, fashion. The reason for this is linked to one of the major goals of this study: to reintroduce the categories of the Blumhardts' theology into Barth studies. With this goal in mind it is appropriate to describe the Blumhardts' history in the fashion that Barth himself thought about the various events that had shaped their lives. Thus, there are many suggestive events and aspects of the narrative histories that are left undeveloped, because though Barth may have been aware of those dynamics, they did not become central to his own theological appropriation of their thought.

Weaved into the narrative flow are synthetic depictions and elaborations of many of the key themes developed by the Blumhardts. Thus, in these chapters the thought of the Blumhardts is presented in the flow of their lives enabling a coherent picture of their central theological insights and convictions. As will be seen, these convictions revolve around the theological themes "Jesus is Victor" and "Thy kingdom come."

In chapters 4 and 5, we focus on the early and mature theology of Barth to outline and reveal the influence and significance of the Blumhardts on Barth's theology. Chapter 4 is particularly concerned with exploring the Blumhardtian influence on Barth as he broke away from theological Liberalism and Religious Socialism. In this chapter, careful analysis and elaboration of key texts from Barth's early period (1916–1919) is combined with attention to contextual factors that help to illumine an overall theological dynamic: that Barth's new theological orientation after his break with theological Liberalism and Religious Socialism was in large measure shaped and inspired by the Blumhardts' theological vision.

In chapter 5 we focus primarily on the Blumhardtian themes that resurface in the late volumes of the *Church Dogmatics*. Our exposition assumes the undeniable presence of Blumhardtian themes, especially in *CD* IV/3 and in the unpublished *Christian Life* lecture fragments. Our primary goal here is to show the profound level of continuity that exists between Barth's appropriation, elaboration, and deployment of these themes and the Blumhardts' own understanding of the same. Through a close reading of key sections of the *Dogmatics* we show that Barth does not slavishly repeat the Blumhardts, but neither does his understanding evince a total and therefore disjunctive reinterpretation of the key Blumhardtian theologumena "Jesus is Victor" and "Thy Kingdom Come." Rather, Barth exercises a kind of loyal freedom in his re-interpretation and re-contextualization of the major themes of the Blumhardts. When seen together, our exposition in chapters 4 and 5 shows that during his early development and in his mature theology, Barth was substantively engaged with the theological themes and concerns of the Blumhardts. To our study we now turn.

1

The Understanding of the Blumhardt Influence in Barth Studies

Preliminary Remarks

THE INCLUSION OF AN ENTIRE CHAPTER ON THE VARIOUS INTERPRETATIONS of the Blumhardt influence on Barth should immediately alert one to the possible complexity of the problem at hand. As we noted in the Introduction, it is widely accepted that the Blumhardts were influential on Barth. The depth of their significance and importance for Barth's theology, however, has not been fully understood nor has it been explored to any great effect in Barth studies. This lacuna is revealed in large measure in what follows. At the same time, the explication of many commentators, however limited, can give some guidance about a direction of inquiry as much because of what they don't say as what they do. This is especially the case with two of our commentators. Thus, our engagement with these sources is not meant to be entirely negative, but will also provide some positive orientation for our own exploration of the Blumhardts' influence on Barth.

In what follows we will take as our guiding conviction the fact that the Blumhardts were indeed significant theological interlocutors for Barth throughout his theological development. This conviction, which our later chapters will show is no mere assertion, will guide our analysis of the various interpreters. It assumes that the whole of Barth's theology has been affected in one way or another by the Blumhardts. Because of this presupposition, we will be drawing across a wide spectrum of secondary sources. For the purpose of coherence, therefore, we will assume that these secondary sources fit loosely into three different categories with the understanding that these categories are relatively fluid and are being constructed in an *ad hoc* manner. These categories are: 1) historical/developmental studies; 2) studies of particular doctrinal loci and the interconnection of doctrine and ethics; and 3) Barth's relationship to socialism. To these we now turn.

Interpretations focusing on the Historical and Theological Development of Barth's Thought

Barth's break with Liberalism, coupled with the modern preoccupation with theological method, has led to a focus on Barth's theological development with the express purpose of understanding how he freed himself from the most dominant and influential theological tradition of the nineteenth century. Thus, some of the most influential studies of Barth have attempted to map the changes in his theology, particularly those that resulted in his break with Liberalism. This interest has also been accompanied by searching investigation into how Barth moved from his theological position as developed in the first *Römerbrief* to his later mature theology as found in the *Church Dogmatics*. These questions focus not only on content and substance, but also style and methodology. It is with the most well known of these historical and developmental studies that we will be dealing here.

Hans Urs von Balthasar

Some of the oldest and most well known interpretations of Barth's theology take almost no account of the Blumhardts' influence on Barth. This is certainly the case with Hans Urs von Balthasar's famous *The Theology of Karl Barth: Exposition and Interpretation.* Von Balthasar's work, originally published in 1951, was well received (even by Barth) and has been very influential, even down to the present day.[1] Though von Balthasar

---

1. For Barth's positive comments on von Balthasar's book, see Barth, *How I Changed My Mind*, 69–70; Though von Balthasar's central thesis that Barth underwent two "conversions" in his theology has been challenged by Bruce McCormack, it continues to exert substantial influence. For an example of this one need only see Graham Ward's, *Barth, Derrida and the Language of Theology*, in which Ward argues that the center of Barth's theology is the doctrine of analogy (14), a point that can only be seen as in continuity with Balthasar's interpretation. See von Balthasar, *Theology of Karl Barth*, 107. For a recent defense of von Balthasar's thesis against McCormack, see Reinhard Hütter, "Between McCormack and von Balthasar," 105–9.

does not include a discussion of the Blumhardts, it is still worthwhile to include him if for no other reason than the dominance his interpretation has exerted over Barth studies. This influence has in part been due to the fact that von Balthasar argued for the ecumenical relevance of Barth's theology and that he explicitly sought to engage Barth from a sympathetic, though not uncritical, Roman Catholic position.[2] This ecumenical agenda helped to shape von Balthasar's own exposition of Barth and led him to focus almost exclusively on Barth's theological methodology in an attempt to show the near rapprochement between Barth and Catholicism.[3] Von Balthasar's belief was that Barth's theological methodology (shaped, according to von Balthasar, in large measure by his study of Anselm in 1930–1931),[4] was pushing his theology much closer to Catholic formulations, thereby holding within it the promise of a possible theological reconciliation between the two western traditions of Protestantism and Catholicism. Though von Balthasar's aim was admirable and fruitful,[5] it did not necessarily lead to a proper exposition of Barth's theology, for it focused too much on questions that were more in the background for Barth—i.e., those related to methodology.[6] In von Balthasar's exposition of the specific content of his theology, Barth is portrayed as concerned primarily with working out the methodological implications of his "turn to analogy," which von Balthasar argues occurred in the 1930's. Barth's Christocentrism is read as a vehicle for developing his more basic commitment to the analogical relationship

2. For a discussion of the ecumenical significance of Barth's theology for Catholic theology, see Lamirande, "Impact of Karl Barth," 112–41.

3. As von Balthasar says, "We have in Barth, then, two crucial features: the most thorough and penetrating display of the Protestant view and the closest rapprochement with the Catholic. On the one hand, we have the fullest and most systematic working out of the contrasts that distinguish Protestant and Catholic views: not merely in individual doctrines, even less in merely historical or psychological or even cultural perspectives, but in a strictly *theological* structure. That is why dialogue with someone else might seem more promising than with Barth. On the other hand, he formalizes these contrasts in such a way that occasionally the form almost dissolves in the content, so that the Protestant aspect seems reducible to a 'corrective' or a 'dash of spice' lending piquancy to the Catholic dough" (23).

4. For von Balthasar's thesis on the significance of Anselm, see von Balthasar, *Theology of Karl Barth*, 143–45. For Barth's study of Anselm, originally published in 1932, see Barth, *Anselm, Fides Quaerens Intellectum*.

5. See Lamirande, "Impact of Karl Barth," 112–14, 119–34.

6. See McCormack, *Karl Barth's Critically Realistic Dialectical Theology*, viii.

that supposedly exists between God and man. This would seem to be a reversal of Barth's own approach, which was to place methodological questions in the service of the specific theological content that was being discussed at any one time.[7] Thus, Barth's methodology was far more *ad hoc* than von Balthasar's thesis allows.

Our concern here, however, is with the role of the Blumhardts in Barth's theology, and it should come as no surprise that von Balthasar does not mention these figures. When von Balthasar does turn to consider the influences that helped shape his theology, the central figures are those associated with German Idealism (i.e., Kant, Hegel, and Fichte) as well as Schleiermacher and Kierkegaard. There are a number of probable factors that would lead von Balthasar to this interpretation of Barth's theological origins. The first has to do with the peculiarities of von Balthasar's own Catholic context. As a Catholic theologian, von Balthasar would have undoubtedly been schooled under the assumption that theology needs philosophical presuppositions for its own constructive work. Thus, an investigation into the philosophy most likely to have affected Barth—German Idealism (especially neo-Kantianism)—would have been a matter of course. Second, and closely related, is the simple fact that von Balthasar's preoccupation with Barth's theological method would have naturally required an investigation into the philosophical sources that contributed to it. Finally, von Balthasar was probably unfamiliar with many of the lesser-known figures that Barth wrestled with, especially in his early development. Thus, not only is there no mention of the Blumhardts, but J. T. Beck, Johann Bengel, Friedrich Oetinger, J. C. K. von Hofmann, G. L. Mencken, and Kohlbrügge are all ignored in favor of Schleiermacher and Kierkegaard (with scant reference also to Feuerbach and Overbeck). Again, this lack of knowledge is probably due to the overly philosophical thrust of von Balthasar's interpretation.

The influence of von Balthasar's interpretation of Barth's work may in fact account for much of the lack of understanding of the Blumhardts role in shaping Barth's theology. Because he chose to focus

7. Barth's "loose" approach to methodological questions can be seen from his 1921 statements about Kierkegaard's "infinite qualitative distinction" (*Epistle to the Romans*, 10) all the way up to his discussion of what exactly he means by "Christological" thinking (i.e., Christocentrism) as found in the *CD* IV/3.1, 174–75. These statements do not point to a person who doesn't care about methodology, but rather one who seeks from the subject matter itself the proper theological methodology appropriate to the task at hand, rather than the other way round.

on questions of philosophical influence, his interpretive scheme lacked the categories to give an account of how Barth was related to some of the more radical elements of the nineteenth century, among whom we must include the Blumhardts. This will not be the case in many of our other interpreters.

G. C. Berkouwer

Our next interpreter, G. C. Berkouwer, also received attention, and praise, from Barth for the "goodwill and Christian *aequitas*"[8] found in his 1956 monograph, *The Triumph of Grace in the Theology of Karl Barth*. Berkouwer's work is important for a number of reasons, not the least of which is that it also constitutes an attempt to read the whole of Barth's theology in the light of a central theological or methodological principle, namely "the triumph of grace." This is sharpened when we realize that the principle Berkouwer discerns in Barth comes very close to the impulse Barth received from the Blumhardts in their slogan "Jesus is Victor." Barth himself noted this fact in his rebuttal to Berkouwer's interpretation in *Church Dogmatics* IV/3.1: "He has well seen my initial and constant concern to display the superiority of God and His saving will and Word and work over the ruinous defensiveness and rejection, over the power of chaos, which meets Him on the part of the creature."[9] Barth's critique of Berkouwer, and that which ultimately divides them, is that they are focusing on two different realities. For Barth, and this is decisive, the emphasis is on the *person*, "Jesus Christ," so much so that he is "not dealing with a Christ-principle, but with Jesus Christ Himself as attested by Holy Scripture."[10] Whereas for Berkouwer, the emphasis appears to be on the *principle* of "grace" as determined in "the eternal counsel of God."[11] Despite this difference, which in the end is decisive, there is agreement that Barth is primarily concerned, "that from the very first, at every point, and therefore in this question too, we should take with unconditional seriousness the fact that 'Jesus is Victor.'"[12]

---

8. *CD* IV/2, xii.

9. *CD* IV/3.1, 173–80, esp. 174.

10. *CD* IV/3.1, 174.

11. Berkouwer, *Triumph of Grace*, 381; Berkouwer's work was originally published in Dutch in 1954.

12. *CD* IV/3.1, 175.

Thus, Berkouwer has put his finger on one of the central impulses of Barth's theology, which Berkouwer argues is inextricably linked with the Blumhardts.[13]

In light of this insight, as well as Berkouwer's belief that Johann Christoph Blumhardt's theology represented for Barth an essential "break with the entire consciousness-theology of the 19th century," it is remarkable that only two pages are given to a discussion of the Blumhardts' theology.[14] Even more remarkable is the fact that Barth believed that Berkouwer had misunderstood him because, among other reasons, "the story and influence of the Blumhardts have not yet penetrated effectively the very Calvinistic environment to which he owes his development."[15] Thus, even though Berkouwer saw the Blumhardts as one of the fountainheads of Barth's theology, which he read as working out the central principle of the "triumph of grace," at least according to Barth, he had not understood them correctly, and because of this, he had not understood Barth correctly.

In much the same way as with von Balthasar, this is due in part to Berkouwer's context. As Barth pointed out, Berkouwer's Dutch Reformed context had conditioned him to think that theology was the working out of certain basic *a priori* principles.[16] In contrast to von Balthasar, these principles did not have to be philosophical in nature, but they were, nevertheless, determinative for the explication of the content of theology. In Berkouwer's particular case it was probably the logic of the Reformed stress on the "divine decrees" as found in the doctrine of predestination, which led him to surmise that Barth was also assuming an *a priori* principle (i.e., the triumph of the principle of grace) which in turn formed both the basis and goal of the whole of Barth's theology.[17] We are not concerned here to delve much further into the actual

13. Berkouwer, *Triumph of Grace*, 45.

14. Ibid., 45–46.

15. *CD* IV/3.1, 175.

16. *CD* IV/3.1, 174–76.

17. As Barth says, "Perhaps he cannot do so because he is more deeply rooted than I am in the older Reformed tradition which would have it, on what are thought to be good biblical grounds, that already in the doctrine of election we have a principle which has priority over the person and work of Jesus Christ, so that Jesus Christ is to be understood only as the mighty executive organ of the divine will of grace, and only a secondary place can be given to Christological thinking" (*CD* IV/3.1, 175). For a good description of the theology of the "divine decrees," see Heppe, *Reformed Dogmatics*, 133–49.

content of this debate, but simply to point out that Berkouwer, and he is not alone here,[18] misunderstood the nature of the Blumhardtian "Jesus is Victor" motif and therefore, (according to Barth himself!) misunderstood Barth's theology.[19]

Hans Frei

Our next commentator, Hans Frei, never published his 1956 dissertation, "The Doctrine of Revelation in the Thought of Karl Barth, 1909 to 1922: The Nature of Barth's Break with Liberalism." Nonetheless, this did not diminish its influence, since Frei was a central figure in what has come to be known as the "Yale School" of Post-Liberalism, a peculiarly American school of theology. Though this school was shaped more by Frei's other works, *The Eclipse of Biblical Narrative* and *The Identity of Jesus Christ*, his interpretation of Barth seeped into the collective consciousness of those students who came under the sway of Post-Liberal theology.[20]

Though Frei's work focuses on the doctrine of revelation, it is essentially a developmental study interested in the process by which Barth extricated himself from Liberal theology. He posits a two-stage theory for Barth's development, which consisted of a dialectical period, begin-

18. I am thinking here of the recent, very fine work of John C. McDowell. McDowell's work, which will be discussed further below, is one of the best explications of Barth's eschatology available in English. However, he too misunderstands the "*Jesus ist Sieger*" of the Blumhardts, and, in the end, claims that Barth's eschatology is too "triumphalistic." See chapter 8 of McDowell, *Hope in Barth's Eschatology*.

19. It should be pointed out here that there may be another dynamic which underlay Berkouwer's critique of Barth. It is important to note this, since Berkouwer's critique, as we shall see, resurfaces in different interpreters of Barth. It is quite possible that what is of utmost concern for Berkouwer is not that Barth's theology is over-determined by an abstract principle (i.e., the "triumph of grace"), but that the implications of such a principle would seem to lead necessarily to universalism. When Berkouwer's critique is recycled by other commentators, it is more often than not, this concern, rather than a concern about the nature of sin, that seems to be the motivation behind its use.

20. This can be seen in the work of, among others, George Hunsinger, who essentially recapitulates Frei's dissertation at the beginning of his essay, "Toward a Radical Barth," in *Karl Barth and Radical Politics*, 181–233. Bruce McCormack contends that Frei's dissertation has gone on to exercise a far more salutary influence on Barth interpretation through Hunsinger's later work. See McCormack, "Beyond Nonfoundational and Postmodern Readings of Barth, part 1," 67–95, esp. 71–84; and idem, "Beyond Nonfoundational and Postmodern Readings of Barth, part 2," 170–94, esp. 189–90.

ning in 1915, and an analogical shift that culminates in 1931.[21] Frei is clearly echoing von Balthasar's developmental thesis.

His dissertation is important here because he offers one of the most comprehensive engagements with the question of the Blumhardts influence on Barth in English. Furthermore, according to Frei's thesis, the Blumhardts, along with other "biblical realists," constitute the primary tradition in which Barth stands after his break with theological Liberalism up to 1929–1931. Within Frei's taxonomy of nineteenth-century theology, the Blumhardts find themselves included in a group that Frei calls the "biblical realists."

In Frei's understanding, biblical realism was an essentially non-academic, non-formal theological tradition, which read the Scriptural narratives in the Bible as realistic narratives, within the framework of something akin to the *heilsgeschichtliche* approach developed in the covenant theology of Johannes Cocceius (1603–1669), though without concern for questions of theological method.[22] This way of reading the Scriptures was accompanied by—and modified through—the eschato-logical realism (or chiliasm) found in Württemberg Pietism, with its attendant stress on the social aspect of the kingdom of God and its vision of the unity of body and soul.[23] The witness of the Scriptures points to a God who works in the world "realistically." If this was the case *then*,

---

21. Frei, "Doctrine of Revelation," iv–v.

22. As Frei notes, "Unlike the other traditions we have mentioned—skepticism, relationalism, and idealism—Biblical realism has no distinct methodological convictions. Instead, it represents an outlook and mood which each of its adherents has to recreate for himself in terms of his own thought-forms, mental and spiritual patterns. Biblical realism derives a connected system of Christian thought and interpretation as immediately as possible from the exegesis of scripture. Usually this systematic framework is historical, i.e., a factual-historical interpretation of Heilsgeschichte. The climax and consistently urgent motive of this historical system is the factually understood eschatological event which is about to come upon us all. The urgency of this event derives as much from the command to 'go therefore and make disciples of all nations' as from the fact that he who issued this command is himself active, in complete independence from the human instruments through which he fulfills his gracious purpose" (ibid., 488–89). For a discussion of Cocceius's theology, especially his understanding of the relation between God and history, see Asselt, *Federal Theology*, 197–302.

23. Frei is quite explicit about linking "biblical realism" with Württemberg Pietism. When speaking about the "biblical realists," Frei says, "The group we are about to consider is, with one notable exception (Hermann Friedrich Kohlbruegge), associated with the tradition of Wuerttemberg Pietism, a tradition with which both Mencken and Beck had considerable affinity" ("Doctrine of Revelation," 387).

why should it not be the case *now*? The "biblical realists" argued that if God was at work in the Scriptures in a "realistic" fashion, so too must he be at work in the world here and now. Thus, their piety emphasized *Reichsgottesarbeit*, or "kingdom work," which aimed at the amelioration of suffering and the humanization of the world in preparation for the coming of Christ.

The role of the Blumhardts and the group of men that Frei includes as "biblical realists" (Mencken, Beck, Kohlbrügge, Kutter, Ragaz, etc.) was to provide the eschatological content and realistic approach to the scriptural narratives that, during Barth's early development, gave the inner core of his thought its orientation and verve, despite the shifting forms that constituted the differences between the first and second *Römerbrief*. Thus, biblical realism (i.e., Württemberg Pietism) is for Frei that which links together the first and second *Römerbrief*.[24] This is in contrast to a number of scholars (including Barth himself!) who have argued that one of the elements that differentiates the second *Römerbrief* from the first lay in the formers perceived movement away from Beck and Württemberg Pietism.[25] But Frei believes that it was the eschatological and biblical realism that Barth learned from the "biblical realists," and above all from the Blumhardts, which provided the content for both the first and second *Römerbrief* and therefore gives them a greater continuity even in discontinuity. As Frei himself says, "there can be no doubt whatever that it is by recapturing this tradition—in contrast to the liberalism of his earlier days—that one finds that continuity between the first and second edition of Der Roemerbrief, upon which Barth has so stoutly insisted, despite the fact that the two editions are obviously unalike (even to him!) both in form and (perhaps) in content."[26] A more ringing endorsement for the importance of the

---

24. Frei: "It is in regard to 'ultimate intention' that Barth stood and stands in the tradition of Biblical realism" (ibid., 488).

25. This is the opinion of among others: Eberhard Busch, *Karl Barth and the Pietists: The Young Karl Barth's Critique of Pietism & Its Response*, 80–81; Jürgen Moltmann, *The Coming of God: Christian Eschatology*, 18; and Hendrikus Berkhof, *Two Hundred Years of Theology: Report of a Personal Journey*, 185-198; for Barth's comments, see his *Karl Barth/Rudolph Bultmann Letters, 1922-1966*, 155.

26. Frei, "Doctrine of Revelation," 494.

theological influence of the Blumhardts would be hard to find.[27] There are, however, some problems and one key limitation with Frei's thesis.

According to Frei, the "biblical realists," "with one notable exception (Hermann Friedrich Kohlbruegge), [were] associated with the tradition of Württemberg Pietism, . . ."[28] For Frei, this means that "Johann Christoph Blumhardt is the central figure in this movement." Upon closer inspection, one finds that it is really the thought of the Blumhardts (especially as they are interpreted by Barth), which gives shape to Frei's understanding of what "biblical realism" is. This is problematic primarily because it exposes the artificiality of the descriptor "biblical realism." The Blumhardts would have never described themselves as "biblical realists" in the way that perhaps J. T. Beck would have. In regard to the Blumhardts' relationship to Barth, this becomes problematic because it obscures those aspects of the Blumhardts' thought that fall outside the realm of the artificial category "biblical realism." If we are to understand the Blumhardts' influence on Barth, then we need to develop categories that can do justice to the Blumhardts' thought independently of Barth.

Frei comes close to this in his identification of "biblical realism" with Württemberg Pietism. However, he does not fully understand the dynamics of this form of Pietism and therefore cannot do justice to certain aspects of the Blumhardts' thought. For instance, Frei notes that Württemberg Pietism was essentially located within the state church.[29] While this is partly true, there were significant strands of this tradition that were just as separatistic as other forms of Pietism. This is certainly the case with the separatist Korntal settlement, with which both Blumhardts had extensive dealings. This is important primarily because separatists tended not to identify the kingdom of God with the church.

---

27. This quote was preceded by the following qualifier: "Nor do we want to speak here of a simple genetic 'descent' of Karl Barth. While his background is largely conservative and, by his own admission, more closely related to conservative than liberal thinkers, he has always sought to maintain his independence over against both tendencies. There is no thought here to absorb Barth into the cross-sectional lines of those who went before him. If we say that Biblical realism gave Barth a good deal of the content of his theology, we mean by this an affinity for a certain type of unpietistic, realistic, and heilsgeschichtliche tradition in scriptural exegesis. Many men could partake of this common tradition, and yet each could remain within it as a creative thinker" (ibid., 493–94).

28. Ibid., 387.

29. Ibid., 388.

Thus, even though they might shun "the world," they were also more open to the possibility that God was at work outside of the state church. The non-identification of the kingdom of God with the church is readily discernible in both Blumhardts, and Christoph Blumhardt's "turn to the world" during his phase of socialist engagement becomes more easily comprehensible when this fact is taken account of. The separatist impulse also enabled both the elder and the younger Blumhardt to be highly critical of the church.[30]

This has ramifications for our understanding of Barth, because both of these tendencies can be discerned in his theology, at least in its earliest phase. Indeed, Barth relates an encounter with Christoph Blumhardt in which he inferred from Christoph's critique that the only path open to him was to leave the church. But Christoph counseled against such an idea saying, "remain in the church and become a pastor. The church needs pastors that have hope for her and for the world."[31] Though Christoph's counsel reveals that his critique of the church was always for the sake of the church, nonetheless, the sharpness of the critique is incomprehensible without reference to the separatist impulse found in the context of Württemberg Pietism, and Barth's own lifelong distinction between the church and the kingdom is more easily understood in the light of the Blumhardtian influence. Frei's analysis lacks the categories to illumine these particular dynamics.

Frei also argues that there were no *schwärmerisch* (i.e., enthusiastic, spiritualistic, visionary) elements in Württemberg Pietism. This is false, since one of the early significant elements of the Pietism of this region was the work of the "Inspired," a group of lay preachers who often had visions and other ecstatic spiritual experiences, and who could

---

30. Though Johann Christoph Blumhardt stood essentially within the tradition of Bengel in asserting that Pietism must be lived within the state church, one has to keep in mind that he was eventually run out of the very same due to the various events associated with the Möttlingen "*Kampf*" and revival. This led Johann to a more independent relationship vis-à-vis the church and the various pietistic groups he had been associated with before the Möttlingen experiences. Christoph, following the logic of his father's initial independence, was even more critical of the state church. See Ising, *Johann Christoph Blumhardt*, 343; for Christoph, see Lim, *'Jesus ist Sieger!'*, 64. See also Macchia, "The Secular and the Religious," 60–61.

31. Barth and Thurneysen, *Suchet Gott, so werdet ihr Leben!*, 170. For a comparison of Barth and Christoph Blumhardt's critique of the church, see Sauter, *Theologie des Reiches Gottes*, 238–51.

certainly be described as *schwärmerisch*.[32] This is problematic for an understanding of the Blumhardts, because Frei's conception of "biblical realism" puts more weight on the role of the Scriptures, while, at times, not paying sufficient attention to the element that was most important to the Blumhardts: the role of the Holy Spirit in illuminating the reader of Scripture.[33] The role of the Spirit was so emphasized by Christoph that it often led him to some controversial positions.

Christoph was not at all afraid to assert that in certain instances, the Bible was wrong. This brought down on him the condemnations of many of his colleagues, not the least that of his friend and colleague Friedrich von Bodelschwingh (1831–1910), and certainly fueled his own peculiar construction of universalism.[34] At the same time, however, it gave Christoph the freedom he needed to move into solidarity with the world as represented in the socialist movement.[35] It cannot be denied that in both of these elements—i.e., universalism and solidarity with the world—Barth was influenced by Christoph, even if he did not adopt the same attitude toward Scripture.

Finally, Frei's dissertation is limited primarily because it deals only with the early phase of Barth's theological career. As you will see, this will be a repeated criticism of many of the studies in this section. In fact, the dissertation itself was completed before the publication of *Church Dogmatics* IV/3, arguably the volume most strongly influenced by the Blumhardts. Frei, however, does seem to leave open the possibility that

---

32. For a discussion of the role of the "Inspired" in the beginnings of Württemberg Pietism, see Ward, *Protestant Evangelical Awakening*, 163–73.

33. As Lim notes about Christoph, "He is much more concerned with 'beholding God,' by which one senses something of God and is touched by God. The reader of the Bible will become captivated by the living God; and in reverse the authority of the Bible becomes evident" (*'Jesus ist Sieger!'*, 95).

34. As Lim describes it: "Understanding God's Word this way, Blumhardt takes the liberty to contradict several thoughts in the Bible, which contradict God's relationship to the world. These are e.g. the idea of wrath and condemnation. They contradict God's love for the world. He also does not agree with some of the Apostle Paul's expressions. He criticizes his development of God's wrath in the letter to the Romans . . ." (ibid., 97–100, esp. 98). See also Stober, *Christoph Friedrich Blumhardt*, 237. For a good introduction to von Bodelschwingh see Crowner and Christianson, *Spirituality of the German Awakening*, 333–62. A more hagiographical introduction can be found in Bradfield, *Good Samaritan*.

35. Lim, *'Jesus ist Sieger!'*, 68–71.

Barth's later theology, at least in content if not form, was still shaped by the "biblical realism" that he ascribes to the Blumhardts.[36]

Joachim Berger

Joachim Berger's massive 1956 dissertation, written under the tutelage of Heinrich Vogel, "Die Verwurzelung des theologische Denkens Karl Barths in dem Kerygma der beiden Blumhardts von Reich Gottes" constitutes the most substantive single engagement with the questions with which we are concerned. It is the only book-length study on the topic of the influence of the Blumhardts on Barth. Concentrating on Barth's early theology (1915–1924), Berger does an admirable job of highlighting many of the substantive similarities in theological methodology and content between Barth and the Blumhardts, analyzing their theologies separately and then offering a lengthy and detailed comparison in a final section. Berger's work gives serious weight to our thesis that Barth was substantially influenced by the kerygmatic theology of the Blumhardts. His central thesis is that Barth's theology is "rooted" (*verwurzelt*) in the *kerygma* of the two Blumhardts. This image implies two dialectically related insights that are developed especially in the final section. First, Barth's theological imagination was fired in a decisive fashion by the proclamation of the Blumhardts, such that he can be seen as the theological heir of the Blumhardts—appropriating, correcting, and extending the deepest insights of their theology.[37] Second, Barth's development of the Blumhardts' thought is not a slavish repetition, nor even a specific service to a "Blumhardtian" theological tradition. Rather, like the growth of a new vine out of the same root, it is a decidedly independent development with its own aims, methods, and conclusions. It is genuine theological reconstruction. Berger develops this two-fold thesis first by briefly analyzing the textual evidence in Barth's early corpus and then by extending this analysis out to a broader consideration

36. For what else could Frei mean when he says, "It is in regard to 'ultimate intention' that Barth stood and *stands* in the tradition of Biblical realism" ("Doctrine of Revelation," 488 [emphasis mine]; see also, 487–504)?

37. Berger goes so far as to describe this as an "arch" that extends from the *kerygma* of the elder Blumhardt, through the changes found in the younger, to the final development of their thought in Barth's so-called "dialectical" phase exemplified by the second edition of the *Römerbrief.* See Berger, "Verwurzelung des theologische Denkens Karl Barths," 365.

of similarities and differences between Barth and the Blumhardts in the material content and formal structure of their respective theologies.

Berger begins with an assessment of three key early works in which Barth directly engages the life and thought of the Blumhardts. These include the 1916, "Action in Waiting for the Kingdom of God";[38] the 1919 essay, "Past and Future: Friedrich Naumann and Christoph Blumhardt,"[39] written upon the death of Christoph; and the very important 1920 "Unfinished Questions for Theology Today" in which Barth compares the thought of Blumhardt and the atheist church historian Franz Overbeck.[40] Berger's analysis of these early writings yields four conclusions.

First, Berger notes that all three of these works reveal that Barth paid careful attention to the Blumhardts' thought, especially that of the son; and that he was not merely an observer of their theology, but was also personally moved by them.[41] Indeed, Berger's second point develops this notion further as he points out that by Barth's own admission, his early theology should be considered deeply indebted to the Blumhardts. The literary evidence for this is found in the preface to the reprint of Barth and Thurneysen's *Suchet Gott, so werdet ihr Leben!* There, they seek to explain the inclusion of "Action in Waiting for the Kingdom of God" (a review of Christoph Blumhardt's *Hausandachten*[42]) in the new edition. Barth and Thurneysen note that they have chosen to include this review because it sheds light on the theological debt that they owe to Christoph Blumhardt. Furthermore, and important to Berger, is the fact that their relationship to Blumhardt, "was not disrupted, as we continued on"[43] and thus, the dialectical theology of Barth and Thurneysen should not be seen as a break, but rather an extension of some of the central insights developed by Blumhardt.

In his third point, Berger clarifies the nature of the dependence of Barth on the Blumhardts. His basic contention is that Barth's relationship cannot be understood as a straightforward literary or spiritual

38. English translation in *Action in Waiting*, by Barth and Blumhardt, 19–48.

39. English translation in *Beginnings of Dialectical Theology*, 35–45.

40. English translation in *Theology and Church*, 55–73.

41. For the following, see Berger, "Verwurzelung," 332–39.

42. C. Blumhardt, *Haus-Andachten nach Losungen und Lehrtexten der Brüdergemeinde.*

43. Barth and Thurneysen, *Suchet Gott*, 2.

dependence. Rather, it is a relationship of appropriation and reconstruction. There is genuine difference even in the similarity, and theological resonance in forceful creativity. This insight receives further clarification in Berger's final point that especially in light of his essay "Unfinished Questions for Theology Today," which was a review of Franz Overbeck's *Christentum und Kulture*, Barth can be seen engaging other key figures who give him the conceptual tools to take the positive eschatological insights of the Blumhardts and put them to use in creative and independent ways, thereby contributing to a new theological starting point. In Overbeck, Barth saw the negative counterpart to Blumhardt, who along with the same must be heard and taken equally seriously if a way forward was to be found for theology. Thus, "Barth combined the message of the Blumhardts with the knowledge of other theologians, and thereby expanded and deepened it."[44]

Berger's textual analysis gives way to a broader inquiry into the similarities and differences between Barth and the Blumhardts in the material content and formal structure of their respective theologies. The material content of Barth and the Blumhardts is ordered according to some of the classical *loci* of systematic theology: sin, soteriology (in both its objective and subjective dimensions), Christology, eschatology, Christian ethics, and the kingdom of God. Despite some differences, there is a common underlying theme that shows up in Berger's analysis of the various *loci*: the centrality of eschatology.[45] "It can be clearly felt through the expressions of the Blumhardts that it is in eschatology where their original concerns are verbalized. The same observation can be made about Barth's convictions."[46] For example, the depth and reality of sin are seen not through a consideration of an abstract notion of original sin nor through the deleterious effects of human sin on humanity and creation (though both have a more actualistic notion of sin); rather, in the view of the eschatological judgment aimed at its eradication, the depth of the problem of sin is revealed and the ultimate intention and nature of God's judgment is revealed as reconciling rather than destructive.

---

44. Berger, "Verwurzelung," 339.

45. Berger seems only to be implicitly aware of this interconnection as he leaves it relatively undeveloped.

46. Ibid., 347.

Similarly, Berger argues that Barth and the Blumhardts understand the objective dimension of soteriology in the light of the universal reconciliation intended for the whole inhabited earth, which has been inaugurated and completed in the Reconciler, Jesus Christ. The Christology of both is summed up in the conviction that in Jesus, "The Kingdom of God has become actual, is nigh at hand."[47] The completed work of redemption will add nothing to the actuality of the reconciliation effected in Jesus Christ, but will be the full disclosure and transformation of creation in the living light of the resurrection, which reveals the cross as the fulfillment of the eschatological judgment and subsequent liberation of humanity and creation.[48] Berger notes that in distinction from the Blumhardts, though not in contradiction to them, even in this early period Barth has already linked eschatology with protology, such that his doctrine of election as seen in the second *Römerbrief* roots the completed work of redemption back in the intention of God for creation as determined in the eternal counsel of God.[49] "Election and rejection," though still undeveloped at this point as compared to the later deliberations in *Church Dogmatics* II/2, are a protological way of speaking about the eschatological judgment and new creation actualized in the history of Jesus and revealed in his resurrection.[50]

Likewise, the subjective dimension of salvation is described as the eschatological impossible possibility that has dawned in the resurrection of Jesus Christ, and which is now mediated through the Holy

47. Barth, *Epistle to the Romans*, 30; see also Berger, "Verwurzelung," 344–46.

48. It should be noted that this interpretation is decidedly shaped by Barth's theology, since it is highly questionable whether the Blumhardts' had thought through the relationship between their eschatological Christology (Jesus=the kingdom of God) and the idea that in his person, as the kingdom of God, God's eschatological judgment had been enacted and completed. This is especially the case for the elder Blumhardt, who believed that God's eschatological judgment was still future. Though questionable as to the Blumhardts' understanding, this is certainly one of the directions that Barth took their theology. For the elder Blumhardt, see for instance J. C. Blumhardt, *Blätter aus Bad Boll*, 4:218–19.

49. Berger, "Die Verwurzelung," 342. See also Barth, *Romans*, 117–18, 132–35, 415; see also idem, *CD* II/2, 3–506 passim.

50. "The kingdom of God means to the Blumhardts: the concern is about God Himself, God appoints what happens to His world, and He carries it out on earth. The same conclusion is developed in Barth, which comes in the direct connection of the kingdom God and the doctrine of predestination: God's will alone decides, and if God wills something, it also occurs" (Berger, "Verwurzelung," 361).

Spirit. The Christian can neither create the possibility for knowledge of God and salvation, nor possess it, but only receive it as a gift and hope in it as a promise that moves towards its fulfillment.[51] Christian ethics is also developed by both Barth and the Blumhardts along the lines of hope for the kingdom of God.[52] These constructions place the emphasis on the work of God, even in the subjective realm, such that synergism is ruled out.[53]

Other connections can also be discerned in the formal loci of eschatology and the kingdom of God. For instance, both Barth and the Blumhardts refuse to comment on what the eschaton will be like, considering such speculation dangerous and unwarranted. Both placed an emphasis on the redemption of this world, such that, "creation will be redeemed, man does not enter heaven, rather, heaven comes to man who becomes a citizen of the kingdom of God."[54] Berger also notes the commitment of both to the *apokatastasis ton panton*—which contributes to the interweaving of eschatology, Christology, and soteriology—and the addition of protology in the case of Barth. The reconciliation effected in Jesus Christ, the establishment of the kingdom of God, is the salvation of the whole world intended by God from the beginning. At the same time, Berger notes some differences between Barth and the Blumhardts, especially regarding the developmental dynamic in the Blumhardts' notion of the kingdom of God and the central role of the Holy Spirit.

51. "Because the world is the world, and time is time, and men are men, and so long as they remain what they are, my new life must exist 'beyond' them; as the deadly and incommensurable power of the Resurrection, my new life presses upon my *continuing in sin*, and, as the criticism of my temporal existence and thought and will, determines also its meaning and significance.... Grace, then, is not a human possibility for men by the side of which there is room for such other possibilities as, for example, sin. Grace is the divine possibility for men, which robs them, as men, of their own possibilities" (Barth, *Romans*, 195, 200).

52. Ibid., 457; see also Berger, "Verwurzelung," 356–60.

53. Importantly, Berger notes that the Blumhardts were far more ambivalent about human cooperation with God than was Barth. This was especially so in the case of the younger Blumhardt, who during his so-called third period (1896–1906) came close to identifying struggle for the kingdom of God with struggle for social justice as exemplified by Social Democracy. Thus, human cooperation and struggle was in some sense constitutive of the coming of the Kingdom. In Berger's interpretation, however, Christoph sought to rectify this during his fourth phase (1906–1919), emphasizing the distinction between all human constructions and work and the coming kingdom of God. See ibid., 347, 349.

54. Ibid., 349.

According to Berger, the Blumhardts conceived of the kingdom of God as a living reality that moved the world toward its final end, embracing both this world and the world to come. This led the Blumhardts to speak of the kingdom as the "organic" work of God to bring the world to its intended goal. Though Barth would have agreed with the spirit of the Blumhardts conception, Berger notes that by his so-called "dialectical phase" (1920–1924), Barth saw a danger in such constructions because they ran the risk of identifying immanent this-worldly realities and possibilities, like Religious Socialism, with the transcendent and trans-historical other-worldly kingdom of God, which breaks into the world as a *novum*.[55] According to Berger, this danger was made evident at times during the third phase (1886–1906) of the younger Blumhardt, in which struggle for the kingdom of God was over-identified with the struggle for social justice.[56] Berger interprets the younger Blumhardt's fourth phase (1906–1919) as motivated by a desire to rectify the over-identification of the kingdom of God with this-worldly endeavors. Berger implies that this motivation is what led Christoph to withdraw from party politics during the later period of his life.

In accounting for this difference between Barth and the Blumhardts, Berger is not forced to leave the Blumhardtian sphere to search for another influence. This is because Berger argues that, at least during the early phase of Barth's theological development (1915–1924), he was most decidedly shaped by the thought of the younger Blumhardt as exemplified in his fourth phase, a phase that was more concerned to emphasize the *diastasis* between the kingdom of God and all human work. Thus, Berger surmises that the distinction between Barth and the Blumhardts here is relative rather than absolute.

Berger also notes a difference in the conceptions of the eschatological role of the Spirit in Barth and the Blumhardts. In the Blumhardts, the eschatological outpouring of the Spirit of Pentecost was a signal

55. In his brilliant discussion of Barth's genetic development between *Romans I* and *Romans II*, Bruce McCormack argues that there is a shift from a "process eschatology" to a "consistent eschatology." This shift could also be described as a shift from a developmental model to a more static "time-eternity" construction. As McCormack shows, however, the former was never meant to construe the kingdom of God as a this-worldly possibility, but always as an "other-worldly" possibility actualized by God's work in Christ such that the latter is no more static than the former. See his *Karl Barth's Critically Realistic Dialectical Theology*, 141–55, 180–82, 245–80.

56. See note 53 above.

that the kingdom was about to dawn in its final cosmic form. This is one of the central concerns and emphases of the elder Blumhardt, even in distinction from his son. According to the elder Blumhardt the Spirit will be poured out again—importantly, "on all flesh"—in a kind of "second Pentecost" whereby the eyes of the blind will be opened and the ears of the deaf made to hear. Through this direct act of God, the world will be prepared to receive the coming kingdom of God. For the elder Blumhardt, this second outpouring of the Spirit was also meant to begin the work of extending the victory of Jesus over death through the occurrence of the miraculous. These miraculous works were understood *primarily* as "signs of the coming kingdom," but the elder Blumhardt was sufficiently ambivalent about their function such that they could be understood as in some way contributing to or even being constitutive of the coming kingdom of God. The younger Blumhardt retained this conception, though he downplayed the underlying theology of history on which the conception of a "second Pentecost" was built and became progressively suspicious of the miraculous as more than a "sign" of the kingdom. The outpouring of the Holy Spirit, however, retained a central place for the younger Blumhardt and was conceived as a work that would contribute to the work of redemption by extending and revealing it to the whole of creation.

According to Berger, the idea of a final outpouring of the Spirit or "second Pentecost" is absent from Barth and though the "miraculous" is not necessarily denied by Barth, it is of little importance. Despite these differences, Berger detects a more fundamental agreement. For both, the work of the Spirit represents God himself acting in his creation to bring about the desired end of the knowledge of God's reconciling and redeeming act in Jesus Christ, the kingdom of God come on earth. According to Berger, both the Blumhardts and Barth emphasize, "that no new work of God is done through the Spirit, but alone through Him God's work of reconciliation and redemption becomes man's very own."[57] Likewise, for both Barth and the Blumhardts, the universal de-

---

57. Berger, "Verwurzelung," 351. "But one thing may be said of both with certainty: they both see the Spirit as *God Himself* at work, who continues and reveals His work in Christ. This work of God through the Spirit helps itself by the effective means, which related entirely to the work of God in Christ and bring this home to man, making it understandable; the Holy Scriptures, the human proclamation of the Word of the Holy Scriptures, man's celebration of the sacraments installed through the Holy Scriptures" (351–52).

termination of God is for a new heaven and a new earth, which means the restoration of creation. Thus, salvation is healing and healing is salvation, an insight that implicitly affirms the miraculous.

Finally, Berger turns to a comparison of what he calls the formal structure of the theologies of Barth and the Blumhardts. By "formal structure" Berger means the theological epistemology that shapes the material content of their respective theologies. His argument is that both share a similar theological epistemology that moves around the twin foci of actualism and realism, but that each begins from a different starting point: Barth from actualism, the Blumhardts from realism. Furthermore, it is Berger's contention that Barth's beginning point is more fundamentally in line with the Blumhardts' theology than their own starting point, the implication being that Barth's position represents a needed corrective to the Blumhardts'.

Berger is quite murky in his use of these terms, but he says enough for one to grasp his central point.[58] Actualism refers to the act of God that makes possible our knowledge of the true God, while realism refers to the reality of the God who acts. According to Berger, actualism is more objectivistic and seeks to understand the truth of God from God's perspective, arguing that only the God who acts to establish knowledge of himself in the world can be the real God. Realism is more intuitive, rooted in the fact that there is a real God, but that the reality of God only becomes known through his actions in the world.

To begin from the perspective of realism is thus to affirm an innate knowledge that there is a "real" God. It thus implies a human possibility or "point of contact" within humanity, or the forgotten memory of the "real," to use Platonic imagery. Though this point of contact may be innate, it necessarily requires the acting God to transfigure and fulfill it. It is thus dialectically related to actualism. To begin with actualism is to begin with the utter incapacity of humanity to know God. Whatever "innate" knowledge we have is utterly incapacitated by sin and therefore useless so that the knowledge we have is not the knowledge of God, but of the No-God. It is idolatry. Therefore, unless God acts, His reality will not be known; and conversely, because He acts He is the real God. As

---

58. Berger does not comment on or develop the ontological grounding for either of these epistemological motifs. But it is clear that his relatively undeveloped reflections would resonate with the more detailed analysis of these concepts given by George Hunsinger in his *How to Read Karl Barth*, 30–32, 43–49.

can be seen, each is mutually constitutive of the other and Berger argues that both Barth and the Blumhardts, though departing from their different starting points, arrive on the shore of the other.[59] Thus, in Barth, actualism leads necessarily to realism, while the Blumhardts' realism leads necessarily to actualism.[60]

It was the act of the true or "real" God at Möttlingen that had inaugurated the Blumhardts' ministry and theology.[61] This event called into question many of their own preconceived notions of who the "real" God is, how this God works, and where He works. According to Berger, the younger Blumhardt began more and more to move in the direction of actualism through his conviction that the kingdom of God was at work in the world, especially in the great social upheavals of the late nineteenth and early twentieth centuries. Barth took up this conception of the kingdom of God as the act of the true God and after a brief flirtation with Religious Socialism, re-rooted it even more firmly in Christology than Christoph had. This shift, in Berger's view, is what allowed the Blumhardts' kerygmatic theology of the kingdom of God to become the basis for an objective and scientifically oriented theology.

There is a great deal to be learned from Berger. His analysis of Barth's early *oeuvre* provides a number of helpful insights, though they need further development and explication. His comparison of the material content and formal structure of the respective theologies of Barth and the Blumhardts' also brings out the deep continuities between their theologies. Above all, his analysis points to the seminal influence that the Blumhardts' eschatology and concept of the kingdom of God had on Barth in a way that is almost unequalled in the secondary literature. That the kingdom of God has broken into this world in the life, death, and resurrection of Jesus Christ and is continuing to move forward through history towards its final universal revelation was the theological vision of the Blumhardts and became that of Barth, at least during the early phase of his theological development.

59. "These common factors reduce the difference between Barth and the Blumhardts for the idea of God, to the question: is the true God standing in the center of theology, He who reveals Himself to man by His deeds, or is the acting God, who by so doing becomes the determining reality, the center of theology" (Berger, "Verwurzelung," 371)?

60. Ibid., 370.

61. See chapter 2, subsection "The Outpouring of the Holy Spirit," for a discussion of this.

We would be remiss if we did not note some of the problematic aspects of Berger's work. I will briefly highlight two. The first is that Berger's method of explication does more to obscure than to clarify, because it forces the Blumhardts' kerygmatic theology into the categories of systematic theology, which necessarily leads to some distortion. Discussing the Blumhardts highly idiosyncratic, lyrical, aphoristic, and kerygmatic theology in terms of sin, soteriology, Christology, etc., is a method that is simply unable to do justice to the constant interweaving of themes evident in their thought and the role of experience and existential struggle by which they arrived at their theological insights. Gerhard Sauter notes that this does not necessarily lead to a "misinterpretation" of the themes, but certainly to a misunderstanding of their intention.[62] Whether or not that is the case, Berger's analysis does favor the more systematically structured theology of Barth, such that in his desire to show continuity between Barth and the Blumhardts, it seems clear that a misreading of the Blumhardts is at work. Two examples of this should be considered.

The first is the question of the relationship between the kingdom of God as embodied and present in Jesus and the event of eschatological judgment. In Barth these two things are almost synonymous.[63] In the

62. This distinction is difficult to make sense of since the intention and meaning of a specific theological theme are usually closely related. Meaning would seem to refer to the coherent use and identifiable content of a key theological theme in a given context, while intention would seem to imply the direction or movement intended by the deployment of that theme. The former, the meaning, seems to be more open to mutability and change, while intention appears to be rooted in a more basic orientation or direction along which multiple meanings for a single concept or theme could be organized or made coherent. Rather than misunderstand the intention, Berger's method seems more prone to misunderstanding the meaning of given theological concepts or themes as found in the literature of the Blumhardts. See Sauter, *Theologie des Reiches Gottes*, 238.

63. Consider the following: "The new Day which has dawned for men in the resurrection, the Day of Jesus Christ, this—according to my gospel—is the Day that ushers in the transformation of all time into eternity. This is the Day when the *secrets of men* are laid bare and it is revealed that men are known by God. *Through Jesus Christ* men are judged by God. This is their KRISIS, but it is both negation and affirmation, both death and life. In Christ there has appeared an end, but also a beginning, a passing to corruption, but also a becoming new; and both are for the whole world and for all men. For the Redeemer who has been manifested in Christ is the Creator of all things. There is no residue. In Christ, high and low, the just and the unjust, after they have received the same command to halt before the unknown God, have the same access to

Blumhardts the relationship was never systematically thought through, allowing for statements that placed the judgment still in the future and statements that placed it in the past in the event of the cross.[64] Despite Berger's intentions, this ambivalence in the Blumhardts is lost sight of because of the need for a tidy systematic comparison. Likewise, the contribution of the Spirit to the work of redemption was not systematically developed in the Blumhardts so that Berger's contention that for both Barth *and the Blumhardts,* "no new work of God is done through the Spirit, but alone through Him God's work of reconciliation and redemption becomes man's very own,"[65] requires a highly tendentious reading of their *corpus.* There are places where this position can be found, but there are also places where the work of the Spirit is seen as adding something to the work of Christ, especially in the elder Blumhardt.[66] Furthermore, Berger's analysis of the formal structures of the theologies of Barth and the Blumhardts is also anachronistic and skewed towards Barth's systematic concerns, since the formal categories of actualism and realism were unknown to the Blumhardts. All these examples raise a very important question that has no easy answer and will confront our own interpretive work: Is Berger's thesis about the importance of the Blumhardts for Barth based on a misreading of the Blumhardts themselves, a reading that one could describe as "Barthian"?

Another limitation of this work is that it does not move the investigation beyond Barth's so-called "dialectical phase," which Berger marks as ending in 1924, just before the first lecture cycle in dogmatics given at Göttingen from 1924 to 1925. In this, his work shares in the same limitation we noted with Frei and will find with Jüngel, to whom we are about to turn. Though we cannot fault Berger for choosing to delimit his area of inquiry, it is nonetheless problematic for our understanding of Barth and the Blumhardts since the period discussed is well before Barth published *Kirchliche Dogmatik* IV/3 in 1959, or the posthumously published lecture fragment *The Christian Life.* These sources are significant because together they contain the most mature

---

the Father. ALL flesh is as grass; and it is the will of God that ALL should be saved (i. 16, iii. 29, x. 2)" (Barth, *Romans,* 69).

64. For the former, see J. C. Blumhardt, *Die Verkündigung,* 62–64; for the latter, see C. Blumhardt, *Vom Reich Gottes,* 66–67.

65. Berger, "Verwurzelung," 351.

66. See J. C. Blumhardt, *Verkündigung,* 69–75.

and explicit discussion of the Blumhardts in the whole of Barth's theological corpus. Berger's investigation, therefore, represents a good start which, when its limitations are recognized, can prove instructive for further research, but it does not show, because it does not intend to show, whether the Blumhardts were more than a merely episodic influence on Barth's theology.[67]

Eberhard Jüngel

Our next commentator, Eberhard Jüngel, studied with Barth at Basel and is an important systematic theologian in his own right. His article "Von der Dialektik zur Analogie," was the first study to successfully challenge the two-stage theory of von Balthasar.[68] The alternative offered by Jüngel was to argue that Barth's break from Liberal theology in 1915 was the only break he experienced in his theological development. After this initial break, the emphasis must be placed on the continuity of Barth's thought, rather than on the discontinuity, as Balthasar had done by contrasting the dialectical and analogical modes of theological thinking found respectively in the young and mature Barth.

Another study more directly related to our concerns was included in the same book in which Jüngel's ground-breaking study appeared.[69] This article focused on "Barth's Theological Beginnings" and includes a discussion of the Blumhardts' role in Barth's theological development during the 1910's and 1920's. The essay itself is broken down into three parts, focusing on what Jüngel calls, "three convictions that emerged," before Barth moved into his formal dogmatic stage.[70] These include: 1)

67. To be fair, Berger acknowledges this point in the final section of his dissertation. However, he goes on to argue that he believes that Barth's development since the 1920's took the path it did because of the initial influence that the Blumhardtian theology had on him: "Barth, who began in *this* manner, who came into *such* contact with the Blumhardts' message, *had to*, sooner or later, on whatever dangerous and obscure way, end *there* where he stands today [1955]" ("Verwurzelung," 388)!

68. Eberhard Jüngel, "Von der Dialektik zur Analogie," in idem, *Barth–Studien*, 127–79. For an outline and analysis of Jüngel's thesis, see McCormack, *Karl Barth's Critically Realistic Dialectical Theology*, 5–7.

69. "Barth's Theological Beginnings," in Jüngel, *Theological Legacy*, 53–104.

70. Ibid., 53. Jüngel's thesis about Barth's break with Liberalism allows for various shifts in methodological style within an overall continuity of theological content and intention. Thus, Jüngel also offers a three-fold schema for tracking Barth's development: 1) beginnings to 1919; 2) dialectical theology to *Münster Dogmatics* of 1927; 3)

theology as an "impossible possibility"; 2) theology as a kind of "herme-neutical meta-criticism"; and 3) theology as the "theory of praxis." We will focus here on the first.

Jüngel's argument is that Barth came to the conviction that theology is an "impossible possibility"—which nonetheless is established through the self-speaking of God (*the* impossible as far as human intention and action is concerned)—through the influence of the Blumhardts and Franz Overbeck.[71] According to Jüngel, Overbeck, the radical atheist and church historian at the University of Basel, pointed out in the strongest possible terms that the theology of culture-Protestantism, with which Barth had been grappling since 1915, was in fact not Christian. This was due to the fact that it sought to justify theological knowledge, and therefore Christianity, through historical knowledge and the various methods of historicism. But for Overbeck, this was an impossibility, for history did not found, but dissipated and disintegrated religious truth.[72]

Dogmatic theology. See "Barth's Life and Work" in *Theological Legacy*, 27. This idea of "shifts" in Barth's thought has been further developed by Gerhard Sauter and used to trace further re-orientations or shifts in Barth's later theology. See Sauter, "Shifts in Karl Barth's Thought," 111–35. The extent to which this differs from von Balthasar's idea of "breaks" in Barth's thought is briefly discussed by McCormack in his *Karl Barth's Critically Realistic Dialectical Theology*, 7.

71. The principle text that Jüngel is concerned with here is Barth's published review of Carl Albrecht Bernoulli's edited volume of Overbeck's *Christentum und Kultur*, published as "Unsettled Questions for Theology Today." Jüngel also points to Barth's 1920 address "Biblical Questions, Insights, and Vistas," however, as also bearing evidence of the influence of Overbeck and Blumhardt. See Karl Barth, "Biblical Questions, Insights, and Vistas," 51–96. H. Martin Rumscheidt has pointed out that in the public correspon-dence and debate between Harnack and Barth that followed this address, one of the reasons that Barth had deviated from Harnack was due to the influence of Blumhardts' eschatology. As he says: "Here lies the second point where we must pause in tracing Barth's 'estrangement' from Harnack. As he worked on his sermons and studied, in-terpreted as he tried to fulfill his commission to preach the gospel, he came under the influence of the two Blumhardts.... It is in this insistence on God's otherness and in the double emphasis—God *on earth* and on earth *God*—that there is to be sought the element that influenced Barth and that was so distasteful to Harnack, namely eschatol-ogy." See Rumscheidt, *Revelation and Theology*, 7–14, esp. 8, 10. For his discussion of the significance of Overbeck, see 67, 134–39.

72. Jüngel, "Theological Beginnings," 57–58. As Barth notes, "Overbeck denies such a possibility categorically. Inflexibly he confronts us with the choice: If Christianity, then not history; if history, then not Christianity. 'Historic Christianity—that is Christianity subjected to time—is an absurdity' (242). History is precisely the basis on which Christianity can *not* be established; . . ." (Barth, "Unsettled Questions for Theology Today," 61).

This was especially true of Christianity, the religion whose content was "wholly eschatology" and whose origins and destination stood "in the history before history, the super-history (*Urgeschichte*)."[73]

Though for Overbeck the implications of this critique were tragic, since he did not believe that theology as Christian theology was possible, for Barth this became a new starting point that contained within it the seed of promise for his own new approach to theology. But Barth's conscious misreading of the intention of Overbeck was only made possible insofar as he read Overbeck "as a backward-looking, critical Blumhardt," and Blumhardt "as a forward-looking and hopeful Overbeck."[74] Thus, Barth read Overbeck through the lens of the escha-

---

73. Barth, "Unsettled Questions for Theology Today," 62.

74. Ibid., 56. There is some debate about whether Barth's misreading of Overbeck was intentional or not. The evidence appears to lean towards a "creative" appropriation that was a misreading which Barth was willing to defend. There are at least two witnesses that seem to contradict one another in this matter. The first is Barth's letter to Thurneysen, dated April 20, 1920, in which he reports that Frau Professor Overbeck "portrayed her husband for [him] in a way that simply tallies to the hairbreadth with our conception of him." This would seem to indicate that Barth did indeed seek some support—whether historical, biographical, or psychological—for the theological importance that he would ascribe to Overbeck in "Unsettled Questions for Theology Today," and that his "mis-reading" was not necessarily meant to be totally arbitrary. See *Revolutionary Theology in the Making*, 50.

The second witness points in a different direction. Barth's "creative" appropriation and his awareness that he might have misread Overbeck's intentions come to the fore in his published response to Eberhard Vischer's 1922 critique of Thurneysen and himself. Vischer's point was that Barth had misunderstood Overbeck's intention and that his appropriation was precisely the kind of intellectual arrogance that Overbeck despised in a theologian. Barth's 1922 response is telling and deserves to be quoted at length: "I have for *my* understanding of the historical Overbeck someone as witness, who really knew him *still* somewhat better than Eberhard Vischer. But I don't insist, since I cannot present the related document and *my* interest in Overbeck is actually just the same even if Vischer were correct on the entire line.... We are interested in the history of Overbeck as much and as little as everything that is historical; it does not interest us *in itself*, but in its *importance*.... He is the bearer of a very specific concept, namely the eschatological understanding of Christendom. He carried this so clearly, at least in its negative range—but what is here to be called 'positive' and 'negative'?—which we have not seen anywhere, except (with a somewhat different accentuation) with Blumhardt... . As the knowledgeable one, he presented questions to them to which he never received an answer: the question, if Christendom, as a great historical reality, is possible, and if it wants to be such at all.... Is the root of these questions to be found in the psychological subject of Overbeck rightly understood as enthusiasm or scepticism? Did Overbeck take a 'positive position' toward Christendom, or was he an 'atheist'? Whoever expects a decision on the debate of *this* problem, has not heard what was asked. Who may, who

tologically oriented theology of the Blumhardts. As Jüngel points out, Barth "had already found in the Blumhardts those Christians and non-scholarly theologians who made it possible for him to stand up to 'the Overbeckian negation' and even to recommend it as 'an introduction to theology.'"[75] It was thus the Blumhardts' belief that the impossible could become possible (i.e., that God could speak, making theological speech possible, just as God had done that which was impossible in Möttlingen), which enabled Barth to see that the radical negation and criticism that Overbeck leveled at theology was an essentially positive thesis. This was Barth's interpretation in spite of the fact that Overbeck's intentions may have been quite different.[76]

In developing this thesis, Jüngel emphasizes that Barth was deeply influenced by the Blumhardts, and that "Barth remained theologically close to the two Blumhardts for the rest of his life. He knew that he was in their debt."[77] Thus, Jüngel ascribes to the Blumhardts a central place in Barth's theological development. If there is any weakness to his thesis it is related primarily to the limitations of the study itself, which admittedly focuses only on Barth's "theological beginnings," an issue we have already noted in connection to Frei and Berger. However, even in light of this, Jüngel manages to point to the fact that Barth would remain, to some extent, under the influence of the Blumhardts' theology, and that "in his last lectures on the *Church Dogmatics*, which expounded his ethics of the doctrine of reconciliation (later published as a fragment from his literary remains), Barth offered a thankful testimony to how much his own theology was influenced by 'the two Wurttembergers.

---

can and who wants to remain here? I sense that the giving of weight to this is an attempt to *avoid* the seriousness of the matter. For what does all the material help, which can be brought together from one side or the other for the challenge presented by Overbeck? Would it carry less weight if Overbeck would have died as a total skeptic" (Barth, "Immer Noch Unerledigte Anfrangen," 61–63)? Here, Barth reveals that his reading of Overbeck doesn't need to square with Overbeck's own intentions, because that is not where the true significance of his work lies. The "related document" to which he refers was a letter that he had received from Frau Overbeck.

75. Jüngel, "Barth's Theological Beginnings," 65.

76. For a discussion of Overbeck's relationship to theology, see Henry, *Franz Overbeck*. It is also, of course, a question as to whether or not the Blumhardts would have desired to be "appropriated" in this fashion, for their concern was not primarily with providing a new foundation for theology.

77. Jüngel, "Theological Beginnings," 63.

…'"[78] Jüngel, therefore, is to be read in continuity with the interpretations of Berger, Frei, and Berkouwer in his estimation that the Blumhardts were of great theological importance for Barth.

Bruce McCormack

Our last commentator in this group pays scant attention to the Blumhardts' influence on Barth. This would not be a problem were Bruce McCormack's *Karl Barth's Critically Realistic Dialectical Theology: It's Genesis and Development 1909–1936* not so influential. McCormack's work is conceived principally as a critique of von Balthasar's two-stage thesis for Barth's development. The problematic element in McCormack is not that he recognizes that Barth's break with Liberal theology should be, at least symbolically, linked with his 1915 visit with Christoph Blumhardt at Bad Boll. It is rather that beyond recounting this meeting, McCormack pays absolutely no attention to the role of the Blumhardts' theology in shaping Barth's own theological development. Thus, McCormack places the Blumhardts (and I should point out that it is only Christoph Blumhardt and not the significant influence of his father Johann Christoph that McCormack mentions) at the moment of genesis in Barth's theological revolution, but draws no conclusions about their significance in Barth's theological development.

McCormack argues that there was only one real "break" in Barth's theological development—i.e., his break from Liberal theology occurring sometime around 1915—and that the shift from dialectical theology to doctrinal or analogical theology was merely a shift of emphasis. McCormack builds on the work of Ingrid Spiekermann and Michael Beintker to argue that even in the dialectical phase there was a form of analogy at work and that analogical thinking is always already dialectical thinking.[79] Furthermore, McCormack shows that within Barth's doctrine of revelation is the *Realdialektik* of the veiling and unveiling God. Thus, even when Barth moved towards the more stable forms of theological expression, as found in the *Christliche Dogmatik* and be-

---

78. Ibid., 63.

79. See McCormack, *Critically Realistic Dialectical Theology*, 8–14 for his discussion of Spiekermann and Beintker. See also Beintker, *Die Dialektik*; and Spiekermann, *Gotteserkenntnis*.

yond, he never left behind dialectical thinking precisely because he understood that God was Himself dialectically present in His revelation.

McCormack, unlike von Balthasar, is not unaware of the many "outsiders" who contributed to the shaping of Barth's theology. However, he prefers to place the weight of his exposition regarding Barth's early development on "one of the true outsiders of the nineteenth century," Franz Overbeck, completely ignoring the role that the Blumhardts' eschatology had in shaping Barth's appropriation of Overbeck.[80]

There is no doubt that McCormack's work is judicious and erudite. And he has done a great service in clarifying the nature of the "shifts" in Barth's thought, not the least being his excellent treatment of the role of Protestant Scholasticism in the emergence of Barth's dogmatics from the mid-1920's on.[81] But his oversight of the Blumhardts, especially when seen in light of emphasis given them by Frei and Jüngel—let alone Berger and Sauter—would seem to leave a fairly large hole in McCormack's picture of Barth's development. There may be at least three reasons for this oversight. The first has to do with the focus of his study.

Though McCormack makes it quite clear that he does not believe that Barth was ever all that concerned about methodological issues, his study is nevertheless conceived and executed as an attempt to explicate the "development and genesis" of Barth's so-called "critically realistic dialectical theology." Thus, McCormack's study is concerned above all with the critical realism that he believes orients Barth's various *ad hoc* methodological engagements. That is, McCormack's study is focused on the question of theological method in Barth, though this is explicated primarily in the context of the doctrine of revelation.

In light of this concern, the Blumhardts would seem to provide absolutely no guidance whatsoever, especially if we take seriously Hans Frei's estimation that, "Biblical realism has no distinct methodological convictions."[82] Thus, McCormack never thinks to take seriously the possibility that the Blumhardts' own eschatological "orientation" could have

---

80. McCormack, *Critically Realistic Dialectical Theology*, 226–35. Though it should also be pointed out that McCormack pays extensive attention to Marburg neo-Kantianism and to Barth's brother Heinrich Barth, as well as Søren Kierkegaard. See ibid., 218–40.

81. See ibid., 327–67.

82. Frei, "Doctrine of Revelation," 488.

influenced Barth's so-called "critical realism."[83] However, one need only think here of the theological axiom "God is God," which Barth ascribed both to the Blumhardts and Hermann Kutter, as evidence of a possible methodological influence.[84]

The second possible reason for McCormack's oversight is due to the fact that his study is far too over-determined by his desire to dislodge the von Balthasar thesis from its place of prominence. The logic here is quite simple: because von Balthasar did not deal with the Blumhardts, McCormack has no reason to do so either.

Finally, McCormack has expressed that he did not deal with the Blumhardts principally because he sought to follow closely Barth's own description of the key interlocutors, as found in the preface to the second edition of the *Römerbrief*. In that famous preface, Barth describes four reasons that led him to revise his study. Those included: 1) his ongoing engagement with the writings of Paul; 2) his encounter "with the warning addressed by Overbeck to all theologians"; 3) his closer reading of Plato and Kant through the work of his brother Heinrich, as well as further exposure to the writings of Kierkegaard and Dostoevsky; and 4) the various reviews of the first edition.[85] This would certainly provide some justification for his decision to ignore the Blumhardts, but one has to wonder why they were not taken up later, especially in the exposition of the *Christliche Dogmatik*, since Barth expressly identi-

83. Though I do not necessarily wish to challenge the *content* of McCormack's particular descriptor here, it does seem to me a bit dubious to utilize the philosophical terminology of neo-Kantianism to describe Barth's theological orientation. Perhaps a better way of describing Barth's theological orientation still awaits us?

84. For an excellent discussion of this theological axiom, see Busch, "God is God," 101–13. The point of Busch's essay is to show the way in which this saying provided a theological axiom that guided Barth in his deliberations on the possibility of theology, a possibility that was wholly under the shadow of the eschatological proviso. This judgment converges with Jüngel's analysis of Barth's reflections on the "impossible possibility" of theology, which was developed in conversation with Blumhardt and Overbeck. This axiom, according to Busch, extended beyond the early dialectical period. As he notes, "The theological principle 'God is God' not only did NOT exclude the later Christocentric theology but was *and* remained its *premise*, a premise which neither dropped nor even corrected the basic structure of that principle" (103).

85. Karl Barth, "The preface to the second edition," in idem, *The Epistle to the Romans*, 3–4. McCormack related this fact to me in a private conversation (Private Conversation at Princeton Theological Seminary, 10/7/02). It should also be noted that McCormack admitted that he may have overlooked the importance of the Blumhardts in his interpretation of the influence of Overbeck on Barth.

fies the Blumhardts as part of the theological lineage out of which he was working in that volume.[86]

~

Thus ends our discussion of the various interpreters of Barth's theological development and the way in which they have chosen to deal with the acknowledged influence of the Blumhardts. A few concluding observations are in order.

First, of the five interpreters that we looked at, only one (von Balthasar) seemed totally unaware of the substantive contribution of Blumhardts to Barth's theological development. McCormack, though aware of the importance of the Blumhardts—especially Christoph Blumhardt—in Barth's break from theological Liberalism development chooses not to incorporate that influence into his overall description of the development of Barth's "critically realistic dialectical theology." Frei, Berger, and Jüngel are very explicit in their accounts as to both the substance and importance of the contribution of the Blumhardts to Barth's theological development, whatever their shortcomings. Of the five, perhaps the most puzzling is Berkouwer, whose theme "The Triumph of Grace" appears to come closest to the Blumhardtian impulse found in Barth's theology. In spite of this, there is no extensive explication of the Blumhardts' theology and their contribution to Barth's theology is mentioned only in passing. Barth's own confirmation that Berkouwer not only seemed to have come close to capturing an essential aspect of his theology, but that it was an aspect which was certainly shaped by the Blumhardts, adds the puzzling question of why Berkouwer did not explore these figures in more depth. As noted above, Berkouwer comes close to the heart of Barth's theology, but manages to fundamentally misunderstand it because, at least in Barth's eyes, he had not understood the true significance of the Blumhardts and the meaning of their theology.

Our second observation regards the insights culled from these various interpreters about the importance of the Blumhardts for Barth's theology. Frei points us to the importance of the Blumhardt's realistic interpretation of the Bible and the combination of their "biblical real-

---

86. See Karl Barth, *Die christliche Dogmatik im Entwurf*, vi. For McCormack's treatment of this, see *Critically Realistic Dialectical Theology*, 375–449 passim.

ism" with a consistent eschatology for Barth's own approach to Scripture. In Berger, we see that there are multiple connections and theological affinities ranging across the theologies of Barth and the Blumhardts that are shaped above all by the eschatology and reality of the kingdom of God that the *kerygma* of the Blumhardts sought to point to. In Jüngel we are shown that the Blumhardts, far from making no methodological contribution to Barth's theology, are in fact at the center of his concept of theology as an "impossible possibility." Berkouwer's thesis echoes Berger (even if it was the most problematic from Barth's point of view!) given that he sought to trace the thematic "the triumph of grace" throughout the whole of Barth's thought, arguing that it was the heartbeat of his theology. Finally, though McCormack chooses to ignore the Blumhardts on the whole, he is still comfortable with attributing to them a constitutive role in shaping Barth's "spiritual atmosphere," and that is no small point.[87]

Finally, none of our interpreters, with the possible exception of Berkouwer, reveal to us very much about the possible role and influence of the Blumhardts on Barth's later theology. This is due almost exclusively to the fact that most chose to focus on the early significance of the Blumhardts in the context of exploring Barth's own theological beginnings and subsequent break with theological Liberalism. The distortions that we noted in Berger's analysis of the Blumhardts' theology showed us that in our readings of both Barth and Blumhardts we must be aware of possible distortions in our interpretations and should be careful to allow their respective theologies to speak freely.

Now that we have dealt at some length with those interpretations focusing on Barth's overall theological development, we will turn our attention to those commentators who focus primarily on Barth's construction of specific doctrines and his understanding of the interrelation of doctrine and ethics.

Interpretations Focusing on Specific Doctrinal Loci and Ethics

In this section we will engage studies that are not so much interested in Barth's theological development, as in the specifics of his doctrinal and

---

87. This was the basic point that McCormack made in a private discussion (Private Interview, Princeton Theological Seminary, Princeton, NJ, 10/07/02).

ethical proposals and constructions. For many, Barth is single-handedly responsible for restoring dogmatic and doctrinal theology to a central place in Christian theology. Given this assessment and Barth's expressed suspicions about discussions surrounding theological methodology, it should not be surprising that engagement with the substance of Barth's doctrinal and ethical theology constitute a large percentage of the secondary literature on Barth. We have chosen to limit our discussion to only three of the most relevant sources.

Gerhard Sauter

Our first commentator, Gerhard Sauter, came to know Barth's theology through his study of the Blumhardts.[88] This fact, coupled with his own theological acumen and insight, makes his work on the question of the relationship between the thought of the Blumhardts and Barth superior to any of the commentators that we have or will consider in this study, including Berger.

Sauter's 1962 dissertation, *Die Theologie des Reiches Gottes beim älteren und jüngeren Blumhardt*, was for many years considered the standard treatment of the theology of the Blumhardts. Contained within it, in dense and tangled German, is a section entitled, "Reflections on the Relationship of Ch. Blumhardt and Karl Barth."[89] This text has been augmented more recently by his 1997 address to the Karl Barth Society of North America, "Why is Karl Barth's *Church Dogmatics* Not a 'Theology of Hope? Some Observations on Barth's Understanding of Eschatology,"[90] in which he returns to the question of the Blumhardts influence on Barth. In these two texts we find a wide-ranging and complex discussion of the influence and the importance of the Blumhardts for understanding Barth's theology. His reflections on the Barth-Blumhardt relationship span a number of theological themes, including

88. Gerhard Sauter's father, who passed away in 1945, was a close friend of Ludwig Hönig and Otto Salomon, both of whom were married to granddaughters of Christoph Blumhardt. This family connection was what originally drove Sauter to do his doctoral thesis on the Blumhardts' theology. It was through his intensive work on the Blumhardts, done under the supervision of Otto Weber at the University of Göttingen, that he was eventually introduced to the work of Barth. (Private Interview, Center for Theological Inquiry, Princeton, New Jersey, 12/11/02).

89. Sauter, *Die Theologie des Reiches Gottes*, 235–67.

90. See Sauter, "Why is Karl Barth's *Church Dogmatics* Not a 'Theology of Hope?"

ecclesiology, anthropology, and eschatology. While in his dissertation he focuses almost exclusively on the influence of Christoph Blumhardt on Barth's ecclesiology and anthropology, in his more recent essay he turns his attention to consider the elder Blumhardt's role in shaping Barth's eschatology.

In his dissertation, Sauter makes it clear that he is not interested in a "genetic relationship" between Barth and Christoph Blumhardt. Rather, he wants to indicate the historical and thematic "dependencies" between the two.[91] He divides his investigation into two periods: 1) the "dialectical period"; and 2) the period of Christological concentration. Throughout his considerations of these themes, Sauter stresses that Barth took the pastorally motivated proclamation of the Blumhardts and sharpened it, thereby changing it in some measure, for his own systematic use. Thus, though there was an undoubted identity, there was also to be found a real difference between Barth and the Blumhardts.

During the dialectical period the primary motif shared by Barth and Christoph Blumhardt was the antithesis "God-humanity." As Sauter notes, "Blumhardt's antithesis 'God-humanity' which was dominant in the second phase of his preaching might have systematically concentrated itself in the dialectical thinking of the young Barth."[92] This antithesis was worked out systematically by Barth and was the real source for his use of Kierkegaard's "infinite qualitative distinction," according to Sauter.[93] Barth's appropriation of this antithesis would lead him to expand in a more general direction, so that it was no longer the dialectical confrontation between God and the people of a specific congregation, but rather God's confrontation with the whole of the cosmos.[94]

91. Sauter, *Die Theologie des Reiches Gottes*, 239. Even in his attempt to assert the historical dependencies, the real interest of Sauter is to show the continuity and, to a lesser extent, discontinuity of their specific theologies. This intention changes only slightly in the later 1997 address, as the focus is almost exclusively on the continuity between Barth and Johann Christoph Blumhardt.

92. Ibid., 240.

93. Sauter: "The reference to Kierkegaard is mainly a road sign that points to a more memorable and specific philosophical concept. The relevant starting point, therefore, corresponds with a theological thematic, as it came to prominence in Christoph Blumhardt: God's righteousness over the righteousness of man" (ibid., 240–41).

94. It is indeed strange that Sauter would make this claim given the fact that Blumhardt himself would turn more and more away from a position that emphasized God's confrontation within the fellowship of believers to include God's confrontation

Internal to the antithesis of "God-humanity," Sauter finds another dialectic, through which the former works itself out in the world: the guilt and hope of the Church. Both Barth and Blumhardt shared this dialectic, though Barth placed far more emphasis on holding the two together *within* the Church, while Blumhardt tended to allow the two to fly apart, thus identifying the hope of the Church with the *Gemeinde*. The area of their closest agreement regarded the "guilt" of the Church.

Both Barth and Blumhardt were motivated in their reflections on this guilt by their shared critique of religion as the attempt of man to reach God. Only insofar as the Church (and religion for that matter!) had succumbed to this attitude was either Barth or Blumhardt interested in discussing its guilt. Thus, their critique was meant to be a critique *for the sake of* the Church, rather than its outright repudiation as an institution. For both, the Church falls under this guilt when it either becomes self-satisfied with its place in society and loses its critical edge and prophetic charge, or when it begins to believe that the true answers to the problems of the world are to be found in a conversion to "churchliness," whether that was in a liberal or conservative form. When the Church begins to believe that only from it and by it may the world be saved, it transforms into that form of religion which is the arrogance of humanity.[95] Both found this attitude in the conservative "Inner Mission" movement of Wichern and, to some extent, in the Liberal culture Protestantism of their day.[96] In contrast, they were concerned to emphasize the fact that the Church exists as a witness of God *for the sake* of the whole world, not for the sake of the Church. Thus, if the Church has a vanguard function in the world, it is not for its own sake, but for that of the whole of humanity. Its task was to humanize

---

with the whole of humanity. This is most clearly evident in Blumhardt's turn to socialism as a parable of the kingdom.

95. As Barth notes: "The wealth of religion has, however, its own peculiar danger, for its proper function may be misunderstood. Instead of pointing beyond itself, it may be erected, like some great pyramid, as an immense sepulchre within which the truth lies mummified in wood and stone. True religion is a seal, reminding men that they have been established by God and that they will be established by Him; it reminds them also of their dissolution and of their redemption, and of the daily renewed faithfulness of God" (*The Epistle to the Romans*, 129–30). Sauter points out that Blumhardt even places part of the blame for the social problems of the day on the Church's repudiation of its true role in the world. See Sauter, *Die Theologie des Reiches Gottes*, 243.

96. See Bentley, *Between Marx and Christ*, 15–35.

rather than to Christianize the world.[97] Thus both were in close proximity to the Religious Socialists who critiqued the optimistic collusion
of Christianity and bourgeois society. At the same time, however, both
Barth and Blumhardt detected in Religious Socialism another form of
the same kind of arrogance that believes that humanity can reach God
through its own efforts and striving.

The difference between Barth and Blumhardt becomes apparent
when considering the *hope* of the church. In Barth's case, guilt and hope
are both dialectically applied to and found in the Church, whereas,
Blumhardt is far more ambivalent about the hope of the Church, choosing in good pietist fashion to emphasize that hope is found primarily
in the *Gemeinde*, though his understanding was considerably different
from the traditional pietist concept.[98] For Sauter, this distinction is
further problematized by the relative lack of emphasis that Blumhardt
places on working out the positive content of the hope to be found in
the *Gemeinde*. Thus, Blumhardt was often accused of spiritualism owing
to the lack of a concrete description of the real hope of the *Gemeinde*. In
comparison, Sauter briefly mentions Barth's "fleshing out of the poverty,
despair, and hope represented by the church"[99] as found in his exposition of Romans 9–11 in the second *Römerbrief*.[100]

When he turns to consider the proximity of Barth's thought to
Blumhardt during the period of "Christological concentration," Sauter

---

97. One finds this contrast powerfully communicated in Christoph Blumhardt's letters to his son-in-law, Richard Wilhelm, a missionary to China before the outbreak of
World War I. See Christoph Blumhardt, *Christus in der Welt*.

98. *Gemeinde* is a notoriously difficult word to translate. It can mean, "fellowship,"
"congregation," "local authority," "community" and even "municipality." In Christoph's
thinking the meaning of the term moves from being focused on the local congregation,
to a concept which is more cosmopolitan and universal, and then back to an open
fellowship which is loosely connected through the unifying power of the Holy Spirit.
This shift meant that the concrete fellowship which bore the hope of God into the
world shifted out of the Christian context and into the world, specifically the SPD, and
then again shifted back to a more localized and Christian context, though it retained
its openness to the world as the realm of advance of the kingdom of God. In all three
of these stages, Christoph emphasized the role of the Holy Spirit as the one who called,
formed and sent forth these differing forms of the *Gemeinde*.

99. Sauter, *Die Theologie des Reiches Gottes*, 246.

100. See Barth, *Romans*, 330–423; see also Barth and Thurneysen, "Unsere Hoffnung
und die Kirche," in *Suchet Gott, so werdet ihr Leben!*, 160–75.

focuses on Barth's anthropology.[101] He begins his reflection with the question whether or not Barth's Christological-anthropology is too abstract, since its construction seems to obscure the existential aspect of human life. Barth's contention—that *real* (ontological) humanity is found only in Jesus—would seem to lead to the accusation that Barth has opened himself up to the critique of Feuerbach: Jesus is simply the idealization of humanity. Sauter points out that Barth's answer to this critique is bound up with his general response to the criticism leveled at him by Berkouwer: that his thought was static, because based on the assumption of an *a priori* principle, i.e. the triumph of grace. Thus, Sauter's discussion of Barth's anthropology is necessarily bound up with a consideration of his eschatology, as he turns his attention to the section "Jesus is Victor" found in *Church Dogmatics* IV/3.

The turn to this late volume of the *Church Dogmatics* is motivated primarily by Barth's contention that "the being of man is a history"—a fact that is secured Christologically and therefore finds its content in Barth's description of the history of Jesus Christ.[102] The highpoint of his description of this Christological history is found in the sub-section "Jesus is Victor."

In contrast to his later reflections on this section, Sauter believes that Barth, in the end, does not escape Berkouwer's critique of triumphalism. Furthermore, Barth misconstrues the thought of the elder Blumhardt because he re-contextualizes the Blumhardtian concept of the "warfare history of Jesus" in an ontic-noetic dialectical teleology. According to Sauter, Barth views the victory of Jesus as a reality (ontological) that asserts itself inexorably through history as a form of living knowledge (noetic). Thus, through the march of history the truth or reality of Christ's victory becomes more and more progressively known, with the implication that it also becomes more and more secure and that the powers of opposition are more and more fully subdued. According to this logic, Barth's threefold-*parousia* of Christ is constructed as a kind of successive revelation in which the teleology of the ontic-noetic dynamic overtakes the more restrained Blumhardtian dynamic of

---

101. In a footnote, Sauter points out that one could also focus on the shape of Barth's doctrine of predestination and his doctrine of creation to find similarities between Blumhardt and Barth. See Sauter, *Die Theologie des Reiches Gottes*, 251.

102. *CD* III/2, 157, as quoted by Sauter, ibid., 255.

promise-fulfillment.[103] In contrast, the elder Blumhardt understood the theological catchphrase "Jesus is Victor!" neither as a superior noetic standpoint in history, nor as a kind of hidden knowledge coming to light. Rather, it was seen as an illumination of the dynamic at work in the "time between the times," the time of warfare.[104] Thus, the work of the Christian is not merely to "publish" the Word abroad, but to join in the fight and prepare for the restoration of the whole cosmos.

Whether or not one can really divide Barth from Blumhardt here is questionable, given the fact that Barth's own description of the "warfare history of Jesus" provides the necessary restraint to refute the claim that he is a triumphalist. Barth emphasized that the inevitability of Jesus's victory is also a genuine struggle occurring in history here and now that has deadly consequences, just as the elder Blumhardt had understood it.[105] Furthermore, Barth's use of an actualistic idiom in describing Jesus Christ—so much so that he is rendered and known only as an "event" and "history"—must at least give one pause when accusing him of "a-prioric thinking." One gets the sense that Sauter himself is not altogether comfortable with his own assessment here. This is confirmed in light of his later 1997 address in which he softens his critique regarding the distance between Barth and the elder Blumhardt.

Sauter has expressed that his 1997 address was the culmination and conclusion of his work on Barth and the Blumhardts.[106] In this later essay, he comes to see that Barth's theology is shot through with

103. Sauter: "Barth's construction of a 'threefold parousia' of Jesus Christ (337 ff.) describes this teleology of revelation so to speak as successive steps, one revealing more respectively than the previous one" (ibid., 258).

104. See ibid., 258–59. Part of Sauter's criticism of Barth is that he stands too closely to the younger Blumhardt in regards to this. By so doing, he loses the dynamic tension that was more clearly evident in the elder Blumhardt. See ibid, 259–60.

105. Barth: "By this environment the Son of God and Man, Jesus Christ, is Himself challenged and assaulted as He challenges and assaults it by His existence and with His Word. His life is constantly confronted by death, the covenant by unfaithfulness and apostasy, reconciliation by strife. . . . This does not mean that absolute and final limits are set to Him, but it does mean that He has to contend with limits of relative and provisional seriousness. He is noticeably though not invincibly confined. And as His Word contradicts the contradiction, it seems for its part to subject itself even to a certain bondage and conditioning, and to be spoken with a relative and provisional but unmistakable restraint" (CD IV/3.1, 166–67).

106. Private Interview, Center for Theological Inquiry, Princeton, New Jersey, 12/11/02.

precisely the kind of reticent, though hope-filled, dialectic of "promise-fulfillment" which he had ascribed to the elder Blumhardt.[107] Not only was this the case in his eschatology proper, but it also permeated Barth's understanding of theology in general. According to Sauter, Barth argued that all theological knowledge was to be seen under the shadow of the eschatological proviso that placed a question mark over against all theological declarations. Theological speech was built on the eschatologically derived insight that, "dogmatics can only be an approximation of the truth of theology *by God*,"[108] thus, "'eschatology' did not signify a doctrine of the last things. Rather it was the place holder for the question about the truth of Christian theology."[109] For theology to be true in any sense, it must be taken up into the economy of the *Deus dixit*, who is the "true witness" to himself. The implication of this being that Barth was not and indeed could not be committed to a-prioric thinking, since his conception of theological speech was that it was only possible insofar as it pointed beyond itself to the present self-speaking God.

Something of this dynamic was also at work in Barth's musings on "the doctrine of last things." Sauter's description of Barth's eschatology deserves to be quoted at length:

> I cannot say whether Barth thought he had found a sufficient solution to this problem or not. In any case, Barth was convinced that he had pointed out the problem in a way that could not be overlooked, that is, by impressing upon us what *we*, in any case, must *not* say—namely, that what occurred with Jesus Christ actually leaves nothing to be expected. Or the exact opposite— namely, that with the coming of Jesus Christ certain things

107. Whether or not the particular conception that Barth and Blumhardt are now seen to share is adequate, is an open question. The reason for Sauter's change of position is unknown. He has noted that the order by which he engaged the Blumhardts and Barth (i.e., Blumhardt first, then Barth) may have contributed to the overstatement in his dissertation (Email Correspondence, February 2, 2006). It may also be that though he had been exposed to *CD* IV/3, and its explicit engagement with the Blumhardts, he was not able to gain access to *The Christian Life* lecture fragment (published only in 1975), in which Barth amplifies and deepens his engagement with the Blumhardts. Whatever the case may be, Sauter retained a critical though appreciative stance towards Barth's eschatology in his own constructive work. For an assessment of Barth that seems to confirm this conclusion, see Sauter, *What Dare We Hope?*, 68–80. See also, Barth, *CL*, 256–60.

108. Sauter, "Karl Barth's Church Dogmatics," 412 (emphasis original).

109. Ibid., 410.

occurred, some of which are highly significant for the progress of world history, though the rest and possibly what is most decisive, remains outstanding; and that we could even determine under the circumstances how far we have already come, and what yet remains to be anticipated, to be hoped for, and—by the power of this hope—to be done.

With that two possibilities of speech are strictly excluded. Either on the one hand, basically everything has already occurred, so that at long last we should be satisfied—everything else may be a matter of indifference to us! Or on the other hand, something has in fact been completed, possibly even that which is decisive, yet it requires supplementation, completion, or at least continuation through that which we have to accomplish.[110]

Gone is the ontic-noetic conceptuality in his exposition of Barth's eschatology in general, and of Barth's understanding of the Blumhardts' "Jesus is Victor!" in particular. Barth's position (and Blumhardt with him) moves between an over-description of the "last things," on the one hand, and a tentative agnosticism about the ultimate end and final outcome, on the other. Though Sauter does not formally retract his critique that Barth's theology was over-determined by an abstract concept of "Jesus is Victor!," he leaves open the possibility that Barth was himself a "theologian of hope," constrained to think and speak neither more nor less than hope would allow.[111] Thus, the sense of the "impossible possibility" of theological language is translated into the idiom of hope in the context of eschatology, so that Barth was constrained to speak of Jesus's victory, but only in faith and hope.

In this context Sauter also notes that Barth took two questions from Johann Christoph Blumhardt's eschatology. The first was "How can we speak of God's kingdom?"[112] The answer:

110. Ibid., 425.

111. Barth takes the same kind of hope-filled dialectical approach in regard to the possibility of an *apokatastasis* or universal reconciliation. However, the logic is reversed since our knowledge of the final end is not certain. On the one hand, we do not know and therefore cannot rightly proclaim that in end the whole cosmos will be reconciled to God. But, on the other hand, such a hope is not to be denied: "If we are certainly forbidden to count on this as though we had a claim to it, as though it were not supremely the work of God to which man can have no possible claim, we are surely commanded the more definitely to hope and pray for it as we may do already on this side of this final possibility. . . ." (CD IV/3.1, 478).

112. Sauter, "Karl Barth's Church Dogmatics," 417.

It asserts itself—it breaks in and simultaneously opens the suffering human being for faith, for the expectation of the coming kingdom. . . . With Blumhardt the confession of 'Jesus is Victor!' and the cry 'Our Lord, come! (1 Cor. 16:22; cf. Rev. 22:20) penetrate each other: the certainty of the presence of Christ and the imminent expectation of the coming Christ, with whom the creation will be redeemed in the consummation of the kingdom of God. The victory of Jesus does not bring the battle to an end, but rather leads it creatively forward. This view is directed 'towards the whole,' when God will be all in all.[113]

We speak of the kingdom of God because we are constrained to do so, because it forces itself upon us, and only in light of the fact that *our* speaking is limited and provisional, always open to correction and emendation.[114] Sauter explicitly identifies Barth's position with the dynamic teleology of the elder Blumhardt, thus leaving behind another aspect of his earlier critique. His description focuses more on the role of confession in the explication of their mutual understanding of the catchphrase "Jesus is Victor!" "Jesus is Victor!" is neither more nor less than an "assertorical judgment. With it we affirm as definitive who Jesus Christ is—not only for us, but for the whole world—as he will appear irresistibly, even if he has not yet appeared as such for all; that is, who Christ is at the goal of the last time."[115] The difference between this assessment and Sauter's earlier critique is subtle.

In his dissertation, Sauter argued that Barth's position was based on a systematic deduction from his Christology, which in turn had ontological implications (i.e., the ontic-noetic dynamic), notwithstanding Barth's protests to the contrary.[116] Thus, according to Sauter, it was *de facto* an abstract principle. In this later essay, Barth's position is more closely aligned with an exegesis of Jesus' confession from the cross: "it is finished." "Jesus is Victor!" becomes synonymous with the promise of God as revealed in Jesus's victory on the cross. So that, "if we repeat it as-

---

113. Ibid., 417.

114. The parallel here to Barth's early discussion of the problem of Christian preaching is obvious: "As ministers we ought to speak of God. We are human, however, and so cannot speak of God. We ought therefore to recognize both our obligation and our inability and by that very recognition give God the glory." Karl Barth, "Word of God," 186.

115. Sauter, "Karl Barth's Church Dogmatics," 423.

116. See *CD* IV/3.1, 173–80.

sertorically, that is, as confession, we thus attune ourselves to that which really is, of which, however, we can only speak in hope."[117] The shift here is one of emphasis, rather than substance. For the latter position (i.e., that "Jesus is Victor" is a confession of faith) is but a hair's breadth from the former (i.e., that "Jesus is Victor" because of a predetermined, presumably pre-temporal, principle). The difference, if one can call it that, is that the latter chooses a kind of agnosticism about the way in which the victory of Jesus will work itself out in history, while the former seeks to explain too much, foregoing the tension and genuine struggle that occurs within history. The problem is that the ontological category of "reality" still creeps into Sauter's new interpretation, leaving the real difference between this new interpretation and the older one unresolved. The difficulty in distinguishing the two positions may explain Sauter's lingering doubt about whether or not Barth and Blumhardt are to be helpful for constructing a contemporary eschatology.

The second question Barth takes from the elder Blumhardt is: "How is it possible to think hope theologically?"[118] The answer to this question is rooted in Blumhardt's insight, that "he could understand everything which confronted him in pastoral caregiving solely out of the irrefutable expectation of God."[119] The objective confrontation with the demonic and its confession that "Jesus is Victor!" was only understandable under the arch of the hope of God's coming. The attempt to invent hope in the face of this was futile. Only as Blumhardt hoped in the coming of Christ, in the penultimate form of Gottliebin Dittus' exorcism, was his pastoral care possible. Sauter notes a parallel between Blumhardt's understanding of the role of hope in pastoral care giving and Barth's understanding of hope in theological language. According to Sauter, for Barth the very possibility of theological confession and construction is based on the petition, "Thy kingdom come," which is permeated by hope in the coming Christ. Again, the "impossible possibility" found in both the utterance of faith and in theological language

117. Sauter, "Karl Barth's Church Dogmatics," 424.

118. Ibid., 417.

119. Ibid., 417. Sauter goes on: "Pastoral caregiving would be impossible without grounded hope; it would be groundless and unfounded, if it would not hold on to the victory of Christ over the powers of sin and death, and if it would not proclaim this victory in and through the presence of God. Hopeful speech indicates a neediness that cannot be expressed otherwise than as extending towards the coming Christ" (418).

is permeated by hope in the living and coming One. Hope that faith and witness are true and truly useful to the self-witnessing God.

Thus ends Sauter's treatment of the relationship between Barth and the Blumhardts. The significance of his interpretation is not only that he goes a long way in locating the influence of the Blumhardts in the various stages of Barth's career as well as within the various theological loci. But that he also shows that it was their eschatology and "theology of hope" that gave to Barth the tools he needed to re-conceptualize the possibility and task of theology itself. Thus, Sauter further confirms and extends the thesis that we have already met in Jüngel—even though part of his work precedes Jüngel's by twenty years—that the Blumhardts had a constitutive role in helping Barth to navigate many of the issues surrounding theological methodology. It also confirms and offers some corrective to Berger's thesis by giving a clearer picture of the Blumhardts' concerns and how their eschatology was deployed in key areas of Barth's theology, not the least being his Christology.

John C. McDowell

Our next commentator, John C. McDowell, is a relative newcomer to Barth studies. His dissertation, *Hope in Barth's Eschatology: Interrogations and Transformations Beyond Tragedy*, was published in 2000. In McDowell we have a masterful discussion of Barth's eschatology and the "theology of hope" contained therein. He is not afraid to tangle with Barth's critics, giving a five-fold response to the two central critiques of Barth's eschatology: i.e, that it is either too filled out by a Christological event already having taken place or that it is merely a progressive "noetic" event with no real new "ontic" content. These criticisms are linked especially with Berkouwer, Moltmann, Richard Roberts, and Philip Rosato.[120]

McDowell's response is as follows: 1) Barth's eschatology is highly personalistic in that it finds its focus in Jesus Christ. The eschatological future is not some general future, but the future presence of Jesus Christ; 2) these critics fail to note that Barth's Christological focus provides a form of human provisionality since redemption has come in Christ *alone*, and is yet to come *for us*. We wait, therefore, not as those

---

120. See McDowell, *Hope in Barth's Eschatology*, 40–57. For Roberts's critique, see his, "Karl Barth's Doctrine of Time: It's Nature and Implications," in Roberts, *A Theology on It's Way?*, 1–58. For Rosato, see *The Spirit as Lord*. For Moltmann, see his *Coming of God*, 13–16.

who "possess" salvation, but as those who have received it as *promise*; 3) the criticism that Barth's understanding of the eschatological future is merely a "noetic" event misses the fact that this future entails a "coming to *be* that which Christ has redeemed one for."[121] The eschatological future, therefore, also contains a new ontological dimension; 4) none of these criticisms takes seriously the "practical and ethical *function* of Barth's eschatology."[122] He argues that Barth's doctrine of time is eschatologically structured, that is, it is a period "between the times" (*zwischen den Zeiten*), between Easter and the Consummation. The time "between the times" is provisional and fragile insofar as our knowledge of the eschatological future is only given to us in an outline form under the name Jesus Christ. "Predictive eschatology" is thus ruled out because we cannot know the exact or even definitive shape of our future. We can only know the future of the humanity of Jesus Christ, and even that is only known dimly. Nevertheless, it is known and this knowledge creates the context in which time is known and informs the *way* in which we are to use it: the provisional re-humanization of society; 5) McDowell argues that these critics also fail to notice Barth's account of the provisional nature of human activity which occurs within this eschatologically structured time. He traces Barth's understanding of eschatological provisionality from his early emphasis on the divine No, through to his later refusal to over-describe the eschatological future ending in his description of "good" human action as "parables of the kingdom." Both of these moves secure the contingency and provisionality of human action in light of the promised end since they call into question a simple identification of human actions with the kingdom of God.

Throughout the Blumhardt name appears in conjunction with some of the groundbreaking insights that Barth is described as arriving at. This includes Barth's early integration of theology and ethics, or theory and praxis, as seen in his theologically motivated move toward Socialism in 1910's as well as in his conception of faith and theological discourse as an "impossible possibility."[123]

For the most part, however, McDowell shows only slight interest in the Blumhardts themselves and their role in shaping Barth's eschatology and doctrine of hope. His knowledge of their theology is essentially

121. McDowell, *Hope in Barth's Eschatology*, 56.

122. Ibid., 56.

123. Ibid., 60–61, 83–88 passim.

secondhand, and he gives no account of the question of an identity or difference between their thought and Barth's, such as we saw in Berger and Sauter.[124] The only place at which he appears to be aware of a possible difference is in the use of the Blumhardtian catchphrase "Jesus is Victor!" He notes that "if left unqualified these metaphors can break free from their pastoral context of providing hope with confidence, and imply a more logical 'predictive style' eschatology."[125] It is in fact, the presence of this theme that finally becomes the target of McDowell's only substantive critique of Barth's eschatology.

Though McDowell does not revert to the primitive criticisms of Berkouwer and others, he presses the point home that Barth appears at times to over-emphasize that "Jesus is Victor" at the expense of the sense of tragedy and contingency that inhabits human life. The irony here is that this criticism works to undermine McDowell's interpretation of Barth as having sufficiently guarded himself against such a critique.[126] McDowell shows, in the chapter before his conclusion, how Barth had integrated the confidence emanating from Easter Sunday with the crushing despair of Good Friday. But apparently, in McDowell's view, the continuing presence of the Blumhardtian thematic constantly threatens to overwhelm. McDowell offers an alternative model in D. M. MacKinnon, the venerable dean of contemporary English theology. Whether or not the corrective found in MacKinnon is sufficient, or even needed, is beside the point here.[127] What is important is that McDowell believes that the presence of the Blumhardtian theme "Jesus is Victor" creates an imbalance in Barth's eschatology which leads him to a position that is essentially triumphalistic. Thus, according to McDowell, if there is a problem with Barth's eschatology it comes from the influence of the Blumhardts and the abiding presence of the *Christus Victor* motif of the elder Blumhardt.

---

124. That his knowledge of the Blumhardts is essentially secondhand is seen in the fact that at both of the points listed above, his textual evidence for these claims come from Jüngel and Gorringe, rather than from primary sources. This is further confirmed by the absence of Blumhardt texts in his bibliography. See ibid., 60–61, 83–88 passim, 241–59.

125. Ibid., 88.

126. This becomes exceptionally clear in chapter 7; see ibid., 180–213.

127. Alan Lewis would seem to provide a far more judicious and balanced attempt to integrate Easter Sunday with Good Friday in his *Between Cross and Resurrection*.

By way of concluding our discussion of McDowell, two observations are important here. First, whether or not the Blumhardts' influence on Barth is detrimental to his eschatology,[128] the argument that their thematic is what needs critical corrective in Barth's theology points to their significance for understanding his thought. Thus, that McDowell did not engage them in a serious manner is a significant oversight, though understandable in view of McDowell's own aims. Second, it also highlights, both in reference to McDowell's work and that of others, that if Barth's eschatology is really to be comprehended, a true picture of the Blumhardts' eschatology in comparison with Barth's is needed, even if this leads to the conclusion that Barth misused or misappropriated their thought. A critical comparison of this sort would provide more light by which to understand the dynamics at work in Barth's theology in general and in his eschatology in particular.

John Webster

Rounding out our second group of interpreters of Barth's theology is John Webster, whose work, *Barth's Ethics of Reconciliation* (Cambridge: Cambridge University Press, 1995), argues that Barth's theology will only be fully understood once the role of human agency found therein is taken seriously. Webster is representative of a growing field of literature on Barth's ethics and moral theology.[129] His work constitutes that part of our second interpretive category that focuses on the question of the integration of theology and ethics.

---

128. Had McDowell worked through the actual context and meaning of the catch-phrase "Jesus is Victor" in the Blumhardts themselves, he might have found that the charges of "triumphalism" were baseless. This is due, at least in part, to the fact that the cry "Jesus is Victor!" arises in the midst of those who are marginalized, rather than those who stand in the center. Württemberg Pietism in general and the Blumhardts in particular always saw the thematic "Jesus is Victor!" as a cry to be identified primarily with the destitute, the sick, the poor and the oppressed. Thus, rather than being a cry of triumphalism, it was a cry that sought to make sense of the vicissitudes, violence and utter senselessness of life, not by orienting hope on a kingdom that was outside of history, but, rather, on one that was to be engaged in fighting for in the "here and now," precisely because God was fighting and warring for such a kingdom, regardless of the deadly consequences of such a struggle.

129. Other full-length monographs include: Willis, *The Ethics of Karl Barth*; Macken, *The Autonomy Theme*; Matheny, *Dogmatics and Ethics*; Biggar, *Hastening that Waits* ; and Webster, *Barth's Moral Theology*.

Webster's work deals with the role of ethics in Barth's dogmatic theology, and is especially concerned to explicate the integration of theology and ethics as found in what Webster has described as Barth's "moral ontology—an extensive account of the situation in which human agents act."[130] This requires him to take into account three mutually dependent points, which, though asymmetrically unfolded, are necessary to one another and are therefore, in some sense, equally important in Barth's theological ethics:

> (1) The *Church Dogmatics* as a whole is one lengthy exposition of the statement which in a very particular way is 'at once the basis and the content of all the rest', the 'hardest and most comprehensive statement', that 'God is'. One of the ways in which the *Dogmatics* can be construed is as a massively ramified reassertion of the aseity of God: as an intense pursuit of the truth that neither in the realm of being nor in the realm of knowledge is God contingent or derivative, but rather axiomatically real, true, and free.... (2) Because—and only because—it is an exposition of the statement 'God is', the *Church Dogmatics* is also all along the line an anthropology. For the form of God's aseity, the chosen path of the divine being, is specified in the history of Jesus Christ; God's freedom is freedom for fellowship.... And so part of Barth's exploration of the logic of 'God is' is an exploration of how a Christian doctrine of God cannot be simply a doctrine of God.... God moves towards humanity by establishing covenant fellowship between himself and his creatures; God is true God 'only in this movement'. Dogmatics thereby acquires a double theme.... (3) Because the theme of the *Church Dogmatics* is *this* God in covenant with humanity, the *Dogmatics* is intrinsically an ethical dogmatics, and includes description of the human covenant partner as agent.[131]

Thus, Barth's theology is a theory of practice insofar as it is implicitly concerned with human action as it is caught up into a prior divine action: the move of God toward humanity as signified in the history of Jesus Christ. This prior move toward humanity calls forth a faithful, non-coerced response to follow in deliberate and meaningful action.[132]

130. Webster, *Barth's Ethics of Reconciliation*, 1.

131. Ibid., 2–4.

132. As Webster notes: "Put another way: *from the very beginning, Barth's theme is God and humanity as agents in relation.* Even at the furthest reaches of his protest against anthropocentric reduction of God to a function of human piety, consciousness

This becomes clear as Webster focuses on the central motif and posture of Christian action: prayer.

Prayer is the most characteristic form of Christian action because it is both a response to a prior divine gift of grace and a genuinely free human venture, predicated on the belief that we are called to ask in anticipation of an answer and in response to the prior fact of God's own action. The action to which we refer is the prayer of Jesus. Because Jesus prayed and continues to pray, prayer is more than simply a human action, it is also a divine action to which we are called to correspond.[133] The concrete description of the divine action to which human action should correspond, "is centrally and decisively the coming of the kingdom of God in Jesus Christ; and around this center, and with reference to it, it is God's gracious overruling of all world-occurrence. In this action God speaks His Word to which man must reply and to which his active life must correspond if lived in obedience."[134] This divine action is the subject of the first three petitions (i.e., free human responses) of the Lord's Prayer, though it obviously finds its most direct parallel in the second petition, "Thy kingdom come."

Though the subject of prayer occupies Webster's attention, he is also concerned to unravel the inner-logic of Barth's ethics of reconciliation, and in particular the reasoning which lay behind his decision to disavow Reformed sacramental theology and the practice of infant baptism, choosing rather to argue for believer's baptism. The basic logic for this move lies in Barth's concern to guard both divine and human freedom. Barth argues that the only sacrament, or medium of divine grace, is Jesus Christ himself. Thus, there can be no other vehicle of di-

---

or moral projects, Barth is attempting to safeguard not only the axiomatic divinity of God, but also the authenticity of the creature" (ibid., 33).

133. As Barth describes it: "It is constituted by the fact that it knows and acknowledges and affirms His intercession as that of the great High-priest, that it is posited on this basis, that it cannot posit itself on any other. . . . The Son of Man teaches it to pray, and therefore to ask. It allows itself to be taught by Him. And as He prays with it, it can now pray with Him. . . . Therefore it will not allow its Lord to be alone in prayer, but it will be at His side with its own asking, however imperfect and perverted and impotent this may be compared with His. And both with heart and mouth the asking of the community which is elected together with Him will be a true and genuine asking, because and in the very fact that it is merely a repetition of His petition, that it is enclosed in His asking, that it is associated with it, that it lives by its seriousness and power, that it is related to the gift and answer of God present within it" (*CD* III/3, 277).

134. *CD* III/4, 475.

vine action (i.e., baptism, and by implication, the Lord's Supper) except the living Jesus Christ, who is made present to us by the Holy Spirit. Baptism is thus an active response on the part of one who has already been "baptized by the Holy Spirit."[135] Therefore, infant baptism is "not correct; it is not done in obedience, it is not administered according to proper order, and therefore it is necessarily clouded baptism."[136]

The Blumhardts do not figure into Webster's account of Barth's "ethics of reconciliation." This is understandable since there is no textual basis for their influence in Barth's various discussions of baptism. It would, however, seem to be an oversight given the prominence of the Blumhardts in Barth's explication of the second petition of the Lord's Prayer, "Thy kingdom come."[137] Nevertheless, Webster cannot be blamed here for overlooking the Blumhardts, since his work is essentially an explication of the inner-logic of Barth's ethics of reconciliation, rather than a genealogical account of its development and influences.

That the Blumhardts might have had some role in helping Barth to shape his understanding of the integration of theology and ethics becomes clearer if we take into consideration a few issues: 1) Christoph Blumhardt undoubtedly influenced Barth in his understanding of the relationship between theology and socialism. Barth's identification of socialism as a "parable of the kingdom" could be interpreted as a concise form of Christoph Blumhardt's own judgment that socialism was "a prophetic voice from the world."[138] And certainly the designation of socialism as a "parable of the kingdom" has something to say about the relationship between divine and human action, however obliquely it may say it; 2) Barth's emphasis on the role of hope in ethics led him to place great stress on another Blumhardtian theme: "hastening and waiting." The first time that this formula appears in Barth's work is in his 1916

---

135. See Webster, *Barth's Ethics of Reconciliation*, 131.

136. Karl Barth, *Regarding Baptism*, 40. This quote is taken from an admittedly earlier discussion of Barth's position on baptism, though it still catches the spirit of his final position in *CD* IV/4.

137. Barth argues that his entire exposition of this petition was formed and inspired by the Blumhardts. See idem, *The Christian Life*, 256–60. Webster does not take this up, even in passing, in his own explication of this section of *CL*. See Webster, *Barth's Ethics of Reconciliation*, 201–13.

138. Christoph Blumhardt, "Der vernünftige Gottesdienst," in *Auswahl* III, 288–89 (unpublished translation by the Bruderhof and Plough Publishing).

review of Christoph Blumhardt's *Haus-Andachten nach Losungen und Lehrtexten der Brüdergemeinde*, in which Barth describes Christoph as a man who pleads, "unceasingly and unwaveringly before God and to God 'Thy Kingdom come!' and waiting and hastening with men toward this coming";[139] 3) Barth's interpretation of the role of prayer in the elder Blumhardt's exorcism of Gottliebin Dittus shares some structural parallels with his own more elaborate systematic discussion of the nature of prayer.[140] This coupled with the fact that the Blumhardts were central to Barth's own interpretation of the second petition of the Lord's Prayer tells us that the Blumhardts taught Barth something significant about the nature of prayer, and therefore about true Christian action.

~

In this second category we have been dealing especially with those interpreters of Barth who were concerned with the construction of specific doctrines as well as his understanding of the relationship between theology and ethics. We have dealt with fewer interpreters in this section, though this has allowed us to go into more detail in exploring their interpretation of the influence of the Blumhardts on Barth. This was especially the case with Gerhard Sauter, who justified such attention due to the special nature of his concerns. Because his work focused first on the Blumhardts and then on Barth it shed the most light on our question regarding their influence. Echoing and refining Berger, his work shows the pervasive influence of the Blumhardts on Barth, moving from his ecclesiology and critique of religion, through anthropology and into his eschatology. At the same time, Sauter gives added justification to Eberhard Jüngel's argument that Barth's description of theology as an "impossible possibility" and the methodological implications of such a description are to be credited to the influence of the Blumhardts in conversation with Franz Overbeck.

McDowell's work is more enigmatic in regard to our question, and perhaps even more so in light of Sauter's discussion of the central

---

139. See Karl Barth, "Action in Waiting for the Kingdom of God," 22–23. This formula reappears in Karl Barth, *Ethics*, 474–75, 487–88, and was the inspiration for the title to Nigel Biggar's *Hastening that Waits*, though he also pays no attention to the Blumhardts.

140. See *CD* IV/3.1, 176.

role the elder Blumhardt played in shaping Barth's mature eschatology. McDowell is aware of the Blumhardts (even following the methodological thesis of Jüngel), but they do not provide any real categories for his interpretation, and their thematic "Jesus is Victor" becomes the central problem of Barth's eschatology, for which McDowell offers his own corrective.

Webster's work is representative of the growing literature on Barth's ethics. Unfortunately, it is also representative in its relative lack of dealing with the Blumhardts' influence on Barth in the context of theological ethics. However, the role of prayer and Barth's emphasis on the "parabolic" nature of human action in relation to divine action does leave open the possibility that here also, the Blumhardts' influence may be detected. This will become more evident as this latter theme comes up again in the context of the discussion of Barth, the Blumhardts, and socialism.

Interpretations Focusing on Barth's Relationship to Socialism

In our final section we will focus on those interpreters who have sought to take account of Barth's relationship to socialism, and in particular whether or not that relationship had any determinative impact on Barth's theology. This has been one of the most hotly contested areas of Barth scholarship since it first appeared in the early 1970's in connection with the work of Friedrich-Wilhelm Marquardt, with whose work we will begin.

Friedrich-Wilhelm Marquardt

The appearance of his *Habilitationsshrift, Theologie und Sozialismus: Das Beispiel Karl Barths* in 1972, ignited a storm of protest and affirmation in the politically charged atmosphere of cold-war Germany.[141] Following its publication, a meeting was convened in Leuenberg outside Basel at

---

141. The events surrounding the refusal to accept Marquardt's *Habilitationsshrift* at the *Kirchliche Hochschule* in Berlin, which led to the resignation of Helmut Gollwitzer, Marquardt's Doktor Vater, contributed to the sensational atmosphere surrounding the debates of Marquardt's thesis. For a full discussion of this see Markus Barth, "Current Discussion on the Political Character of Karl Barth's Theology," in *Footnotes to a Theology*, 77–94.

which Marquardt's thesis was hotly debated, "by some of the weightiest names in Continental theology."[142]

The net result was that many of the followers of Barth in the German context were divided—much as had happened to the followers of Hegel—into "right-wing" and "left-wing" camps of interpretation. Some of the literature resulting from this debate was eventually published in English in 1976, under the editorial direction of George Hunsinger. There are five essays on the question of socialism in the theology of Barth included in his *Karl Barth and Radical Politics*. We will look at the contributions of those most closely associated with Marquardt's controversial thesis: those of Helmut Gollwitzer and Marquardt himself.

Marquardt's relatively simple, though far-reaching, thesis was that Barth's theology was "in fact rooted (as Barth was aware on the theoretical level) in his political involvement (praxis)."[143] It is an attempt to take seriously Barth's own verdict that his "own theology always had a strong political side, explicit or implicit."[144] Marquardt develops his argument with four points: 1) Barth was a life-long socialist; 2) the existential setting for Barth's theological development was to be found in his socialist activity; 3) Barth's turn to theology was meant to work out the integral connection between "the Bible and the newspaper"[145]; 4) Barth's construction of the doctrine of God was along what were explicitly socialist lines.

With the first point Marquardt is attempting to do away with a picture, prominent especially in the Anglo-American context, wherein Barth was understood to have left his socialist commitments behind when he left his Safenwil pastorate and moved into his academic post at the University of Göttingen. In making his point, Marquardt goes so far as to argue that Barth was dismissed from his position at Bonn in 1935 due more to his political association with the socialist party (which he

---

142. Hunsinger, "Introduction," in *Radical Politics*, 10. The debate was so contentious that one of its participants, Eberhard Jüngel, stormed out in protest. See M. Barth, "Political Character of Karl Barth's Theology," 92.

143. Marquardt, "Socialism in the Theology of Karl Barth," 49. This essay, published in English in 1976, was the first attempt to mediate the debate occurring in the German context into the Anglo-American context.

144. Karl Barth, "Music For a Guest–A Radio Broadcast," in idem, *Final Testimonies*, 24.

145. Marquardt, "Socialism in the Theology of Karl Barth," 59.

had joined in Germany in 1932) than with any purely religious or theological qualms he might have had with the Hitler regime (i.e., his refusal to take the oath).[146]

Marquardt's second point is to make clear the real genesis of Barth's theology, which he argues is not found in Barth's anxiety over theological speech, but rather is found in his anxiety over what it meant to belong "to that socially comprehended religious organization, the church."[147] This anxiety came to a head with the failure of "empirical socialism" in the face of World War I and due to Barth's growing distance from the religious socialists in Switzerland. According to Marquardt, the failure of international socialism to stop the First World War did not lead him to fundamentally deny the correspondence between socialism and the gospel. Rather, it radicalized his commitment to socialism, while at the same time it tempered his understanding of the relationship between empirical socialism and the kingdom of God. Marquardt argues that this can be seen in Barth's exegesis of Romans 13 in the first *Römerbrief*, which was executed in dialogue with Lenin's *State and Revolution*.[148]

Barth's misgiving towards socialism was that it sought to merely replace the existing social order with another. He affirmed the need to fundamentally replace the existing social order, but not with another all-too-human construction. Rather, the "new man became the object of Barth's thinking and acting," and thus, "the Christian community became the agent of revolution."[149] The Christian community, therefore, became the vanguard movement in the world, seeking to make concrete that which the gospel had proclaimed. However, at the same time, Barth placed the Christian community on the same level with the socialist movement. That is, both were seen in a subordinate position to God's socialism, or the kingdom of God. No direct identification between either the kingdom of God and socialism or the kingdom of God and the church was possible. Rather, both, for better or for worse, were now understood as parabolic witnesses to *the* kingdom of God.

146. Of course, part of Marquardt's thesis is to argue that in Barth there is no such thing as a "purely religious or theological position" which is somehow separate from a political orientation.

147. Ibid., 51.

148. This assertion has been sharply contested by Eberhard Jüngel. See his "Theological Beginnings," 97.

149. Marquardt, "Socialism in the Theology of Karl Barth," 56.

This position was more fully worked out in the second edition of the *Römerbrief*, and continued to distance Barth from the Swiss religious socialists, who were both anti-ecclesial and too unclear about the relationship between the kingdom of God and socialism.[150] They identified the socialist movement with the inbreaking kingdom of God. In face of this, Barth was forced to turn to theological work in order to work out the relationship between the Bible (i.e., the kingdom of God found therein) and the newspaper (i.e., the real material existence of humanity). It is in this third point that Marquardt's thesis has received the greatest challenge. For it implies that the relationship between Barth's exegesis and his political praxis is reversed, thus reducing both his exegesis and his theology to their political function.[151]

The final point is Marquardt's attempt to show that Barth's theology retained its indelibly socialist imprint into his mature dogmatic work, and that it is most clearly seen in his construction of the doctrine of God.[152] That God is the "one who loves in freedom," is a direct appropriation of Barth's early articulation of ethical (read "socialistic") action, the implication being that what was formerly the goal and intention of human action for the kingdom of God is now given solely in the being of God.[153] Human action, however, is not abrogated, but called into

150. Barth's break with the religious socialists was not amicable. And though his tone would become softer toward them, he retained the judgment that an over-identification between socialism and the kingdom of God was evident among the religious socialists. See Barth, *CL*, 243.

151. See Hunsinger, "Conclusion: Toward a Radical Barth," in *Karl Barth and Radical Politics*, 189–91; and Eberhard Jüngel, "Theological Beginnings," 82–104.

152. The questions raised by Marquardt's work have led other commentators, under the influence of his thesis, to explore in detail both why Barth, after his sharp dialectical turn and move to Göttingen in 1921, focused on dogmatic theology; and the way in which his radical political commitments were theologically grounded and constitutively influential in his later theological constructions. One of the best examples of this is Peter Winzeler, *Widerstehende Theologie*. For Winzeler's response to his critics see his "Der Sozialismus Karl Barths in der neusten Kritik," 262–72.

153. This is found in his 1923 essay, "Problem of Ethics Today," in which the kingdom of God is described thus: "It is as a task and not as an object of desire, as a goal and not as a termination of the moral struggle, that enthusiastic, idealistic, communistic, anarchistic, and, it is well to remember (all true Lutheran doctrine to the contrary notwithstanding), even *Christian* hope envisages reality here on earth. The cry of Western humanity is one: let freedom in love and love in freedom be the pure and direct motive of social life, and a community of righteousness its direct objective!" ("The Problem of Ethics Today," 160).

parabolic correspondence to the God who "loves in freedom." "Barth's concept of God, in other words, elaborates the ethical and social goal of human action."[154] This leads Marquardt to argue that the concise summation of Barth's doctrine of God is to be found in a relatively obscure passage in which God is called "the fact that not only sheds new light on, but materially changes, all things and everything in all things."[155] For Marquardt, this parallels Marx's eleventh thesis on Feuerbach in which theory and praxis are inextricably linked and asymmetrically ordered, with praxis in the primary position.[156] However, the agent of change for Barth is God, who "is not a basis for interpreting the world, but the fact which really transforms it."[157]

Marquardt's thesis offers more than an explication of the relationship between theology and politics, or even theology and socialism in Barth. His work is an attempt to offer an overarching principle through which Barth's theology as a whole may be interpreted. Whether or not he is successful in the details, his work has been extraordinarily influential and intellectually productive for other interpreters of Barth's theology.[158]

Though Marquardt recognizes the importance and influence of Christoph Blumhardt in shaping Barth's approach to socialism,[159] he is far more interested in the influence of Kutter and Ragaz. But even these two figures are finally subordinate to Barth's own "theological existence in Safenwil," which was one of "socialist praxis."[160] Nevertheless, of the five "Marxist" elements in Barth's thought that Marquardt outlines at the end of *Theologie und Sozialismus*, a case could be made that all of them were directly or indirectly inspired by the Blumhardts (though Marquardt only recognizes that fact in the case of one, "historical mate-

154. Marquardt, "Socialism in the Theology of Karl Barth," 67.

155. Ibid., 67. The quote is found in *CD* II/1, 258.

156. "The philosophers have only *interpreted* the world in various ways; the point is to *change* it" (Marx, "Theses on Feuerbach," 571).

157. Marquardt, "Socialism in the Theology of Karl Barth," 68.

158. Some examples which were influenced by Marquardt to varying degrees and with varying results are: Lehmann, "Theologian of Permanent Revolution"; Bentley, "Christian Socialist"; Dannemann, *Theologie und Politik*; Hood, *Contemporary Political Orders and Christ*; Petersen, "Theology and Socialism," 59–74; Villa-Vicencio, "'Revolution of God'" 45–58; Gorringe, *Karl Barth*; and Dorrien, *Barthian Revolt*. We will turn to consider Gorringe's work below.

159. Marquardt, *Theologie und Sozialismus*, 70–71.

160. Marquardt, "Socialism in the Theology of Karl Barth," 58.

rialism"), or that Barth's own peculiar interpretation of "Marxist" ideas was tempered by the influence of the Blumhardts.[161] In reality, it is not Marquardt himself who proves most interesting in regard to accounting for the Blumhardts influence on Barth, but others who have been influenced by him. This is especially the case of our next interpreter.

Helmut Gollwitzer

Helmut Gollwitzer, it could be argued, was the real source of inspiration behind Marquardt's thesis. After Barth's retirement, Gollwitzer was not allowed to succeed Barth because key figures in Switzerland feared that he was a communist. When Marquardt's thesis was rejected at the *Kirchliche Hochschule* in Berlin, Gollwitzer resigned in protest as a sign of solidarity with his student Marquardt, but also as a sign of solidarity with the thesis put forth by Marquardt. His 1972 essay, "Reich Gottes und Sozialismus bei Karl Barths," is his mature reflection on the questions raised both by Marquardt and by his own personal experience with Barth.[162]

Throughout this meandering essay, all the while identifying with Marquardt's thesis, Gollwitzer is concerned to show that, "In reality the entire direction of Barth's thought leads to *praxis*: to faith as the praxis-determining element, not to faith as the enabling of dogmatic utterances—the latter is only a stage on the way to praxis."[163] Thus, an integral connection exists between Barth's Safenwil existence and his later dogmatic work, a connection that is to be found in the "socialist" element in Barth's thought. In contrast to Marquardt, Gollwitzer does not leave himself open to the charge of reducing Barth's theology to its political function. He is clear that socialism "is a predicate of the gospel. God wants socialism. True socialism is the kingdom of God—both as the goal of God's history with man, and as the present movement on earth here and now."[164]

---

161. Marquardt, *Theologie und Sozialismus*, 313–32, esp. 314.

162. ET, "Kingdom of God and Socialism in the Theology of Karl Barth," in *Karl Barth and Radical Politics*, 77–120. Note: this essay is an abridged version of the German original.

163. Gollwitzer, "Kingdom of God and Socialism in the Theology of Karl Barth," 97.

164. Ibid., 77–78.

Gollwitzer is aware of the shifting of perspective that occurs between the first and second *Römerbrief* and the later shift encountered in the *Church Dogmatics*. However, he argues that Barth retained his insight that an essential link exists between the kingdom of God and socialism. He notes two things that are evident throughout Barth's career:

> First, the contention that the God of the gospel wants socialism led to a penetrating consideration of evangelical talk about God and to its Christological and Trinitarian contents and foundation; yet this reflection was always aimed toward determining what the kingdom of God is, the kingdom of God in heaven *and* on earth, transcendentally *and* immanently, as a prototype of the grace to be imitated in praxis here and now. Second, the search for the revolutionary agent defined the Christian community as such, and gave her direction for her social action following from the highest and no longer questionable authority, from the revelation of this God himself in his Word, namely, Jesus Christ. This is what has persisted. This is the unity of Barth's theology through its various, living phases, progressing in constant self-correction.[165]

In connection with these, there are at least two points that deserve to be highlighted.

The first is Barth's interpretation of "revolution." Gollwitzer notes that, for Barth, revolution referred to the "fundamental transformation," of the whole of existence, rather than its immanent reform.[166] In Gollwitzer's estimation, this put Barth in continuity with the Reformation tradition, which stressed the radical newness and transformation of the individual not through human action, but by grace alone. This insight, however, led Barth to make two decisive corrections to Reformation theology. The first was to extend the notion of the revolutionary transformation of the individual by grace, to humanity as a whole. Gollwitzer notes that it was under the guidance of Ragaz, Kutter, and Blumhardt that Barth was able to conceive of the kingdom of God in "material, universal and social terms," over against the individualistic emphasis found in the Reformers.[167] And though the voice in which Barth spoke

---

165. Ibid., 90.
166. Ibid., 91.
167. Ibid., 93.

about such a revolution changed over time, he retained this emphasis all the way up to the final sections of the *Church Dogmatics*. That this revolution occurred through God's action alone meant that a simple identification of the kingdom of God with socialism was impossible. Nevertheless, human action is set on its way toward its goal of "correspondence" to God's action in the world, which is conceived in socialist terms.

This corrective implied Barth's second complaint about Reformation eschatology: its total lack of implications for political and social life. According to Gollwitzer, Barth increasingly saw the "kingdom of God" as having implications for the social arena of human life, almost at the expense of individual life. Here again, the problem of the correspondence between God's action and human action comes to the fore. This leads us to Gollwitzer's second point, the importance of the concept of "parable."

According to Gollwitzer, "parable" and "correspondence" are central to Barth's theology and to his theological ethics in particular. These concepts were used by Barth to map the relationship between divine and human agency. "Parable" has both a positive and negative aspect when applied to the relationship between God's action and human action. The negative is simply that there can be no identification between divine and human action; God is God and man is man.[168] It is the eschatological proviso in its ethical and political form. According to Gollwitzer, and contrary to most Barth interpretation, this form takes precedence in Barth's thought over against the *analogia fidei*, its correlate from the theory of knowledge. Over-attention to the latter, "is indicative of academic theology's idealist way of thinking."[169] The positive implication of "parable," and that for which the negative exists, is that human action really can point to divine action in a meaningful and "parabolic" fashion. Furthermore, this "correspondence" is not to be found in an interior and immanent relationship to God, but in real, objective, social, and historical acts. God's kingdom, which brings the material, social, and universal transformation of reality, is both the basis and goal of all human action.

168. Ibid., 97.
169. Ibid.

The Blumhardts are of central importance for Gollwitzer's interpretation. According to Gollwitzer, they (along with Ragaz and Kutter) formed Barth's understanding of God's kingdom as a materially, socially, and universally transformative power.[170] As part of his continuity thesis, Gollwitzer also points out that Barth never lost the eschatology he had learned from the Blumhardts, though it did undergo some alteration in its form. This fact leads him to surmise that had Barth written *Church Dogmatics* V it would have been an eschatology close to that found in the first *Römerbrief*, implying the continuity both with the Blumhardtian influence and the socialist impulse of Barth's early work in a way that seems to imply a mutual interpenetration of the two.[171] That is, the Blumhardtian impulse and the socialist impulse appear to be inextricably intertwined for Gollwitzer. Whether or not this is definitely the case for him, it is most certainly the judgment of our last commentator.

Timothy Gorringe

Timothy Gorringe's *Karl Barth: Against Hegemony* represents the first full-scale appropriation of the Marquardt thesis into the Anglo-American context. Though others, most notably George Hunsinger, have sought to integrate the Marquardt thesis into their interpretative work on Barth, no one has sought to offer an overarching interpretation of Barth that emphasizes the political character of Barth's theology in the way that Gorringe does. His central thesis is to argue that, "From first to last his [Barth's] work is 'against hegemony.' It is this above all which distinguishes his work as a contextual theology, as a response to his context."[172] For Gorringe, "hegemony" constitutes those cultural, social, and political realities that have become accepted as the "norm" through a process of historical and ideological crystallization. When these realities assert themselves as unquestionable, they become ideologies, or "world views," and enslave humanity. According to Gorringe, Barth, as a "theologian of freedom," is concerned with both a negative and a positive response to these ideological realities. The negative response is his calling into question the legitimacy and ultimacy of the

170. See ibid., 80, 93.
171. See Ibid., 94–95.
172. Gorringe, *Karl Barth*, 1.

various hegemonies to which humanity is enthralled. The positive response is Barth's account of how humanity is to take up their liberation that has been won through Jesus Christ.[173]

Gorringe's goal is to show the specific ways in which Barth sought to respond as a theologian to the hegemonic forces that he encountered in his context. All the while, he is concerned to attack the various pictures of Barth as an idealist (read: "neo-orthodox") concerned only with theories of knowledge, arguing instead that theory and praxis are embedded in one another in Barth's theology (a la Marquardt and Gollowitzer).[174] This overarching approach guides his reading of Barth's *oeuvre*, and leads him to pay particular attention to the social, cultural, and especially the political events that were simultaneously occurring as Barth's theology unfolded.[175] Thus, Gorringe reads the first *Römerbrief* in light of the First World War, while the second *Römerbrief* is read in light of the various revolutionary failures in Germany and Russia. All the while, Gorringe attempts to retain a focus on the content of the two texts and to show the internal continuities and discontinuities, developments and breaks that are evident in Barth's thought during this period. This is repeated, to provocative effect, as Gorringe gives an account of the development of Barth's theology all the way through his final volume of the *Church Dogmatics*.[176]

173. See ibid., 2–3.

174. Gorringe: "The very structure of the *Dogmatics*, the integration of theology and ethics, the refusal to separate law and gospel, is a sign of his determination not to allow so much as a knife blade between theory and praxis" (8–9). This thesis has recently received more verification in fact with the publication of the small volume, *Ever Against the Stream*, by Frank Jehle. Jehle does not offer an elaborate thesis about the relationship of theology and socialism or theology and politics in Barth's thought. Rather, he is concerned simply to give an account of the specific historical instances wherein Barth can be seen to be engaged in political issues in a public fashion, which he does to great effect, confirming in many ways the thesis that Barth's theology includes within it an imperative to engage in political struggle.

175. Gorringe has received considerable negative reaction because of this methodology. See McCormack, "Review of *Karl Barth: Against Hegemony*, by Timothy Gorringe." For a more favorable assessment, see Selinger, "Review of *Karl Barth: Against Hegemony*, by Timothy Gorringe."

176. Some of the most interesting parallels, which will need further detailed scholarly analysis are: The development of Barth's theology of the Word and his doctrine of God as seen against the background of his struggle with Fascism (117–63); the development of Barth's doctrine of creation and anthropology in light of the devastation of the Second World War and the Shoah (164–216); and the development of Barth's

Throughout, Gorringe takes notice of the Blumhardts as especially important interlocutors for Barth in his theological development. As he notes, "The impact of the Blumhardts on Barth can hardly be overestimated."[177] They are, in fact, the progenitors of both the negative and positive responses to hegemony that are found in Barth, though Gorringe does not point this out explicitly. They also help to shape the ordering of the relationship between the negative and positive; that is, that the former exists only for and in light of the latter. Christoph Blumhardt's intense critique of religion, culture, and society comes to Barth both directly and mediately—through Ragaz and Kutter—and was very influential on Barth's own negative response to the various cultural and political hegemonies he encountered. In Christoph Blumhardt, Barth encountered a person who took with upmost seriousness the fact that "God is God"; a person who sought to live in the light of that reality—a reality that radically relativizes all others.

The Blumhardtian inheritance was also very important in shaping Barth's own positive vision of what human liberation should look like and how human freedom was to be used. For Gorringe, this is most clearly spelled out in *Church Dogmatics* IV/3, which he offhandedly describes as a volume concerned above all with the message of the Blumhardts.[178] According to Gorringe, Barth "read the atonement as a *history* of the assault of light on darkness, a history of liberation."[179] This history occurs under the watchword, "Jesus is Victor!," which points not only to the divinely ordained fact of human liberation, but also indicates that human freedom is to be used to participate in this "battle history."

The Blumhardts were also responsible for the way in which Barth understood the relationship between the negative and positive response to hegemony. In both Christoph and Johann Christoph Blumhardt, the negative critique of the world, its culture, politics, philosophies, etc.,

---

theology of reconciliation and its attendant concept of freedom in the light of the rapid industrial and cultural change experienced in Europe during the 1950's and early 1960's as well as the growing antagonism between East and West with their varying attempts to legitimize the justness of their cause, through religion or Marxist theory, etc. (217–67).

177. Ibid., 34.

178. See ibid., 224.

179. Ibid., 242.

has its reason for being only in the light of God's "redeeming love."[180] Thus, the negative critique does not exist merely as an epiphenomenon of some wider cultural anxiety, but rather as the first in an ordered response to the onslaught of God's love. The negative gives way to the positive articulation of both human liberation and human freedom, both of which occur in response to God's act in Jesus Christ who is himself the kingdom.[181]

The above means that the continuity of Barth's theology of liberation (or "socialist impulse" as in Gollwitzer) is inextricably bound to the continuity of the Blumhardts' influence on Barth. But unlike Gollwitzer, Gorringe is explicit about this fact. He ends his work with the following observation:

> I believe that Barth's work from first to last makes a profound contribution to human liberation. It does this, of course, in the many-sidedness of its approach to *die Sache*, Jesus Christ, from which springs its depth and its spirituality, and in its ability to generate questions. It is liberative, however, especially in its hostility to abstraction and its concern for the concrete. In this connection the role that the Blumhardts play in Barth's theology from his first commentary on Romans to the final fragments is of crucial importance.[182]

With this assessment, Gorringe gives a central place to the influence of the Blumhardts on Barth, making this fact one of the key elements that gives coherence to his own interpretive project. In light of this, it is both surprising and unfortunate that he does not devote any significant time to discussing the Blumhardts more directly. He is content primarily to discuss them in the light of Barth's own presentation of their ideas. This is of course entirely understandable, since his project is concerned with Barth, and only tangentially with the Blumhardts. However, one is left wondering if more attention to the Blumhardts would have strengthened his case that Barth was a liberation theologian ahead of his time.

~

180. Ibid., 34.
181. See ibid., 289.
182. Ibid., 288–89.

In this final section we have dealt with those interpreters who have sought to elucidate the relationship between socialism and the kingdom of God in Barth's theology. All three of our interpreters have argued that Barth's theology as a whole can only be properly understood when his commitment to "socialist" or "liberative" praxis is taken into account as the practical outcome of his dogmatic theology. Though Friedrich-Wilhelm Marquardt was the first to offer a substantive account of this interpretation of Barth, the work of Gollwitzer and Gorringe proves to be the most interesting as regards the role that the Blumhardts' influence on Barth might play in such an interpretation. For Gollwitzer, the Blumhardts fundamentally shape Barth's understanding of the kingdom of God as that which is materially, socially, and universally transformative. Also, as mentioned in connection with Webster, Barth's use of "parable" as a way of coordinating human action with divine action has generally been interpreted as something he learned from Christoph Blumhardt.

In Gorringe, the Blumhardts are seen as one of the central influences that shaped Barth's theology and gave it its "anti-hegemonic" contours. They provide a loose outline for Barth's negative response to his context, whereby God is seen as he who puts a question mark to the whole of the cosmos. They also provide Barth with a positive vision of the kingdom of God as embodied in the midst of the real needs of humanity. Their vision of the victorious Christ is not a victory that hails from the center of the cultural, social and political power centers, but from the margins. This is a victory in which humanity is called to participate as those who struggle for righteousness and love, even in the face of overwhelming odds, devastation and demonic powers. Thus, human freedom is freedom in response to the free love of God that has conquered and is conquering even in the midst of the shadows of this world.

A Common Thread?

Rather than summarize the above material, I would like to give a very brief indication of the direction our study of the influence of the Blumhardts on Barth might move in light of our preliminary investigation. The one central theme that has continued to re-surface in different contexts and with different implications is the influence that the

Blumhardts' eschatology had on Barth. Their focus on the in-breaking kingdom of God was not a theology of the "last things," but was the impulse which inhabited the whole of their theology and was summed up, with its theological, practical, and methodological implications in the slogan, "Jesus is Victor!" and in the petition, "Thy kingdom come!"

The victory of Jesus—a victory that is not open to human manipulation, but must be waited for and hastened toward—is the victory of the risen, coming Christ. This victory is a material, social and universal victory, in which real life is addressed. It is also a victory that continues to work itself out in temporal life through the struggle that human beings are called to participate in. It does not, therefore, abrogate human action, but inspires and directs it, envisioning a transformed life on the earth. At the same time, this victory is a social victory, for it is the victory of Jesus Christ who is himself the kingdom of God. Thus, the material transformation that occurred in the victory of Jesus on the cross and in the resurrection has implications for the larger social and political life in which human beings find themselves. It calls for "parabolic" correspondence to the being of the God "who loves in freedom." Furthermore, this victory is universal. There is no area of human life that is not affected and taken up into the transformation wrought in Jesus Christ. And, to the scandal of many, this victory also includes all of humanity. Though Barth and the elder Blumhardt differed in their belief in an *apokatastasis ton panton* from the younger Blumhardt, as will be shown, all three operated in the hope for such a universal reconciliation.

The influence of the Blumhardts eschatology reaches across doctrinal lines.[183] This is no less the case in its influence on Barth's theology. It affected his approach to theological language; it contributed to the shape of his particular integration of doctrine and ethics; and it most certainly shaped certain aspects of Barth's Christology, ecclesiology, anthropology, creation and theology of election. This plurality means that any investigation of the influence of the Blumhardts on Barth will have a number of areas to focus on, but must keep at its center the seminal affirmation, "Jesus is Victor!"

Our preliminary investigation of the various secondary sources, therefore, compels us to focus our attention on the eschatology of the Blumhardts. In this, Berger, Sauter, and Jüngel will be of special impor-

---

183. See Gollwitzer, "Christoph Blumhardt," 259–75, esp. 264–65.

tance, but so also Gollwitzer and Gorringe. Berger, Sauter, and Jüngel all point us to the substantive theological contribution that the Blumhardts proclamation of the kingdom of God made during the formative period of Barth's theological development, while also giving intimations—and in at least one case substantial reflection (i.e., Sauter)—that the Blumhardts continued to be important theological interlocutors for Barth even up to the final volumes of the *Church Dogmatics*. Gollwitzer and Gorringe are less relevant, but their essential point that Barth's theology was always concerned to envision human action and human reflection on the God who acts in His Word is no less salutary, since it forces us to remember that Barth was not above all interested in constructing dogmatics as an exercise in theological epistemology. Rather, reflection was always meant to ground action, and action was what made reflection real. As both commentators show, such an approach to theology resonates deeply with the practical, pastoral and theological concerns of the Blumhardts.

2

The Life and Thought of Johann Christoph Blumhardt

The Blumhardts' Context: Pushing the Boundaries of Württemberg Pietism

THE BLUMHARDTS WERE NOT AHISTORICAL FIGURES. THEY CAME FROM a specific tradition, which contributed to their peculiar theological vision. That tradition was Württemberg Pietism. At the same time, however, it is widely acknowledged that though children of their time and context, both Blumhardts were nonetheless innovators who strained at the boundaries of the tradition they inherited. The novelty of their message has contributed to some confusion as to their relationship with their immediate environs and the theological tradition in which they were nurtured. Early in the twentieth century, some interpreters almost portrayed the Blumhardts as though they were men "without father or mother, without genealogy, without beginning of days or end of life" (Heb 7:3).[1] This understanding, though rhetorically effective, has fallen by the wayside as more research has emerged showing the profound influence that Württemberg Pietism exercised on both the father and the son. Though a presentation that shows the pervasive influence of the Württemberg tradition on the two Blumhardts is beyond the limits of this project, it is still important to devote some time to a discussion of the Württemberg tradition out of which the Blumhardts arose and to seek to clarify their relationship to it.

---

1. Leonhard Ragaz was particularly guilty of this, as was Eduard Thurneysen. See Ragaz, *Der Kampf um das Reich Gottes*, and Thurneysen, *Christoph Blumhardt*.

What is Württemberg Pietism?

Dieter Ising begins his assessment of Johann Christoph Blumhardt's relationship to Pietism with the following observation:

> It has become accepted practice to account Johann Christoph Blumhardt as among the Pietists—according to the prejudices of one's own opinion of Pietism—and thus to approach it in a positive or negative manner. That 'Pietism' does not exist, but rather, that there is a many faceted movement which reaches from the 17th century to our very present day that experienced changes in its history, is not seen.[2]

Ising's point, echoed by others, is that when one speaks of a historical or theological relationship to Pietism, one has to take into account that Pietism was and is an internally diverse phenomenon. The type of Pietism that exerted a profound influence on the Blumhardts was the nineteenth-century Württemberg Pietism that was rooted in the life and thought of Johann Albrecht Bengel (1687–1752), Friedrich Christoph Oetinger (1702–1782) and Nicholas von Zinzendorf (1700–1760).

Frank Macchia provides a succinct description of the nineteenth-century Württemberg Pietism that we have in mind here, when he says: "Perhaps it would not be too simplistic to say that Pietism near the turn of the nineteenth century in Wuerttemberg had its roots in the eschatological fervor of Bengel, the vision of cosmic transformation in Oetinger (that was connected with living the life of God through wisdom principles), and the revivalistic and missions-oriented impulses of the Bruedergemeinde Herrnhut."[3] The key motifs of this form of Pietism were centered on the question of the in-breaking of the kingdom of God in history. They include: 1) the belief that the kingdom of God was already related to history in a very intimate fashion, so that God was active in the world not only as the reviver of souls, but also as the transformer of the world; 2) that when the kingdom came in its fullness, it would consist in the universal outpouring of the Holy Spirit, which, for some, implied a universal restoration of all things or "apokatastasis";

---

2. Ising, *Johann Christoph Blumhardt. Leben und Werk*, 340; Eberhard Busch echoes this sentiment in his *Karl Barth and the Pietists*, 4–5, originally published as *Karl Barth und die Pietisten: Die Pietismuskritik des jungen Karl Barth und ihre Erwiderung*; See also Stoeffler, "Pietism," 3–24, esp. 3–10.

3. Macchia, *Spirituality and Social Liberation*, 22.

3) because God was so intimately at work in history, many within this tradition sought to overcome the perceived dualism of classical Pietism between the soul and body, thus making space for healing and the miraculous; 4) God's work in the world and history also constituted a call to missions, which included a definite concern for the political and social issues of the day; and 5) a nascent critique of some of the motifs of classical Pietism, especially the subjectivistic orientation of the practice of piety (i.e., the concern over one's own salvation, etc.).[4] Though many of these motifs can be found in one way or another in other forms of Pietism, it is the predominance of the eschatological and social concept of the kingdom of God that gives them their particular configuration in Württemberg Pietism and which distinguishes it from other types of Pietism.[5] This is the theological and ecclesial tradition from which the Blumhardts emerged and which exercised such a profound influence on their life and ministry.

Clarifying the Relationship of the Blumhardts to Württemberg Pietism

The ministry of both of the Blumhardts has long been seen as a challenge to the more conservative circles of Pietism. This challenge has led to differing assessments of their relationship to their pietistic environment. Within the contemporary secondary literature there are two ba-

---

4. I am indebted here to the work of Frank Macchia. See his *Spirituality and Social Liberation*, 21–42; for a discussion of the Württemberg version of the "apokatastasis" doctrine, see Groth, *Die 'Wiederbringung AllerDinge' Im Württembergischen Pietismus* and idem, "Chiliasmus und Apokatastasishoffnung"; for a discussion of the rich history of political and social activism in Württemberg Pietism, see Hartmut Lehmann, *Pietsimus und weltliche Ordnung in Württemberg*.

5. It should be noted here that the primary theological motif of classical Pietism is what is called the "New Birth." This is the belief in the conversion of the individual through an existential/spiritual encounter with Jesus Christ in faith as mediated by the Holy Spirit, which includes an emphasis on a synergistic conception of divine sanctification through which the individual "grows in grace and spiritual maturity." It is from the belief that the individual can be changed (empirically!) that many of the insights and distinctive motifs of the later Württemberg Pietism stem. It is not a far step from the belief in the transformation of the individual to the belief in the transformation of society and the world. For a discussion of the theological motifs of Pietism, see Gerdes, "Theological Tenets of Pietism," 25–60. For the corporate dimension of the kingdom spirituality of Württemberg Pietism, see Macchia, *Spirituality and Social Liberation*, 38.

sic orientations: the first, associated most notably with Karl Barth, and following him, Eberhard Busch and Gerhard Sauter, argues that both Blumhardts were essentially outside of Pietism; and the second, here associated with Frank Macchia, Martin Stober and Dieter Ising, locates them within the circle of Württemberg Pietism, with the qualification that they are to be seen as pushing the boundaries.[6] The more recent scholars of this second group (Macchia, Stober, Ising) have argued that it was often the contemporary debates, which were polemical in nature (this is especially true of Barth and his Religious Socialist predecessors), which shaped the older assessments of the Blumhardts, rather than the actual subject matter itself.[7] Both groups agree that the two Blumhardts were critical of certain aspects of what they understood to be the "Pietism" of their day.[8] The question of their relationship to Pietism, therefore, can be formulated as follows: Does the life and thought of the Blumhardts constitute a critique of Pietism that fundamentally breaks with pietistic thought or is their work to be understood as an extension of pietistic themes and therefore still within Pietism, especially the Württemberg version of it?[9]

6. These two contrasting orientations show up fairly early in Blumhardt interpretation. One can see them in the differing approaches of Eugen Jäckh and Eduard Thurneysen in the mid-1920s. Thurneysen's early work, *Christoph Blumhardt*, was explicitly conceived as a response to the work of Jäckh (*Blumhardt Vater und Sohn und ihre Botschaft*). As Thurneysen wrote to Barth: "I intend to write something about Blumhardt within a reasonable time, now more than ever since the publication of the book by Jäckh who simply makes a religious Pietist out of him. . . ." (*Revolutionary Theology in the Making*, 201). Thurneysen's approach is surely rooted in the overall approach of the Swiss religious socialists and especially Leonhard Ragaz who describes Christoph Blumhardt as finishing the work of his father by dispensing with the thought and language of Pietism. See Ragaz, *Der Kampf um das Reich Gottes*, 35–36.

7. See Ising, *Johann Christoph Blumhardt*, 340; see also Sauter, *Die Theologie des Reiches Gottes*, 65.

8. The question of what the Blumhardts meant by "Pietism" is also a very complicated and difficult question that is simply beyond this work. An example of the awareness of this problem is noted by Ising, who has observed that the elder Blumhardt could understand "Pietism" in a negative fashion, generally identifying it with both self-righteous spirituality and the separatist impulse, though at the same time, he could take for granted many positive elements of Pietism. See Ising, *Johann Christoph Blumhardt*, 340–47.

9. It is to be noted here that Eberhard Busch, in his *Karl Barth and the Pietists*, is essentially asking the same question about the critique of Pietism found in the first edition of Barth's *Römerbrief*. See Busch, *Karl Barth and the Pietists*, 24–25; In a more recent essay, published as an epilogue to the English translation, Busch moved this

Karl Barth sets the pace for the interpretation of the Blumhardts as located outside the circle of Pietism. This thesis is developed primarily in his chapter on Johann Christoph Blumhardt in *Protestant Theology in the Nineteenth Century*.[10] Barth notes at least three ways in which Blumhardt is to be seen as deviating from Pietism: 1) His discovery of the theme "Jesus is Victor" and its stress on the objective battle of Jesus with the powers of darkness and the subsequent cosmic dimensions of liberation are, according to Barth, in contrast to Pietism's stress on the conflict between Jesus and the unconverted heart.[11] 2) His transformation into a "theologian of hope" was, according to Barth, another diversion "from the way of Pietism."[12] Barth argues that Blumhardt's response to the fading of the Möttlingen revival set him apart from other men involved in the revival movements (*Erweckungsbewegungen*) of the nineteenth century, in that Blumhardt saw the revival and all the miraculous events connected to it as signs of the coming of Christ, but not as the coming itself. Thus, Blumhardt would not be cast into depression over the end of revival, but instead would begin another chapter of his ministry at Bad Boll, which above all was determined by his chiliastic hope in the coming of Christ into the world. 3) Finally, according to Barth, Blumhardt differed from Pietism in that he saw Jesus's work in the world as a struggle with darkness, which included help for the embodied and social dimensions of human life. Blumhardt was just as concerned with relief from illness as he was in relieving persons of their guilt over sin. This emphasis on the embodied being of man also helped Blumhardt to be sensitive to the issues of poverty, though his son would become more aware of the systemic nature and origins of this problem. According to Barth, Johann Christoph Blumhardt's conception of sin

---

insight further by characterizing Barth as a "critical friend or friendly critic" of Pietism. See idem, "Hope for the Conversion of the Converted: Karl Barth and Pietism," 286.

10. 643–53. Barth's interpretation here should be seen in continuity with that of Eduard Thurneysen and Leonhard Ragaz (see note 6). Also, it is assumed here that Barth's judgment about the elder Blumhardt should also be applied, perhaps even more so, to the younger Blumhardt. Thus, according to Barth, both Blumhardts are outside of Pietism.

11. As Barth notes, "According to Blumhardt it is a 'petty view' to treat Christianity as the private concern of every individual. Even the salvation of the individual is bound up with the innermost content of the whole of human history, with the consummation of the victory grounded in Christ's redemptive death and resurrection" (ibid., 650–51).

12. Ibid., 646.

and the human person was far more holistic and more concerned with relief from poverty than that of the representatives of Pietism.

Gerhard Sauter essentially echoes this position in his major work on the Blumhardts, while Eberhard Busch also appears to follow Barth when he discusses the influence of Christoph Blumhardt and Johann Tobias Beck (1804–1878) on Barth in his turn from theological Liberalism and in the first *Römerbrief*.[13] Both Beck and Blumhardt are characterized as critics of Pietism. However, Beck is more clearly identified as a Schwäbian pietist, while Blumhardt is not.[14] In conjunction with Barth's turn away from the Schwäbian influences that permeated his first *Römerbrief* to the more dialectical orientation of the second *Römerbrief*, Busch never describes Blumhardt as one of the influences that Barth sought to leave behind. This is in contrast to the influence of Beck. In fact, Busch points out that in the second edition of the *Römerbrief* Barth "breaks away from his 'association with Beck.'"[15] The implication here is that when Barth breaks with the Schwäbian Pietism of Beck, he is not breaking with Blumhardt, who, in Busch's estimation is not a pietist. Furthermore, in the context of his discussion of the second *Römerbrief*, Busch does not mention Blumhardt in his section on "The Quotations of the Pietists," the implication being that he is not a pietist.[16]

13. See Sauter, *Die Theologie des Reiches Gottes*, 24; see also Busch, *Karl Barth and the Pietists*, 30–35. It is worth noting that Sauter later changed his position on this issue. See his, "Was hat Johann Christoph Blumhardt der Kirche und Theologie heute zu sagen?" 92.

Of further interest in this context is the dissertation of James Carroll Cox, *Johann Christoph Blumhardt and the Work of the Holy Spirit*. Cox wrote this under the supervision of his *Doktorvater*, Karl Barth. His work shows a real awareness of the historical tradition of Württemberg Pietism and its approach to the doctrine of Scripture and the work of the Holy Spirit. Though he follows Barth in his belief that Johann Christoph Blumhardt is to be seen at least as an outsider of the Württemberger tradition, he does argue that, prior to "the fight", Blumhardt's theology is basically that of the revival theology of his day. This position is remarkably similar to the other orientation that we will discuss below. The proximity of these positions and the fact that Barth could be involved in both of them in a determinative fashion should help us to understand that the two orientations are more fluid than they may appear and that perhaps Barth's own opinion on these questions shifted over time, since Cox's work was published in 1959.

14. Busch, *Karl Barth and the Pietists*, 31, 92–93.

15. Ibid., 80.

16. Ibid., 89–91. A further indication that Busch is following Barth and the whole tradition that runs back to Ragaz, is that Blumhardt is discussed (in connection to

In contrast to this, a strong consensus has emerged over the past twenty years that the Blumhardts are to be interpreted as essentially within Württemberg Pietism.[17] This position (with which this author identifies), represented here by Frank Macchia, Martin Stober and Dieter Ising,[18] has shown that all of the issues that Barth points to as un-pietistic actually have antecedents within Württemberg Pietism.[19]

---

the first *Römerbrief*) *primarily* in the context of Barth's position vis-á-vis the Religious Socialism of Kutter and Ragaz (ibid., 57–60). Also, it should be mentioned that Busch himself, in a private conversation (Private Conversation, in Klein Schneen 5/25/00), told the author that he does not consider Christoph Blumhardt as a pietist.

17. This more recent position goes back further in the secondary literature. See for example, Roessle, *Vom Bengel bis Blumhardt,*; Lehmann, *Pietsimus und weltliche Ordnung in Württemberg*; Groth, "Chiliasmus und Apokatastasishoffnung"; and Haug, *Gestalt und Botschaft.*

18. All of these works represent the most up-to-date discussion of this question having been published within the last ten years. Macchia, *Spirituality and Social Liberation*; Stober, *Christoph Friedrich Blumhardt d.J. zwischen Pietismus und Sozialismus*; and Ising, *Johann Christoph Blumhardt.* There is one important distinction that needs to be acknowledged here. Dieter Ising, though comfortable with placing the elder Blumhardt within the Württemberg tradition is not so comfortable with locating the son in the same. His basic position is that the elder Blumhardt, though located within the older Württemberg Pietism, was essentially a pariah to many of his contemporaries, such that his position within the Pietism of his day was tenuous. This tension came to a breaking point with the son since he moved the thought of his father, already under suspicion by many, in directions that would have been barely recognizable to many of the Pietists of his day (Private Letter from Dieter Ising, November 6, 2003).

19. At least three underlying issues make this position more persuasive: 1) the contemporary scholars discussed below are not shaped primarily by the polemical and constructive needs of Religious Socialism. That is, in the prior position discussed above, it was above all the Religious Socialist's opposition to the "Pietism" that they knew which shaped their judgment about the relationship of the Blumhardts to Pietism. This negative attitude toward Pietism can be readily seen in Leonard Ragaz's 1919 essay, "Gottesreich und Politik. Gespräch zwischen Quidam und einem Pietisten," in which Quidam, a religious socialist, takes a Pietist to task because he shows great concern for his soul, but none for his fellow man (see Ragaz, *Weltreich, Religion und Gottesherrschaft*, 1:80–104); 2) a second issue is that the scholars in this second group take with a grain of salt the opposition of the Blumhardts themselves to "Pietism." That is, this second group is able to show that though both of the Blumhardts register protests against "Pietism", their definition of what "Pietism" is was not based on historical research, but their own immediate concerns, and, furthermore, that these protests fit in with the distinctive form of "Pietism" that was Württemberg Pietism. That is, their protests (against "piety", etc.) often are working out of the logic of other Württembergers and are therefore already within Pietism; and 3) finally, this position is emerging now simply because there has been more time to construct a well-rounded picture of Württemberg Pietism and better source materials with which to do it. See Ising, *Johann Christoph Blumhardt*, 341.

At the same time, and in contrast to some earlier interpreters (most notably Jäckh), this position does not deny that there are aspects of the Blumhardts' thought that are critical or discontinuous with Pietism in general and Württemberg Pietism in particular.[20]

Macchia's work provides the most detailed discussion as it is specially intended to be a reading of the Blumhardts, "in the Light of Wuerttemberg Pietism." The publication of his work marks an advance in English language reception of the Blumhardts, since he attempts to interpret both the father and the son as *within* the tradition of Württemberg Pietism.[21] His assessment, similar to that of Stober and Ising, is that the Blumhardts "may be characterized as Pietists, but with a somewhat atypical drive toward a radical realization of the kingdom of God in the deliverance of the poor and the oppressed."[22] Thus, Macchia provides a lengthy and detailed introduction to the tradition of Württemberg Pietism as rooted in Bengel, Oetinger, and Zinzendorf as well as a solid introduction to the second generation of Württemberg Pietism that immediately preceded the elder Blumhardt. This second generation of leaders, which included Phillip Matthaus Hahn (1739–1790) as well as Blumhardt's relative Christian Gottlieb Blumhardt (1779–1838)—one of the founders of the famous Basel Mission—were the primary mediators of Schwäbian Pietism to the elder Blumhardt and, to a lesser extent, his son.[23]

20. William G. Bodamer Jr. gives an excellent summary of this position when he says of the elder Blumhardt: "The distinctiveness of Blumhardt is, therefore, not the distinctiveness of beginning a new tradition in theology. He stood in the same tradition as his contemporaries and dealt with similar themes. The distinctiveness of Blumhardt is in his use of the themes and his unwillingness to come to the end of theological work too soon" (idem, "Life and Work of Johann Christoph Blumhardt," 144–45).

21. Within the English-language literature on the Blumhardts the dualistic typology described here is also valid. Those who approach the Blumhardts as located outside of Pietism are generally concerned with the son. Examples of this approach include: Bentley, *Between Marx and Christ*; idem, "Preacher of Hope"; Lejeune, "Christoph Blumhardt, 1842–1919," in *Christoph Blumhardt and His Message*; Cox, *Work of the Holy Spirit*; and Regehr, "Preaching of Christoph Blumhardt". Those who approach the Blumhardts as located essentially within Pietism include: Bodamer, "Life and Work of Johann Christoph Blumhardt"; Dayton, "Radical Message of Evangelical Christianity"; and to a lesser extent those connected to the various Brethren movements and churches: Arnold, "A Letter Concerning the Blumhardts"; Eller, "Who are These Blumhardt Characters Anyhow?"; Krüger, "A Man for the Kingdom".

22. Macchia, *Spirituality and Social Liberation*, 1.

23. See ibid., 23–42.

In the thought of this second generation the earlier emphases on eschatology, cosmic transformation, and healing found in the work of Bengel, Oetinger, and Zinzendorf were transformed and made even more prominent. Macchia argues that Hahn had already emphasized the objective-historical nature of the in-breaking of the kingdom of God, including its cosmic dimensions.[24] And Christian Gottlieb Blumhardt had brought the themes of deliverance from suffering through miraculous healing and the "gospel for the poor"—a theme of great importance to Christoph Friedrich Blumhardt—to greater prominence.[25] The elder Blumhardt differed from this second generation and some of his own contemporaries, in that he kept a cosmic orientation in his "theology of hope" in the line of Oetinger and Zinzendorf, with a new emphasis developed by Ludwig Hofacker (1798–1828). In Hofacker, the Spirit was understood more to create repentance than to be a result of it.[26] This insight was coupled with the idea that the various repentance movements inspired by the Spirit were provisional in nature and thus looked forward in hope to a final outpouring of the Holy Spirit which would be universal in extent. This was in contrast to the more common revivalist emphasis on the need for repentance so that the Spirit would be poured out. However, since this cosmic orientation began with Oetinger and Zinzendorf and was further mediated to Blumhardt via Hofacker (also a Schwäbian pietist), Barth's claim that it is unpietistic is incorrect. Thus, the three central points at which Barth saw Blumhardt as deviating from Pietism—i.e., 1) the objectivism of the in-breaking of the kingdom of God; 2) the emphasis on hope for a final cosmic outpouring of the Holy Spirit; and 3) the emphasis on both physical and social healing—are already found in one form or another in the Württemberg tradition.

Both Stober and Ising echo this judgment.[27] Stober actually argues that in certain respects, for the first half of his life, Christoph was more pietistic than his father: "For the father actually preferred certain reformation concepts to the pietistic ones—i.e., as with the objectivity of absolution—a typical pietistic insecurity in regards to the certainty of salvation remains. Therefore, Christoph Blumhardt's call, so typical of

24. See ibid., 24–25.

25. See ibid., 25–28.

26. See ibid., 30.

27. See Stober, *Christoph Friedrich Blumhardt*, 232–35; Ising, *Johann Christoph Blumhardt*, 340–47.

the revival movement to challenge the unconverted to repentance and salvation, was much more emphatic than with his father."[28] Thus, according to this interpretation, not only should one see the elder Blumhardt as rooted in Württemberg Pietism, but also the son. Furthermore, the ethical and spiritual orientation of both Blumhardts—described as "hastening and waiting" by Barth—as well as Christoph Blumhardt's radical critique of religion can be found, in nascent form, in the thought of other Württemberg pietists.[29]

Ising also notes ways in which the elder Blumhardt could be said to have deviated from the Schwäbian tradition. For the most part he sees Blumhardt's departure as occurring after the Möttlingen *Kampf*. These departures include: 1) a desire to downplay, if not deny, the distinction between the saved and the unsaved, so popular among the revivalists; 2) a downplaying of eschatological predictions, which had been associated particularly with Bengel; and 3) a stronger sense of God's desire and power to work in *this* world.[30] Nevertheless, in light of Macchia's work, all three of these departures were already evident in one form or another in other Schwäbian forerunners. With this picture in mind, however, the distinctiveness of the Blumhardts from their Schwäbian forbearers and Württemberg Pietism should not be totally dismissed. Perhaps the best way to describe their relationship to it would be to say that it is not the presence of each of these themes individually in the Blumhardts, but rather, their *combination*, together with the Blumhardts emphasis on a universal hope for all of humanity which makes them distinctive and therefore unique among the Schwäbian pietists, though, nevertheless, still within the pietist circle.

---

28. Ibid., 235.

29. For Barth's discussion of Christoph Blumhardt's spirituality, see his "Action in Waiting," in *Action in Waiting*, by Karl Barth and Christoph Blumhardt, 19–48, esp. 22–23; Macchia points out that this spiritual orientation was already evident in the thought of the leader of the Korntal separatists, Johann Michael Hahn (1759–1819), with whom both Blumhardts had extensive contact. See Macchia, *Spirituality and Social Liberation*, 33–34. Stober echoes this. See his *Christoph Friedrich Blumhardt*, 233. In regard to the critique of religion, Macchia points out that there was an intense critique of piety already in Ph. M. Hahn's work. Macchia, *Spirituality and Social Liberation*, 37.

30. Ising, *Johann Christoph Blumhardt*, 340–47. For Ising, the latter is the most decidedly un-pietistic.

Having clarified the relationship between the Blumhardts and the pietistic context in which they were nurtured we now turn to a discussion of the life and thought of the elder Blumhardt.

Johann Christoph Blumhardt, Theologian of Hope[31]

As we noted in the introduction, our account of the historical narratives of the two Blumhardts will be portrayed in a straightforward and even naïve, fashion. The primary reason for this is linked to one of the major goals of this study: to reintroduce the categories of the Blumhardts' theology into Barth studies. This goal necessarily limits the amount of investigation and interrogation that normally accompanies historical studies. What will strike the reader of the Blumhardt stories is the way in which they too show signs of having the same dynamics of power that are evident in all social relations, whether inter-personal, spiritual, domestic, or political. Our goal, however, is to recount and portray the Blumhardts' history in a way similar to how Barth himself thought about the events that had shaped their lives. Therefore, many suggestive events and aspects of the narrative histories will be left undeveloped because though Barth may have been aware of those dynamics they did not become central to his own theological appropriation of their thought.

Blumhardt's Early Life and Ministry

Johann Christoph Blumhardt was born on July 16, 1805. His father, Johann Georg Friedrich Blumhardt (1777–1822) was a poor tradesman in Stuttgart, and his mother Johanna Luise Blumhardt (1779–1857), was the daughter of a tailor. According to Friedrich Zündel, on the day of Blumhardt's birth, foreign troops entered Stuttgart and even went into the home of his parents.[32] Johann Christoph's parents' interpretation of this and other events shows quite clearly that they were immersed in the eschatological expectations associated with Johann Albrecht Bengel. Bengel, "the soul of Swabian Pietism,"[33] had predicted that the

---

31. This is Barth's description of the elder Blumhardt. See his "Blumhardt," in *Protestant Theology in the Nineteenth Century*, 646.

32. Zündel, *Johann Christoph Blumhardt, ein Lebensbild*, 9.

33. Stoeffler, *German Pietism During the Eighteenth Century*, 102. Stoeffler notes that, "Bengel's influence was disseminated throughout his native Württemberg, and ter-

millennium would begin in 1836, preceded by great tribulations that the faithful would be required to experience.[34] Because his family was deeply religious and steeped in the Pietism of the region, they saw the events surrounding the Napoleonic Wars in apocalyptic terms.[35] In light of the imminent end of the world, Blumhardt's "father gathered all the children around his chair and told them the time of the Antichrist was coming. He then earnestly exhorted them that they should allow themselves to be decapitated rather than deny Christ."[36] Social upheaval and eschatological interpretation of the same would be a common theme in the lives of both Johann Christoph and Christoph Friedrich Blumhardt,[37] and though both Blumhardts would move away from Bengel's apocalyptic eschatology, they would nevertheless consistently seek to read the "signs of the times" in light of the kingdom of God.

Another early influence on Blumhardt that was also eschatologically inclined was the separatistic Kornthaler movement. In 1819, under the leadership of Gottlieb Wilhelm Hoffmann (1771–1846) and others, a community that was to be free from state control and ecclesiastical oversight (i.e., separatistic) was established by the Württemberg government at Korntal. Established to stem the tide of immigration to America, which many of the more separatistically inclined Pietists had been doing for some time,[38] the community is described by Frank

---

ritories contiguous to it, by a considerable group of able followers" (104). Mary Fulbrook echoes this when she notes that, "through his teaching at Denkendorf Bengel directly influenced the education and outlook of more than three hundred future theologians as well as many others" (Fulbrook, *Piety and Politics*, 137).

34. See Bengel, "Toward an Apocalyptic Chronology" in *Pietists—Selected Writings*, 272–73.

35. Blumhardt himself is purported to have read the whole Bible through twice by the age of eleven. See Zündel, *Johann Christoph Blumhardt*, 10.

36. Bodamer, "The Life and Work of Johann Christoph Blumhardt," 6.

37. The elder Blumhardt experienced the Napoleanic invasions, while he and his son both experienced the revolutions of 1848, the Franco-Prussian War and the creation of a united Germany in 1870–1871, and the upheaval caused by the Industrial Revolution, which finally began to make its way into Germany in the last third of the nineteenth-century. Christoph would also live to see the horrors of the First World War.

38. The most famous of the millennial émigrés from Württemberg was George Rapp (1757–1847). In 1803–1804 Rapp, founder of the Harmony Society, convinced a sizeable group of separatists from the village of Iptingen, where Blumhardt would later be pastor, to settle in America on explicitly apocalyptic grounds. Rapp's message was that the Second Coming was drawing close and the faithful of the Lord should separate

Macchia as, "a quasi-communistic settlement, a social experiment more novel than the rigid hierarchical structure of the Herrnhutter settlements." Macchia goes on to note that it was the Kornthaler's emphasis on the in-breaking of the kingdom of God that accounted for their different approach to organizing their social relations.[39] This idea—that the kingdom of God can and should make a difference in this world—was a novel aspect of early nineteenth-century Württemberg Pietism. Hoffmann's son, Wilhelm Hoffmann Jr. (1806–1873), would become one of Blumhardt's closest friends during his preparatory schooling at Schönthal from 1820–1824, and through Wilhelm and his father the eschatological ideas of Korntal would impact Blumhardt so deeply that he is purported to have claimed, "I owe them everything."[40] Later, both Blumhardt's brother-in-law and father-in-law would serve as overseers of Korntal assuring close contact to the community throughout his life.

After studying theology at the University of Tübingen from 1824 to 1829 and a one-year pastorate served in Dürrmenz, Blumhardt went to serve in Basel in 1830. Blumhardt's relative, Christoph Gottlieb Blumhardt (1779–1838), was a principal architect and founding member of the Basel Missionary Society, the leading missionary organization of the German-speaking world.[41] Johann Christoph would hold a teaching post at the Basel Mission house from 1830 to 1837 teaching Hebrew, physics, chemistry, and mathematics. His passionate interest

---

themselves from the world, go out into the wilderness and await the Lord's return. This exodus would eventually result in the founding of New Harmony, in the Territory of Indiana, in 1814. For a discussion of Rapp and New Harmony, see Taylor, *Visions of Harmony*, 5–39. Importantly, Rapp's community was distinct from Korntal in that it was far more authoritarian than the latter. I owe this distinction to Dieter Ising (Email correspondence, 7/19/06).

39. Macchia, *Spirituality and Social Liberation*, 31–38, 61–62.

40. Fritz Grünzweig, *Die evangelische Brüdergemeinde Korntal*, 26; as quoted in Macchia, *Spirituality and Social Liberation*, 61.

41. There is some confusion in the literature about the actual relationship of Christian Gottlieb Blumhardt and Johann Christoph Blumhardt. Zündel describes him as his cousin (8–9), Macchia an uncle (24), and Ising "the cousin of his father" (388). For purposes of clarity, I will follow Ising's judgment since his work represents the most recent scholarship. Either way, the influence of Christian Gottlieb on the younger Blumhardt is clear and significant. For a good discussion of the deep and pervasive interest in and commitment to missions in Württemberg Pietism, see Macchia, *Spirituality and Social Liberation*, 38–42.

in missions, which he saw as one of the precursors to the fulfillment of the kingdom of God, would later find literary expression in his *Handbüchlein der Missiongeschichte und Missiongeographie*. He would also maintain a lifelong connection to the mission movement through his involvement in the Basel Mission conferences, which he attended yearly. His Basel residency was also important because during this time Blumhardt was able to clarify his own call to the ministry, occasionally stepping in to preach in churches in the surrounding area,[42] and because he would meet his future wife, Doris Köllner (1816–1886) during this period.

There is evidence that some of the roots of Blumhardt's particular theology of the kingdom of God can be seen already during this period. There are three interrelated aspects worth mentioning. The first was Blumhardt's passion for missions among the Jews. This was motivated by a two-fold emphasis on the humanity of Jesus as well as an apocalyptic eschatology. Blumhardt showed a predilection for focusing on the humanity of Christ, the evidence of which comes to us primarily through a story that the Missionhaus committee disciplined Blumhardt for being "too enthusiastic in teaching about the humanity of Jesus."[43] This incident highlights both Blumhardt's Incarnational/practical thrust, but it also points to the fact that Blumhardt took the humanity of Jesus seriously, which in turn caused him to take to heart the need to love the "blood brothers" of Jesus, which was what Jewish missions represented to him.[44]

The other motivation for Blumhardt's enthusiasm for Jewish missions was his belief that their general conversion would be a sign of the soon-dawning kingdom of God. This notion, which was espoused by Bengel and Karl Köllner (1790–1853), Blumhardt's future father-in-law, points to the conviction that the coming kingdom of God was not without effects this side of the eschaton. In fact, it may be that Blumhardt's conception of the "time of grace" before the coming of the kingdom, which we will discuss below, is rooted in his hope for the conversion of the Jews.[45]

42. Zündel, *Johann Christoph Blumhardt*, 39.

43. Bodamer, "Johann Christoph Blumhardt," 12.

44. Zündel, *Johann Christoph Blumhardt*, 43.

45. Indeed, the conviction that the Jews would experience a mass conversion is a recurrent theme found throughout Blumhardt's writings and is almost always in close

A second major aspect of Blumhardt's later theology that is rooted in this period was Blumhardt's interest in the Hebrew Scriptures. Because of his responsibilities in teaching Hebrew, Blumhardt spent a great deal of time working through the First Testament while at Basel.[46] Many commentators have noted that Blumhardt's mature eschatology is shaped by a Christocentric reading of the expectations of the Hebrew prophets.[47] In regards to his notion of the kingdom of God, this may be the period during which Blumhardt turned more towards the eschatological expectations of the prophets over against the prevailing interest in the book of Revelation, the central text for Bengel and many of Blumhardt's contemporaries. Whether knowingly or not, this is undoubtedly the period in which Blumhardt gained a deep appreciation and understanding of the Hebrew Scriptures, on which he later would base many of his ideas about the soon-coming kingdom of God, preceding gift of the Holy Spirit, and the general restoration of the cosmos.[48]

The final aspect of Blumhardt's later eschatology that must be seen as rooted, in some measure, in this period was Blumhardt's refusal to give a fixed date to his hopes for the soon-coming kingdom of God. Here the year 1836 is paramount. This was the year that Bengel had

---

proximity to his notion of the great "time of grace," during which the whole earth would be renewed in preparation for the coming of the Lord.

Ising notes that Blumhardt's conception of the "salvation of the Jews" was not necessarily a conversion to Christianity, but rather a greater faithfulness to the God of Abraham. This understanding could go some way in obviating the contemporary accusation that Blumhardt's hope shares in a form of Christian imperialism. See Ising, *Johann Christoph Blumhardt*, 297.

46. Ibid., 77.

47. See Zündel, *Johann Christoph Blumhardt*, 280, 285–86; Rüsch, *Die Erlösung der Kreatur*, 7–8; and Groth, "Chiliasmus und Apokatastasishoffnung," 81.

48. A good example of Blumhardt's approach to these themes in the light of the Hebrew Scriptures in contradistinction to the book of Revelation is in his discussion of Isa 65. In his reflections on the eschaton, Isaiah and the prophets are accorded more authority because, according to Blumhardt, their descriptions are more straightforward, concrete, and filled with hope, whereas the descriptions in Revelation are more ambiguous, difficult to understand, and may or may not have to do with conditions on the earth. This approach means that those passages in Revelation that sound more like the concrete hopes of the prophets, like Rev 21, have more authority while those sections that do not, like Rev 20, are downplayed. See *Besprechung wichtiger Glaubensfragen*, 332–37, 340–44.

argued the millennium would begin.[49] Blumhardt would later remark that, "Nothing is so naïve as trying to calculate the approximate time of the Lord's second coming."[50] Though Dieter Ising notes that there is no mention of 1836 in any of Blumhardt's letters from this period, nor from his exegetical lectures on the book of Revelation in 1832, nonetheless, Blumhardt still flirted with developing an apocalyptic chronology just after the events at Möttlingen.[51] This anecdote indicates that though Blumhardt may not have pinned his hopes on the year 1836, the desire to develop a time-scheme by which to predict the second coming of Christ and to interpret the "signs of the times" had still affected him. Nonetheless, though Blumhardt flirted with the idea, he immediately rejected it, never making his chronology public. His rejection of this temptation was certainly rooted in some measure in the failure of Bengel's hopes to materialize in the year 1836, a failure that Blumhardt had witnessed first hand.[52]

In 1837, Blumhardt left the Basel Mission for a pastorate at Iptingen, a center of the separatist movement in Württemberg. During his time there, Blumhardt came into direct contact with the crushing poverty of the region. He also became aware of the plight of the poor as he himself was quite poor during this period, using much of his modest salary to support some of his extended family.[53]

Blumhardt was chosen vicar of Iptingen because of his pastoral gifts and especially his congenial nature. The state church (*Landeskirche*) was hoping to reestablish ties with the local separatists and the current rector had proven unable to accomplish the task. Blumhardt was brought in to assist and given free reign to try and rebuild the community's relationship with the church.[54] After a period during which he won over

49. See Groth, "Chiliasmus und Apokatastasishoffnung," 58–59.

50. Johann Christoph Blumhardt, *Besprechung wichtiger Glaubensfragen*, 368 (unpublished translation by the Brüderhof and Plough Publishing).

51. Ising, *Johann Christoph Blumhardt*, 100–101, 207–8.

52. Groth quotes from an essay in which Blumhardt recounts the effects that the year 1836 had on many people who went so far as to cease getting married, attending to their fields, or running their businesses. See Groth, "Chiliasmus und Apokatastasishoffnung," 82.

53. Macchia, *Spirituality and Social Liberation*, 63–64.

54. As noted above, Iptingen was the village from which George Rapp had led a group of separatists to America to establish a new religious community (see note 38). Apparently, the relationship between the separatists and the local church had not im-

their trust, Blumhardt succeeded in healing the rift between the local separatists and the state church. An excerpt from a letter reveals the down-to-earth approach Blumhardt used by which he successfully won the hearts of many of the Iptingers:

> When visiting the sick, you must be really outgoing—ask about the family situation, listen to what they tell you, and talk about their work problems. Don't give yourself spiritual airs! And, please, no 'official' face! Even if the spiritual does at times have to take second place—you know quite well how little I care for small talk—you will still leave a blessing behind. Above all, one should meet no one with a face that says: I know all about you—from dubious sources. It's better to be specially nice to those of whom bad things are told. Don't forget this![55]

Though most would not officially rejoin the church, many would attend services to hear Blumhardt preach and receive the sacrament, a great accomplishment in view of the fact that before Blumhardt came many of the separatists would not even set foot in the church building.[56]

Because of his desire to marry, Blumhardt searched for a pastoral position whereby he could more ably support a family. After a number of failed applications for a position that would afford him the means to support a family, he was fortunate to make the acquaintance of the well-known Christian Gottlob Barth (1799–1862), pastor of Möttlingen, while attending the Basel Mission conference in 1838. Barth encouraged Blumhardt to apply for the post at Möttlingen from which he was about to retire. After following Barth's advice, in early July 1838, Blumhardt received word that he had been appointed the new pastor of the parish of Möttlingen and Unter-Haugstett. He moved to Möttlingen on July 31 and was married to Doris Köllner on September 4, 1838; his uncle Christoph G. Blumhardt conducted the wedding. Blumhardt's ministry would now begin in earnest and his experiences at Möttlingen would transform his life and ministry.

---

proved much since that time, as Blumhardt noted that some of the separatists, "have not been inside a church for thirty years. . . ." (Zündel, *Johann Christoph Blumhardt*, 52, unpublished translation by the Brüderhof and Plough Publishing).

55. Zündel, *Johann Christoph Blumhardt*, 52 (unpublished translation by the Brüderhof and Plough Publishing).

56. See the chapter on Iptingen in Zündel, *Johann Christoph Blumhardt*, 48–89; see also Ising, *Johann Christoph Blumhardt*, 111–30.

The Möttlingen "Kampf" and Awakening

Blumhardt's early years in Möttlingen were relatively uneventful. The congregation at Möttlingen suffered from a kind of spiritual lethargy, and often slept through Blumhardt's sermons.[57] Zündel describes it as follows:

> The task Blumhardt had in Möttlingen was obviously much harder than the one at Iptingen. He faced a congregation that had learned to go to sleep while listening to one of the most brilliant preachers of the day; an air of surfeit, weariness, and discontent all around; a small circle of pietists; a group of parishioners who continued to regard Barth as all in all, and side by side with them a considerable number who felt disgruntled at the preferential treatment given the others and therefore were not so friendly disposed toward the new rector those others had specially asked for.[58]

Blumhardt sought to counter this state of affairs with pastoral visits, public readings as well as practical work to help with illness and poverty, but to little "spiritual" effect. The spiritual lethargy that had marked the community continued up to 1842 when Blumhardt became embroiled in the case of Gottliebin Dittus.

Gottliebin Dittus (1815–1872), a well-known member of the community,[59] came to Blumhardt in the fall of 1841 complaining of spiritual struggles that she was experiencing at night. Initially Blumhardt felt repelled by her and sought to avoid her.[60] However, because of the petitions of her family and a local doctor, in April of 1842 Blumhardt took her under his care and decided to investigate some of the strange happenings that had been reported by a number of her neighbors. Blumhardt arranged a surprise visit to the Dittus house accompanied by the mayor and some members of the village council. The visit revealed the extent of the problem, as so many paranormal

---

57. Macchia, *Spirituality and Social Liberation*, 64.

58. Zündel, *Johann Christoph Blumhardt* (unpublished translation by the Brüderhof and Plough Publishing), 106.

59. Zündel notes that she was highly esteemed in the community because of her Christian character and that she had been one of Pastor Barth's best parishioners. See Zündel, *Johann Christoph Blumhardt*, 121.

60. Zündel, *Awakening*, 27–28. This volume is a highly condensed version of the chapters in the Zündel biography dealing with the events at Möttlingen.

events occurred that Blumhardt was forced to end the meeting somewhat prematurely for fear that he was exposing some in his entourage to events that could have grave consequences. This visit would be the first of many for Blumhardt, though he was often at a loss to know what to do for Gottliebin. Having sought medical help for Dittus, Blumhardt eventually became convinced that something demonic was involved in the woman's struggles. He recounts the decisive moment as follows:

> It became clear to me that something demonic was at work here, and I was pained that no remedy had been found for the horrible affair. As I pondered this, indignation seized me—I believe it was an inspiration from above. I walked purposefully over to Gottliebin and grasped her cramped hands. Then, trying to hold them together as best as possible (she was unconscious), I shouted into her ear, "Gottliebin, put your hands together and pray, 'Lord Jesus, help me!' We have seen enough of what the devil can do; now let us see what the Lord Jesus can do!" Moments later the convulsions ceased, and to the astonishment of those present, she woke up and repeated those words of prayer after me.[61]

Blumhardt noted that this particular encounter was only the beginning of his battle with the forces at play in the case of Gottliebin. Many of her symptoms would intensify and become worse over the next year and a half, especially when Blumhardt was present.[62]

During this time, as Blumhardt recounts, all of his theological conceptions were exploded:

61. Ibid., 36.

62. A detailed description of the paranormal events and psycho-somatic symptoms exhibited by Dittus can be found in Blumhardt's own recounting of the story. See his *Blumhardt's Battle: A Conflict with Satan*, passim. Blumhardt wrote this account because some of the details of what had happened at Möttlingen were circulating in the form of rumors and were becoming the source of some anxiety and sensation. The Zündel biography draws almost exclusively from this source for its descriptions.

In the early twentieth century, because of the lively conversation about the Blumhardts' life and thought, these events were subjected to various interpretations, including those using psychological, physiological, and mythological categories. A detailed record of the events, including Blumhardt's recollections and consistory reports, as well as a definitive series of studies from differing perspectives and disciplines has been published together as, Johann Christoph Blumhardt, *Der Kampf in Möttlingen*. James Carroll Cox also provides an excellent overview of the various interpretations given to these events in his *Johann Christoph Blumhardt and the Work of the Holy Spirit*, 51–84.

What I suffered in spirit and soul at that time, cannot be expressed in any words. My desire to end the whole thing became even stronger.... I felt myself in a net out of which I could not possibly extricate myself by merely retreating without danger to myself and others. In addition, I felt ashamed before myself and my Savior, to Whom I prayed so much, and in Whom I trusted so much and Who had given me so many proofs of His help—I confess it openly—to give in to the devil. 'Who is the Lord?' I had to ask myself many times. And with faith in Him, Who is the Lord, the words were formed in me again and again, 'Forward! Forward! It has to lead to a good end, even though it will lead into the deepest depths, unless it were not true that Jesus had crushed the head of the serpent.'[63]

Though tempted to counter what he saw and experienced with other forms of folk magic, Blumhardt became more and more resolute that the only sufficient weapons at his disposal were prayer, the reading of Scripture, and fasting. For Blumhardt, the use of these was neither magical nor instrumental, but rather pointed to the true actor in the whole drama that he had been forced to witness, the living and risen Jesus Christ.[64] Blumhardt expressed it in a letter to his friend Barth, saying, "Whenever I write the name of Jesus, I feel overcome by a holy awe and by a joyous, fervent sense of gratitude that I know this 'Jesus!' is mine. Only now have I really come to know what we have in him."[65] Through the Möttlingen "Kampf", Blumhardt came to the conviction

63. Johann Christoph Blumhardt, *A Conflict with Satan*, 21–22.

64. It is important to note that Blumhardt never saw the ability or motivation to engage in the struggle into which he was drawn as arising from himself. Rather, he always felt that he had been compelled, enlisted, even forced into the conflict. "It had never occurred to me until then, and even then it was an immediate impulse that guided me. The impression of that impulse has stayed with me so strongly that later it was often my only reassurance, convincing me that what I undertook *was not of my own choice or presumption.* At that time I could not possibly have imagined that it would escalate so dreadfully" (Zündel, *Johann Christoph Blumhardt*, 128, unpublished translation by the Brüderhof and Plough Publishing [emphasis mine]).

65. Ibid., 138. Zündel's interpretation of this reference is instructive: "In the phrase, 'this "Jesus!" is mine' Blumhardt puts 'this' into the neuter form (dieses) of the accusative instead of the masculine one would normally expect (diesen). Now the term 'my Jesus' is used very frequently in Christian literature, both poetry and prose, but occurs nowhere in the New Testament—an example of how very often our concept of Christianity as mainly devotional or edifying in character deviates from what is represented in the Bible. Blumhardt saw Jesus as too great and himself as too small to let himself speak of his relationship to him in this manner" (138).

that the living Christ was both present and active, bringing his kingdom into the world through deeds of power. Furthermore, such deeds were not merely transformative, but also illuminative, giving Blumhardt an entirely new take on Scripture and reality. All of his future thoughts on the kingdom of God and his hope for a universal outpouring of the Spirit for the renewal of the cosmos are rooted in this event.[66]

The fight came to a decisive conclusion on December 28, 1843. By this time some of the symptoms experienced by Gottliebin had spread to other family members, including her brother Hans and her sister Katharina. Blumhardt describes it in the following way in the official report that he prepared for the Church Consistory in August of 1844:

> Finally, the most moving moment came, which no one can possibly imagine adequately who was not an eye and ear witness. At two o'clock in the morning the supposed angel of Satan roared, while the girl bent her head and upper part of her back over the backrest of the chair, with a voice of which one could hardly have believed a human throat capable, "Jesus is Victor! Jesus is Victor!"—words that sounded so far and were understood at such a distance that they made an unforgettable impression on many people. Now the power and strength of the demon seemed to be broken more with every moment. It became ever more quiet and calmer, could only make a few motions and finally disappeared unnoticed like [when] the life-light of a dying person goes out, however not until eight o'clock in the morning.[67]

Though some symptoms persisted in the following months, the battle had come to a conclusion. The confession uttered by Gottliebin's sister Katharina, or the force inhabiting her, became shorthand for what Blumhardt and others had experienced in the *Kampf*. For Blumhardt, the inner meaning of all that had transpired revealed itself in the watchword: "Jesus is Victor!"[68] Jesus, who had revealed himself as victor over the forces of darkness through the cross, had manifested himself anew in the case of Dittus and her siblings. Blumhardt would spend the rest of his life thinking through the meaning of these events. However, the

66. As Cox notes, that Blumhardt would subject his experiences—which included the case of Dittus, the awakening and various other miracles recounted in Zündel (117–254)—to serious theological reflection is another indication of Blumhardt's pietistic orientation. See Cox, *Work of the Holy Spirit*, 52.

67. Johann Christoph Blumhardt, *A Conflict with Satan*, 56.

68. See Cox, *Johann Christoph Blumhardt*, 60.

Kampf would not be the only event connected to this theme, for in the following months of 1844 a revival movement focusing on the confession of sins, repentance, and the laying on of hands by Blumhardt broke out in Möttlingen and the surrounding region.

Though there were some indications of a definite change in his congregation from 1842 on, it was only after the fight had concluded that the revival really began. The conversion of one of the most notorious men in the village would spark the movement and eventually people from the entire region were coming to Blumhardt to confess their sins and receive absolution through the laying on of hands, a practice that caught the attention of church authorities. Those who came to receive absolution were later followed by others seeking healing. It was in fact in the context of offering absolution that Blumhardt came to realize that he had been given the gift of healing.[69] This would prove extremely significant for Blumhardt as he would later link healing with forgiveness in both a soteriological and eschatological context.

Soteriologically, the close relationship between healing and forgiveness found expression in Blumhardt's emphasis on a holistic spirituality:

> Jesus generally did two things: he preached and he healed. What he said in words about the newly bestowed mercy of God was to be shown in his deeds of healing.... Jesus' acts of healing were to show how it would be in the Kingdom of God, where the whole man, body and soul, would be free from the yoke of darkness. ... If his body remains in pain and torture, how can the soul be open to receive the most glorious words?[70]

Healing was the outward manifestation of the holistic salvation that Jesus proclaimed. The transformed life given in the reality of "rebirth" could also be found in physical or mental restoration. Thus, miraculous healing was organically connected to forgiveness and rebirth, though not in a mechanical way. Forgiveness was granted by God's grace, but this did not automatically guarantee healing. Both were the direct gift of God, with forgiveness having priority, for there was no healing without forgiveness. At the same time, both the miracle and the person's trans-

---

69. See Zündel, *Johann Christoph Blumhardt*, 182.

70. Johann Christoph Blumhardt, *Blätter aus Bad Boll*, 2:17–18 (unpublished translation by the Brüderhof and Plough Publishing).

formed life functioned *together* as signs that pointed to Jesus Christ, so that the real *telos* of salvation was neither human wholeness nor salvific blessedness, but rather the coming Lord.

The eschatological significance of healing and forgiveness had both a positive and a negative side. Positively, as the quote above makes clear, in the universal appearing of the kingdom of God the whole person will be set free from the powers of darkness. Thus, the historical instances seen in the midst of the community here and now are pointers to the final reality that will come there and then. Furthermore, rejecting the apocalyptic eschatology of Bengel, Blumhardt argued that the transformation and healing experienced in his community had a wider, even universal, significance. Thus, these were signs not just of the final transformation of the church or the "faithful" but for the whole world. For Blumhardt, the kingdom comes not for our or the world's destruction but rather for the restoration and healing of all things.[71] Thus, God's grace and healing were for all, even for the whole cosmos.[72]

71. Blumhardt: "People think, probably correctly, that our time is the end time, but what they mean by it is that God has now done all there is to be done to convert men and that all to be expected from now on is judgments. Wrath and nothing but wrath is approaching, they say, since God does not care to do any more for those that until now have proved unruly. What this leads up to is that God will have regard only for the few that still believe. All the others he will let go to hell, not caring to still do anything extraordinary out of love for them. Those few, it is thought, will then be allowed to enjoy all the benefits of the saint's inheritance in the light. There is no mercy, no weeping and sighing over the lost ones, no love that would still hope, or plead with God, for them. It is regarded as foolishness and wild-eyed enthusiasm to believe that God might once more stretch out loving arms to save the lost before the day of wrath is upon us. According to that, the day of wrath is here before it is due!" (Zündel, *Johann Christoph Blumhardt*, 257–58, unpublished translation by the Brüderhof and Plough Publishing). See also Macchia, *Spirituality and Social Liberation*, 88–89.

72. The universal horizon of healing worked itself out in Blumhardt's pastoral counseling. As Zündel notes: "Blumhardt regarded each individual case as a reflection of the *general* distress; he saw in one sufferer all those afflicted similarly, and felt for them all. When, for instance, he would meet an individual epileptic, with his mind's eye he saw before him the scourge of epilepsy in general. Hence it was against that whole scourge that he would pray and also expected the patient and his family to pray. Of course that did not mean that all those so afflicted would suddenly and without knowing why be healed; it rather expressed a hope that the Lord would once more give his church power over this scourge and that entreaty against it might at least find an open door" (*Johann Christoph Blumhardt*, 265). Healing for the whole cosmos found expression in each individual case that Blumhardt encountered.

Negatively, the correlation of healing and forgiveness raised a very thorny issue for Blumhardt. If Jesus's death and resurrection were the foundation of forgiveness and healing, why was there so little of the latter in evidence in his day? We will take this question up more directly below. In anticipation, however, we should note that the lack of healing that Blumhardt saw in the world, and experienced in his own ministry, drove him to call out more fervently—as he had during his time with Dittus—for the Lord to act by pouring out the Holy Spirit, which would restore the gift of healing to the church. This restorationist longing was coupled—especially in Blumhardt's late years—with an irrepressible hope that God would draw all people to himself through the same Spirit. Thus, again, the universal occurrence of healing was organically connected to the hope for a universal pardon.

Zündel paints the picture of a unique revival movement due largely to the approach of Blumhardt.[73] Great emphasis was placed on the fact that conversion and repentance was not to be beaten out of people but should be voluntary. Just as with the events associated with Dittus, Blumhardt believed that manufacturing revival or repentance was a waste of time. People should not be pressured to repent; they will either repent by the leading of the living Christ or they will not. Zündel notes that this approach gave the renewal movement a sense of objectivity:

> An overview of the movement as a whole seems to bring out one outstanding characteristic—its *objectivity*, a distinguishing mark hard to put into words. One might say that it bore the imprint of divine origin. There was nothing fabricated in it, neither with Blumhardt nor with the people coming to him; what he, and they, did was something that simply came upon them. Blumhardt on his part had never so much as dreamt of such a movement, much less attempted to provoke anything like it.[74]

Blumhardt sought to avoid factionalism, disavowing the distinction between the "converted" and the "unconverted." Because the movement had simply "come upon them," there was no sense that they were special or that they deserved what had been given to them. Rather, Blumhardt and the community saw themselves as in solidarity with the rest of the

---

73. Zündel, *The Awakening*, 67–147.

74. Zündel, *Johann Christoph Blumhardt*, 179 (unpublished translation by the Brüderhof and Plough Publishing).

world, hoping that what they had received would eventually be given to all.

Blumhardt interpreted the *Kampf* and the awakening movement as internally related.[75] In the *Kampf* the living Christ had broken into history to free Dittus. In the awakening movement and the attendant miracles, the living Christ was at work sowing healing and bringing about repentance, extending the work begun in the *Kampf*. Both represented the liberating work of the living Christ to free the earth from bondage. The liberative power of Jesus was at work freeing humanity from the bondage of dark forces *and* giving forgiveness of sins, healing the sick *and* granting repentance and reconciliation in the life of the community.

In the light of the *Kampf* and the awakening movement, Blumhardt came to believe that the kingdom was at work in ways that had real physical consequences. As noted above, an important aspect of Blumhardt's interpretation, which would have great significance for the later ministry of both Blumhardt and his son Christoph, was the universal context in which Blumhardt placed the events that he experienced. Just as Blumhardt understood the manifestations of demonic power seen in the case of Dittus and the other forms of illness he encountered during the awakening movement as instantiations of the power of death that held the world in thrall, so also did he see the positive aspects of the *Kampf* and the awakening in a wider context.[76] What was occurring at Möttlingen was a penultimate outpouring of the Spirit and thus a provisional in-breaking of the kingdom of God.[77] Blumhardt firmly believed that God was preparing to pour out the Spirit in a decisive fashion and

75. Blumhardt: "The relationship between my struggle and the awakening is not at all an outward one. The awakening was in the fullest sense won by the struggle. Through battle and victory satanic powers were broken that now either cannot work at all or but very feebly. A spell that had darkened hearts and minds has been removed; people's minds, formerly dull and closed, have become responsive" (Zündel, *Johann Christoph Blumhardt*, 178, unpublished translation by the Brüderhof and Plough Publishing).

76. "To be sure, he was made aware of the power and curse of sin, which, also in the case of his Möttlingen folk, lay like a pall over everybody, including the so-called believers. Even more, however, he came to know an overwhelming Grace that was earnestly concerned for the sins of all the world to be put under forgiveness" (ibid., 256, unpublished translation by the Brüderhof and Plough Publishing).

77. Zündel notes that Blumhardt's universal view was fueled by his confession that he had produced neither the *Kampf* nor the awakening, but rather both had simply "come upon him" (ibid., 191–92).

the battle and awakening movement were to be seen as preparing the way for the cosmic transformation of the world.[78]

The penultimate status of these events became clearer as the awakening movement began to wane in the summer of 1844. Although he had sought to avoid the sensational and was always respectful of the church authorities Blumhardt was eventually ordered to cease laying on hands for absolution and praying for the sick publicly. These restrictions, imposed in 1847, effectively curtailed Blumhardt's ministry and the revival. Though there was a brief reawakening following the revolutionary events of 1848,[79] Blumhardt felt that a new context in which to carry on his ministry was necessary to circumvent the restrictions placed upon him by the consistory. With the help of generous benefactors, he was able to purchase Bad Boll, a spa located about 70 miles (100 km) from Möttlingen. Bad Boll would become synonymous with the Blumhardt name and from there his ministry would continue to have a profound effect even after his death in 1880.

Bad Boll, "The House of God"[80]

Blumhardt, his family, and a small group from Möttlingen moved to Bad Boll in 1852. There is some truth to James Cox's statement that, "At Bad Boll, the biographical details fade away into the background and into the foreground steps Bl.'s proclamation through sermons, devotions and letters."[81] Nevertheless, we will give a brief description of what might be called the spirit of the house at Bad Boll.

According to numerous eyewitness descriptions the house at Bad Boll was characterized by a sense of hope and peace, naturalness and hospitality.[82] Blumhardt, in keeping with the patriarchal social mores

---

78. Macchia, *Spirituality and Social Liberation*, 70–71.

79. For an excellent discussion of Blumhardt's political response to and theological interpretation of the Revolution of 1848, see Ising, "Eine 'Weckstimme durch alle Völker'," 286–308.

80. This description is taken from Jürgen Moltmann's essay, "Hope for the Kingdom," 5.

81. *Johann Christoph Blumhardt*, 92.

82. The description of one guest at Bad Boll paints the picture of a remarkable place: "The gathering of many people of both high and low estate; the pervasive peace and tranquility; the general atmosphere of an unpretentious family life, heightened by the unaffected and relaxed mingling of all classes; the quiet, inward, tolerant, unpietistic attitude felt in most persons; in addition the free, open, genial, cheerful bearing of

and style of the day, set the tone of the house. There were others, however, who contributed greatly to the overall spirit of the house at Bad Boll. Doris Blumhardt and especially Gottliebin Dittus, later Brodersen,[83] should be mentioned here. Both women were intimately involved in overseeing the daily work of the large house, which was able to accommodate up to 150 guests.[84] Having been eyewitnesses of the events at Möttlingen, they also contributed to the remarkable eschatological atmosphere of the house. Gottliebin was intimately involved in raising the children and even assisted Johann Christoph in assessing some of the cases of those who came to him for healing. Hansjorg, Katharina, and herself had been adopted by the Blumhardt family almost immediately after the events of 1842–1844. The emotional and spiritual response to her death in 1872 reveals that she had become an intimate part of the family and indispensable to Blumhardt's ministry.[85] As will

---

Pastor Blumhardt, the owner of Bad Boll, richly gifted as he is with faith and trust in God and far removed from sectarianism—all this made me decide to spend my two weeks of vacation here in Boll" (Zündel, *Johann Christoph Blumhardt*, 418, unpublished translation by the Brüderhof and Plough Publishing).

83. Dittus married Theodore Brodersen in 1855. Theodore became the manager of the spa facilities at Bad Boll, and the three children born from this marriage were raised as part of the Blumhardt family.

84. Krüger, "A Man for the Kingdom," 16.

85. Because of the events she had experienced, Gottliebin was accorded a special authority and respect from those in the Möttlingen and Bad Boll circles. According to most accounts, she exhibited a spiritual strength that matched Blumhardt's own. It is worth quoting a passage from Johann Christoph Blumhardt's testimony to Gottliebin's life: "As regards outer activity, she so became the heart and soul of everything that it is not too much to say that every arrangement and plan made was fully and solely hers. Nothing either big or small escaped Gottliebin's careful eye, and her inner gifts, too, contributed significantly to the blessing resting on the house. To be sure, not everybody understood her or was at ease with her, for she had (if I may say so) a natural dislike of certain spirits, as though her nerves, which had remained sensitive to such influences, were unfavorably affected by them. For that reason she could assume a forbidding manner to such people. But whoever found the right approach to her could benefit from contact with her and would retain for her a special love and appreciation. She was of great help to us by evaluating quickly and accurately the state of mentally ill or disturbed persons, especially as to whether we could have hopes for them or not— one of the most difficult parts of our task. Besides, she was able to give clear and definite advice in physical problems; in particular, her counsel and services were outstandingly successful in cases of bodily injuries to children and others. Thus, she was of great help to us in every respect, and because of that we could never regard her otherwise than as a special gift of the Lord" (Zündel, *Johann Christoph Blumhardt*, 420–21, unpublished translation by the Brüderhof and Plough Publishing).

be noted below, Christoph Blumhardt was especially affected by events surrounding her death.

Notwithstanding the contributions of Doris Blumhardt and Gottliebin Dittus, it was above all Blumhardt who gave to the house the special character noted by all who visited. The principle reason that Blumhardt had moved to Bad Boll was to more adequately accommodate the large numbers of people who were coming to him for spiritual counsel and healing at Möttlingen. Thus, he continued in his role as a pastor at Bad Boll.

In the light of the events at Möttlingen, Blumhardt had come to see the body and spirit as intimately related, such that he emphasized a holistic spirituality. This emphasis was also evident in Blumhardt's approach to pastoral counseling at Bad Boll. The everyday and the spiritual were brought together, and as Rudolph Bohren notes, Blumhardt's counseling began and ended at table.[86] In the fellowship of mealtime, worship and song, conversation on a wide variety of political and spiritual issues, devotional reflection and especially eating were all suffused together and seen as contributing to the authentic human life that was the ultimate aim of the kingdom of God. Jürgen Moltmann gives a succinct description of the method of both Blumhardts:

> Blumhardt's table talks, as far as they have been handed down, are neither too narrowly intimate nor too generally political. For him the personal issues of the heart and mind belong together with the broader issues of the kingdom of God. He saw the one in the other, as we say today: Think globally—act locally! He viewed the most intimate personal details in the light of the coming kingdom and he saw the dawning kingdom in the small matters of every day life. And—most importantly—there was no religious mediation inbetween. The small personal life and the great arch of the kingdom of God confront each other in unmediated fashion.[87]

This description, which also characterizes Bad Boll under the direction of Christoph if not in detail certainly in spirit, also points to the pervasive theme of hope for the kingdom of God that is ubiquitous in Blumhardt's writings after 1844. Prayer, worship, counsel, labor, amusement and eating were all done in the expectation that God's kingdom

86. See Bohren, *Preaching and Community*, 140–58.
87. Moltmann, "Hope for the Kingdom," 6.

wished to break into the world in the form of the everyday just as much as in the form of the miraculous exception. Because of the ebb and flow of renewal and revival that could be seen as much at Möttlingen and Bad Boll as in any of the revivals associated with the *Erweckungsbewegung*, Blumhardt emphasized that the kingdom did not come to make "super-Christians" but rather authentic human beings.[88] His famous statement that, "Humankind must convert twice: first from the natural to the spiritual and then back again to the natural",[89] is evidence of this holistic approach, and Blumhardt viewed every event, great and small, that he saw at Bad Boll in the light of his hope for the coming kingdom of God. In this light, the spirit of Bad Boll should be described as a spirit of hope.[90]

Blumhardt died February 28, 1880. One of the last words he is purported to have uttered expresses the spirit of hope that characterized the house at Bad Boll: "the Lord will open his mild hand in mercy over all nations."[91] To conclude our discussion of the elder Blumhardt we will turn to consider the specific nature of Blumhardt's hope.

88. It should be noted here that though Blumhardt welcomed the many developments associated with the *Erweckungsbewegung*, he was also critical of them. For example, he rejected the notion that they represented the final outpouring of the Holy Spirit and the return of apostolic gifts for which he fervently hoped. See Ising, *Johann Christoph Blumhardt*, 297, 346–47. He was also critical as these movements took on nationalist overtones, especially during the Franco-Prussian war of 1870–1871. For examples of this, see Ising, *Ein Brevier*, 207–9.

89. Harder, "Einleitung," in Christoph Blumhardt, *Ansprachen, Predigten, Reden, Briefe*, I:12; as quoted in Macchia, *Spirituality and Social Liberation*, 92.

90. Zündel: "He had come as a man of hope, and in Bad Boll, too—indeed more and more as time went on—he saw every divine help he experienced on behalf of others as a gift and power imparted in advance of what was yet to come. In his eyes, one—and not the least—of Bad Boll's missions was to be a focus for the expectation of God's kingdom. . . . On the contrary, it was his inmost longing that the battles still facing the kingdom of God—not battles with opponents of flesh and blood but with that power he had taken the field against in Möttlingen—go forward in victory. One might say that this spirit of hope was the pulse governing the life in Bad Boll: it animated the small band that had moved from Möttlingen to Bad Boll" (*Johann Christoph Blumhardt*, 419–20, unpublished translation by the Brüderhof and Plough Publishing).

91. Ibid., 536.

Blumhardt's Hope

As emphasized above, Blumhardt's theology was rooted in his experiences at Möttlingen. The cry "Jesus is Victor!" was the leitmotif of the whole of his theology, summarizing both the concrete historical experiences of Möttlingen as well as the subsequent theological and pastoral reflection given to those events. The conceptual apparatus and context in which the dynamic reality that the saying "Jesus is Victor!" pointed to was worked out by Blumhardt in the idiom of eschatology, specifically his pietistic hope for the kingdom of God.[92] The eschatological hope for the kingdom of God found expressed in Württemberg Pietism gave to Blumhardt the categories, motifs, and conceptual tools whereby he was able to interpret what he had experienced at Möttlingen. At the same time, and importantly, it was the historical-concrete experience itself, coupled with a fresh re-reading of Scripture, which was the controlling source of Blumhardt's theological reflections, such that, despite his debt to the Württemberg tradition, Blumhardt's reflections and proclamation evidence a great deal of originality vis-à-vis his pietistic environment. There are four interrelated aspects that need to be highlighted: 1) Blumhardt's distinct understanding of the kingdom of God; 2) his emphasis on the universal outpouring of the Holy Spirit; 3) his theology of history; and 4) the extent of his hope.

The Kingdom of God

Blumhardt's hope revolves around two poles, a hope for the in-breaking kingdom of God and for the universal outpouring of the Holy Spirit. These two poles gain Christological coloring through the catchphrase "Jesus is Victor!"[93] In both of these concerns, Blumhardt evidences that he is not as interested in the kingdom of God as the state of existence that awaits humanity after the end of history, but rather with the power of the same as it breaks into history to transform the spiritual and physical conditions of humanity in preparation for the coming of the Lord. Thus, one will search long and hard to find descriptions of the ac-

---

92. This is the essential insight of Gerhard Sauter. See his *Die Theologie des Reiches Gottes*, 24.

93. A number of commentators have aptly noted that the elder Blumhardt emphasizes the pneumatological effects of Jesus's victory, while the younger Blumhardt focused more in the Christological grounding of those effects. See Macchia, *Spirituality and Social Liberation*, 115–18.

tual kingdom of God in its eternal dimensions as one might find in the visionary Emmanuel Swedenborg.[94] Furthermore, those that one does find are almost exclusively based on the historical and earthly descriptions found in the prophets of the Hebrew Scriptures as opposed to those found in the book of Revelation.[95] This produces a very particular vision of the kingdom of God that one could describe as actualistic and moving along the lines of a dynamic teleology.

In its most basic sense, the kingdom is the reign of God in the individual, the community, history, and the cosmos. This reign will be a healing reign of peace in which humanity and the cosmos will be restored and transfigured. Blumhardt conceived of the kingdom as both an internal reality in which the heart of the individual was ruled by God *and* as an external reality instantiated in physical and historical moments of transformation that will find their consummation in the "Day of the Lord," which is the end of history.[96] Both the Reformers and many of the early Pietists had spoken of the kingdom of God as an internal reality working on the heart of the individual, based on the faulty translation of Luke 17:21 as "the kingdom of God is within you," rather than the better translation, "the kingdom of God is in your midst."[97] As Frank Macchia has shown, the physical-historical manifestation of the kingdom was a major emphasis of much of later Pietism, especially the Württemberg version of it.[98] Blumhardt combines both of these under-

94. The Swedish scientist and mystical philosopher, Emanuel Swedenborg (1688–1772) was one of the most influential esoteric thinkers of the eighteenth century. His thought, though not universally accepted, was not unknown in the Pietistic environment of Blumhardt. His thought is an attempt at "spiritual physics" whereby the workings of the spirit-world and the world of the hereafter are laid out in a systematic fashion. See for example, Swedenborg, *Four Leading Doctrines*.

95. As mentioned before, Blumhardt's discussion of Isaiah 65 is instructive in regards to this. See his *Besprechung wichtiger Glaubensfragen*, 332–37.

96. The relationship of the "kingdom of God" to the "Day of the Lord" is worked out most clearly in Blumhardt's sermon, "Wann kommt das Reich Gottes?" in *Die Verkündigung*, 298–309.

97. For an example of this, see Martin Luther, *Dr. Martin Luther's Small Catechism*, 155–56; one of the central texts for Johann Arndt, the grandfather of German Pietism, is Luke 17:21, which he renders as "within you." See his *True Christianity*, 49–51; for a discussion of the interpretation of Luke 17:20–21, see Kümmel, *Promise and Fulfillment*, 32–36.

98. For a discussion of the Württemberg tradition's interpretation of the kingdom of God, see Macchia, *Spirituality and Social Liberation*, 21–42.

standings of the kingdom, but places the former in service to the latter. That is, the coming of the kingdom in the individual person is not the goal, but rather the start whose goal during the interim is found in the longing prayer for the coming of the kingdom for all of creation. Thus, individual salvation, which Blumhardt understood as an aspect of the kingdom of God, was not the be-all-and-end-all of the Christian gospel or the Christian life.[99] Rather, the individual is caught up in a larger "history of development" that is sometimes quiet and secret, and sometimes public and revolutionary.[100]

99. Gerhard Sauter offers an interesting discussion and critique of the younger Blumhardt's non-systematic understanding of the relationship between "Justification by Faith" and the "kingdom of God" in which the former offers a critique of synergistic notions of salvation, while the latter roots the former in concrete-historical events whose aim is finally the transformation of the universe. In his discussion he notes that the elder Blumhardt provides a better basis for linking these two themes together, presumably because Johann Christoph favored the Reformation understanding of "Justification by Faith," while the younger Blumhardt's ideas are clearly shaped by the more synergistic aspects of pietism. See his *Die Theologie des Reiches Gottes*, 271–78.

The salvation of the soul is not what preoccupies either of the Blumhardts' thoughts or ministry. Rather, it is the coming of the kingdom for the whole cosmos. As Rüsch notes in reference to the elder Blumhardt: "Pointedly said: Blumhardt does not ask: 'How do I receive a gracious God?', rather: 'How will the sighing creatures of God finally receive their day of redemption?'" (*Die Erlösung der Kreatur*, 5).

Blumhardt puts it as follows: "Ah, how self-seeking and egotistic our hope usually is! Most Christians hope for nothing other than that which concerns them, and them alone; they are not concerned about any other hope. Nobody asks as to what is the hope of the whole of mankind, the whole creation, but only about the hope that 'I' may be saved—'I,' 'I,' and nobody else but 'I!' But how un-Protestant this is, for there also the Reformers have such a wide vision! They strove not only for their own salvation but that entire nations might be snatched from the fetters of darkness.... On the whole, people know of no other hope than that of working for forty to fifty years and then of lying down and dying peacefully. But each one should be zealous for all; each one should be concerned that Christianity's great hope should be fulfilled and that more and more the arm of Jesus clears the way for the deliverance of all creation and the conquest of the Satanic powers, until at last comes the great refreshment of His countenance. If we do not have this hope, then we are not in the light" (*Die Verkündigung*, 103–4, unpublished translation by the Brüderhof and Plough Publishing).

100. Johann Christoph Blumhardt, *Blätter aus Bad Boll*, 3:293 (unpublished translation by the Brüderhof and Plough Publishing). Macchia discusses this text on pages 87–89 of his *Spirituality and Social Liberation*.

A comment here about the relationship between the "history of development" of the kingdom of God and history in general is in order. In Blumhardt, the category of development functions on two levels, while revolution is that which ties the two levels together. On the first level is the development of history in general, which includes together the history of the world and the church. All events in this history develop

The basis and form of that history of development is Christological. The history of the kingdom of God, though anticipated in the Hebrew prophets and the history of Israel, really begins with the coming of Christ: "The appearance of Jesus upon the earth marked the beginning of this Kingdom." Though the goal towards which the kingdom moves finds a provisional fulfillment in the cross and resurrection of Jesus, it will only be consummated when, "throughout the whole creation 'God will be all in all.'"[101] The interim, then, is a battle of struggle seen along Christological lines, so that "Jesus is Victor!" points to the battle that Jesus continues to wage to actualize the subjection of the powers and principalities that his cross effected.[102] Thus, the kingdom as God's

---

or move towards their end, which is the kingdom of God. On the second level and concurrently, the kingdom of God has a developmental character of its own. There are events that happen in history that are intimately related to the coming of the kingdom (i.e., the history of Jesus, and later events like the Reformation and Möttlingen), which when seen together can be said to have a progressive or developmental character. Importantly, the relationship between these events is not sequential, such that one could predict what comes next. Rather, each event is an irruption, sometimes greater, sometimes lesser, of the kingdom of God in the world. The factor that inter-relates them is that they are all forms of the coming of Jesus Christ and they all contribute to the final *parousia*. The relationship between the different levels of history is also important. The kingdom of God breaks into general history unexpectedly and miraculously. The various forms of in-breaking are not the result of the development of humanity, the cosmos or history itself (as in Hegel). Rather, the kingdom of God is revolutionary in relation to the history of the world. These dynamic irruptions are guided and fueled by a divine monergism that seeks a faithful human response in the form of longing, prayer or action. At the same time, because the history of the kingdom is the history of the coming of Christ, the real inner meaning of history in general is found in the history of the kingdom of God that occurs in its midst. See Rüsch, *Die Erlösung der Kreatur*, 20–21; see also, Macchia, *Spirituality and Social Liberation*, 88–89.

101. Johann Christoph Blumhardt, *Die Verkündigung*, 316 (unpublished translation by the Brüderhof and Plough Publishing).

102. One of the most important texts dealing with the connection between the Cross of Christ and the warfare of the kingdom of God is in the Good Friday Sermon of 1872. In it Blumhardt declares: "What the Lord endured here (on Golgotha), will be revealed some day. But exactly through this the Savior gained the authority over this darkness, so that exactly here at the cross the possibility opened up that some time it will happen, that *all* knees must bow in heaven, as well as on earth and *under the earth*, and *all* tongues confess, that Jesus Christ is Lord to the glory of God the Father. This is so great that we cannot express it, and hardly dare to conceive it. But Good Friday proclaims a general pardon *over the entire world*, and this general pardon will be yet revealed, for Jesus did not hang in vain on the cross" (Johann Christoph Blumhardt, *Evangelienpredigten auf alle Sonn*, 190; as quoted in Groth, "Chiliasmus und Apokatastasishoffnung," 91).

reign is assured because in Christ's death and resurrection, the powers of darkness were, "weakened to the very root."

> The victory is won. Our Lord sits at the right hand of God and has received gifts to bestow—also upon those who have fallen away. He fights from above until at last He has laid all His enemies at His footstool; until all those spirits of sickness and all powers that in any way deform or destroy men in body and soul are removed; until all of creation, all heaven and earth can rejoice. Oh, who can conceive the greatness of this victory of Jesus which we inherit as soon as we believe and as soon as we learn to grasp the victory which has been laid open before our eyes.[103]

For Blumhardt, the kingdom of God consists of the liberative powers associated with the "there and then" life, death and resurrection of Jesus Christ, that are at work in the "here and now" of the hopeful community and that move towards their consummation in the final universal appearing of the Lord.

The dynamism in Blumhardt's conception of the kingdom of God that we spoke of earlier is also the result of his re-conceptualization of the *parousia*. The kingdom is present within history, both in the history of Jesus but also in later instantiations that come about as God's in-breaking action. Through the resurrection, the further development of the "battle history" of the kingdom was inaugurated.[104] The end of this history will be the final coming of the Lord, but the interim history of conflict that consisted of multiple events—think here of the events associated with Möttlingen—was intimately related as internally connected moments of "advent" or "appearing" that contribute to the final universal appearing. Thus, the resurrection inaugurates Christ's *parousia*, but it does so in order that the struggle begun in the life, death, and resurrection of the Messiah might be passed on to his people. The vocation of the community is to further the liberating power and effects of the kingdom of God, not as their own creation, but as servants of the living God who is waging war on behalf of all humanity. This struggle,

103. Johann Christoph Blumhardt, *Die Verkündigung*, 13–14 (unpublished translation by the Brüderhof and Plough Publishing).

104. ". . . his coming began in reality with his resurrection and transfiguration; for there and then was the beginning of an actual continuous coming toward the final goal: his true and visible coming" (Johann Christoph Blumhardt, *Besprechung wichtiger Glaubensfragen*, 319, unpublished translation by the Brüderhof and Plough Publishing).

therefore, could not entail waging war against humanity, but rather for its ultimate liberation from the cosmic power of death. There can be no infidels here. Blumhardt's hope was to see these liberating powers and effects given to the whole of humanity. For this, he believed that a fresh outpouring of the Spirit was desperately needed because the power by which the community was enabled to pray and act in hope for the kingdom of God was the Holy Spirit.

The Outpouring of the Holy Spirit

This brings us to the second aspect of Blumhardt's theology of hope: the Holy Spirit, or better, the power and effects of the Holy Spirit. For though Blumhardt affirmed the divine nature of the Spirit as the third person of the Trinity, his real interest was in the work that the Spirit does in history to further the kingdom of God. The Spirit is intimately related to the progress of the kingdom of God in two ways: it was involved in the victory over the powers and principalities in the life of Christ, and it is the power by which the disciples of Jesus are taken up into the history of struggle of their Master.

Blumhardt was careful to emphasize that though Christ had glory from on high, it was only after his baptism, in which he received the Spirit that he began to perform miracles.[105] This same Spirit is promised to the Christian community and according to Blumhardt the moment of inclusion of the community of Christ in the struggle for the kingdom of God was historically localized in the event of Pentecost, which functions as a kind of second resurrection.[106] At Pentecost, the same

105. Blumhardt doesn't deal in any depth with the ontological question of the relationship between the Word and Spirit in the life of Christ. Though he affirms the divinity of Christ as the Son of God, his preoccupation is with Christ's humanity, which was assisted in its kingdom mission by the presence, guidance and power of the Holy Spirit. See Johann Christoph Blumhardt, *Die Verkündigung*, 87–88. Nonetheless, as James Cox notes, "when Blumhardt uses the terms 'Teacher,' 'Comforter' or 'personal Holy Spirit,' these—one could almost say—offices of the Holy Spirit are Christocentrically conceived. As the Teacher, the Holy Spirit makes it possible to accept and understand the revelation of Jesus Christ presented in the Scriptures. As the Comforter, the Holy Spirit was sent by Christ and represents His personal presence, making it possible for one to continue within the Body of Christ. As the Spirit of Pentecost, the Holy Spirit is the herald for the return of Christ and is, so to speak, the subjective side of the Kingdom of God" (Cox, *Work of the Holy Spirit*, 100).

106. The relationship between the outpouring of the Spirit and the resurrection of Christ as two forms of the *parousia* is not sharply delineated. It could be argued that

Spirit that enabled Christ to struggle with and overcome the powers of darkness was given to the Christian community, "in an outwardly visible manner."[107] In the Spirit of Pentecost, Christ continues his struggle through the community and thus moves history closer to his final appearing in which all things will be made subject to him. The purpose of the struggle that the Spirit empowers is to extend the rule of Christ physically and spiritually, so that at his coming the transition will be smooth rather than cataclysmic.[108]

There are three key aspects to the work of the Spirit of Pentecost that need to be highlighted here: (1) the presence of the Spirit; (2) the gifts of the Spirit; and (3) the longing for the kingdom. The Spirit is the Spirit of Christ because through the Spirit Christ is made present to the community and the believer. Commenting on John 14:18, Blumhardt says: "Now the Savior will still come to them. They will still have him in all need, perplexities, and weaknesses through the Holy Spirit whom He will send to them as someone personally from God. The Holy Spirit will so represent His Person that they would really have Jesus Himself, though not being able to see Him."[109] Blumhardt's understanding of the presence of the Spirit of Pentecost is linked to his hope for the kingdom of God. When we come to faith in Christ, we receive the Spirit of God who makes Christ present to us, confirming that we are God's children. The Spirit of Pentecost—as distinct from, though building upon this first gift—is a more intense and palpable sense of Christ's presence, which overcomes all doubt and contributes to the struggle for

---

for Blumhardt the resurrection of Christ can only properly be called the first form of Christ's coming, while the gift of the Spirit could be seen as the effect and extension of that coming on the community and then out into the broader world. Nevertheless, Blumhardt does at least see a two-fold *parousia* (resurrection-final appearing) between which is a history of struggle.

107. Johann Christoph Blumhardt, *Besprechung wichtiger Glaubensfragen*, 23 (unpublished translation by the Brüderhof and Plough Publishing).

108. It is important to note that Blumhardt makes a distinction, sometimes unclear, between the power of the Spirit that sows rebirth in the individual and the Spirit of Pentecost whose purpose is, "primarily the growth and fulfillment of God's Kingdom." Blumhardt notes that, "the Spirit of Pentecost himself has no direct link to a person's rebirth, but rather he bestows extraordinary gifts, so that through this the convert experiences a kind of divine transformation although the Spirit has not himself brought about the rebirth" (ibid., 29–30).

109. Johann Christoph Blumhardt, *Die Verkündigung*, 147 (unpublished translation by the Brüderhof and Plough Publishing).

the kingdom by assuring us of Christ's ever-present help. The purpose of this palpable sense of Christ is not to give an inner assurance simply to assuage ordinary doubts, but rather to equip the Christian to engage in struggle for the kingdom of God.[110] That is, through the Spirit of Pentecost, the Christian is encouraged to engage in the difficult struggle for the kingdom. One hears the echoes of Blumhardt's Möttlingen experiences in this.[111]

Along with the presence of Christ, the Spirit of Pentecost gives the gifts of the Spirit, whose central purpose is to liberate humanity and the cosmos and thereby to contribute to the ultimate coming of the kingdom of God. The gifts of the Spirit of Pentecost are miraculous and include not only gifts of healing and wonderworking, but also absolution (or the "Keys of the kingdom"), unity, and the so-called fruit of the Spirit.[112] Here the influence of the Möttlingen experience surfaces again. Through the events at Möttlingen, Blumhardt came to believe that the power and gifts of the Spirit were more nearly like they are portrayed in the New Testament than not.

Lastly, the Spirit of Pentecost motivates the cry for the kingdom to come, which contributes to the dawning of the Kingdom:

> I would almost say that the Spirit never speaks without impelling us to say, 'Come!' Otherwise only human thoughts are expressed, human feelings, human endeavors, but no true divine thought. The Holy Spirit does not speak without the little word, 'Come' being laid upon everyone's lips, whatever kind of Christian belief we follow. The Spirit is always ready to say to each one, 'Think of the coming Savior.'[113]

110. See Johann Christoph Blumhardt, *Besprechung wichtiger Glaubensfragen*, 30. In this excerpt entitled, "Etwas von der Geburt aus dem Geist" ("Regarding Spiritual Rebirth"), Blumhardt describes the palpable nature of the Spirit of Pentecost as the, "gift of the incarnate Holy Spirit" (29), referring to the objective nature of the effects of the outpouring of the Spirit at Pentecost.

111. Blumhardt described the source of courage he found during the Möttlingen *Kampf* in terms similar to this: "And with faith in Him, Who is the Lord, the words were formed in me again and again, 'Forward! Forward! It has to lead to a good end, even though it will lead into the deepest depths, unless it were not true that Jesus had crushed the head of the serpent'" (*A Conflict with Satan*, 22).

112. See Ising, *Johann Christoph Blumhardt*, 351.

113. Johann Christoph Blumhardt, *Die Verkündigung*, 285–86 (unpublished translation by the Brüderhof and Plough Publishing).

The Spirit produces groaning for the coming of the Lord. At the same time, however, Blumhardt emphasized the need to cry out for a general or universal outpouring of the Spirit. The need for this prayer was the result of Blumhardt's conviction that the Spirit of Pentecost had been withdrawn from the church. The Möttlingen experience had indicated to Blumhardt that the withdrawal was not God's intention. Blumhardt combines all of the aspects of the Spirit's work to note that the overall work of the Spirit is to prepare the earth for the coming of the Lord. This becomes clearer when we consider Blumhardt's theological interpretation of history.

Blumhardt's Theology of History

Blumhardt's hope for the kingdom and the Spirit of Pentecost are both linked to a theology of history that is a variant of the chiliastic hope found in Württemberg Pietism.[114] Blumhardt divided history into three epochs of revelation in accord with the three persons of the Trinity, similar to the medieval chiliast Joachim of Fiore.[115] The epoch of the Father was associated with Moses and the history of Israel, while that of the period of the Son referred to the time of Christ and the history of the church. The third epoch of the Holy Spirit was conceived by Blumhardt as a time of great grace that precedes the final revelation of the kingdom of God. During this third epoch, the Church would be restored to its supposed original state, enabling it to fulfill its calling to prepare the earth for the coming of the Lord, and the Spirit of God would be poured out on all flesh (Joel 3:1ff.), indicating that many outside of the church would also be included in God's final restoration.[116] This epoch was necessary, for Blumhardt argued that the Lord would not come to a world that was not ready to receive him.[117]

As noted above, Blumhardt believed that the Spirit of Pentecost had been withdrawn from the church. His argument was a way to account for the lack of real power among Christians of his day, which events at

114. For a discussion of chiliasm in Württemberg Pietism, see Groth, *Wiederbringung AllerDinge.*

115. See Mcginn, *Apocalyptic Spirituality*, 97–148; see also Reeves, *Joachim of Fiore,* 1–28.

116. This raises the question of Blumhardt's universalism, which we will consider below.

117. See *Die Verkündigung,* 306–7.

Möttlingen had highlighted. He attributed this withdrawal to a lack of faith during the time following the apostles that persisted up to his own day, in which he argued that heartfelt prayer for the coming of the Lord had waned and the Spirit of Pentecost had thereby withdrawn.[118] The church had been entrusted with the mission of extending the kingdom of God through doing "even greater works" than Jesus had done. In the wake of its failure, however, the Church was now to be compared to the widow in the parable of the unjust judge (Luke 18:1-8), and the question posed to the church was whether it would have faith to cry out to God to send the Spirit and bring the kingdom to its fulfillment.

From time to time, the longing cry for the return of the Spirit could be seen in the history of the Church. The two key examples repeatedly mentioned by Blumhardt were the Reformation and the events at Möttlingen.[119] Both of these events were instances in the battle history of the kingdom of God in which the longing cry for the return of the Spirit was rekindled. As noted above, the return of the Spirit of Pentecost would mark the final stage before the universal revelation of the kingdom of God in all its fullness that would occur as the end of history. Aside from his more general hope for the coming of the Lord, the immediate motivation for Blumhardt's exhortation and pleading for the Church and the individual Christian to cry out for the Spirit of Pentecost was that he judged the Reformation a failure in this regard. Though it had been a moment when faith was rekindled, before long the flame had gone out. He was determined that the Möttlingen experience should not be squandered in a similar fashion. This orientation is highlighted in Blumhardt's famous exhortation to "wait for and hasten on" towards the coming of the kingdom.[120] Though the kingdom and the Spirit come from God alone, and so we must wait for them, nonetheless our waiting is filled with longing and therefore is also an active hastening towards the coming of the Lord. The exhortation to wait and hasten applied to both prayer and action.

---

118. See Johann Christoph Blumhardt, *Besprechung wichtiger Glaubensfragen*, 312–22. This is the source and motivation for Blumhardt's Church critique.

119. For an example of this, see Blumhardt's Reformation Day sermon of 1856, "Seid nüchtern und wachet!" in *Die Verkündigung*, 93–105.

120. See ibid., 364–73.

Blumhardt's thought is distinct from many forms of chiliasm.[121] Consider the following: He refused to develop a time-scheme, like Bengel and others, by which to predict when the third epoch of the Spirit would begin, thus the epochs of revelation and when he expected them to begin were more flexible and more closely linked to human longing and prayer. He did not attribute the lengthy delay of the coming of this great time of grace to God's doing or providence, but rather to the failure of the church.[122] He rejected the idea that this period must be preceded by destruction, choosing rather to emphasize that the outpouring of the Spirit, which will occur suddenly and is really a period of grace that precedes the final judgment by which many who are far off might be brought back.[123] Related to this was his reticence regarding a millennial kingdom.

Though the coming time of the Spirit of Pentecost is closely associated with the prophecies of Joel 3:1ff., Blumhardt was very wary of describing this period in terms of a "millennial kingdom." This was because the description of the millennium in Revelation 20 was closely connected to tribulation and destruction, but also because the millennial period is described as coming to an end with a cataclysmic conflict and judgment.[124] By contrast, Blumhardt emphasized that the period of the Spirit of Pentecost would be a great time of grace during which the kingdom of God would progress to its fulfillment in history such that the transition into eternity, which is marked by the "Day of the Lord," would be more a day of pardon than condemnation.[125]

121. For a detailed discussion of Blumhardt's relationship to the chiliastic thought peculiar to Württemberg Pietism, see Groth, "Chiliasmus und Apokatastasishoffnung," 75–82.

122. Blumhardt: "When the majority in Christendom do not keep His commandments, then things are at a standstill. But when His commandments are done on earth, then the wheel turns" (*Die Verkündigung*, 283, unpublished translation by the Brüderhof and Plough Publishing).

123. See ibid., 63–64.

124. See Johann Christoph Blumhardt, *Besprechung wichtiger Glaubensfragen*, 340–44.

125. Blumhardt: "The hope of the New Testament refers to the expectation of the end of all things when all will again be brought into harmony, when all pain ceases, all mysteries are revealed, and the fullness of God's mercy in Christ Jesus will unfold over all creation, and this shall be revealed to the children of God when the groans of all creation are quieted. And when it says here 'hope of salvation,' it is not meant in the sense that we hope for salvation after death; the Holy Scripture means by this salvation

The Extent of Blumhardt's Hope

Finally, the extent of Blumhardt's hope also needs to be considered. Is the kingdom of God and its work of restoration and salvation meant for all creatures or are only a few to be saved? Over the course of his life, Blumhardt gave conflicting answers to this question, so that there is some debate about the universal extent of his hope. One thing is clear: Blumhardt emphatically rejected the doctrine of double predestination.[126] Friedhelm Groth has shown that Blumhardt's thought evolved over time, moving closer and closer to affirming the *apokatastasis ton panton* ("restoration of all things"). At the same time, however, he refused to hold to a systematically or logically required doctrine of universalism. There are a couple of aspects worth mentioning.

Blumhardt's thought, at least as early as the 1850's, is clearly sympathetic with the *apokatastasis* doctrine espoused by many leading Württemberg Pietists, most notably Bengel and his most important student Friedrich Christoph Oetinger (1702–1782).[127] This sympathy moved to the foreground in Blumhardt's 70s. In the last decade of his life, Blumhardt became more and more explicit that, "By sending Jesus

---

the final deliverance of all groaning creation from its torments and need, its misery and distress" (*Die Verkündigung*, 102–3, unpublished translation by the Brüderhof and Plough Publishing).

Karl Barth, Gerhard Sauter, and Frank Macchia have all rightly pointed out that Blumhardt's focus on the time of grace before the final *parousia* is problematic because Blumhardt describes it in such terms that it is difficult to know how the *parousia* transcends the preceding epoch, or if there is even a difference between the two. It should be noted however, that the source of Blumhardt's reticence to speak about the time after history is rooted in the Württemberg tradition. Bengel's eschatology, which focused primarily on the time after the millennium, tended to cut the nerve for fervent engagement in prayer, mission, and social work for the poor. Blumhardt would have opposed these implications because of his interests in missions, but especially because of his experience at Möttlingen. To resign oneself to the transformation of all things in eternity meant that not much hope for change in the here and now could be expected. Though Blumhardt may have overemphasized the this-worldly and historical work of transformation of the kingdom and the Spirit, he certainly had his reasons. For Karl Barth, see his *Protestant Theology in the Nineteenth Century*, 652–53; for Sauter, see his *Die Theologie des Reiches*, 50–51; for Macchia, see his *Spirituality and Social Liberation*, 86–87.

126. See Johann Christoph Blumhardt, *Besprechung wichtiger Glaubensfragen*, 199–200.

127. See Groth, "Chiliasmus und Apokatastasishoffnung," 82–96. I am closely following Groth for my analysis here.

Christ His Son, our Lord, to us, He became not the Father or God of judgment but the Father and God of mercies, the God of all comfort. Nothing but mercy pours down from above, nothing but comfort awaits us! And gleaming brightly before us is mercy and comfort for poor, sinful, suffering mankind."[128] In fact, the third epoch of revelation, in which the Spirit would be poured out over "all flesh", was conceived of as a time of general repentance, during which the whole of creation would be brought back to God.

Though Blumhardt was sympathetic with the *apokatastasis* doctrine, he did not downplay the significance of judgment or the reality of hell, rather, he reinterpreted them in light of it. Blumhardt understood judgment as a "making right" rather than a condemnation. Blumhardt's comments on the Twelve Thrones of Judgment set aside for the Apostles described in Matt 19:27–30 deserves to be quoted at length:

> One may ask what kind of judging the disciples were supposed to do while sitting on their thrones. Here we must remember that according to Paul at the end all of Israel will be saved (Rom. 11:26). And, Romans 11:32: 'For God has consigned all men to disobedience, that he may have mercy on all.' Thus this judgment by the disciples is no judgment toward damnation; rather it is a preparation for submission and for acceptance of salvation.... Even in the Old Testament the word 'judging' (richten) is sometimes used in the sense of 'setting right,' as for instance when it says 'Zion must be judged by right and justice.'... The 'judgment' shall be a means to bring as many as possible back into the fold. Finally, all knees shall be bent and all tongues confess that Jesus Christ is Lord. In order to make this possible there will have to be a lot of judgment-work done.[129]

Judgment, then, which Blumhardt held as both necessary and real, was not for the destruction, but rather for the restoration of God's creation.

Following Bengel and other Württembergers, Blumhardt understood hell as God's prolonged judgment, which would not necessarily be an unending torment. In his reflections on the parable of the great judgment in Matthew 25, Blumhardt refused to say what would happen to those who wound up on the left hand of the judgment seat of

---

128. Johann Christoph Blumhardt, *Die Verkündigung*, 58 (unpublished translation by the Brüderhof and Plough Publishing).

129. Johann Christoph Blumhardt, *Blätter aus Bad Boll*, 4:218–19 (unpublished translation by the Brüderhof and Plough Publishing).

the Lamb. He simply affirms the reality of judgment, while at the same time emphasizing that hell was not originally created for humanity but rather for the devil, that it does not have an eternal character, and that "even in judgment he [God] cannot deny his mercy."[130] Though it would be wrong to say that Blumhardt held to a systematic doctrine of the *apokatastasis ton panton*, it is clear that his hope for creation was sympathetic with it. It is also clear that he believed that, "the Lord Jesus is nevertheless the compassionate and gracious One, even if the whole world is not so clearly aware of it and able to experience it. At last, however, His countenance will shine upon all men."[131]

This universal horizon caused Blumhardt to see his struggles and prayer for the Spirit to be poured out and the kingdom to come as something that had relevance for all humanity and thus led him to severely criticize the concern for individual salvation that he encountered in many of his contemporaries. The vocation given in new birth was not to rest in the assurance of one's salvation, but to beg and plead that God might bring his kingdom to renew the face of the earth, a renewal that would include far more of humanity than it excluded.[132]

Blumhardt's hope for the outpouring of the Spirit and the coming of the kingdom was a hope and struggle engaged on behalf of all people. Through the coming of the Spirit and the kingdom, humanity and creation would experience liberation from the powers of darkness and death. The whole person would be healed and restored both spiritually and physically, thus becoming authentically human. Though there are indications in the elder Blumhardt that he saw some of the social im-

---

130. Ibid., 125 (unpublished translation by the Brüderhof and Plough Publishing).

131. *Die Verkündigung*, 126 (unpublished translation by the Brüderhof and Plough Publishing).

132. Blumhardt: "Nobody asks as to what is the hope of the whole of mankind, the whole creation, but only about the hope that 'I' may be saved—'I,' 'I,' and nobody else but 'I!' . . . But each one should be zealous for all; each one should be concerned that Christianity's great hope should be fulfilled and that more and more the arm of Jesus clears the way for the deliverance of all creation and the conquest of the Satanic powers, until at last comes the great refreshment of His countenance. If we do not have this hope, then we are not in the light" (ibid., 103–4).

plications of his thought, it was Christoph who would work this out in surprising ways.[133] To his life and thought we now turn.

3

Christoph Friedrich Blumhardt and the Healing of the Body Politic

Christoph Blumhardt's Early Life and Ministry

Christoph Blumhardt was born in 1842 in Möttlingen during his father's struggle with Gottliebin Dittus's condition. He would grow up in the midst of the awakening movement that followed hearing the stories from the Möttlingen days told to him not only by his mother and father but also by Dittus herself. His most formative years were spent at Bad Boll, where the family lived after 1852. Growing up in this context would leave its mark on the younger Blumhardt. Arthur Wiser's estimation that the father and son be interpreted as a single witness to Jesus Christ is not far off the mark, for the single greatest influence on Christoph was clearly his father.[1]

Compared to his father, Christoph was much more ambivalent about his call to ministry. He did not enjoy his theological studies at the University of Tübingen. He did, however, find a kindred spirit in J. T. Beck, under whom he studied at Tübingen. Martin Stober's estimation that, "No other Tübingen professor shows so many great parallels to Blumhardt as Beck," is correct.[2] This was especially the case in terms of their eschatology, though disagreements can still be discerned.[3]

---

1. Arthur Wiser, "Introduction," in *Action in Waiting for The Kingdom of God*, by Karl Barth and Christoph Blumhardt, 1.

2. Stober, *Christoph Friedrich Blumhardt*, 176.

3. See ibid., 181–91, for a discussion of the various parallels between Blumhardt and Beck. Christoph rejected the "organicological" language that Beck used in reference to the kingdom of God, and his father before him had already rejected Beck's prediction of the 1840's as the end of the process of the development of the kingdom of God. See also Meier, *Christ, Sozialist, Theologe*, 36.

Despite misgivings, Blumhardt was ordained in 1866. After a few years of service in a number of parishes, Christoph was called home to assist his father at Bad Boll.[4] Before the death of his father in 1880, the most important event to happen to Christoph was the death of Gottliebin Dittus in 1872. Gottliebin's first serious illness had occurred in 1862, and though she had recovered, she had not received complete healing, to the consternation especially of the elder Blumhardt.[5] She was diagnosed with stomach cancer in November of 1871. Though Gottliebin had expressed serious doubts about Christoph's pastoral and Christian calling during his student days, when he returned to Bad Boll in 1869, he worked closely with her, gaining a new appreciation for the woman who had been intimately involved in raising him. Christoph's newfound appreciation reached its zenith in the events surrounding her death, as he experienced what is described by Stober as a "strange birth."[6]

The actual events surrounding the night of Gottliebin's death are unknown to us, but they were of central importance to Christoph.[7] He interpreted the experience as his baptism into the events at Möttlingen that until then he had viewed only as an outsider. Through the events at the bedside of Dittus, Christoph had "experienced" God in a fashion similar to his father: "There was one thing which brought about the change in Möttlingen with the breakthrough of the overpowering

4. It appears that Christoph came home in the fall of 1869, but continued to do pastoral work in some of the villages near Bad Boll (Dürnau and Gruibingen) at least up to 1871. See Macchia, *Spirituality and Social Liberation*, 112; see also, Ising, *Johann Christoph Blumhardt*, 333.

5. Ising, *Johann Christoph Blumhardt*, 303–4.

6. Stober, *Christoph Friedrich Blumhardt*, 253.

7. Stober notes that one cannot understand Christoph apart from this experience (ibid., 254). It is significant that there is no literary account of these events as it reveals an aspect of Christoph's personality that would come more to the fore later in his career. Many of those associated with the inner circle at Bad Boll expressed a certain pang of guilt and aggravation that the account of the Möttlingen *Kampf* had ever been published, as there was general agreement that not everyone was able to understand what had happened, and for many it was simply a kind of sensational curiosity. This interpretation comes out forcefully in Christoph's *Damit Gott Kommt*, 67–68. The reason for this feeling was that the experiences themselves were not what was important, but what they pointed to and were supposed to move one toward: the kingdom of God. It seems clear that Christoph felt the same way about his experiences at Gottliebin's death, thus he did not repeat the mistake of his father by committing those experiences to paper.

victory of Jesus. It was called: 'Jesus is Victor!' Yet a greater battle was fought on that night and ended again with 'Jesus is Victor!' and hereby we live till today." Blumhardt saw himself as given a taste of what his father had experienced and thereby commissioned to proclaim the gospel with the same power and freshness that his father had: "My thirst for true life was suddenly quenched with one drop of heavenly water, which sufficed, to awaken that motivated life, which had captured those older Möttlinger friends. . . . But when this occurred to me, I knew more in 8 days, than all theologians. At that time I also understood, what the Apostle's preached."[8] According to Stober, this event would serve as an important pre-requisite for Christoph taking over after his father's death in 1880.[9]

Since the publication of Robert Lejeune's four volume collection of Blumhardt's writings, it has become customary to see his development in four phases: 1) the first phase, from 1880–1888, is marked by continuity with his father; 2) the second phase, 1888–1896, is a phase of critical rethinking of his father's proclamation and the meaning of the events at Möttlingen vis-à-vis the kingdom of God which continues forward; 3) the third phase is marked by Christoph's explicit "turn to the world" and involvement in socialist politics; and finally, 4) the last phase is seen as a critical re-thinking and re-assessment of the development of his thought during the second and third phase. We will follow this four-phase demarcation in our explication and will also follow the broader scholarly opinion that these phases, though showing real development from one to another, do so within a much deeper continuity.[10]

---

8. Christoph Burnhardt, *Eine Auswahl*, I:458; and vol. 2, 10; as quoted in Stober, *Christoph Friedrich Blumhardt*, 253.

9. Ibid., 255.

10. Gerhard Sauter, in emphasizing the continuity between the stages, described Blumhardt's first stage as, "the 'exegetical preparatory' one (see p. 91ff.), the second is the 'meditative clarification' (p. 111ff.), the third the 'homiletic honing' (p. 131ff.) and the fourth the 'critical after-thought' (p. 215ff.)" (Groth, "Chiliasmus und Apokatastasishoffnung," 99). This opinion is shared by a number of theologians. See also, Meier, *Christoph Blumhardt*, 132; see also, Macchia, *Spirituality and Social Liberation*, 110–11.

The First Phase: 1880–1888

Johann Christoph Blumhardt died in February of 1880. Theophil (1843–1919), Christoph's younger brother, was present with him at his father's bedside. After Christoph and Theophil were blessed "for victory," the elder Blumhardt passed away.[11] Upon the death of his father, Christoph took over pastoral leadership at Bad Boll. Continuity with his father's message is the primary characteristic of this first phase of the younger Blumhardt's life and ministry. Christoph sought to carry on as his father before him had done. In the eulogy for his father, Blumhardt recounted the struggle at Möttlingen to give comfort and courage to his hearers and to indicate that he intended to carry on in his father's footsteps.[12]

In some of the earliest sermons after the death of the elder Blumhardt, one senses that Christoph was looking for a way forward, a sense of direction that would guide his own ministry and calling to witness to the kingdom of God. As one reads through the sermons from this period one is also struck by Christoph's conviction that this new way would only be found by holding to the legacy of Möttlingen-Bad Boll:

> This I apply to our household. It should not be that we are now overcome. Believe me, that hurts the Majesty of Jesus Christ in Heaven. I have felt this several times recently. We must not act as though for us the Savior were dead, however weak, poor, and insignificant we may feel ourselves to be. . . . Today I want to ask all of you to take possession of this sense of victory so that sorrow is not allowed to become master! We must stand above this! We must in truth remain people of victory, for we have experienced something of the Majesty of Jesus Christ. We know that it is He who lives and with Him the faithful, here and beyond. He is with us and around Him a cloud of the faithful, who for us are not dead, even when they have died. For us, Papa is not dead! . . . The Lord's cause must go forward triumphantly![13]

11. Zündel, *Johann Christoph Blumhardt*, 536–37.

12. Christoph Blumhardt, *Auswahl*, I:7–8.

13. Ibid., 13 (unpublished translation by the Brüderhof and Plough Publishing). Macchia provides an excellent example of this sentiment in a quote of Blumhardt's: "I stand firmly in a particular calling as successor of my father's thoughts, which for me were inspired of God" (Christoph Blumhardt, *Ansprachen*, I:37; as quoted in Macchia, *Spirituality and Social Liberation*, 113).

Nevertheless, Blumhardt's desire to find direction for his own struggle for the kingdom was also a powerful theme. His searching and seeking for a new impetus came to expression more and more and finally burst into full view around the time of the death of Doris Blumhardt in July of 1886:

> But now things are changing; it is a distressing situation, and we are far, far away from those early days. Think about it for a moment! All those we could lean on to some extent until now, are gone. We remain here, but I am the only one left of our inner fellowship. Humanly speaking, if I were to die today we could no longer be what we are. Well, let us therefore hold firmly together in the expectation that something will come to us.[14]

Möttlingen and the history and events associated with it—as well as the many after-effects—were not to be despised, but Christoph believed it a mistake to simply dwell on the past. As with his father, Möttlingen was a *sign* that something new could be given in greater measure; that the kingdom of God was breaking anew into the world; that the living Christ was struggling in the midst of history to free his people. As such a sign, it held a special place, but Blumhardt was dead set against it becoming anything more than a reminder to press forward to the continuing and new work that God was doing in the world.[15]

Coupled with this positive desire to hear something new from God, Blumhardt also began to express a great dissatisfaction with the culture of piety that had come to surround Bad Boll. Macchia notes that, "He was tired of the people who came to Boll to find a refuge from the world or to find answers to needs which Christoph viewed as self-centered."[16] As Blumhardt stated it:

14. Ibid., 257 (unpublished translation by the Brüderhof and Plough Publishing).

15. Blumhardt: "When I speak of Möttlingen, I can well imagine how it was at the time of the apostles. It is not true that the Spirit of God flows, as it were, from generation to generation. The Spirit of the Möttlingen time will simply cease after the death of all those who received it, unless a new gift is given. I cannot thank our dear God enough for having permitted us children to taste a very small portion of this. But, great as this was, it is still not quite the same; we are in need of a new stimulus, a new foundation. Now, cry out, you children! Cry out with us all that the Heavens may open; it will otherwise go hard with us" (ibid., 260, unpublished translation by the Brüderhof and Plough Publishing).

16. Macchia, *Spirituality and Social Liberation*, 113.

I am not here to maintain a nice house with a crowd of people; our purpose is something else. Whoever wishes to belong to me and to be a friend in my house must learn to look up into Heaven and away from himself. We must look upon the misery of the world in order to understand it. But then we must turn our gaze toward Heaven so that we may receive something from above—not for ourselves, in self-love—but for the world, that the darkness of the world comes to an end! He who sets to work on this is actually praying.[17]

As the last witnesses of the Möttlingen events died, a subtle shift in Christoph's thinking occurred. During most of the first phase, Christoph had emphasized the presence of God in creation, a theological implication Christoph had drawn from the *Kampf* and later revival; but with the loss of the Möttlingen witnesses, this recedes into the background. In its place Christoph can be seen puzzling over how God could be present, and yet nothing happening; worse still, how could the events at Möttlingen now be the basis for expressions of piety and devotion that were motivated only by individual concern? These questions reach their greatest intensity from May 1887 to March 1888. In May of 1887, Hans Broderson, son of Gottliebin Dittus, died from an unknown illness. Blumhardt interpreted this death as a sign of judgment from God that a new way forward needed to be found.[18]

Christoph's dissatisfaction and longing reached their highest point after the death of Hans-Jörg Dittus, brother of Gottliebin and the last remaining eyewitness of the events at Möttlingen. After his death on March 3, 1888, a period of spiritual and theological transition began during which Christoph more prominently emphasized the theme of judgment and the distinction between God and humanity. This was also the period in which he would submit his father's hopes to a critical rethinking in search of a new orientation that was both faithful to what he inherited, though clearly an innovation. Discerning and clarifying what

17. Christoph Blumhardt, *Auswahl*, I:271 (unpublished translation by the Brüderhof and Plough Publishing).

18. "Today the burial of our beloved Hans is uppermost in our hearts. I have the feeling that we stand at the conclusion of a significant time, both inwardly and outwardly. Inwardly, because I can see it as nothing other than a rebuke from God for our whole household. . . . I can only say that in certain areas there must be a change; otherwise, we will have to undergo other trials" (ibid., 381, unpublished translation by the Brüderhof and Plough Publishing).

this new way was to be vis-à-vis his father, the extended circle of Bad
Boll followers, and the larger church would be the central occupation of
Blumhardt throughout his second phase.

Before we turn to this second phase, we should note that some of
the familiar characteristics of his father's thought can be detected during
this first phase. Christoph emphasized the need for a new outpouring of
the Holy Spirit for the kingdom of God to progress in the world.[19] He
also continued in his father's legacy by arguing that the kingdom does
not come by human effort, but by divine action, while simultaneously
stressing that the priority of divine action cannot lead one into quietness.[20] Rather, human action and longing are enclosed in divine action
and are engaged in for the sake of the whole world.[21] At the same time,
there are also some changes in Christoph's thought vis-à-vis his father.

The Hope for the apokatastasis ton panton

As will become evident during our discussion of Christoph's life and
thought, the development of his thought was not so much the result
of explicit change, but of a sharpening and intensifying of many of the
insights already evident in the elder Blumhardt. This is undoubtedly
the case with the hope for the *apkatastasis ton panton*. Christoph shows
almost no ambivalence in his hope for the universal restoration of all
things. He takes over this hope from his father, seeing it as one of his
essential insights, and proclaims it almost violently.[22] "In our thinking

19. See ibid., 24–26.

20. "There are no developments, no human institutions, that have achieved anything
in the Kingdom of God, but only deeds of God, glories that came down from Heaven;
these bring it about, and it is for these that we wait" (ibid., 16, unpublished translation
by the Brüderhof and Plough Publishing).

21. Ibid., 115. "Those lazy Christians who run around thinking that nobody will
bother whether they do anything or not, will get more than they bargain for! . . . I
just don't see why we should dispense with works. What is the purpose of my faith?
Somehow it must prove itself. Believing does not mean thinking; belief is being, and being means that things happen. If I am in the good spirit then good things will happen.
But it is God who brings about faith, and it is God who brings about works, and only
then will we become true men" (ibid., 106–7, unpublished translation by the Brüderhof
and Plough Publishing).

22. For a detailed discussion, see Groth, "Chiliasmus und Apokatastasishoffnung,"
96–103; Christoph also subjects the early misgivings of his father regarding the *apokatastasis ton panton* to critique. He describes those early misgivings as a misguided attempt to make the newly arrived at hope harmonize with traditional church doctrine.
See his *Damit Gott Kommt*, 38–42.

we should not be unsure about the world, about the souls of mankind in general. The surest thing in the Bible is that God will save the whole of mankind, yes, all of creation."[23] One of Christoph's central critiques of Christianity is that it has lost contact with the universal intention of God to save humanity. The loss of this biblical truth has led Christianity to concern itself only with the individual's salvation, rather than being concerned for the universal restoration of creation.[24] Christoph roots his conviction in the second key development that can be discerned during this period: a renewed concentration on the person and work of Jesus Christ.

"Eschatological Christology"

Whereas in the elder Blumhardt eschatology and particularly the reality of the kingdom of God functioned as the controlling concepts over Christology, in Christoph eschatology is more resolutely grounded in the Incarnation. The distinction here is subtle but important. With Christoph, "Jesus is Victor!" takes on a decidedly Christocentric flavor that is in keeping with his father's intentions, but is nonetheless more pronounced, leading him in a new direction. As Macchia notes, "There is a subtle shift . . . from the absence of God (in the elder Blumhardt) to the radical implications of the presence of God through the incarnation of God in Christ (in the younger Blumhardt)."[25] The elder Blumhardt had identified the dynamic nature of the kingdom of God with the life of Jesus. The emphasis on the Spirit of Pentecost as well as his three-stage theology of history, however, had occupied Johann's attention, rather than the Christological basis of the kingdom. The latter becomes more of a concern for Christoph. It is difficult to know exactly when

23. Christoph Blumhardt, *Auswahl*, I:54.

24. "The idea of eternal damnation also does not come from the Bible; it is purely a concept of the churches. On that day of the Lord everything will become good; the wicked will become good; it will be a tremendous time of conversion. All the nations of the earth will then go to Jerusalem. God will change hearts. . . . The idea that God's creatures will no longer be respected is one of the most barbarous thoughts that has ever been. . . . It is peculiar, though, that those people who speak so much about the justice of God always regard themselves as being saved" (ibid., 92, unpublished translation by the Brüderhof and Plough Publishing).

25. Macchia, *Spirituality and Social Liberation*, 116.

this shift occurs, but it is evident as early as 1882 and reaches maturity during Christoph's third phase.[26]

Whether motivated or not by his hope for the *apokatastasis ton panton*, the shift towards the Incarnation is first evident in connection with the same. The hope for the restoration of all things is grounded firmly in the event of the Incarnation:

> The fact of His becoming man relates Him to all flesh, with all that is called man. When He, who is now bound to all flesh, is named Jesus by God, then salvation is thus proclaimed to all flesh. We can avail ourselves of this and allow the name Jesus to enter our consciousness with fullest impact. We must never allow a contradictory teaching to arise in us. I beg of you, do not be led astray, especially in times of corruption when sins seek to become powerful, when seductions are so great! . . . Who can separate himself from his fellowmen? If you would once damn one another seriously, just think—if your neighbor is to have no salvation because of his present nature, how much of your nature has also to go down into Hell? . . . The Father in Heaven has secured the world with the name Jesus—to begin with, through the proclamation of all-encompassing redemption, but finally also through the promised breaking in of salvation in the future of Christ Jesus.[27]

Emphasis on the Incarnation was not meant to portray a crystallized or static reality. Rather, Christoph's focus on the Incarnation occurs within the wider matrix of what might be called an "eschatological Christology,"[28] which emphasizes the dynamic presence of the living

26. In the early 1880's, one finds the common theme of the elder Blumhardt, the crucial role of the Holy Spirit in bringing about the kingdom of God, alongside a new emphasis on the person and work of Jesus as an eschatological and universal reality. As time moves forward, however, though it remains important, not as much emphasis is given to the epochal significance of the Spirit. See Blumhardt, *Auswahl*, I:24–26.

27. Blumhardt, *Auswahl*, I:56–58 (unpublished translation by the Brüderhof and Plough Publishing).

28. Though I am in agreement with Macchia's analysis of the presence of at least two different forms of Christology (Incarnational and symbolic) I would argue that they come together as two foci in the single ellipse of an "eschatological Christology," that is greater than the sum of its parts. The two types that Macchia describes form a dialectically related pair between which Christoph moved back and forth. Both, however, are subject to a concern to see Jesus in the most intimate relationship to the kingdom of God, even identifying Jesus as the kingdom of God enfleshed. See Macchia, *Spirituality and Social Liberation*, 115–20. I take the phrase "eschatological Christology," with some

Lord who is both moving the kingdom of God forward *within* history, while also being the "One who comes" from *without*. Within his mature "eschatological Christology," the experiences at Möttlingen and Bad Boll were interpreted through a dynamic Christology and eschatology, while world history was more and more of interest to Christoph as the realm in which the Spirit of God was at work bringing the kingdom into concrete expression.

We will develop Christoph's "eschatological Christology" under the following points: (1) Jesus Christ, the *autobasilea*; (2) the resurrection and the Holy Spirit as the mediation of the kingdom to history and the world; (3) the relationship between world-history and the history of the kingdom of God; and (4) "the living God" is the One who comes.

1) Jesus was/is the kingdom of God on earth (i.e., the *autobasileia*) as both the apocalyptic judgment of the eschaton and the new life for all of creation. The kingdom of God though hoped for and occasionally seen in parabolic form in the history of Israel, has been enfleshed in Jesus Christ, the Last Man.[29] The root of this insight was lodged in the exorcism experience of the elder Blumhardt and subsequent reflection on it. In the cry, "Jesus is Victor!" the elder Blumhardt believed he was confronted with an unmistakable sign of the inbreaking of the kingdom of God. This "sign" placed the struggle at Möttlingen in a longer history that stretched back into the Hebrew Scriptures, but which had come to a decisive and climactic point in the crucifixion and resurrection of Jesus Christ. For the elder Blumhardt, Jesus Christ begins the kingdom of God: "The appearance of Jesus upon the earth marked the beginning of this kingdom."[30] Christoph moved this insight in an even more Christocentric direction, such that when he used the phrase, "the kingdom of God" he meant "the history of Jesus Christ." "The history of Jesus' life is the history of God's kingdom then and now."[31] This history

---

hesitancy, from Jürgen Moltmann. See his *On Human Dignity*, 5. Though I do not fully agree with his critical reading of Barth, I do think that the description and much of the content associated with it can be readily applied to Blumhardt's Christology. See also Sauter, *Die Theologie des Reiches Gottes*, 24, 33.

29. See Christoph Blumhardt, *Auswahl*, I, 48–49.

30. Johann Christoph Blumhardt, *Die Verkündigung*, 316 (unpublished translation by the Brüderhof and Plough Publishing).

31. Christoph Blumhardt, *Action in Waiting*, 3. "He lives among men and he is the kingdom of God. He does not make it; He *is* the kingdom!" (Christoph Blumhardt, *Auswahl*, III:61, unpublished translation by the Brüderhof and Plough Publishing).

referred to the whole life of Christ as depicted in Scripture, marked above all by the resurrection as the sign of God's triumph.[32]

Crucially, however, by the "history of Jesus Christ" Christoph did not mean a harmonized form of the apostolic memory and proclamation, but a *living* reality. That is, the phrase "history of Jesus Christ" did not mean a proto-narrativist Christology (though it does undoubtedly share characteristics with such a Christology), rather it referred to an ongoing living reality outside of the historical continuum whose subject continues to penetrate ongoing history. As Christoph puts it: "Behind the veil of world-history, as it were, stands the Cross of Christ; now and then the veil parts and this history of the Crucified presses through into our world."[33] This passage sheds some light on the implications of Blumhardt's identification of Jesus with the kingdom of God.

First, that Jesus was the kingdom of God meant for Blumhardt that in the cross of Christ, the apocalyptic judgment of the "Last Day" has been effectively poured out on all of humanity. When the history of the living Christ presses into this world, it does so as the history of the One who was judged and now is alive. Thus, its presence in history is the presence of a history that both judges and transforms the world.[34] The judgment experienced in the here and now and the final cosmic judgment when Christ comes together constitute our share in that which Christ has already experienced, and thus they are a judgment unto life.[35] Furthermore, this judgment is not simply for Christianity or for some small pocket therein, but for the whole of creation.[36]

32. Importantly, and in keeping with his father, Blumhardt included the history of Israel in the history of the kingdom of God enfleshed in Jesus. See Lim, *'Jesus ist Sieger!'*, 139.

33. Christoph Blumhardt, *Vom Reich Gottes*, 66 (unpublished translation by the Brüderhof and Plough Publishing).

34. See Christoph Blumhardt, *Auswahl*, II:28–30. See also, Macchia, "Shadow of the Cross," 63.

35. "We want to enter the day of Jesus Christ! That will also be a day of judgment, but it is a day of judgment that He Himself has endured. It is the day of His blood to which we must submit and let ourselves be punished as godless people. In this judgment, however, we are able to life ourselves up because the day of Christ Jesus is also the day of life in Christ Jesus" (Christoph Blumhardt, *Auswahl*, I:49, unpublished translation by the Brüderhof and Plough Publishing). See also Christoph Blumhardt, *Vom Reich Gottes*, 66–67.

36. "If only Christians would believe and expect that in the future of Jesus Christ, the glory of God will be made manifest to all creation! . . . Then we shall remain faithful

Second, the kingdom of God *is* history. That is, it is the specific process of judgment and reconciliation enacted in the life-history of Jesus Christ, the living and risen Lord who is Yahweh among men.[37] The "kingdom of God" is not a cipher or empty container into which to place all kinds of speculations or hopes, but rather is Christologically shaped and filled out by the details of the history of Jesus that are portrayed in the witness of the apostles. Furthermore, it is dynamic and not static, because it is a *living* history. When this history connects to the world, it does not receive anything from the world, but rather extends the power and effect of the work of reconciliation on the cross into the world, thus reclaiming humanity and the whole cosmos for the end that God has determined for it, i.e., to live in his presence. The Blumhardts were not entirely clear as to whether this extension referred primarily to the revelation of God's work of reconciliation on the cross, or to the actualizing of that event in the here and now. There is evidence to suggest that both are implied, thus meaning that the cross is both the one-time event of reconciliation, while simultaneously representing the origin or foundation of the process of reconciliation that will end in universal restoration.[38]

In sharper lines than his father, therefore, Christoph developed the notion that the "history of the kingdom of God" was a self-enclosed and self-sustaining entity that encountered the world from outside in the form of the living and risen Christ. At the same time, "the history of the kingdom of God" was ongoing because it had entered into the world through the resurrection and in the outpouring of the Holy Spirit.

2) Through the resurrection and subsequent outpouring of the Holy Spirit, the living Christ, the kingdom of God enfleshed, was now present in the world secretly working its way toward God's intended goal, thus linking together the acts of creation and redemption through a dynamic teleology. The resurrection was both the reality of the victory of the kingdom of God, but also the sign of promise that the history of the kingdom, as displayed in Jesus in his life and death, was still active

---

to the end, and we shall all be engulfed in the Savior's great history of victory on the earth" (ibid., 90, unpublished translation by the Brüderhof and Plough Publishing).

37. See Lim, *'Jesus ist Sieger!'*, 109.

38. See Christoph Blumhardt, *Auswahl*, I:48–49, and *Vom Reich Gottes*, 68–69, for texts in which both a once-and-for-all *and* a process doctrine of reconciliation are entwined with one another.

in the here and now. If Christ's life and death are the fulfillment and enactment of the kingdom of God, then his subsequent resurrection and mediation through the outpouring of the Holy Spirit meant that the kingdom had not been lost to us, but rather was alive and active in the world. As Lim describes it:

> The resurrection of Jesus is the "seed", from which a new history develops. It germinates and grows through the effectiveness of the living person of Jesus. This means concretely, that history, which originated from the living person of Jesus . . . has actually entered the affairs of world history. In this way the being and deeds of Jesus on earth develop.[39]

The resurrection begins the process of God's reclamation of the cosmos, while the Spirit extends and completes it. Christoph saw the Holy Spirit as God's presence in the community and in the individual extending the kingdom and working to prepare the world for the coming universal restoration.[40]

In deep continuity with his father, Christoph believed that the Spirit's presence in the community and individual was necessary for humanity to participate in the history of God's deeds on earth. Thus, though the kingdom moved forward by a kind of divine monergism, humanity was not excluded, but rather included as God's free creatures and covenant partners who struggled with the living Christ to see the kingdom of God enter into the world.[41] This was nowhere more evident than in the Spirit's work in moving the community to pray, "Thy Kingdom Come!" Prayer for both the elder and the younger Blumhardt, however, was not passive, but an active waiting. Especially during Christoph's third phase, the prayer for the kingdom of God became almost synonymous with action among the poor in the world. But even during this period, struggle for the kingdom of God was still only possible because of the empowering presence of the Holy Spirit. The question of the relationship between divine and human action connects to the broader question of the relationship between the history of the kingdom of God and world-history.

39. Lim, 'Jesus ist Seiger!', 142.

40. See ibid., 172–75.

41. For multiple examples of this, see Christoph Blumhardt, *Vom Reich Gottes*, 84–114.

3) The relationship between the history of kingdom of God and world-history was dialectical in nature. The history of humanity moves forward at its own pace, but is preceded, encapsulated and penetrated by the history of God's kingdom, which both judges and transfigures the history of humanity.[42] Though the progress of the "history of the kingdom of God," the living Christ, was not always discernible, it was nonetheless at work in the world, moving inexorably towards its intended goal: the world's redemption.[43] Thus, the inner meaning and promise of world history was the history of the kingdom of God, which Blumhardt no longer identified with Christianity, but only with the living and active Christ.[44] In this way, God's intention for creation was accomplished in the Incarnation. "This is the man Jesus Christ: he is fixed in the creation where his true nature is grounded. . . . He is in the creation, and it must go as he goes."[45] The history of the crucified messiah was constantly breaking in upon human history to show the latter its true end and bring it to its fulfillment:

> The Savior is coming. He is not sitting on some celestial throne, resting somewhere in eternity, waiting for some particular time before he acts or a certain moment when he will suddenly plunge in. The coming of the Savior runs like a thread throughout history, through God's working in the world (Matt. 28:20). If this thread is not to break, then Jesus must always be coming. . . . And there will indeed come a time when our waiting and watching, which has prepared the coming of the Lord, will be consummated.[46]

The event of an inbreaking was seen to be a life-giving revelation of God's purpose for the earth, such that the knowledge of God's presence meant receiving both new life and a new orientation and anticipation

42. Macchia, "Shadow of the Cross," 63.

43. "We do not know how this victory will finally take place. We do not even know how this victory goes forward in secret, or how such words as 'Forgive them!' go on working. But we do know that God does not give up the plan to redeem mankind just because for centuries sin has not understood and does not accept Him. God carries through His cause in Christ in the face of all disbelief, in the face of all sin" (Christoph Blumhardt, *Auswahl*, I:102, unpublished translation by the Brüderhof and Plough Publishing).

44. See ibid., 199–202.

45. Eller, *Thy Kingdom Come*, 12.

46. Christoph Blumhardt, *Action in Waiting*, 38–39.

of God's coming cosmic transformation and rule. God's act of creation *and* redemption are not merely once-and-for-all events in history, but rather once-and-for-all events that are progressively moving towards their final cosmic goal. The humanity of Jesus was the criterion for discerning where the kingdom of God was at work in the world.

Both Blumhardts, but especially Christoph, emphasized that in the humanity of Jesus we see the shape and form of the kingdom of God at work in history. This stress on the humanity of Jesus as the locus of God's presence in the world meant that his life and work were the pattern and criterion for both discerning and participating in the move of the God in history.[47] Because of this, the church and church history were on the same level as the world and world history. The kingdom of God could just as well work with the church as against it. The kingdom was no longer mediated to the world through the church as church, but only as it was obedient to Jesus Christ. What is more, during his third phase, Christoph would be led to radically emphasize that the kingdom of God could even be found at work under realities that were very different from the church (i.e., Socialism), insofar as these other realities conformed to the humanity of Jesus. This allowed for both a universal horizon when considering the relationship of the kingdom of God to the world as well as a more holistic appreciation of the life of humanity. The arena of God's action was no longer only in the church, but included the whole inhabited earth. The *oikonomia* is already God's possession, thus the kingdom of God is for the whole earth and all who live in it.

4) Christoph's eschatological Christology is shaped by and gives shape to a dynamic understanding of God's nature. Like his father, Christoph stressed that God is the "living God." This idea was rooted in the experiences at Möttlingen and Bad Boll, where Christ had broken into the world in the case of Gottliebin Dittus and the later revival. Johann deepened this insight through exegetical reflection on key passages in the Torah. Bodamer has shown that the elder Blumhardt's understanding of God's being was shaped by his reading of Exodus 34. In this passage, the name of God is described as God's action towards humanity:

47. Macchia calls this a "symbolic Christology" and notes its emergence during the second phase of Blumhardt's development. See his, *Spirituality and Social Liberation*, 119–20. He also notes that during Christoph's third phase, Jesus' humanity is so emphasized that Blumhardt almost rules out His divinity.

> Then the LORD came down in the cloud and stood there with him and proclaimed his name, the LORD. And passing in front of Moses, proclaiming, 'The LORD, the LORD, the compassionate and gracious God, slow to anger, abounding in love and faithfulness, maintaining love to thousands, and forgiving wickedness, rebellion and sin. (Exodus 34:5–7, NIV)

According to Bodamer, "Blumhardt has no interest in an abstract God. He deals with the God who deals with man. The way of God to man is what is important to him. . . . God *is* what He *does*."[48] Or, as Karl Barth would eventually formulate it, "God's being is in His act."[49] Christoph's thinking continues in the line of his father,[50] but he further identifies God's nature with the eschatological coming of the kingdom of God who is Jesus Christ:

> What God is, we carry in our hearts; it is the coming of Jesus Christ. This is God, whether you believe it or not! And even if I were the most miserable of widows, I would still stick to this! The coming of Jesus Christ is God; and when this comes about, all creation will know what God is and who God is![51]

God is the coming God, an active God who lives. Christoph's emphasis on Jesus Christ as the living and coming One was a further elaboration of his father's thoughts on the "living God" revealed in the Torah, for Jesus was the concrete manifestation of the living God of Israel precisely because he had overcome death and continued to appear in the here and now as the victor.[52] The implications of this are many.

---

48. Bodamer, "The Life and Work of Johann Christoph Blumhardt," 59, 62, emphasis mine. Bodamer argues that Blumhardt took for granted that God's name reveals God's being, and thus his preference for Exod 34 over against Exod 3 shows a person who wanted to avoid the abstract in favor of the concrete.

49. *CD* II/1, 257–72.

50. "Our general name 'Lord' or 'God' is not sufficient; it means very little to most people, whereas when an Israelite spoke of 'Jehovah', it immediately brought to mind a history interwoven with the life of the people" (Christoph Blumhardt, *Auswahl*, I:237, unpublished translation by the Brüderhof and Plough Publishing). This passage shows the influence of the elder Blumhardt, as well as Christoph's own deep appreciation for the pattern of engagement between God and Israel in the Hebrew Scriptures which is seen throughout his work.

51. Ibid., 322 (unpublished translation by the Brüderhof and Plough Publishing).

52. See Christoph Blumhardt, *Auswahl*, II:328–29.

The first is an emphasis on divine precedence. Because God is living and active it is His life and action that are decisive, rather than human life or action. Divine precedence and human subsequence was the only proper way to order God's interaction with humanity because for both Blumhardts it was in God's very nature to act. God lives, God acts, and the direction of his life and action are towards his creatures in love. That God acts was a truth that both Blumhardts believed was rooted in the Scriptures. The events at Möttlingen forced them to take those depictions seriously again as indicating something essential about God.

This insight also qualified their emphasis on the kingdom of God as "history" and thereby distinguished it from a *Heilsgeschichte* approach. The kingdom was an event because God lives and acts and the actions of God constitute a history. This history does not develop, however, in a linear fashion that can be readily detected on the surface of the flow of world-history. Rather, it develops through the interaction of promise and fulfillment.[53] When the living God encounters the world as the history of the kingdom of God whose goal is the final cosmic restoration, he does so by further impregnating the world with his promise to bring this kingdom to its fulfillment.[54] This finds its conceptual corollary in the physical resurrection of Christ, which is both the *sign* of promise, while also being an initial *fulfillment* of God's universal promise. The way from death to life, as exhibited in the death and resurrection of Jesus, is not self-evident and certainly not known through conceptual or systematic mapping. It is only the act and promise of God that allows one to move from the one to the other.

Likewise, what links one episode of the kingdom together with another is not their external linear development, but the fact that it is the living God who is acting through them. More specifically, the irruptions of the kingdom of God are occurrences or forms of the "advent" of Jesus Christ. "The coming of the Savior runs like a thread throughout history, through God's working in the world (Matt. 28:20). If this thread is not to break, then Jesus must always be coming."[55] This meant that the kinds of calculations and predictions developed by Bengel and oth-

---

53. See Sauter, *Die Theologie des Reiches Gottes*, 301–25.

54. Blumhardt often referred to this by using the metaphor of the kingdom as a "seed." For examples of this see Christoph Blumhardt, *Auswahl*, I:213; II:90, 140, 241; III:61, 384–85.

55. Christoph Blumhardt, *Action in Waiting*, 38.

ers about the final coming of the kingdom were never of great interest to the Blumhardts, and especially not to Christoph. At the same time, however, though the kingdom does not develop out of necessity and at a predictable rate, it does move forward because it is *God's* kingdom and God's purposes will not be thwarted. Furthermore, though the coming of Jesus into history was primarily the action of God, it also sought corresponding human actions, which were enfolded into God's history.[56] This inclusion of humanity into the work of God means that God's history is embodied in world history through the faithful actions of humanity.

Finally, the Blumhardts' understanding of the living God led them to emphasize that the kingdom of God was God's own future. "What God has spoken must be fulfilled. God will glorify Himself. The creation is *His*, not ours. The earth is *His*, not ours. Life belongs to *Him*, even your life. It does not belong to you; it is His! It belongs to God!"[57] This meant that eschatology and the hope for the kingdom could not be reduced to anthropology or ethics, even if the same could be included in it. As mentioned above, human longing, prayer and action were essential, but in the end the kingdom comes because God brings it. Thus, it is not a doctrine or idea, but a reality whose coming is sure even if sometimes hidden, because it is rooted in the promise of God, which was revealed in the event of Christ's resurrection: "In Him, everything lives! Even the dead will return to life."[58] That the resurrection of Jesus could already be experienced in penultimate forms in history was a truth that both Blumhardts believed the Scriptures witnessed to and the events at Möttlingen had brought back into view.

Though Christoph's "eschatological Christology" was developed over the course of his life, it should be noted that even during the first phase a palpable shift towards Christology can be detected in the younger Blumhardt. This shift highlighted, among other things, God's presence in the world moving the cosmos towards its intended end. Why the effects of the living Christ experienced at Möttlingen appeared to be receding more and more from view became a central problem for Christoph towards the end of his first phase. He would spend all of his

---

56. See Christoph Blumhardt, *Auswahl*, II:303.

57. Ibid., 321.

58. Christoph Blumhardt, *Auswahl*, I:201.

spiritual and intellectual energy in understanding and addressing this problem during his second phase.

The Second Phase: 1888–1896

During his second phase, Blumhardt was consumed with developing, refining, and sharpening his answer to the question of why God's kingdom has not come and even seems to have receded as an effective power in history. His answer: human nature impedes the kingdom. The devil and the powers of darkness—the primary opponents of the elder Blumhardt—were vanquished by the living history of the kingdom of God that flared up at Möttlingen and later at Bad Boll. Though still problematic, they are nevertheless pushed to the side as the primary opponents to be fought against; while sinful human nature, which refuses to bow before the immanently present Lord who wants to bring His kingdom into the world for the salvation of all, becomes the central opponent to be fought against. This shift in orientation is captured in Blumhardt's new watchword: "Die, that Jesus may live!"

How does one die? Christ's cross, which before had been the sight of the eschatological judgment, is now the pattern by which that eschatological judgment is brought into the life of the faithful Christian: "The Cross of Jesus Christ points only to the narrow way, and this Cross stands outside the town, outside the gates and among the pagans, among the people. There we see His flesh sacrificed for the sins of the world, and there we are clearly told: You, too, sacrifice your flesh to the God who wants to make you blessed!"[59] This death cannot be manufactured through piety however. Rather, the disciple has to surrender that they may receive it, for only God can bring about this death and the new life of the kingdom that comes through it.[60]

In keeping with the cosmic orientation and emphasis on embodied existence, Christoph understood this discipleship of the cross as aimed not at making the individual righteous, but rather as equipping them to continue the struggle for the kingdom of God, which comes to bless the whole world. This meant that the human willfulness that had to be put

---

59. Christoph Blumhardt, *Auswahl*, II:48 (unpublished translation by the Brüderhof and Plough Publishing). This is the key element of what Macchia describes as the shift to a "symbolic Christology," whereby Jesus becomes the pattern by which the kingdom is received into the world. See his *Spirituality and Social Liberation*, 119–20.

60. See ibid., 49–53.

to death would include not only personal sinfulness, but also social institutions and traditions that impeded God's kingdom from advancing.[61] Meier notes that this concern with the social and embodied aspects of humanity represents a reformulation of the traditional question, "Who's will reigns? The will of God or the arbitrary will of man? Now Blumhardt simplifies the question: Who lives in man, in their conditions? Blumhardt's answer was obvious: Christ is to live everywhere. He has to enter into bodily life, into the life of the people, into social life."[62] Two traditions and social institutions that undergo critique during this period are Christianity in general and the heritage of Bad Boll and the elder Blumhardt.

The Gedanken aus dem Reich Gottes ("Thoughts on the kingdom of God")

Throughout Christoph's career, a severe critique of both the history of Christianity and the present day church is evident. This is certainly rooted in Christoph's own pietistic heritage. Blumhardt's critique, however, lumps together both mainline Christianity and Pietism.[63] Both forms of Christianity attempt to get a handle on God, rather than waiting for God to act. Both are guilty of being mechanical and of over-identifying themselves and their efforts with the kingdom of God.

> It is a reproach to those Christians who say they can lead us to life and can bring the Kingdom of God. No—we do not want this from you—we want it from Christ! His light and His life must be revealed; only then are we justified in inviting all the people. Then will come the Kingdom of God. There is no life without the revelation of the Risen One, Jesus Christ. Christianity and piety cannot create life. This we can see everywhere in the world—everything human sinks back into death. Even when individuals make a new effort, as was given, for example, in the Reformation, it does not endure. Today we are again in night and darkness, in disunity and misery.

61. This is the root of Blumhardt's understanding of the social and systemic nature of sin.

62. Meier, *Christoph Blumhardt*, 40.

63. As Macchia has shown, Blumhardt's critique of both mainline and pietistic Christianity was not unusual within Württemberg Pietism, as it can be found already with Ph. M. Hahn (1739–1790). See Macchia, *Spirituality and Social Liberation*, 37.

> No! Jesus must live! Jesus must rise! Jesus Himself must speak—and He will speak! In the spirit of the living God He will reveal Himself in our hearts. He will become mightier and mightier in those who are His and in many, many others who give themselves to His blood. Thus will the Kingdom of God be filled with the thanksgiving of those for whom Jesus laid down His life.[64]

Nothing, no person, no community, no movement can be univocally identified with the kingdom of God, and thus every community, every movement, and every person must be critiqued in light of it, in order that it may "die, that Jesus may live." Nowhere does the seriousness with which Christoph intended to apply this negation become clearer than in his *Gedanken aus dem Reich Gottes*.[65]

Published in the tradition of the *Blätter aus Bad Boll* as a single volume in 1895, this work is a sustained theological engagement, critique, and rethinking of the elder Blumhardt's message and experience in the new context in which Christoph found himself. It is by far the single most important document for understanding the development of Christoph's thought vis-à-vis his father. There are, however, three different fronts that Christoph is simultaneously engaged in critiquing: 1) his father's legacy; 2) the friends of Bad Boll and the larger community of the *Erweckungsbewegung*, many of whom suspected that Christoph had strayed from his father's legacy; and 3) the state church and the history of Christianity that it represented. We will deal with all three of these together in what follows.

As a historical phenomenon, Christianity was no different than any other historical entity. It was not the kingdom of God on earth, but a mixed history characterized more as a history of deterioration than a history of triumph. Following in the wake of his father's theology of history, Christoph emphasized that through the Spirit of Pentecost the church had been empowered to preach the gospel and witness to the coming of the kingdom of God in the form of miracles. These were not the goals of the Spirit of Pentecost, however, but were to empower the community to continue to move towards the true goal: the coming of

64. Christoph Blumhardt, *Auswahl*, II, 121–22 (unpublished translation by the Brüderhof and Plough Publishing).

65. See the recently re-published edition of Christoph Blumhardt's *Damit Gott Kommt*.

the kingdom of God in the appearance of Jesus Christ. According to Blumhardt, the first gift of Pentecost was given only as a *signum* and not the *res*. Through this sign, the Christian communities would begin to embody the kingdom of God in preparation for its final coming.[66] Thus, Pentecost began the fulfillment of the promise of Joel, but was not the thing itself.

After the Apostles' death, however, the church lost sight of the ultimate goal of longing, acting, and praying for the coming kingdom of God and began to settle in for the long haul. This displaced the goal of the struggle for the kingdom of God that began in the life and death of Jesus whose ultimate aim was the restoration of the whole cosmos, and put in its place the goal of the conversion of souls, the building and maintenance of Christian institutions, and the development of Christian doctrine.[67]

All was not lost, however, because God does not abandon the goal for which He created the earth. The kingdom of God, though hidden and difficult to discern, continued to flare up in history in the form of "stations on the way." The most significant of these "stations" were the Reformation, Pietism, and the events at Möttlingen. However, and this was key for Blumhardt's critique, all of these were merely "stations," not the final goal or destination. They had occurred in history as signs of God's continuing presence and as occurrences of the struggle to bring the kingdom of God fully into the world. Unfortunately, throughout history, these stations became the goal: "If, through God's grace and revelation, a station was reached, then rest and refreshment was granted to the endowed ones, but only in the expectation that they then would be so much more zealous to attain the goal. But caught up in sluggishness and self-interest they made themselves at home at this station, forgetting their goal."[68] According to Blumhardt, it was human willfulness that had slowed the kingdom of God and created "detours," not the will of God. Blumhardt believed that this was undoubtedly the case within Christendom and that Bad Boll and the events at Möttlingen were be-

---

66. The resonance with Johannes Weiss's and Albert Schweitzer's conceptions of the eschatological hopes of early Christianity should not be lost sight of here. See Weiss, *Jesus' Proclamation*, originally published as *Die Predigt Jesu*; see also Schweitzer, *Quest of the Historical Jesus*, originally published as *Von Remarius zu Wrede*.

67. See Christoph Blumhardt, *Damit Gott Kommt*, 50–60.

68. Ibid., 49.

ing sucked into the same process of ossification. He would have none of this:

> If we do not know how many stations we still have to pass until we arrive at the goal, neither do we need to know. Enough of that, Möttlingen was a station to us, and we hurry on toward the goal. Of course the direction takes a sharp turn today. Oppositions make themselves known, other surroundings and situations occur which need attention. It is no longer Möttlingen, or the work of Bad Boll, which developed through Möttlingen. It is also not our father Blumhardt which counts now, but only that which brings us closer to the goal. We actually turned our back to Möttlingen in order to advance.[69]

Blumhardt's critique of "established" patterns and forms of church life and Christian struggle had led him to alter his dress, cease calling himself a pastor in 1894, and stop many of the spiritual practices that Bad Boll had become synonymous with, such as healing and counseling. These changes were in part a response to those who came to Bad Boll only for individual physical or spiritual healing, rather than seeing the same as signs and bridges that should open the individual to the rest of the world, to hope for the cosmic Sabbath that would encompass the whole world.[70] Blumhardt was very critical of the lethargy that he believed was creeping into Bad Boll, and he believed that in some measure his father's own attempts to interpret the Möttlingen experiences to the larger Christian community in terms that made such palatable had contributed to the delay in the kingdom's progress.[71] At the same time, however, his changes were not wholly negative, but rather evinced a genuine hope that God would act anew.

Blumhardt's negation and critique of the church and of his father's legacy occurred within a greater positive relationship. This was because the events that had come before, the "stations," were in fact the kingdom of God flaring up in history. If God was truly in them, movement beyond them could not mean their total disregard. "The intervention of

---

69. Ibid., 64.

70. As James Bentley notes, "He soon became impatient with it, believing that a certain spiritual selfishness was afflicting the countless pious Christians who flocked to Bad Boll" ("Preacher of Hope," 577).

71. See Christoph Blumhardt, *Damit Gott Kommt: "Gedanken aus dem Reich Gottes"*, 152–59.

God at Möttlingen was actually like being shaken and awakened out of sleep. In comparison to before, we now stand awake and certain that we always have to be alert at the door, in order to open it when the Lord comes (Rev. 3:20; Lk.12:36f.). For it is we who have to be ready when He comes not He who must be ready when we come."[72] Blumhardt's critique was meant to be salutary because it warned those who longed for the kingdom to expect something new from God, just as God had acted in a new way in the Reformation and at Möttlingen. It was just that they should not expect that God would or had to act in the exact same way.[73] The continuity between the Reformation, Möttlingen, and whatever might come next, was not to be found in external forms, theology or even revered persons, but in the living God who had shown Himself in Scripture and history as objectively acting.[74] This might mean a move-

---

72. Ibid., 47.

73. "But this also has become clear to us: that this life intervention of God will not once for all repeat itself in the same manner or mechanically alone through means of grace alone. Much rather, God's intervention comes as a thief in the night (compare Matt 24:42–44 and others). We have to be alert for new situations and new responsibilities. According to the times and the conditions of times in which people live, God will lead and guide his people to the end of the world. It would make no sense at all, if the Savior would say words like: 'Surely I am with you always, to the very end of the age' (Matt 28:20), if his living intervention and reigning were not necessary. Since he is not willing to be a dead corpse, likewise we also are to be alive and flexible and are not to be dead in temporal arrangements. It is important to remain flexible for His surprises. It is important to make progresses, to dispose of the archaic, and to accept the contemporary. It is important to be armed externally and inwardly, in order to be prepared for the right time and in the proper manner to hear the command of the Commander in Chief. Of course there are also points of rest, which have to be gained individually in battle and assault. Nowhere, however, is a lasting stay granted, until the people of God are at their final goal. All peoples can be drawn into this circle of truth and righteousness through this" (ibid., 47).

74. A number of scholars have argued that in this conception Blumhardt almost identifies the kingdom of God with progress, making him a crypto-Hegelian. But as developed above in our discussion of Christoph's eschatological Christology, and as Meier has pointed out, though sharing certain elements of Hegel's philosophy of history, Blumhardt also had some significant differences. Blumhardt did not see progress as simply a linear development of successive stages. Rather, the kingdom flares up in history, but it does not become a part of the flow of history as though the occurrence, of itself, would simply lead straight into the next in-breaking. The development is predicated neither on a linear nor on a cyclical inevitability, but is predicated on the promise of God to bring the world to its final end. Clearly, Blumhardt also did not believe that humanity or any immanent power of creation could create the progress of the kingdom; rather progress can only occur as God acts. Finally, God's being is not to be identified with history. See Meier, *Christoph Blumhardt*, 37–38.

ment beyond the traditional forms of church life and thought, but this critique and movement beyond was also for the sake of the church, the Bad Boll community, and above all, the kingdom of God.

In continuity and distinction from his father, Christoph argued that the kingdom of God advanced on two fronts. The first was against the cosmic demonic forces that held the world in thrall. The Möttlingen *Kampf* and his father's ministry fell into this camp. On the other front was God's fight for the kingdom within humanity, against the human will to dominate. Christoph saw his own new orientation in this second struggle.[75] Both of these fronts included external and internal dimensions. In the case of the former, spiritual struggles and the work of miraculous healing linked healing with salvation and highlighted the fact that God sought to "save" the whole person. In the case of the latter, the struggle against greed and selfishness and the sinful will was simultaneously linked to a struggle to relieve physical oppression. As a reality in history, the kingdom sought to humanize the internal and external realms of human existence, rather than to create "pious Christians." With this insight, Blumhardt's critique unfolded into a radical affirmation of creation and the world.[76] The true Christian was to be truly and

75. "If therefore the catch-word was previously: 'Jesus is Victor!,' first in the battle against darkness and superstition, and later on the catchword was: 'God is merciful to all creatures, because Jesus is Victor!' Today the catchword is: 'Die! For only then Jesus can live!' But he can only live and reign, be victorious and rise again, if you deny yourselves and die to yourselves, in order that you, being dead to yourselves, come to God with all of your heart and with all of your soul to bring forth fruit which is well pleasing unto God. For only when man submits himself in a totally new and complete manner, will victory come, which makes possible God's mercy to all creation. For, as it was mentioned, Jesus does not only desire victory, Jesus wants life. He wants to live in you people who have flesh and blood, for the benefit of God's righteousness and truth on earth" (Christoph Blumhardt, *Damit Gott Kommt*, 44).

76. Meier describes the significance of this breakthrough as follows: "Now the goal of his thought swings dialectically towards a different orientation: The polarity of the physical life and the right life before God is negated. God does not have to influence this life as an external power. He is already present in human life. God can only begin to do something with man, as they are truly human. With the influence of God's perfect order in the physical life, Blumhardt had overcome the denial of the body in Christian thought. Now he decisively and finally overcame the dualistic worldview, which predominated in Pietism. After putting aside the spiritually oriented worldview, temporal existence gained a theological quality. . . . In truly being human also lies the road to God" (*Christoph Blumhardt*, 40).

fully human. When this happened, God could enter fully and finally into the world where he was already at work.[77]

Though the hope and thought of the elder Blumhardt is subjected to a critique in the *Gedanken aus dem Reich Gottes*, Christoph saw his own new orientation as having far more in common with his father's hopes than not, and thus he rejected criticisms that his new direction was a betrayal of his father's legacy:

> Basically, therefore, we have today the very same hopes as our father had. We cannot say that he yielded to a false conception of the Scriptures and accepted something unjustifiable in his hope. Much rather it was scripturally according to the Spirit. Likewise we have to hope for the same as he. Yes, our hope today has grown entirely out of his. We possibly may say: Our hope is more certain, clearer, freed from our personal desires and therefore has become by far much bolder. Blumhardt saw, similarly to the departing Moses, the promise in the distance in rather nebulous contours (comp. Deut. 34:1-4).[78]

At the close of the *Gedanken aus dem Reich Gottes*, Christoph shows the continuity of his thought with what he calls the three-fold hope of his father: 1) the hope for the outpouring of the Holy Spirit which will renew humanity; 2) the hope for the development of Zion or a people of God obedient to and longing for the coming of the kingdom of God for the whole cosmos; and 3) the hope that death itself would be swallowed up, thus liberating humanity and the earth and bringing God's purposes in creation to their end in the kingdom of God. This three-fold hope continues on in Christoph's thinking because through the call to, "die, that Jesus may live": 1) an attempt is being made to make room for the Spirit to come and renew the whole of humanity; 2) a community of "fighters for the kingdom of God" is being created; and 3) the eyes of those who struggle is taken off of themselves and their own piety and placed on God's true goal of establishing his kingdom on this earth.[79]

With this period of critical reflection and re-orientation behind him, Blumhardt turned away from the churchly world and the pious circles that had surrounded and supported Bad Boll and his father's ministry. He hoped to hear God anew and believed that to do so required

77. See Christoph Blumhardt, *Damit Gott Kommt*, 131–32.

78. Ibid., 166.

79. See ibid., 174–212.

him to disengage from the sphere with which he was most comfortable and which he believed was turning into a cul-de-sac. During his third phase, this turn would lead him out into the world in a revolutionary new direction.

The Third Phase: 1896–1906

Christoph's aggravation with the pious culture that had formed around Bad Boll and his new stress on waiting for God to act again led him to look away from the church and ecclesiastical circles to find where the kingdom of God might be breaking into the world anew. Over the course of his second period of development, the critical watchword "Die, that Jesus may live!" had counter-intuitively issued in a radical affirmation of creation and human life. This shift of accent marked a new openness in Blumhardt to affirm the everyday life of human existence into which God wanted to come and through which the kingdom of God would come. At the end of the second and into the third phase, Blumhardt's emphasis was no longer "die, that Jesus may live," but love that which God has created and will never give up.[80]

God's Revolutionary Love

Though Blumhardt had always emphasized love, it was now seen as the way in which one made room for the kingdom precisely because this was the way that God had acted towards the world in Jesus, the kingdom of God incarnate:

> It will be day in your heart, when you *believe in God's love,* and *live in God's love*—then it will be day. God's love melts everything else, everything bad and everything mean and everything despairing. Love conquers everything, love conquers death, but it must be God's love—a kind of love that even loves its enemies: a love that strides unperturbed like a warrior through everything and can never be insulted or hurt or despised, or thrown

---

80. Robert Lejeune sought to capture Blumhardt's renewed emphasis on God's universal love for all of creation by using the catchphrase "Ihr Menschen seid Gottes!" ("You oh man, belong to God!") to describe the third phase of Blumhardt's development. See Christoph Blumhardt, *Auswahl,* III. Meier notes, however, that this emphasis is already evident in the second phase, illustrating the fact that no stage in the four-fold periodization can be seen as sealed off from the others. See Meier, *Christoph Blumhardt,* 41.

away, and can never be repelled; a love that strides through the world like a warrior with the helmet of hope on his head. That is the love of God, which will never concede there is anyone who is not loved. I say it boldly in the face of the whole world, in the face of heaven and the underworld: *Everything* is loved because Jesus is born. They should all know they are loved and not one single person should feel rejected—*they are all loved, because Jesus is born!* ... Jesus wants to be understood as the boundless love of God, and in this love he wants to conquer; in this love he wants to be the flame that burns pure. There has to be *judgment*, we have to be judged and things have to be put right. But it is only God's love and mercy that take us through his judgment and sets us free from everything that enslaves us and makes us miserable people who live today and tomorrow disappear in the darkness of death.[81]

In keeping with the basic emphasis of his father, but seen now through his new emphasis on God's reclamation of the social and physical dimensions of human life, Blumhardt believed that God desired and would in fact pour out his transforming love into the hearts *and* into the physical and social conditions of humanity. "Today, God's purpose expands world-wide. God's kingdom goes into the alley, there where the poorest of the poor are, those who are rejected and despised."[82] Blumhardt believed that only this love could penetrate into the conditions in which the majority of humanity lived, bringing the process of God's reclamation closer and closer to its final goal. Love was greater and more effective than the pious self-righteousness often shown towards the poor and oppressed, and Blumhardt believed that only love could prevail over the dehumanizing conditions experienced by the same.[83]

In Blumhardt's eyes, when this love penetrated the world it would have revolutionary consequences. In March 1898, Blumhardt contrasted the revolutionary foment in the world with the kingdom of God's love, saying,

81. Christoph Blumhardt, *Auswahl*, III:10–12 (unpublished translation by the Brüderhof and Plough Publishing).

82. Christoph Blumhardt, *Ansprachen*, II:84. This passage, taken from a devotion given on September 17, 1897, is significant because it shows that Christoph saw his shift towards social concern as an extension of the Möttlingen *Kampf*, and therefore in deep continuity with his father's ministry.

83. See ibid., 84–85.

The process of fermentation and change comes with Jesus. The poor, the wretched, the dejected, the sick, and even the mentally deranged shall win respect through Jesus; no longer shall they be despised! He represents God's love, and wants to pour the love of God into every human heart saying: Despise no one, condemn no one, raise the lowly from the dust, help God forward in deed, so that all those who are poor, rejected, despised and suffering shall see help coming. Rebel against the present state of affairs and bring it about that all people are equal— through love! Thus Jesus still stands at the door, needing people to help him do this work; people who, in the strength of the Almighty, will transform everything out of love. Heaven and earth, all things must become new out of love![84]

God's revolution overthrows the conditions of the world because it reclaims the world not for its destruction, but for its recreation.

In keeping with his Christocentrism, Christoph identified the revolution of God with Jesus and the divine mission that He came to fulfill:

Primarily it is a social message which Jesus brings to us, a concern that to each individual member of the human race there comes a true perception of God and God's creation. . . . It shall be the building up of a new social order, which in the end shall include all nations. In contrast to social systems under which we have been rejected, bound and ruined, killed, hated and assaulted on every side as though by the furies. Such is our unhappy society, in which no orderly family life can exist; where the fathers have no idea how to deal with their children; where friendships are formed and friendships are broken; where relationships constantly are faced with heartbreak. In contrast to this hapless social order, this tragic human assembly, Jesus wants to establish a joyful society under which he can say to us, "You belong to God, and not to these fellowships you yourselves have initiated. In the first place you are *God's* people!"[85]

Jesus is the original revolutionary whose kingdom consists, at least in part, of new social relations. These new social relations included not

---

84. Christoph Blumhardt, *Auswahl*, III:106 (unpublished translation by the Brüderhof and Plough Publishing).

85. Ibid., 302–3 (unpublished translation by the Brüderhof and Plough Publishing).

only justice, equity, and freedom from suffering, but also forgiveness of one's enemies and love for all.

At the same time, for the revolution of God to be real and effective, it must be *God's* revolution. It is very important to note here that Blumhardt remained committed to the fact that God's kingdom does not enter into the world in either its penultimate forms or in its cosmic finality through human effort. It must be rooted in a divine act: "Today we want to know nothing, we want to start nothing on earth through assuming it is God's will. . . . In the building up of his kingdom, God shows his sovereignty in sharp outline. I count as nothing, nor do you."[86] Divine action precedes and establishes the kingdom, thus in continuity with his critical negation, no tradition, movement, community, or person can be univocally identified with the kingdom of God.[87] At the same time, in acting, the living God does seek a human corollary. "Side with him; in your heart you can fight for, pray for, seek for the will of God. Now you are part of that, all in the world are part of it if they listen to this voice of God's Son."[88] Divine action encloses and incorporates true human action.[89]

---

86. Ibid., 19 (unpublished translation by the Brüderhof and Plough Publishing).

87. Emphasis on God's act is also rendered in Christocentric fashion. See Christoph's 1898 Christmas eve sermon, "Christ in the Flesh," in R. Lejeune, *Christoph Blumhardt and His Message*, 168–76.

88. Christoph Blumhardt, *Auswahl*, III:22 (unpublished translation by the Brüderhof and Plough Publishing).

89. The asymmetrical dialectical relationship between divine and human action is captured nicely in the following passage:

"We do not want to make anything. We do not want to spend our strength in organizing meetings, in theories, science, art, politics. We want none of all this. Once people gather together, even only a handful, and stand on the rock which is the Father in heaven, then the realities of God's kingdom will appear.

"Do not think that God's cause can just fall from heaven [however]. There has to be a living church. The Savior says expressly, 'To you I will give the keys of the kingdom, to you, man, in whom my Father lives.' It is given into the hands of men in whom the Father lives to bring and to loose on earth so that it is valid also in heaven. What such men do on earth is also valid in heaven. Yet the Father must be fully in them, else it amounts to nothing. It is a great mistake to think that every theologian, every pastor, can loose and bind" (ibid., 66–67, unpublished translation by the Brüderhof and Plough Publishing).

The Turn Towards Socialism

Blumhardt's new emphasis on love and its revolutionary consequences coincides with an important shift towards political engagement. With the theological groundwork laid during the second and into the early part of his third phase, Christoph turned outward to see where God was at work subduing death in the world in order that the life of God could manifest itself. His critique of Christianity and the pious circles associated with Bad Boll and the larger *Erweckungsbewegung* forced him to open himself to hear God's voice from other quarters in the world. He did not have to listen long, for he believed that he heard God at work in world history through the 1899 Haag Peace Conference organized by the Russian Tsar. During the preceding year, Blumhardt had began to read the works of many leading socialists engaged in attempting to solve the "social question," a shorthand term meant to denote the many problems that *laissez-faire* capitalism and industrialization were causing across Europe. According to Lim, in 1898 Blumhardt had begun to "read extensively the writings of Karl Marx, F. Staudinger, F. Mehring and A. Bebel, etc."[90] Though he would never be a theoretical or doctrinaire socialist, Blumhardt would gain a first hand knowledge of the ideas of leading socialist thinkers during this period, even recommending some of them in his discussions.[91]

That Blumhardt should identify himself with the Social Democratic Party or SPD was not a matter of course. There were a number of movements engaged in ameliorating the conditions of poverty with explicitly Christian roots and aims, with which he might have allied himself.[92] What set the socialists apart, however, was their unwavering commitment to restructure society through revolutionary change, and their internationalist agenda in which the building up and betterment of humanity, rather than a single nation, was the ultimate goal. In Blumhardt's view, engagement with the issues of social justice could

90. Lim, *'Jesus ist Sieger!'*, 64.

91. Ibid., 64–65.

92. For a good discussion of Adolf Stöcker (1835–1909) and the *Evangelisch-soziale Kongress*, and the diverse political work of Friedrich Naumann (1860–1919), two leading voices for a "social Christianity" during this period, see W. R. Ward, *Theology, Sociology and Politics*, 44–122; see also Pentz, "Politics of Friedrich Naumann"; Shanahan, "Friedrich Naumann"; Massanari, "Adolf Stoecker's Formulation"; and idem, "True or False Socialism."

not be in the form of piecemeal paternalistic hospice, nor a means for nationalist aggrandizement, but had to aim at the total transformation of society and world because those were the goals of the kingdom of God. In his view, the socialist message and hope resembled his hope for the kingdom of God more than any of the other so-called Christian movements or parties.[93]

The exposure to socialist ideas and his own careful assessment of how those ideas might harmonize with the hope for the kingdom of God, as well as Christoph's growing conviction that God was in fact at work among the socialists, led Blumhardt to become a member of the SPD at some point during the late summer or early autumn of 1899.[94] Before this, Blumhardt had already been explicit that he believed the socialist movement was a word from God that would address the social upheaval experienced in Germany at the time. In a sermon on "True Worship," in April of 1899, he expressed this idea, saying:

> It's very interesting to see how this question has achieved such eminence in the demands of today's society. It is aired especially, and most often, by the greatly-libeled Social Democrats. Actually, they are prophets. With all their might and main they want to bring about a future state; and in everyone's ears they proclaim this foolishness: "If for once we—our bodies—were properly

93. A careful analysis of the sermons and devotions from 1898 reveals that Blumhardt was struggling with how to connect his hope for the kingdom of God with the hopes and longings of socialism. During this year he is more reticent about identifying the hope for the kingdom of God with the hopes of the SPD. See, for example, Christoph Blumhardt, *Auswhal*, III:134–35, 206–10. This reticence, though never lost, does recede in 1899. This is evidenced in the December 12, 1899, letter to his son-in-law, Richard Wilhelm, a missionary in China: "I have already learned to know some very wonderful people, and I am astonished at how folks seem to understand me. The expectation of re-demption and healing of society as well as between nations; the idea that the time must be fulfilled before a new time can be expected and that we must therefore have patience with all men; the idea that Jesus wants the kingdom of God on earth as in heaven; the idea that the masters of capital treat the masses of people only as slaves, etc.—all this binds me to the heart of the proletariat. These people understand what I preach about God although they have never sought him" (Christoph Blumhardt, *Christus in der Welt*, 43, unpublished translation by the Brüderhof and Plough Publishing).

94. There is some debate in the secondary literature as to when Blumhardt became a full-fledged member of the SPD. Macchia recounts that process by which Blumhardt was moved towards an official identification with the SPD from June 1899 to February 1900, while Lim (and Meier to some extent) places it somewhere between June 1899 and October 1899. See Macchia, *Spirituality and Social Liberation*, 123–24; see also, Lim, *'Jesus ist Sieger!'*, 66–68; and Meier, *Christoph Blumhardt*, 60–64.

cared for, then we would all be better people than we are today."
To me, that's a prophetic voice from the world.... Naturally, we
can't support them in the sense of bringing about a revolution.
And we also can't go along with the Peace Conference which is
now meeting in The Hague where they proclaim: "The people
can make peace today on their own terms." But we can agree in
the sense that we can say: "God also wants this to happen; God
also wants to solve the social problem. Therefore I am also a
socialist; and until that is done, our Christianity has not reached
its peak."[95]

Blumhardt's identification with the SPD was very embarrassing for
many of his colleagues and friends and he would be defrocked by the
church consistory because of it.[96] He would interpret the loss of his pension and ecclesiastical privileges, however, as a gift of God that would
free him for work in the world among the poor, where he believed God
was already present bringing his kingdom into being. He expressed this
new relationship between the poor and God in a way that presages the
later constructions of Liberation Theology:

Do we want to follow Jesus on this way? Then we must accept
him in this company. Then the call comes to us to set to work
wholeheartedly, for *here* is Jesus. He himself, speaking about the
time of his absence, does not say, "I was rich and you respected
me." He says, "I was poor, I was hungry, I was thirsty, I was imprisoned, and you came to me, to the poor Savior. You came to
me, who sat as a guest at the table of the lowest men. There you
came to me." Here must be your whole heart; here you must
do the deeds of faith; for it is from here that the power comes
which will overthrow the world, the wretched, *unhappy world.*[97]

The commitment of the Social Democrats to the cause of the poor and
the oppressed, among other things, appealed to Blumhardt as a kind of
parable of God's kingdom. In a letter to his friends who were concerned
about his turn to socialism, Blumhardt proclaimed,

Whoever looks into the elements of social democracy and into
the ideas which necessarily derive from it must recognize that a

95. Christoph Blumhardt, *Auswahl*, III:288–89 (unpublished translation by the
Brüderhof and Plough Publishing).

96. Bentley, *Between Marx and Christ*, 29–31.

97. Christoph Blumhardt, *Auswahl*, III:342 (unpublished translation by the
Brüderhof and Plough Publishing).

follower of Christ can very well empathize with it, actually more than with other political parties. . . . A different order of society is sought for the sake of those who labor and are heavy-laden, for the sake of the outcasts and the downtrodden, for the sake of the infirm.[98]

Discipleship now consisted of discerning that Jesus was at work among the poor and then faithfully joining him there on behalf of the whole world.[99] Because Jesus was at work in a special way among the wretched, it was from there that hope for the whole world would come.

The new enemy or powers against which the disciple now struggled were the social structures that hampered humanity from opening itself to the kingdom of God. That enemy was capitalism and the attendant militarism, nationalism, imperialism, and social inequality that it produced. "Capitalism is the last enemy, mammonism. It kills. . . . with *mammonism* everything now hits the mark. This is the anti-god, which can only be conquered by God."[100] By speaking of capitalism in theological terms, Blumhardt upheld the distinction between the penultimate and the ultimate. The ultimate *telos* of all struggle and hope for the kingdom did not shift to the alleviation of poverty or the betterment of conditions for the working poor. These were penultimate goals, stages of preparation for the final goal that was the liberation of all people, both rich and poor and both humanity and the larger creation, for the freedom of the kingdom of God. During this period this distinction would not always be clear in Blumhardt's speeches, however, leading many to suppose that Blumhardt had identified socialism with the kingdom of God in the same way that others had confused the church or other spiritual movements with the kingdom.[101]

98. Ibid., 449.

99. See ibid., 378.

100. Christoph Blumhardt, *Ansprachen*, II:264.

101. This was evident, for instance, in Blumhardt's 1902 speech, "Christ and the Gospel in the Modern World." See Meier's discussion of this speech in his *Christoph Blumhardt*, 97–98. The speech can be found, along with a transcript of the discussion afterward, in Christoph Blumhardt, *Ansprachen*, II:286–91. In the elder Blumhardt, the coming of the kingdom of God was associated with a period of "great grace" during which the earth was prepared for the final coming of God. During this third phase, Christoph often identifies the hoped for socialist state as that period of grace and peace during which humanity is re-ordered and re-structured so that the Spirit of God can flow through humanity more freely, thus preparing it to receive the coming kingdom of God.

Though he had reservations regarding the revolutionary aspects of the Socialist Party (especially the call for violent revolution) Blumhardt would sit on the *Landtag*, the provincial legislature in Württemberg, as a representative of the SPD from 1900 to 1906. His experience in the *Landtag* would prove to be both positive and negative. It would allow Blumhardt the opportunity to engage in the real questions of social and political policy while at the same time it would expose him to the realities of party politics.[102]

While in the *Landtag*, Blumhardt engaged in political debates on wage reform, tariffs, agricultural policy, and transportation for the working poor.[103] After only two years of work, however, he began to have serious doubts, not about the ideals of socialism, but rather about the practical platform and turbulent party politics he experienced during the violent debates over Eduard Bernstein's Marxist revisionism.[104] Though he would continue to stress that socialism was a "sign" of God's kingdom, he would no longer be able to call it *the* "sign." Rather, it was a parable of the kingdom; limited in its correspondence to God's kingdom, but nonetheless a true *gnomon* or "pointer" to the coming kingdom of God, in which all things would be restored. Because of the limitations of political activism, as well as his disappointment that members of the SPD could not let go of their internal and external animosities, and some serious health issues, Blumhardt retired from political activity in 1907.

Blumhardt's withdrawal from political activity sheds some light on at least two aspects of his thought. First, it reveals that Blumhardt's attachment to the Socialist Party was primarily theological and ethical, rather than ideological. Blumhardt believed that "the socialist movement [was] like a fiery sign in the sky announcing justice."[105] When it proved unable to love its enemies, it too fell under the judgment of God.

---

102. Lejeune, "Christoph Blumhardt, 1842–1919," in *Christoph Blumhardt and His Message*, 71.

103. See Meier, *Christoph Blumhardt*, 110–11.

104. For a discussion of the turbulent debates within the SPD over Bernstein's revisionism, see Schorske, *German Social Democracy*. Blumhardt himself came under fire for being sympathetic with Bernstein's revisionism. Though he had initially rejected Bernstein's program, after the personal attacks that Blumhardt experienced in November 1904, he came to see that his own position had more in common with Bernstein than he originally thought. See Meier, *Christoph Blumhardt*, 107–10.

105. Christoph Blumhardt, *Auswahl*, III:451 (unpublished translation by the Brüderhof and Plough Publishing).

Second, Blumhardt's relationship to socialism reveals a deeper dialectical tension within his thought, for his relationship to the SPD was but a smaller instance of how he viewed the relationship of the kingdom of God to the world. The failure of the SPD to overcome enmity reinforced Christoph's critique of human institutions and traditions. No community, movement, tradition, or person can be univocally identified with the kingdom of God.[106] Instances of the inbreaking of the kingdom, which was what Social Democracy represented, were to be interpreted as provisional and therefore also subject to the judgment of God. This stance allowed for freedom in relation to all forms of social action, while his understanding of faith as organically related to embodied action ensured that the faithful were still to be pushed out into the world to witness to Christ and his kingdom as a present and living reality.

The Fourth Phase: 1907–1919

Blumhardt would remain committed to socialism until his death in 1919. Even after he had retired, he continued to consult a number of leading socialist figures who had been inspired by his theologically motivated work.[107] His conviction about the actual concrete manifestation of the kingdom, however, would be more reticent. He would now move more into the mode of "waiting for the kingdom of God."

106. I agree with Frank Macchia that Christoph never really thought that he could identify any human movement with the kingdom of God. However, it does seem that his experience in the SPD contributed to his clarifying what was already a latent conviction. See Macchia, "Shadow of the Cross," 63.

107. This is particularly evident in the case of Howard Eugster-Zeust (1861–1932), the famous pastor and union organizer of the Appenzell weavers in Switzerland. According to Markus Mattmüller, their correspondence reveals that even into this last period Blumhardt approved of the linkage between the proclamation of the gospel and its concrete realization through social and political activism. See Mattmüller, "Der Einfluss Christoph Blumhardts," 237. Their correspondence has been published under Christoph Blumhardt, *Politik aus der Nachfolge*.

That Blumhardt kept a socialist orientation also finds anecdotal support in the example of Eugen Jäckh, his successor at Bad Boll. David Diephouse points out that in 1930, more than ten years after Blumhardt's death, Jäckh was still a member of the Religious Socialist chapter in Göppingen due to Blumhardt's influence and popularity in the region. See Diephouse, *Pastors and Pluralism*, 299.

"World is world, but God is God"[108]

Blumhardt's experience in the SPD reinforced his conviction that the kingdom of God should not be over-identified with any particular ecclesiastical body, or political or social movement.[109] This does not mean that the initial optimism that had marked Blumhardt's first involvement with the party was totally lost. As Frank Macchia has noted, "Christoph did not mean in the later years to replace hope and fighting with pessimism or mere passive comfort," rather, the same call to action in the world is found in Blumhardt's later thought, though it is transformed into, "deeds done in quiet."[110] This new emphasis could be characterized as a more realistic assessment of penultimate historical instantiations of the kingdom of God and the attendant human efforts inevitably connected to them: though they were an imperative, they were nonetheless flawed, awaiting the coming of Jesus to bring their hopes to fulfillment.

This new dialectical position is evident in Blumhardt's correspondence with Leonhard Ragaz (1868–1945), one of the leading architects of the Religious Socialist movement in Switzerland. In a series of letters written from 1908 to 1912, Blumhardt articulates in outline that his calling now is to wait in "quietness" for the kingdom of God, which means that, "God's kingdom cares for itself. We run alongside and re-

---

108. This phrase comes from Eduard Thurneysen's recollections of conversations with Blumhardt during this period. See Lim, *'Jesus ist Sieger!'*, 101.

109. Lim notes that Blumhardt's position on the relationship between the kingdom of God and socialism had already become more tenuous at least by 1903. This explains his mostly negative reaction in 1904 to Herman Kutter's *They Must*, the central thesis of which Blumhardt considered to be an over identification of socialism and the kingdom of God. See Lim, *'Jesus ist Sieger!'*, 75–79; see also, Blumhardt, *Ansprachen*, II:306. According to Mattmüller, after Kutter got word of this assessment, he and Blumhardt had a falling out, though Kutter's letters betray dissatisfaction with Blumhardt already in 1896. See Mattmüller, "Der Einfluss Christoph Blumhardts," 239. For Kutter's dissatisfaction, see *Hermann Kutter in seinen Briefen*, 157–58. Meier portrays Blumhardt's disagreement with Kutter as formative for his own growing dissatisfaction with the SPD. That is, Blumhardt's enthusiasm for the party had clearly waned, but he had not been able to reformulate how the kingdom of God and socialism related to one another. Kutter's philosophically driven position gave him a negative point of reference away from which he could move. Thus, though he struggled to articulate the relationship between the kingdom of God and socialism, he knew Kutter's position was not it. See Meier, *Christoph Blumhardt*, 112–15.

110. Macchia, *Spirituality and Social Liberation*, 143.

joice and recognize the great move of God's regiment, which does not permit a party anymore, at least not such a one that thinks it represents the only true 'faith.'"[111] Relating the progress of the kingdom of God to progressive political movements or to a reformation of church and society was now problematic for Blumhardt. As Meier describes it, this led to a shift in his theological understanding of the concepts "world" and "progress."

During this last phase, Blumhardt retained a dialectical understanding of the world that had been evident during his earliest period. The world was both the good creation towards which God moved in love, and the realm that resisted and rejected God's purposes. During his third phase, Blumhardt emphasized the former pole of this dialectic. Because the kingdom of God was to be embodied on the earth, the "world" was filled with promise. With the advent of socialism as a sign of the kingdom, Blumhardt believed that the overthrow of the regime of death was imminent and thus the disobedience of the world, though in need of severe critique and judgment, would soon be swept away. After Blumhardt's experiences working in the *Landtag*, and his qualified disappointment with the politics within the SPD, his emphasis shifted to the other side of the dialectic. Because of human sinfulness, God's kingdom, which still comes for the world, is deformed and delayed by the world. Thus, the world is now more of a problem than a sight of promise. It is important to note that there is no retreat into the "eternal" during this phase. The shift to a kind of realism by Christoph does not mean that he relocated his hope for the kingdom of God into the "hereafter." Nor does it mean that he shifted to a kind of Christian Realism, as was later developed by Reinhold Niebuhr.[112] Rather, he simply became more reticent in pointing to where and how the kingdom of God would embody itself on earth, never abandoning the conviction that it would. This reticence implied a sharper distinction between the progress of world-history and the progress of the kingdom of God.

Because the world resists God, progressive movements of any type should not be confused with the kingdom of God. Rather, the kingdom of God comes into the world as the totally new, as the limitation and

111. Christoph Blumhardt, *Ansprachen*, III:70. See also ibid, 25–27, 61–62, and 116–18.

112. For a description of Niebuhr's position, see Lovin, *Reinhold Niebuhr and Christian Realism*.

end of the old. "In Jesus a new reality appears, a reality which is opposed to that of world history. Something new is to begin alongside the old. The old reality does not suddenly disappear; it continues alongside. Yet in Jesus we have a new reality. A new history begins, a new working of God."[113] Progress in the kingdom of God is disruptive of the old world and of the old world's institutions. It is God's own work, not the work of human hands. "World is world, but God is God" as Blumhardt was purported to have said.[114] Though this didn't totally rule out human longing and cooperation in the form of social struggle, as we will discuss below, it made it far more problematic. Blumhardt continued to emphasize the need for people to surrender themselves and to struggle for the kingdom of God in prayer and action, but the emphasis during this latter phase was on the hidden divine movement of the kingdom, rather than in human struggle for the kingdom of God. The kingdom comes because God's purposes will not be thwarted, because in the coming of the kingdom it is God Himself who comes.

Thy Kingdom Come!

During the fourth period, Blumhardt was concerned to emphasize the need for God to break into the world, rather than humanity to build the kingdom. But this did not mean that humanity and especially the small community of the faithful could just sit back and do nothing. The kingdom moves forward as an independent reality, but it continues to search for points of harmony in history. As Macchia describes it, "This implies responsibility on our part to harmonize our efforts with the coming kingdom of God. In this way, the entire 'surface development of peoples' gets 'pulled up into' the realm of the kingdom, creating new avenues of growth not present before."[115] During the third phase, the work of harmonizing tended to be identified more with the political struggle on behalf of the proletariat. At times, this work of harmonizing almost became the real instantiation of the kingdom, blurring the line between divine and human action and leading to a kind of synergism that effectively equated human action with building the kingdom of God on

---

113. Christoph Blumhardt, "The New Reality," in Lejeune, *Christoph Blumhardt and His Message*, 230.

114. See note 108 above.

115. Macchia, *Spirituality and Social Liberation*, 142.

earth. In the fourth phase, Blumhardt reasserts the distinction between God's work and humanity. But this distinction didn't exclude humanity from God's work. Rather, faithful human response was enfolded into it. This understanding was the result of Blumhardt's move away from public political action as well as his retrieval of prayer. During the fourth phase, prayer returns as the central responsibility of the faithful to prepare for the coming of the kingdom of God.

From the beginning of his ministry, Blumhardt had emphasized the necessity of prayer. All along he had conceived of it in the light of his father as "waiting and hastening," which meant that prayer was both passive and active, spiritual and physical. In fact, Johann Christoph Blumhardt's description of prayer as "waiting and hastening" was really a re-description of the whole Christian life as a prayer for the kingdom of God. During his third phase, Christoph remained in this tradition by interpreting his political engagement as a form of Christian discipleship or "waiting and hastening" toward the kingdom. Now, the form of Christian discipleship that Christoph felt led to embrace was more traditional and emphasized the prayer of the faithful community for the coming of the kingdom of God. "All the great things which are to come, we shall already experience today quite certainly in all their glory if we pray and do not falter. But without prayer they will not come."[116] The corollary that the kingdom of God seeks first appears in the cry "Thy kingdom come!"

This cry, however, can be embodied in social relationships, only now Christoph shifts from the socialist movement and returns to the notion of a small community, a vanguard who experiences the inbreaking of God's reign and through whom space is made for the kingdom to come for the whole world.[117] Though Christoph had tempered his assessment of socialism he continued to believe in an initial "beachhead" community. This community could experience new life in their social and physical struggles: "Let us not just look to the distant future, as though something impossible had to come then. Let it come to life now, in our daily life. Let it come to life in your personal experiences. Let it come to life on your sickbed. For the Savior comes also to the sick,

---

116. Christoph Blumhardt, "Our Human Right," in *Christoph Blumhardt and His Message*, 218.

117. See ibid., 219.

the poor, to those who have to struggle for their daily bread."[118] That the kingdom could and would be embodied in history was still Blumhardt's firm conviction, it was just that now he was less emphatic that the utopian socialist state would be that initial embodiment. He was also convinced that the responsibility of the faithful was to harmonize its life through struggle and prayer, both of which were embodied in the cry: "Thy kingdom come!" During this fourth phase, however, the idiom and means through which one engaged in this cry was less political and public and more communal and spiritual.

Furthermore, because the new idiom through which the disciple engaged in struggle for the kingdom of God was prayer, Blumhardt was better able to do justice to the distinction between divine and human action, while simultaneously keeping them together. "Only through a living contact and relationship with the Lord Jesus can we come to this praying without ceasing for the divine things, for the divine growth intended for man."[119] The ability and desire to pray and to pray fervently came freely from God enabling a free human response in the form of prayer and struggle to make space for the kingdom of God to come. God seeks for warriors to fight for the kingdom, when he finds them, he empowers them to pray all the more fervently in thought and deed, thus giving them a taste of the kingdom to come. If they fail to use the initial gift given to them, then God withdraws Himself and seeks others who will be faithful in crying out "Thy kingdom come!"

Blumhardt's new orientation has led to some confusion over his response to the First World War. Some have described his position as essentially a form of "quietism."[120] However, as subsequent studies have shown, during the initial months of the war when the *Kriegsgeist*, or war-spirit, was at a fever pitch, Blumhardt was the lone voice of opposition among Protestant clergy.[121] He rejected the theological claim

---

118. Ibid., 227.

119. Ibid., 214.

120. See W. R. Ward, *Theology, Sociology and Politics*, 126.

121. See Pressel, *Die Kriegspredigt*; Hammer, *Deutsche*. I am indebted to Simeon Zahl for pointing this out. I have been substantially influenced by his interpretation of Blumhardt's response to the war, which he discussed in his unpublished essay, "'. . . dieses Kriegsgeistes, dieses Satans': Christoph Blumhardt's Theological Critique of World War I War Enthusiasm," presented to the Society for the Study of Theology Annual Conference at Cambridge University, 2007.

made by many of his contemporaries that the "Spirit of August" was to be identified in some way with Holy Spirit. Rather, Blumhardt was convinced that the war-spirit was satanic and that the war was a judgment of God against the nationalism, capitalism, and imperialism that had caused it.[122]

As Simeon Zahl has pointed out, Blumhardt rejected the widespread assumption within Germany that Russia or one of the other *détente* powers was to blame for the start of the war. Rather, "We are all to blame for this War; all the nations worked together to cause its outbreak. We [nations] must repent together."[123] The theme of repentance captures the basic theological significance that Blumhardt attached to the war, again in distinction from the vast majority of Protestant preachers. The war would not purify humanity through feats of martial heroism. Rather, humanity could be transformed if in the face of the "shake up" that the war represented, it turned to God in repentance and hope.[124]

The shaking of the foundations of civilization had the possibility of leading humanity to repentance and hope in the kingdom of God. Blumhardt repeatedly emphasized this point.[125] At the same time, he left open the caveat that things may not turn out that way. However, in the face of the war's devastation and seeming endlessness, and his own general agnosticism as to precisely how redemption would come from such a catastrophe, Blumhardt did not surrender his belief that God would in fact use it to accomplish His purpose of renewing the earth.[126] With this hope still burning in his heart, Christoph fell ill in 1918 and died in 1919 at the age of seventy-seven.

Summary of the Blumhardts' Theology: "Jesus is Victor!" and "Thy kingdom come!"

In this final section I will offer a very brief summary of the two key themes in the Blumhardts' theology: "Jesus is Victor!" and "Thy king-

---

122. See Christoph Blumhardt, *Auswahl*, IV:389; see also Macchia, *Spirituality and Social Liberation*, 144.

123. Christoph Blumhardt, *Auswahl*, IV:441, as quoted in Zahl, "Christoph Blumhardt's Theological Critique," 4–5.

124. See Christoph Blumhardt, *Auswahl*, IV:371.

125. See Christoph Blumhardt, *Auswahl*, IV:353–58, 367–75, 381–88.

126. Macchia, *Spirituality and Social Liberation*, 144.

dom come!" These two themes are asymmetrically ordered and represent 1) God's divine movement towards his creatures, and 2) their free response to him.

"Jesus is Victor!": The Primary Theme

As should be evident from the histories recounted above, the Blumhardts' "theology" both originates in and finds crystallization in the slogan "Jesus is Victor!" The elder Blumhardt was confronted by this slogan and the truth to which it pointed in his experiences with the case of Gottliebin Dittus and the later awakening movement at Möttlingen. It became for him a watchword that pointed not to a concept, but rather to the living reality by which he felt himself commandeered and made a witness. Likewise, when Christoph Blumhardt began to develop his own new theological standpoint, he was at great pains to show how the novel direction of his work was in deep continuity with his father. In sermons and devotions, and above all through the *Gedanken aus dem Reich Gottes*, Christoph offered an apologia for his new orientation, which he interpreted as in deep continuity with the witness of his father. Continuity with the theme "Jesus is Victor" was also evident throughout his life. He viewed his work as a continuing witness to the one reality to which this slogan pointed in all of its many facets.

As Gerhard Sauter notes, in the watchword "Jesus is Victor," Christology is embedded in eschatology and eschatology in Christology: "The expression 'God's kingdom' . . . is the *conceptual concentration of the sentence: Jesus is Victor! . . .* By authoritative sermons, through the deliverance of people from the shackles of God-opposing powers, Jesus proves to be the victor, which means that God is Lord. Therefore, the sentence 'Jesus is Victor!' is the Christologically 'filled' explication of the concept of the kingdom of God."[127] The kingdom of God is the living Christ warring in the present to bring the fullness of his reign to fruition. For the Blumhardts, this watchword did not point to a doctrine or teaching, but the reality of Jesus Christ, the kingdom of God who confronted them as alive and active and who compelled them to witness to the in-breaking power of the soon coming Lord. "Jesus is Victor!" means that in the life and death of Jesus Christ the kingdom of God has entered into the world in a decisive fashion. Furthermore, this kingdom,

127. Sauter, *Die Theologie des Reiches Gottes*, 24, 33.

though distinct from the world, is now within the world because Jesus' life and death are no longer enclosed by the grave, but alive through his resurrection and the subsequent outpouring of the Holy Spirit. Thus, the victory won "there and then" strides into the "here and now," transforming the world, moving, sometimes in secret and sometimes openly, to its cosmic dénouement that will include all of God's creatures.

The history of the kingdom of God runs alongside human history as its inner meaning and hope. As the inner meaning and hope of creation it is to be embodied, both penultimately and ultimately, in this world rather than in a "hereafter." That it is *God's* kingdom points to fact that the divine initiative and intention in God's promise to bring His kingdom into the present from the past and the future will in fact finally be fulfilled. That "Jesus is Victor!" is a fact quite apart from our belief in the same.[128]

"Thy kingdom come!" The Secondary Theme

This divine action, however, seeks a human corollary. God brings the kingdom to its final cosmic instantiation when the earth is ready to receive it. This requires the desire and readiness to receive the kingdom on the part of humanity, even if that part of humanity is very small. "Thy kingdom come!" is the human cry that God's victory will be completed and the whole earth be released from its bondage to death. Those who engage in the struggle and prayer will experience penultimate instantiations of the kingdom of God, which are a present blessing, a further promise that God's kingdom comes, and a goad to continue forward for the sake of the whole creation. If we include the history of both Blumhardts, the cry for the kingdom can be described as an active waiting that has spiritual, physical, individual, and social dimensions.

Humanity, therefore, has a role to play in the coming of the kingdom. The ability to engage in the struggle for the kingdom, however, comes as a gift of God. The hope for the kingdom must be birthed in the

128. This is captured nicely in the famous hymn of the elder Blumhardt, "Jesus ist der Siegesheld":

> "Jesus is the conqueror who vanquishes our foe,
> Jesus is the Lord before whose feet the world lies low.
> Jesus comes with victor's might,
> and through the darkness leads to light."
> —Troebst and Ising, *Christoph Blumhardt*, 19

heart by the Holy Spirit. Thus, struggle and witness, even in the affairs of everyday life, is in human terms an "impossible possibility." That it occurs means that God is present. If the individual or the community disregards the gift to cry out and long for the kingdom of God, then the Spirit of God will recede in search of a faithful remnant and the progress of the kingdom of God in the world will go underground. Implicitly therefore, the Blumhardts were arguing that human freedom has only one true *telos*: to hope for the kingdom of God.

As noted above, both Blumhardts clearly judged that Christendom had indeed turned away from the need to cry out in hope for God to bring the kingdom into this world. They envisioned their respective ministries as attempts to recapture and reinvigorate a form of Christian discipleship that they believed had been lost to the church. Whether or not they were successful in their intentions, their kerygmatic witness to the kingdom of God and the novel theological re-constructions found in it, has had a deep resonance and profound influence across traditions and communities. To their influence on Karl Barth, the greatest Protestant theologian of the twentieth century, we now turn.

4

The Significance of the Blumhardts' Lives and Thought for Barth's Early Theological Development

Introduction

IN AN ESSAY PUBLISHED IN 1936, IN WHICH HE SOUGHT TO GIVE A genealogical account of the sources of the "dialectical theology" that was continuing to produce theological renewal in the different currents of Continental European theology, Karl Barth's friend and sometime antagonist Emil Brunner made the provocative claim that, "The real origin of the Dialectic Theology is to be traced, however, not to Kierkegaard, but to a more unexpected source, to a place still farther removed from the main theological thoroughfare—to the quiet Boll of the two Blumhardts."[1] The movement known as "Dialectical Theology" had been associated with a number of rising figures within the German theological world including Brunner (1889–1966), Friedrich Gogarten (1887–1967), Rudolph Bultmann (1884–1976), Eduard Thurneysen (1888–1974), and Karl Barth.[2] All of these men were educated and

1. Brunner, "Continental European Theology," 141.

2. There is some question as to whether or not "Dialectical Theology" was ever really a *school*. No doubt it is used as a descriptor to identify those figures who in the 1920s and early 1930s coalesced around the journal *Zwischen den Zeiten* and who were seen to represent a new and fresh voice in theology. However, from the beginning, the alliances of the various figures involved in this 'school' were tenuous. This has been shown in a number of studies, the classic text being James D. Smart's *The Divided Mind of Modern Theology: Karl Barth and Rudolf Bultmann, 1908–1933*. In the most recent text to take up this question, John W. Hart's *Karl Barth vs. Emil Brunner* shows that, at least in the case of Barth and Brunner, deep differences existed early on. In fact, Hart's central contention is that Brunner was never really very dialectical at all (see chapters

nurtured in the traditions of nineteenth-century German Liberal theology. After the outbreak of the First World War, however, they all, for different reasons, became dissatisfied with what they had inherited from their theological mentors.

For Karl Barth, it was his theological professors' inability to resist the prevailing cultural ideology of Prussian militarism and their attendant acquiescence to the Kaiser's war policy that steeled a growing conviction that he needed to fundamentally rethink his theological orientation.[3] Barth described the moment of his realization in terms of an earthquake: "An entire world of theological exegesis, ethics, dogmatics, and preaching, which up to that point I had accepted as basically credible, was thereby shaken to the foundations, and with it everything which flowed at that time from the pens of the German theologians."[4] Part of the problem for Barth was Liberalism's conception of the theological enterprise. Even at its most critical,[5] the Protestant Liberal tradition understood theology as an essentially cultural task. The implications of understanding the theological enterprise in this way were far-reaching and would take Barth the next fifteen years to explore, but the immediate consequence was that the Christian community's prophetic witness

---

2 and 4 passim). It is probably best to see this grouping of theologians as an *ad hoc* set of alliances, in which the voice of Barth set the pace.

3. Bruce McCormack notes that many of the themes that were important for the so-called "dialectical phase" were already evident as early as 1913. Themes such as the wrath of God, the critique of religion, the priority and otherness of God and the relationship between the kingdom of God and history. However, though these themes were already present during this period, they had not forced Barth to fundamentally rethink his theological orientation. Rather, they were incorporated into the larger matrix of theological Liberalism that Barth had inherited from his mentor Wilhelm Herrmann (1846–1922). Barth doesn't come to the realization of the need for a change until September 1914. This realization develops and culminates in his break with Liberal Theology in 1915. See McCormack, *Karl Barth's Critically Realistic Dialectical Theology*, 78–125, esp. 123.

4. Karl Barth, *Theology of Schleiermacher*, 264.

5. I am thinking here of the defense mounted by Chapman in his *Ernst Troeltsch and Liberal Theology*, in which he argues that Troeltsch, as well as Harnack, had a far more critical relation vis-á-vis Whilhelmine culture than has usually been assumed. Paul Lewis Metzger, in his *Word of Christ*, has persuasively argued that, nevertheless, for Barth the question was not whether or not theological Liberalism was critical of its culture, which it was, but whether or not it was critical *enough*, which it invariably was not. See Chapman, chapters 7–8; see Metzger, 23–27, esp. 24.

to the surrounding culture was eviscerated.[6] Barth later acknowledged that he was most acutely confronted by this problem each Sunday as he prepared to give his sermon. Is the Word of God different from the words of men? If so, can we speak this Word? Does not the fact that all human speech is culturally conditioned mean that our speaking of God is really an un-speaking, that we really do not speak of God, but of the no-God? According to Barth, all of these questions were forced on anyone who claimed to preach the gospel, however, with the outbreak of the First World War, they became more pressing and he became more aware of the fact that Liberal theology provided insufficient answers.

More than just historical factors had contributed to Barth's movement towards the radical new theological position that would be associated with his name however.[7] As Brunner described in his essay, there were a number of theological developments that had led to the exodus out of Protestant Liberalism into unknown territory. Brunner points to five sources that fed the "dialectical theology": 1) the rediscovery of New Testament eschatology by Albert Schweitzer and Johannes Weiss; 2) the rediscovery of the forensic and objective categories in Luther's doctrine of justification by Karl Holl; 3) the continuation of an alternative theology throughout the nineteenth-century associated with the more conservative *Erweckungsbewegung* and people like August Tholuck, J. T. Beck, Martin Kähler and Adolph Schlatter; 4) the reception in Germany of the "dialectical philosopher" Søren Kierkegaard; and 5) the life and thought of the two Blumhardts.[8] To include the Blumhardts in this list and to speak of them as having such seminal importance must have been incomprehensible for many outside observers in 1936 when Brunner penned these words, especially those in the Anglo-American world. But, in reality, almost all of the figures associated with "dialectical theology" had been influenced by the Blumhardts in one

6. When I say fifteen years I am not suggesting that Barth did not understand the central dynamic of theological Liberalism until 1930, but simply that he had not worked out to the genuine depths of the problem of the dynamic of Liberalism (which I understand as the Feuerbachian move to transform theology into anthropology) until his break with the other dialectical theologians in the early 1930's.

7. Gary Dorrien regards the theological break initiated by Barth and the subsequent renewal carried out by him and others, of such importance that he describes it as a "revolt" against Schleiermacher and his theological epigone. See Dorrien, *Theology without Weapons*, 45–46.

8. Brunner, "Continental European Theology," 135–44.

way or another, with the sole exception of Bultmann.[9] In what follows, we will explore their influence on Karl Barth during this early period (1911–1919), noting the contribution their kerygmatic witness made to Barth's own innovative theology.

Barth's Early Encounters with the Blumhardts' Life and Thought

Earliest Encounters with the Blumhardts

In April 1915, Barth visited Bad Boll with his life-long friend and colleague Eduard Thurneysen. Returning from the wedding of his brother Peter to Martin Rade's daughter Helene in Marburg, Barth encountered Christoph Blumhardt and was deeply impressed by his personal presence and the vision that animated him. Though this meeting would prove especially fruitful for Barth's development, it was not the first encounter that Barth had had with the prophet at Bad Boll.

Anecdotal evidence abounds that Barth had encountered many of the rudimentary elements of the Blumhardts' thought prior to 1915. Karl's father Fritz Barth was one of the last students of the Schwäbian theologian Johannes Tobias Beck (1804–1878), who had been a classmate of Johann Christoph Blumhardt and would later be Christoph Blumhardt's most important theological influence, outside of his father, while studying at Tübingen. Though Christoph Blumhardt would reject certain elements of Beck's theology, he shared with him a central preoc-

---

9. Their influence on Barth and Thurneysen is well known and will become evident in what follows. Brunner, however, was even more immersed in the thought world of the Blumhardts. His God-father, Friedrich Zündel, biographer of the elder Blumhardt, introduced Brunner's father to Christoph Blumhardt ensuring a definite family connection to Bad Boll. Brunner also wrote his dissertation under Leonhard Ragaz at Zürich and served as a pastoral assistant to Hermann Kutter. Both Kutter and Ragaz are considered two of the most important mediators of Christoph Blumhardt's thought into the Swiss context. For Brunner, see Hart, *Karl Barth vs. Emil Brunner*, chap. 1 passim; for the role of Ragaz and Kutter as mediators of the Blumhardts' theology, see Mattmüller, "Der Einfluss Christoph Blumhardts," 233–46. In a conversation with Professor Gerhard Sauter it was relayed that Friedrich Gogarten had acknowledged his own indebtedness to the Blumhardts to his students in private conversations (Private Interview, The Center for Theological Inquiry, Princeton Theological Seminary, 12/11/02). In regard to Bultmann's aversion to the Blumhardts, see the letter sent by Barth to Bultmann dated December 24, 1952 in *Karl Barth/Rudolph Bultmann: Letters, 1922–1966*, esp. 106.

cupation with the kingdom of God. Beck emphasized that the kingdom of God was a living organism, present in the world and coming into being in history. In a qualified way, Christoph shared this conviction. The kingdom was present in the world as a living reality. However, Christoph did not believe that the kingdom should become a predicate of history since that seemed to imply that the kingdom's coming could be mapped and predicted. Thus, the organic language of Beck, though evident in Blumhardt, was also qualified.[10] He was also uncomfortable with Beck's hope of creating a systematic biblical theology.

Beck would later make a substantial contribution to Karl's theology as he worked on his first *Romans* commentary.[11] Though this influence would wane considerably after he discovered Franz Overbeck in 1919,[12] it is not implausible, though certainly not provable, that Barth's own spirituality may have been shaped by the eschatology of Beck and the Blumhardts as it was mediated to him by his father.[13]

Aside from Fritz Barth, Karl also mentions that his mother's sister, Elizabeth (Aunt "Bethi") made a deep impression on him. Barth noted that, "She often went to stay in Bad Boll, and especially as a result of meeting Pastor Blumhardt, she increasingly developed an eye for signs of the coming of the kingdom of God. Rather than making her narrow-minded, her devotion kindled in her a love which went out to embrace all men. . . . No wonder that as a result she was welcome anywhere!

---

10. See Stober, *Christoph Friedrich Blumhardt*, 170–91; see also, Meier, *Christoph Blumhardt*, 36.

11. The importance of Beck is captured anecdotally in Barth's famous remark to Thurneysen in 1916: ". . . Discovery of a gold mine: J. T. Beck!! As a biblical expositor he simply towers far above the rest of the company, also above Schlatter. Also in his systematic approach he is in part directly accessible and exemplary for us. I came on the track of him through my work on Romans and will make use of him there along with the other commentators from Calvin to Tholuck and as far as Kutter's *Righteousness*, a whole cloud of witnesses! The older generation may once more have some pleasure in us, but a bit differently from what it intended" (Barth and Thurneysen, *Revolutionary Theology in the Making*, 38)

12. For an excellent and exhaustive account of the influence of Beck on Barth, see Hake, *Der Bedeutung der Theologie Johann Tobias Beck für die Entwicklung der Theologie Karl Barths*.

13. See McCormack, *Critically Realistic Dialectical Theology*, 31. Eberhard Busch recounts a lecture given by in 1905 in which Fritz Barth gave a positive assessment of Pietism, including its doctrine of the kingdom of God. See Busch, *Karl Barth and the Pietists*, 11–12.

Wherever she went, she was loved in no time at all."[14] These remarks, and others made late in his career, have led some to describe the ecclesial and spiritual atmosphere in which Barth grew up as a kind of "moderate pietism," adding to the plausibility that Barth's later attraction to the Blumhardts' thought and life had already been prepared in his youth.[15]

One other anecdotal connection should be mentioned before moving on. During the winter semester 1907 to 1908, while a theological student at the University of Tübingen, Barth visited Bad Boll on three separate occasions, having the opportunity to meet Christoph Blumhardt at least once.[16] In his autobiographical reflections, Barth notes that his "eyes were not fully open," during this first encounter. The encounter still appears to have had some impact on Barth as he includes a reflection on it in his 1916 lecture "Our Hope and the Church."[17]

In this lecture, included in the second edition of the coauthored volume *Suchet Gott, so werdet ihr Leben!*, Barth critiques the church in light of the hope for the kingdom of God that he had learned from Blumhardt. His thesis was that no one takes the church seriously because the church no longer takes God seriously. It no longer looks for the revolution of God that comes for the whole of humanity, but has surrendered this hope for social and physical transformation to the socialists. But Barth's critique of the church is no root and branch rejection rather it becomes clear that he critiques the church for the sake of the church.[18] Without ignoring the concerns of socialism, which were

14. Busch, *Karl Barth*, 19.

15. McCormack uses the term "moderate pietism" to describe Barth's family atmosphere. See his, *Karl Barth's Critically Realistic Dialectical Theology*, 36. A helpful, though preliminary investigation of Barth's inherited relationship to Pietism, and especially the Württemberg version of it, can be found in Eberhard Busch's *Karl Barth and the Pietists*, 9–12.

16. Barth's name is written in the Bad Boll Guestbook (Original in the Archiv der Brüderunität Bad Boll), on November 30, 1907, December 27, 1907 and February 15, 1908. According to Eberhard Busch, Barth definitely met with Blumhardt on December 27th. We don't know if he met with him on the other dates, though it is entirely possible that he did not, as Blumhardt was ill for the better part of 1907 and into 1908. I owe the reference to the Archiv der Brüderunität Bad Boll to Dieter Ising, (Email Correspondence, 11/06/03). For Busch see his *Karl Barth*, 43–44.

17. In Karl Barth and Eduard Thurneysen, *Suchet Gott!*, 160–74.

18. The renewing activity that Barth points to within the church is the small flock of those whose hope reaches out beyond the walls of the church. This notion is clearly rooted in the pietistic cell group reconstructed along the lines of Christoph Blumhardt during his fourth phase. See *Suchet Gott*, 170–74.

almost identical with the concerns of the kingdom, the church "hopes for all, she hopes not only for the poor, she hopes for the wealthy as well," thus she cannot be abandoned, nor can she be identified with a single party or social class. Rather, she can only be identified with the One in whom she hopes: the living God. "The question arises now: why do we remain faithful to the church? The answer is the same which called for the question of our hope. Our hope is the cause of our dissatisfaction and of our pain, but it remains still that which it is: our hope; hope for all and everything, hope also for our church."[19] Importantly, Barth roots his development of this dialectical negation and affirmation of the being of the church in his 1907 encounter with Blumhardt:

> As a student I once heard the old Pastor Blumhardt of Bad Boll. He is a man of hope without comparison and had hard and bitter words against the church. Afterwards I went to him and said: 'Now I know what I have to do. I cannot and will not serve in this church.' He simply said to me: 'You misunderstand me, remain in the church and become a pastor. The church needs pastors that have hope for her and the world.'[20]

Blumhardt's harsh words against the church were meant to be a salutary rebuke that brought life back into the church. Barth heard these words prior to his matriculation at Marburg and after his experiences in Berlin with Adolf von Harnack. That they remained with him is testimony to the impression that Blumhardt had already made on him during this early period.

The Mediation of the Blumhardts via the Religious Socialists and Eduard Thurneysen

Barth encountered the Blumhardt's thought world early on as the above anecdotes make clear. It was after his school days were behind him, however, that the real engagement with their thought happened that would substantively shape his theological thinking. This encounter occurred

19. Ibid., 170.

20. Ibid. Gerhard Sauter explores the commonality of Blumhardt's and Barth's church-critiques, noting that both are really a critique of "religion" as over against the practice of hope. He also notes that Barth's hope for the church is more constructive and descriptive than Blumhardt's, so that Blumhardt is not able to give a positive account of how the faithful church or "Gemeinde" might look. See his *Die Theologie des Reiches Gottes*, 240–47.

within the two-fold context of pastoral ministry and socialist activity in the industrial village of Safenwil, where Barth was pastor from 1911 to 1921. These contexts shaped Barth's reception of the Blumhardts' life and thought as it was mediated to him through the Religious Socialist movement and his life-long friend Eduard Thurneysen.

Barth, Religious Socialism, and the Blumhardts

Barth had shown early on an interest in social and political questions. But his exposure to the working conditions faced by many of his parishioners in Safenwil forced him to take up the cause of the working class and meant that his pastoral ministry would mesh seamlessly with practical political work.[21] Barth's ability to move in this direction had already been anticipated in thought and reflection done in light of his pastoral assistantship in Geneva in 1909.[22] But in Safenwil the theoretical questions took on flesh and blood, and theological reflection had to give way to practical pastoral/political work.[23] During his time in Safenwil Barth gave lectures on human rights and labor issues, hosted readings of books on socialist politics and political economy, delivered informal talks on practical issues like work schedules, domestic finances, and women in the workplace, and contributed to the establishment of at least three different unions in Safenwil. His efforts were so successful that in 1913 he was asked to become the president of the Safenwil Worker's Association, which he declined.[24]

The focus on practical work did not mean however, that Barth was unable to engage in serious theological reflection in Safenwil. As early as December, 1911, not six months after he had been installed, Barth gave the lecture, "Jesus Christ and the Movement for Social Justice."[25]

21. For Barth's engagement with political issues from a sympathetically socialist vantage point during his student days, see Jehle, *Ever Against the Stream*, 18–24.

22. George Hunsinger surmises, rightly I believe, that Barth's stint in Geneva was the first place where he was really exposed to the conditions of the working classes so that by the time he moved to Safenwil in 1911, "he had already developed profound socialist sympathies" ("Toward a Radical Barth," in *Karl Barth and Radical Politics*, 194).

23. Ulrich Danneman highlights three pressing issues that surface in Barth's sermons as practical and existential concerns that faced his parishioners: 1) child labor; 2) alcoholism; and 3) the need for peace and rest from war. See Danneman, "'Den Gefangenen Befreiung!'," 156–57.

24. See Jehle, *Ever Against the Stream*, 25–35.

25. The English translation can be found in Hunsinger, *Karl Barth and Radical Politics*, 19–37.

In this lecture Barth worked out the thesis that, "Jesus *is* the movement for social justice, and the movement for social justice *is* Jesus in the present."[26] Though the lecture is constructed largely in the categories of Liberal theology, especially those of Albrecht Ritschl, it is already moving in another direction.[27] Answering objections that Jesus should not be made into a "social democrat," Barth draws out the close parallels between the ministry of Jesus among the poor and the socialist hope for better material conditions.

In contradiction to the traditional Christian understanding of the kingdom of God as a spiritual or eternal reality with little or nothing to do with the real alleviation of social and material conditions, Barth argues that in Jesus the kingdom of God is not concerned with the opposite of material existence. Rather, "The opposite of God is not the earth, not matter, not the external, but evil, or as he put it in the forceful manner of his day: the demons, the devils who live in man. And that is why redemption is not the separation of spirit from matter; it is not that man 'goes to heaven,' but rather that God's kingdom *comes to us* in matter and on earth."[28] Barth reels off text after text from the Synoptic tradition to ground his argument that the fruit of the kingdom, "is nothing but social help in material terms.... The spirit that has value before God is the *social* spirit. And social help is *the* way to eternal life."[29] Jesus, the partisan of the poor, witnessed to the solidarity of the world with the

26. Ibid., 19.

27. For an account of Ritschl's social doctrine of the kingdom of God see his, "Instruction in the Christian Religion," in *Three Essays*, by Albrecht Ritschl, 219–91, esp. 222–32. The key Liberal category evident in this essay comes from Wilhelm Herrmann and can be described as the conviction that revelation and the truth of the divine in Jesus is to be found in the inner-communion that Jesus had with God the Father as it was lived out in history. That is, the real truth or revelation is not the ethical teachings of Jesus or the New Testament traditions about Him, but that inner-reality which gave rise to the same. For Herrmann, this conception of revelation shielded Christian faith from science and history, as the revelatory significance of Jesus was not the outer-husk, but the inner vitality. This inner-vitality became effective and "revelatory" as the disciples of Jesus experienced it in the event of faith, and then through the lives that they lived, passed it down through history as the call of faith and love. See, Hermann, *Communion of the Christian*, 14–18. Barth's appeal to the social teachings and ministry of Jesus evidences a combination of Herrmann and Ritschl, for whom the Synoptic ethical traditions were extremely important.

28. Karl Barth, "Jesus Christ and the Movement for Social Justice," 27.

29. Ibid., 27–28.

social God, which *is* the kingdom of God. This kingdom, betrayed by Christianity, is actualized by the presence of God's love for the neighbor now overcoming the great obstacle of the kingdom of God in our age: capitalism. If Christianity and Christians are to be faithful to the kingdom, then they must see that socialism is God speaking in our day and age. In fact, "*Real* socialism is real Christianity in our time."[30]

Barth closes by exhorting the members of his audience who are both against and for socialism. The former are exhorted to consider not the actions of individual or collective socialists, but the goals that they long for, which are the same as those of Jesus. To do so will force them to rethink their own position vis-à-vis socialism, because socialism encapsulates the real inner-meaning of Jesus. Barth encourages the latter by pointing out that their aims *are* the will of God. Now, however, they must bring their praxis into line with the great longing for the kingdom of God that the ideals of socialism bear as their inner secret:

> Therefore, Jesus says to you quite simply that you should carry out your program, that you should *enact* what you *want*. Then you will be Christians and true human beings. Leave the superficiality and the hatred, the spirit of mammon and the self-seeking, which also exists among your ranks, behind: They do *not* belong to your concerns. Let the faithfulness and energy, the sense of community and the courage for sacrifice found in Jesus be effective among you, in your whole life; then you will be true socialists.[31]

To be a true Christian is to be a socialist and to be a true socialist is to be a true Christian.

The themes developed in this lecture bear the undeniable influence of Herman Kutter (1863–1931) and Leonhard Ragaz (1868–1945), the leading figures of the Religious Socialist movement in Switzerland. Barth's most intensive engagement with these figures was between 1913 and 1915. But Barth's thesis that, "Jesus *is* the movement for social justice, and the movement for social justice *is* Jesus in the present," bears the fingerprint of Hermann Kutter's famous book, *They Must! An Open Word to Christian Society*, which was the most influential theological interpretation of socialism in Switzerland during the early twentieth

---

30. Ibid., 36.
31. Ibid., 37.

century.[32] The identification of the goals of the kingdom of God with the goals of socialism, to the rebuke of Christendom, was one of the central themes that Kutter worked out in *They Must!*:

> The Social Democrats hunger and thirst after righteous conditions. Is that godlessness? The Social Democrats are advocates of mercy. And shall they not then obtain mercy? The Social Democrats hate what is common, base and greedy. And shall they not be God's children? They are despised and persecuted on all sides. And shall God condemn them to hell? They lay up for themselves no treasures on earth, and declare war on money-getting. And shall they not belong to God? They do what God from the beginning has demanded of his witnesses; they open their whole hearts to the poor and the oppressed. And shall they be without God?[33]

Kutter's work went on to inspire Leonhard Ragaz, the founding editor of *Neue Wege*, the literary organ of the Swiss Religious Socialist movement and a later interlocutor of Barth's.[34] Markus Mattmüller has shown that both men were deeply influenced in their theological interpretation of socialism by Christoph Blumhardt.[35]

Without going into great detail, the thought of both men moves in the direction of Blumhardt by interpreting the socialist movement as the irruption of God's kingdom in modern times. That this irruption was occurring outside of the church among the atheist socialists was a sign of judgment on the church. Where Kutter and Ragaz differed from one another—and perhaps from Blumhardt himself—was in their assessment of what the Christian community and the faithful Christian were called to do. On Kutter's side, the call was to hear the word of judgment spoken by the "living God" through socialism and thereby to lead the church in repentance to hope for the kingdom of God that

32. Kutter, *Sie Müssen!* The book was published in English under the title, *They Must.* It is unknown when Barth read Kutter, but he notes that he knew of Kutter before 1904. See Busch, *Karl Barth*, 30. This is confirmed by a letter of Kutter's in which he notes an unsuccessful discussion of *Sie Müssen!* hosted by Fritz Barth in Basel. See Kutter, *Hermann Kutter in seinen Briefen*, 197.

33. Kutter, *They Must*, 28–29.

34. For a discussion of the relationship between Kutter and Ragaz and the development of religious socialism, see W. R. Ward, *Theology, Sociology and Politics*, 123–64; see also, Mattmüller, *Leonhard Ragaz*, 1:100–107.

35. See Mattmüller, "Der Einfluss Christoph Blumhardts," 237–41.

was socialistic in nature and imminent in its arrival. Thus, socialism was a *sign* of the kingdom of God, rather than the thing itself, whose function was primarily to judge the church and the world, calling them to prepare themselves for the coming of the kingdom that God alone would bring.[36]

On Ragaz's side, the call was to follow the inbreaking of the kingdom of God in history, which meant leaving the church and moving out into the world of Social Democracy to help prepare the world for the final coming of the kingdom, thereby showing Social Democracy how deeply Christian it was. Ragaz, contrary to common misinterpretation, was also hesitant in seeing socialism as the thing itself; rather, it was the *sign*, and after the First World War *a* sign, that the kingdom was struggling to enter the world. The real question was, How do we prepare the world to receive the kingdom of God? Ragaz's answer: Through social and political struggle. The aims of both men had been simultaneously present in Christoph Blumhardt, but when the "waiting" of Kutter became separated from the "hastening" of Ragaz, it would produce a split within Swiss Religious Socialism. In the practical work of party politics what had been held together however tenuously by Blumhardt represented diametrically opposed paths whose centrifugal force tore the Religious Socialist movement apart.

There are parallels between Barth's 1911 lecture and the work of Kutter and Ragaz, especially his identification of the movement for social justice with the kingdom of God. But there is also a key distinction. Though Barth evidences a clear concern for a real inner and outer change in human society that only God can bring about, he does not express the same in terms of an unmediated action of the "living God" or a realistic eschatology. Kutter argued that Social Democracy represented a revelation from God, not because it was, as Barth put it, "a quite direct continuation of the spiritual power which, as I said, entered into history

36. This distinction is not always evident, especially in *They Must!* In considering the role of revolutionary violence for Social Democracy, Kutter makes the extraordinary claim that, "The living God *needs* violence. In the vicissitudes of change and loss we are made wise. The pavilions of our momentary delights we build and rebuild, and God shatters them above our heads!" (114). It was passages like these that caused Christoph Blumhardt to reject the work, calling it an "agitation paper." See Christoph Blumhardt, *Ansprachen*, II:306. Kutter's language may have gotten in the way of his intentions, which he was explicit about with Ragaz from their earliest contacts. See Kutter, *Hermann Kutter in seinen Briefen*, 190–94, 197–98.

and life with Jesus."[37] It is not the inner life of Jesus as mediated through history that animates Social Democracy, but the present and active "living God" who is breaking into history. In this lecture Barth's basic theological orientation, into which he seeks to assimilate the concerns of socialism, clearly reflects the continuing influence of his theological mentor Wilhelm Herrmann and his predecessor Albrecht Ritschl.

Bruce McCormack argues that Barth's interest in social and political questions would have been novel for someone located within the Herrmannian tradition of Marburg.[38] This is right, insofar as one understands that tradition without any connection to Albrecht Ritschl. But if one allows for a reconnection of Herrmann and Ritschl, Barth's argument that what has "entered history through Jesus was a way of life, a basic attitude, an ethos," is no longer all that novel.[39] This is because Ritschl had already moved in this direction by developing the theme of the kingdom of God along ethical and social lines.[40] What *is* novel here is not that the kingdom of God is fundamentally social and ethical, but *socialist* and therefore revolutionary and apocalyptic, placing it outside the realms of church and respectable culture and opposed to the liberal progressive understanding of history. This idea is certainly to be attributed to Kutter and behind him, Blumhardt.[41]

Such a novel conception would have been deeply problematic within a Herrmannian-Ritschlian understanding of the kingdom of God, since the "inner-life" of Jesus was passed down from one person of faith to another, within the general realm of what might be called the "church," but which was more broadly identified with the best aspects of culture. The appearance of the kingdom of God in a way that was radically disconnected from the historical thread that led back to Jesus—which is what the atheist Social Democracy represented—and

37. Karl Barth, "Movement for Social Justice," 20.

38. McCormack, *Critically Realistic Dialectical Theology*, 86–92.

39. Ibid., 87.

40. See Ritschl, "Instruction in the Christian Religion," 222–32.

41. McCormack also notes that the theme of "Judgment" that is present in Barth's sermons and writings from early on is not in keeping with the Ritschlian school, but is probably due to the influence of the Religious Socialists. Kutter and Blumhardt both conceived of socialism as a sign of God's judgment on the present order, but not for its destruction. See McCormack, *Karl Barth's Critically Realistic Dialectical Theology*, 93–98.

the imperative that it produced not just to adjust or reform the world, but to overthrow it, makes the personal and historical mediation of the "inner-life" of Jesus deeply problematic. The implication is that the "kingdom of God" or the "inner life of Jesus" cannot to be understood to move through history in a liberal progressive fashion under the human tutelage of the church or the prevailing culture. Rather, it moves of its own power in history because God is the living One, present in history pressing the kingdom forward to its final cosmic realization. The deeper implication of this was that God was free to bring the kingdom into the world using whatever means were necessary. If God is free to use socialism, then perhaps he is free to use other means, and this raises the question of our knowledge of the kingdom of God. If the kingdom of God cannot be directly identified with any historical movement (this was the position to which Barth would come and which Blumhardt had come to in his fourth phase), then where and how do we find the kingdom of God at work in the world?

In 1911, Barth was not yet aware of the problem that was created for his theology by associating the kingdom of God with socialism. But placing the theo-political themes of Religious Socialism and the Blumhardts within the theoretical framework of Liberalism, which would describe the general theological standpoint of Barth from 1911 to 1914,[42] would prove fatal in the face of the First World War. For the war showed that neither insiders (Culture Protestantism) nor outsiders (Socialism) could resist the ideology of war, and therefore were suspect. Where, then, was the kingdom of God to be found in history? We will return to some of these issues later. Suffice it to say, the presence of Religious Socialist and Blumhardtian themes can be detected in Barth's theological thinking from early on.

Eduard Thurneysen

In connection to the Blumhardts and Religious Socialism, we would be remiss without mentioning Barth's life-long friend Eduard Thurneysen. Thurneysen's influence in regard to Barth's reception of the Blumhardts finds succinct expression in Barth's own remark that Thurneysen "was the one who first put me on the trail of Blumhardt and Kutter and then also of Dostoevsky, without whose discovery I would not have been

42. See Hunsinger, "Toward a Radical Barth," 194–98.

able to write either the first or the second draft of the commentary on Romans, but instead—who knows?—I might actually have embarked on the attractive career of an Aargau trade-union man and councilor."[43] In 1913 Thurneysen had become pastor in the village of Leutwil, not far from Safenwil. Barth and Thurneysen had met during their school days and their families already had connections, but their common struggles over political and theological questions during this period cemented a friendship that would endure throughout their lives.

Though working with Religious Socialist ideas before 1913, Thurneysen would make them more accessible by introducing Barth personally to Hermann Kutter and his literature as well as to the wider circles of Religious Socialism.[44] At this time Barth learned from Kutter, "to speak the great word 'God' once again seriously, responsibly, and forcibly."[45] During the period from 1914 to 1916, as the Religious Socialist movement began to move in different directions, Barth and Thurneysen can be seen hammering out a position that placed them closer to Kutter than Ragaz. This direction was due to at least two factors.

The inter-personal dimension comprises the first. Undoubtedly Thurneysen's own personal connections and loyalty to Kutter gave them a better understanding of his standpoint. Thurneysen had met Kutter while serving in Zürich and felt a particular debt to Kutter for investing in the young pastor that remained even as he and Barth moved in a direction that Kutter could not follow.[46] Barth and Thurneysen also had numerous personal conversations with Kutter, which does not appear to have been the case with Ragaz. Then there is also the manner of Ragaz's rejection of Barth's first public attempt to interpret Blumhardt. We will return to this below, but when, in 1916, Barth submitted a re-

43. Barth and Thurneysen, *Revolutionary Theology in the Making*, 72.

44. See Busch, *Karl Barth: His Life from Letters and Autobiographical Texts*, 75-80.

45. Karl Barth, "Concluding Unscientific Postscript on Schleiermacher," 263.

46. The depth of Thurneysen's regard for Kutter can be seen in the March 1, 1925. letter that he sent to Kutter attempting to answer Kutter's criticism that Barth and he were moving in a direction that he would not be able to follow. See Barth and Thurneysen, *Revolutionary Theology in the Making*, 212–15. For similar remarks, see also *Karl Barth—Eduard Thurneysen: Briefwechsel*, 1:108–9.

Kutter's position vis-à-vis Religious Socialism had also begun to change by 1910, as he began to argue against any ideological identification with the gospel. See Gorringe, *Against Hegemony*, 32–33.

view article of Christoph Blumhardt's *Hausandachten*[47] for publication in *Neue Wege*, it was rejected by Ragaz with the suggestion that it be re-written.[48] Barth resubmitted the article with four minor concessions, but it was still unsatisfactory to Ragaz. Through all of this, Barth appears to have felt insulted, adding to the growing animosity that he felt towards Ragaz.[49]

Though interpersonal ties linked Barth and Thurneysen to Kutter more tightly than Ragaz, it was the material theological stance of Kutter that really appealed to them. That other context in which Barth and Thurneysen lived during this period, the pastorate, and the central work of the Protestant clergyman, the sermon, had become more and more of a problem. Kutter's position gave more guidance to Barth and Thurneysen in the light of the great crisis of this period, the First World War.

With the failure of international socialism and the incomprehensible nationalist cooption of the Protestant church in Germany, Barth and Thurneysen believed that the only way forward was to hear the Word of God afresh in the new situation. To "wait" for *God* to speak as Kutter emphasized, rather than bustling about as they thought Ragaz counseled. But where does one turn to hear that Word? International and Religious Socialism had both failed to stop the war, let alone to create a new humanity, and the theological and ecclesial traditions in which they had both been schooled in Germany were now no longer to be trusted. They found themselves at an impasse. Meanwhile, the daily work of the pastor was still in front of them.

Though difficult, this work would hand them the key whereby they could find a way beyond their impasse. The weekly responsibility to prepare a sermon led them into the Scriptures, forcing them to listen and then proclaim what they heard. This practical work became for Barth, *the* theological problem. Where do we turn to hear the Word? We must turn back to the Scriptures. But how does one read the Bible to hear again a real and objective transforming Word? With the collapse of the Liberal Protestantism that had given them the glasses by which to

47. Christoph Blumhardt, *Haus-Andachten nach Losungen und Lehrtexten der Brüdergemeinde.*

48. See Ragaz, *Leonhard Ragaz in seinen Briefen*, 2:84–85.

49. This is evident in Ragaz's attempt to explain himself in a longer letter sent to Barth after receiving Barth's letter and revisions. See ibid., 86–90, esp. 86–87.

read Scripture, they were in need of a new standpoint and fresh lenses more appropriate to the task at hand than had been the old ones. To hear God's Word, *really* hear the radical and transforming Word of the new world and the new humanity was their desire and would remain the basic orientation throughout the rest of their careers. During this period of ferment, in which they were groping around in the dark looking for the key to open the door on this new standpoint, they had a decisive meeting with Christoph Blumhardt, whom Thurneysen knew personally. To this meeting and its subsequent effects we now turn.

"His life had a secret center around which it moved: God, only God, God alone!": The Decisive Encounter with Christoph Blumhardt[50]

Barth was dismayed with the German theological establishment after the outbreak of the First World War. In a letter written to Thurneysen in September 1914, Barth noted that, "The unconditional truths of the gospel are simply suspended for the time being and in the meantime a German war-theology is put to work, its Christian trimming consisting of a lot of talk about sacrifice and the like. . . . It is truly sad! Marburg and German civilization have lost something in my eyes by this breakdown, and indeed forever."[51] His loss of confidence in the Liberal Protestantism from which he had drunk so deeply during his student days was now no longer a viable option for the pastoral and political work that needed to be done. But Barth's allegiance to Religious Socialism was also tottering. The differing orientations of Ragaz and Kutter had given way to different plans of action in response to the war and different hopes for its outcome.

Ragaz vehemently opposed the war as the expression of godless violence. In fact, the war-experience turned Ragaz into a resolute pacifist, so that by war's end he could say:

> Christianity rejects all use of violence. It makes the truth that it calls for prevail by means of free proclamation, of witness through word and deed, of sacrifice and martyrdom. . . . The central battle of Western history is therefore the battle between

---

50. This was Eduard Thurneysen's description of Christoph Blumhardt given in his *Christoph Blumhardt*, 15.

51. Barth and Thurneysen, *Revolutionary Theology in the Making*, 26.

> Christ's Kingdom, which manifests itself in love and freedom, and Caesar's kingdom, which manifests itself in various forms of violence.[52]

In November of 1914, Ragaz called for the Religious Socialists to present a united front and call for an end to the war. But this call was rejected by Kutter, since it was not the true peace that was needed, which only God could give.[53] The split over the appropriate response to the war was accompanied by a growing split over the status of Germany. Ragaz was pro-Entente and hoped that Germany would lose the war as a judgment of its "war-theology," which impeded the coming kingdom of God. Kutter was pro-German, believing that in its culture, "vastly superior points of contact for the coming Kingdom," could be found.[54]

Barth and Thurneysen found themselves moving between Ragaz and Kutter during the winter of 1914/1915. As McCormack points out, by March of 1915, Barth was exasperated with the debate of whether to "act" with Ragaz, or to "wait" with Kutter.[55] In this context, in April 1915 Barth and Thurneysen traveled north to Marburg to attend the wedding of Barth's brother Peter to Martin Rade's daughter Helene. While there, Barth had a heated conversation with the German nationalist politician Friedrich Naumann (1860–1919), in which the latter made Christianity and the gospel instrumental to the German war effort. On the way home Thurneysen and Barth stopped at Bad Boll, where they stayed for five days (April 10–15), visiting and having many private conversations with Christoph Blumhardt. These would prove decisive for the new orientation of their theology.[56]

What struck Barth at this meeting was later captured in his little essay, "Action in Waiting for the Kingdom of God." "Blumhardt always begins right away with God's presence, might, and purpose: he starts

---

52. Bock, *Signs of the Kingdom*, 50–51.

53. McCormack gives an excellent account of the breakdown within Religious Socialist circles over how to respond to WWI. See *Critically Realistic Dialectical Theology*, 117–25.

54. Ibid., 120.

55. Ibid., 122–23.

56. Barth describes his encounter with Blumhardt in terms reminiscent of a beacon of light that helped to lead him out of confusion: "In the midst of this hopeless confusion, it was the message of the Blumhardts with its orientation on Christian hope which above all began to make sense to me. I owe my acquaintance with it to my friend Eduard Thurneysen" (Busch, *Karl Barth*, 84).

out from God; he does not begin by climbing upwards to Him by means of contemplation and deliberation. God is the end, and because we already know Him as the beginning, we await His consummating acts."[57] Blumhardt, in a totally unsophisticated way, employed a kind of hermeneutical naiveté towards the biblical texts that is sometimes referred to as "Biblical Realism."[58] This wasn't primarily a claim about the nature of the biblical texts, though such a claim was included. Rather, it was a claim that the depictions of God in Scripture were straightforwardly realistic, and, most importantly, what they pointed to was the *living* God who acts in history and on His creation because His goal is to redeem the entirety of it. Thus, the subject matter of the Bible was not human religious experience, but the living and acting God who acts in history to bring about the new world, the kingdom of God. The initial root of these insights, as we have shown in chapters 2 and 3, was the experience of the elder Blumhardt at Möttlingen and Bad Boll, as well as Christoph's later reflections and experiences.

God lives. This was the reality with which one must begin. Though he had heard this before through other mediations, especially Kutter, the recent events of the war and the split among the Religious Socialists prepared Barth to hear it now in a decisive fashion. Immediately upon their return to Switzerland, Barth began to read through Friedrich Zündel's biography of the elder Blumhardt. He was astonished at the work. As he makes clear in letters to Thurneysen, "all of 'our' best thoughts are already grasped and expressed here."[59] It wasn't just the ideas and way of reading Scripture that had impressed Barth, but something of the spiritual life and ministry of the elder Blumhardt fascinated him as well:

> Alongside such a man I see how very small I am. Last Saturday a local drinker greeted me from the window of the first story of his house with balled fists and the following address: 'Get out of here, you beast, you priest, you God-damn fool; where you go, no grass will ever grow again.' There I had it. The elder

57. Karl Barth, "Action in Waiting for the Kingdom of God," 23–24.

58. Eduard Thurneysen is the first to apply this description to the Blumhardts. See his *Christoph Blumhardt*, 25–26. Hans Frei develops this descriptor in his, "The Doctrine of Revelation in the Thought of Karl Barth, 1909 to 1922," 150–55, 386–99. I have noted the problems associated when using this descriptor without qualifications in chapter 1, but I choose to use it here because it captures nicely a key element in their approach to Scripture.

59. Thurneysen, *Briefwechsel*, 1:51.

> Blumhardt would at once have struck up a song of praise in that situation and would have driven the devil out of him. . . .[60]

More than just guides for how to think about Scripture and its subject matter, the Blumhardts were an example of taking seriously the other world, the other reality to which the Scriptures pointed. In the subsequent months, Barth would indeed take the Blumhardts' life and witness so seriously that he would make their concerns his own and seek to recommend them as an example for others.

Barth's Appropriation of the Blumhardts and the New Theological Direction

There were a number of factors that contributed to Barth's move in a new theological direction during 1915–1916. The failure of Liberal theology and International Socialism; the confusion within the Religious Socialist movement; the continual burden of preaching in the wartime environment—all of these contributed to Barth's move. Undoubtedly however, it was Barth's rediscovery of the theme of the New Testament as mediated to him by the Blumhardts' life and witness that made the most impact.

Barth's Turn to Theology

The first evidence that Barth was beginning to integrate the insights of Blumhardt came in May 1915, just after his visit to Bad Boll. He proclaimed:

> God is God and not something other. God is not a beautiful idea of man, the truth and value of which one must first negotiate; not a pious idea which belongs to the peculiarities of religion and church but is only taken seriously within these holy districts. Nor is God a friendly comfort for the incompleteness of human life where one must first ask, 'In this situation will this really in fact be a comfort to me?' No, God is the reality of life, strong and clear as nothing else, experienced and known as the certainty of certainties. He has revealed himself to us, he has shown us how he himself is nothing other than pure freedom. He has said to us: 'Behold, this is and holds unconditionally! You cannot oppose it; you can only accept it thankfully and joyfully

---

60. Barth and Thurneysen, *Revolutionary Theology in the Making*, 30.

by letting freedom completely penetrate you, by placing your-
self wholly in its service.' If we acknowledge this then it becomes
clear that he is our Father, that we belong to him and he to us.[61]

Thurneysen attributed the phrase "world is world, but God is God"
to Blumhardt, first heard by them during their April meeting.[62] As
Eberhard Busch has shown, "God is God" was *the* theological axiom
of Barth's early theology.[63] During this early period, the phrase "God is
God" was meant positively to take seriously the reality of the living God
as witnessed to in Scripture and negatively to distinguish the real God
from all of our conceptions of God. It meant that, "God is not captive to
our imaginations, our fears, or our limitations."[64]

That Barth wanted to take seriously that "God is God," evidenced
that his connection to theological Liberalism was finally coming to
an end. It had already become evident for Barth that the living God
could not be identified with the conception of God developed by the
Protestant Liberal tradition. In light of the misuse of religious-experi-
ence in justifying the German war effort *and* its perilous position vis-à-
vis the critique of Feuerbach, the Herrmannian construal of revelation
as the individual experience of the "inner life of Jesus" could no longer
be considered a legitimate way to understand who God is or what God
wants. What the German Protestant theological establishment called
God, was now seen as simply a projection of their human aspirations,
in this case German nationalism.

The meeting with Blumhardt and his subsequent reading also
contributed to a shift in Barth's thinking about social and political engagement. The reality and priority of the living God did not exclude the
world of humanity, but it certainly qualified human action on behalf of

61. Karl Barth, "sermon, 2 May 1915," in *Predigten 1915*, 174–75; as quoted in
Arthur Marvin Sutherland, "Christology and Discipleship in the Sermons of Karl
Barth: 1913–1916," 86.

62. Lim, *'Jesus ist Sieger!'*, 101. Blumhardt appears to have first used the phrase in
his 1897 morning devotion, "The World of the Children of God." A similar phrase appears in conjunction with the divine initiative in revelation in his 1898 devotion, "The
Revelation of the Living God." The phrase is also employed to emphasize the distinction between God and all others in the 1899 "I am the Lord!" See Christoph Blumhardt,
Auswahl, III:33, 116, 236, 238.

63. "God is God: The Meaning of a Controversial Formula and the Fundamental
Problem of Speaking about God," 101–13.

64. Sutherland, "Christology and Discipleship," 88.

the kingdom of God. One must first "wait" in hope for *God* to act. This would require a clarification of who God is, what the kingdom of God is, and how the kingdom of God related to this world. Such a need led Barth to prioritize the positions of Kutter and Ragaz, as primary and secondary. The first concern would be to "wait" for God's revelation of his own work for the kingdom of God. Once the pattern and quality of God's eschatological action were known, the human correspondence to that action could follow. Thus, Barth was attempting to reconnect the two poles of Blumhardt, the "waiting" and "hastening," that had come uncoupled in Kutter and Ragaz, but in an irreversible relation.[65] His new understanding of the relationship between theological reflection and political action placed theological questions in the foreground and forced him to take even more seriously the question of the knowledge of God and His kingdom.

In his search, sermon preparation and scriptural exegesis would prove critical. Barth had struggled with the task of preaching almost from the beginning of his ministerial career. But now, the problem of proclaiming what he heard in Scripture was intensified. He now realized that what needed to be proclaimed stood on an entirely different footing. As he later reflected, "Over and above the group of problems associated with liberal theology and Religious Socialism, I began to be increasingly preoccupied with the idea of the kingdom of God in the biblical, real, this-worldly sense of the term. This raised more and more problems over the way in which I should use the Bible in my sermons, which for all too long I had taken for granted."[66] The realization of this problem was spurred in part by the critical negation included in the *theologumenon* "God is God." If only "*God* is God," then what words are adequate to express this God? Moreover, if "God is God" and therefore free from human manipulation and constructions, where and how do we have access to Him?

---

65. This is evident, for example, in the typology developed by Barth in September 1915. Barth writes that he now "was forced to place the emphasis where Kutter did but that I was able at no point of importance to regard Ragaz' positions as having to be excluded; moreover, there was one point (not touched on by Bader) which concerned me specially: Ragaz' endeavor to put principles into practice, an indispensable though secondary element in spite of its evident 'danger'" (Barth and Thurneysen, *Revolutionary Theology in the Making*, 31).

66. Busch, *Karl Barth: His Life from Letters and Autobiographical Texts*, 92–97.

At first Barth proposed "conscience" as the sight wherein God was heard. This is evident in his 1916 lecture, "The Righteousness of God" wherein he argued, "There is a fundamentally different way to come into relation with the righteousness of God. This *other* way we enter not by speech nor reflection nor reason, but by being still, by listening to and not silencing the conscience when we have hardly begun to hear its voice."[67] But this proposal was qualified not long after, as evidenced in Barth's sermon "The One Thing Necessary," of March 13, 1916. Here, faith is to be identified with the objective content of the "promises of God." "God's promise to us wants to be seriously taken *a priori*, first above all."[68] The promises to which Barth was pointing were found in Scripture:

> 'In the beginning was the Word and the Word was with God, and the Word was God' (John 1:1). This is not a metaphysical construction, but the deepest practical knowledge of life. In the beginning! From there we can progress to seeing and diagnosing, conceiving and understanding, applying and practicing. From there we can we can go forward to questions, tasks, and conflicts![69]

It was in the Scriptures that the primary witness to the living God was to be found. It would be through expounding the Scriptures that the community could both learn again to seriously "wait" on the living and revolutionary action of God, and thereby to find direction for their own action. "What is faith? Recognizing that God is God! That He is not far from us!"[70] How and where do we find God? The answer to this question comes through realizing that it is not we who find God, but God who found and will find us. This was what the "strange new world" in the Bible witnessed to.

"THE STRANGE NEW WORLD WITHIN THE BIBLE"

In the lecture, "The Strange New World Within the Bible,"[71] delivered in autumn of 1916, Barth resolutely turns in the direction that he believed

---

67. "The Righteousness of God," 23.

68. Karl Barth, "Sermon 13 March 1916," in *Predigten 1916*, 116.

69. Ibid., 116; as quoted in Sutherland, "Christology and Discipleship," 110.

70. Karl Barth, "Sermon 13 March 1916," in *Predigten 1916*, 118.

71. Karl Barth, *The Word of God and the Word of Man*, 28–50.

the truth that "God is God" forced him to go. He seeks to make clear the problems that confront those who would turn to Scripture to know who God is. The essay reveals that, in Barth's estimation, both those on the left and the right of the theological spectrum, despite their very significant differences, share in a common problem. They each only hear part of what the witness of Scripture has to say and therefore do not hear that only "God is *God*."[72]

On the left, the problem with Protestant Liberalism is that they refuse to take seriously that the true subject matter of Scripture is not the religious history of humanity, but the living God: "Not the history of man but the history of God! Not the virtues of men but the virtues of him who hath called us out of darkness into his marvelous light! Not human standpoints but the standpoint of God!"[73] That to which the Scriptures point is not accessible through scientific religious methodologies because such are only capable of finding answers to *our* questions, which are inevitably constructed in *our* image. What confronts us in the Bible, however, is entirely different:

> It is not the right human thoughts about God which form the content of the Bible, but the right divine thoughts about men. The Bible tells us not how we should talk with God but what he says to us; not how we find the way to him, but how he has sought and found the way to us; not the right relation in which we must place ourselves to him, but the covenant which he has made with all who are Abraham's spiritual children and which he has sealed once and for all in Jesus Christ. It is this which is within the Bible. The word of God is within the Bible.[74]

If all the best tools at the disposal of the Christian as seen in religious philosophy, and biblical and historical criticism, are bound only to create a picture of God in our own image, how do we hear this Word of God? By an act of divine grace in which faith is created: "This daring is *faith*; and we read the Bible rightly, not when we do so with false modesty, restraint, and attempted sobriety, for these are passive qualities, but when we read it in faith. And the invitation to dare and to reach toward the highest, even though we do not deserve it, is the expression of *grace* in the Bible: the Bible unfolds to us as we are met, guided, drawn on,

72. Ibid., 48.
73. Ibid., 45.
74. Ibid., 43.

and made to grow by the grace of God."[75] The event of the kingdom of God happens. Revelation happens. But these do not happen as the possibility of the human religious subject or as an internal possibility latent in creation or history. Rather they happen because they are both a possibility of God that is rooted in God's promise to renew the world, and because God has determined to see the same reach its goal.

Barth is not skeptical that the kingdom of God is real or that our knowledge of it is both possible and actual. In fact, following Blumhardt, his presupposition is that the kingdom of God is real and active and we are given knowledge of the same by God. But Barth is deadly critical of the human presumption to make God speak or to identify human action, knowledge, and speech with God's action. To do so is to place the kingdom in human hands, to say that it is "given" rather than "given again and again as gift."

The kingdom of God and our being included in the knowledge of God happens in faith and by God's grace. This is entirely not of our doing, for "There is a river in the Bible that carries us away, once we have entrusted our destiny to it—away from ourselves to the sea. The Holy Scriptures will interpret themselves in spite of all our human limitations. We need only dare to follow this drive, this spirit, this river, to grow out beyond ourselves toward the highest answer."[76] If we will allow this "river" to carry us along, then a "history" of God's deeds will happen among us, the implications of which would be revolutionary: "When God enters, history for the while ceases to be, and there is nothing more to ask; for something wholly different and new begins—a history with its own distinct grounds, possibilities, and hypotheses."[77] The new world of God that is already present in the world can happen in our midst if we will enter into it.

This is not merely an epistemological claim, but an ontological assertion that no amount of ethical idealism or socialist praxis could produce. To *really* know God, would mean to be changed, and furthermore (!) to experience that change in time and history. This is not simply a new way of reading history and the world, but of participating in their transformation. Barth's claim goes far beyond what Liberal

75. Ibid., 34.
76. Ibid., 34.
77. Ibid., 37.

Protestantism ever believed it could deliver. He takes the Biblical texts seriously and dares to ask the prevailing theology: "Do we desire the presence of 'God'? Do we dare to go whither evidently we are being led?"[78]

On the conservative side, things were better, but not by much. Those on the right,

> were right when they struggled so desperately in behalf of the truth that there is revelation in the Bible and not religion only, and when they would not allow facts to be turned upside down for them even by so pious and intelligent a man as Schleiermacher. And our fathers were right when they guarded warily against being drawn out upon the shaky scaffolding of religious self-expression.[79]

Those on the right believed that they had to do with God in the Scriptures. This was an advance over the former position, but unfortunately the answers to the question of who God is and what he has done were constructed along lines that were no less limited because they misunderstood the biblical hope. They also do not allow for the fact that "God is God." In response to them, Barth asks rhetorically:

> Can one read or hear read even as much as two chapters from the Bible and still with good conscience say, God's word went forth to humanity, his mandate guided history from Abraham to Christ, the Holy Spirit descended in tongues of fire upon the apostles at Pentecost, a Saul became a Paul and traveled over land and sea—all in order that here and there specimens of men like you and me might be 'converted,' find inner 'peace,' and by a redeeming death go some day to 'heaven.' Is that all? Is that all of God and his new world, of the meaning of the Bible, of the content of the contents? The powerful forces which come to expression in the Bible, the movements of peoples, the battles, and the convulsions which take place before us there, the miracles and revelations which constantly occur there, the immeasurable promises for the future which are unceasingly repeated to us there—do not all these things stand in a rather strange relation to so small a result—if that is really the only result they have? Is not God—greater than all that? Even in these answers, earnest and pious as they may be, have we not measured God with

78. Ibid.
79. Ibid., 44.

our own measure, conceived God with our own conceptions, wished ourselves a God according to our own wishes?[80]

Conservative Christianity was lost, because, though it knew that it dealt with God in Scripture, it neither understood him nor did it understand the radical implications of that knowledge. It did not want God to speak in the same radical way today that had been exhibited in the strange stories of Scripture. It had forgotten how to hope in God and the radical new world that he brought. If it heard the real *content* to which the Bible points, it would know that what the prophets and the apostles witness to was the *beginning* of a new *world*.

A "beginning" means that something is underway that has not ceased. God's action for the kingdom of God is not locked in the church's memories, but is present because ongoing. It presses itself upon us, constantly asking if we will hear it. Furthermore, what the Bible points to cannot result *merely* in the "renewal" of the individual, or her blessedness and peace in the face of death, because what has begun is a new "world." God's renewing activity is interested in more than the inner life of the individual. Rather, God's concern is with the whole spiritual-material existence of the human person as well as the larger social and political contexts in which humanity lives. Orthodox Christianity moves in the right direction, but it fails to go far enough because it hopes only for the salvation of the spiritual interiority of the pious individual.

Barth offers a corrective to the purported short-circuit in both liberalism and conservatism at the close of the essay. He uses a Trinitarian ordering to answer the question "who is God?" He is the One whose sole purpose (i.e, the Father) of bringing a new world into this world has already begun (i.e., the Son), and continues to unfold in the midst of humanity (i.e., the Spirit). All along the way, the new world and the new humanity have real social and political consequences: "The Holy Spirit makes a new heaven and a new earth and, therefore, new men, new families, new relationships, new politics. . . . The Holy Spirit establishes the righteousness of heaven in the midst of the unrighteousness of earth and will not stop nor stay until all that is dead has been brought to life and a new *world* has come into being."[81] Alongside the conviction that the life-giving Word of God's new world is what is most needed,

80. Ibid., 46–47.
81. Ibid., 49–50.

Barth ends by exhorting the hearers in both camps to come in faith and take hold of that which is promised.

Barth's positive conviction that God does in fact speak in and through the Scriptures brushes aside the understanding of both the starting point (i.e., religious experience) and the course of theological knowledge (i.e., biblical criticism and philosophy of religion) that he had inherited from Protestant Liberalism. The content of what God says—that a new world and a new humanity has begun for *this* world, in the here and now and not after death in eternity—distinguishes him from conservative and orthodox forms of Christianity. God's Word is radical because it shakes up the individual *and* the world, and this revolt has already begun. Christianity, therefore, cannot identify itself with the *status quo*, because that is exactly what is overthrown in Jesus. The actualization of this overthrow does not wait for individual or collective death, but is already surging here and now to change the world.

Barth utilizes phrases and images that are characteristic of Blumhardt throughout this essay.[82] Furthermore, as Hee-Kuk Lim has pointed out, the entire first part of the essay in which Barth recounts the events of salvation history bears striking resemblance to a rhetorical strategy employed by Blumhardt. Lim notes that this is reminiscent of Blumhardt's position on Scripture. According to Lim, "Blumhardt turns the traditional doctrine of inspiration inside out. He no longer speaks of the inspired Scriptures, but of 'inspired people' in the Scriptures: e.g., Abraham, Moses, David, the Prophets, Simon, Joseph and his wife Mary, the Apostles, etc. The people of the Bible were the: 'people, planted in God's garden' who, by every breath from God, understand themselves and turn themselves to God."[83] That is, it was the referent to which they pointed, which was *and is* extra-textual, that made their witness authoritative and inspired. Both Barth and Blumhardt take as central that such things really happened, and therefore will happen again. Such a position passes by the historical questions, not because they are critical, but because they are not critical enough! The occurrence of the events depicted in Scripture lays an impossible burden on us precisely because

82. See Lim, *Jesus ist Sieger!* 101. Lim argues that the phrases "seed," (41) and "God is God," (48) are Blumhardtian in origin. He also notes that Barth's image of the "river in the Bible" and his deployment of it (34), bears striking resemblance to Blumhardt's theme of a "well or fountain" which flows through Scripture.

83. Ibid., 97.

such things point to a "history of God" in the world, and therefore the beginning and end of all things and our responsibility in face of their dissolution.

The themes in the essay also bear the marks of Blumhardt. Recalling our discussion in chapters 2 and 3, one can detect their influence in Barth's understanding of the "content of the contents" to which the Scriptures point. The "strange new world of the Bible" is the world of the kingdom of God which has entered history and is working its way to its final cosmic goal, when God will be "all in all." In contrast to the 1911 essay, Barth's conviction that the new world of the Bible is the kingdom of God with real physical and social consequences is expressed in the form of a realistic eschatology. "The whole Bible authoritatively announces that God must be all in all; and the events of the Bible are the beginning, the glorious beginning of a new *world*."[84] This sound's remarkably similar to the elder Blumhardt's conviction that, "This Kingdom is fulfilled when throughout the whole creation 'God will be all in all.' This will be when all of creation acknowledges or hails the name of God. The Kingdom of God is the consequence of this. . . . The appearance of Jesus upon the earth marked the *beginning* of this Kingdom."[85] The common witness of the Scriptures, which find their pinnacle in Jesus Christ, point to the beginning of a process that continues to this day. As Christoph described it, "From the first to the last chapter, the Bible deals with the coming of God into this world, . . ."[86] Barth's essay is an exercise in adopting and articulating a Blumhardtian reading of the "die Sache" of Scripture. The "content of the contents" of Scripture is God, the One who comes into this world not for its destruction, but for its renewal.

Barth's argument that "a new world projects itself into our old ordinary world," also echoes Christoph Blumhardt's belief that, "In Jesus, however, a new reality appears, a reality that is opposed to the world's history. Something new begins alongside the old. The old reality does not disappear; it continues alongside the new. Yet in Jesus

---

84. Karl Barth, "The Strange New World Within the Bible," 49.

85. Johann Christoph Blumhardt, *Die Verkündigung*, 316 (unpublished translation by the Brüderhof and Plough Publishing).

86. Christoph Blumhardt, *Auswahl*, I:241 (unpublished translation by the Brüderhof and Plough Publishing).

a new history begins, a new working of God (1 Jn. 2:8)."[87] This new world is the *real* reality, and as the real reality it has ongoing effects in this world. "Every word in the Bible guarantees to me deeds of God right here where I stand."[88] Thus, Barth's expectation that the living God will continue to speak today finds further parallels in the hope of the Blumhardts' witness. The identical call of both is "turn to God!" believing that "this promise belongs to our time."[89] We can do nothing but "place ourselves within this truth."[90] The common conviction of both Barth and Christoph is that the *die Sache* of Scripture (i.e., "the content of the contents") is dynamic and progressive, moving towards a real *telos*, and that true knowledge of who God is and the experience of God's new world is accessible only as we faithfully hope in God's promise to renew the world.

Though Barth expresses this realistic eschatology in his own language, it is very difficult to attribute his adoption of this stance to any source other than the Blumhardts. Barth's meeting with Christoph Blumhardt and subsequent reading of F. Zündel's biography of the elder Blumhardt, as well as the *Hausandachten* of Christoph Blumhardt, give multiple sources through which this influence could have been mediated and the remarkable similarity to the Blumhardts' eschatology, which has been outlined in chapters 2 and 3 of this study, strongly indicates that Barth is moving in the thought-forms of the Blumhardts in the "Strange New World" essay.

"Action in Waiting for the Kingdom of God"

"The Strange New World Within the Bible" revealed that Barth had begun to assimilate key theological insights and elements of the Blumhardts' witness. Though unmentioned, the influence of Christoph is everywhere present from the use of phrases and images, to the presence of important themes. Barth's growing appreciation of Blumhardt is further confirmed in the short piece, "Action in Waiting for the Kingdom of God." In this

---

87. Karl Barth, "The Strange New World Within the Bible," 37; Christoph Blumhardt, *Action in Waiting*, 18.

88. Christoph Blumhardt, *Auswahl*, I:241 (unpublished translation by the Brüderhof and Plough Publishing).

89. Christoph Blumhardt, *Action in Waiting*, 15.

90. Ibid., 19.

essay, written just prior to "The Strange New World Within the Bible," Barth reviewed the recently published *Hausandachten* of Christoph Blumhardt. It further confirms that Barth was turning to theological reflection on Scripture as the answer for the current dilemma's facing the Religious Socialist movement and the wider church and that the example of Blumhardt was guiding his thinking.

The essay is less of a review than a wholesale endorsement and recommendation of Blumhardt to those in the circles of Religious Socialism. Many in the movement, however, already knew Blumhardt. Thus, what the essay really represents is Barth's attempt to offer the "Blumhardt" who was influencing his own turn to foundational theological questions as a way beyond the impasse. This was the "Blumhardt" of the fourth phase that we described in chapter 3 as one who had withdrawn from explicit political work in order to "wait" again on God to speak his Word afresh. As his correspondence with Leonhard Ragaz shows, not all within the movement were interested in moving in that direction. Despite the serious misgivings expressed by Ragaz and others, Barth would continue on, but it would remain very important to Thurneysen and himself to show that their new direction was wholly in keeping with the spirit of Blumhardt's theology, revealing the importance that he held for them.[91]

"Action in Waiting for the Kingdom of God"

That this essay is no mere review is confirmed with Barth's first lines: "For me it is the most direct and penetrating Word from God into the need of the world that the war years have produced so far. I have the impression that here is just what we would like to say—if we could!"[92] The "we" here is not just Barth or Thurneysen, but the wider readership of the *Neue Wege*, the literary organ of the Religious Socialist movement, to whom Barth originally submitted the article. Blumhardt's sig-

---

91. This is confirmed by Barth's explanation of the inclusion of "Action in Waiting for the Kingdom of God" in the 1928 (2nd) edition of *Suchet Gott*. "This book review reveals our close relationship to the person and work of Blumhardt the younger during our beginnings. This continuity was not disrupted, as we continued on. This is the reason why we reprint this book-review not only for historical reasons. Besides this we know that Blumhardt himself was able to see this copy, and agreed explicitly with the contents and was happy about it" (idem, 2).

92. Karl Barth, "Action in Waiting for the Kingdom of God," 19.

nificance lay precisely in his ability to redirect the movement back to "the one thing needful," to hear *God's* Word to humanity.

According to Barth, Blumhardt does not give any solution to the problems facing the movement, except to call it back to begin again to the beginning. "My other reason is the conviction that our cause, our hope, is at the moment served better with prayers than with treatises. Our dialectics have come to a dead end, and if we want to become healthy and strong, we have to start from the beginning and become like children. That is where Blumhardt can be of great service to people everywhere."[93] For Barth, Blumhardt's unsophisticated, even "unpractical" little book, is what those in the wider circles of Religious Socialism should seek not merely to hear, but to emulate. One can almost hear the gasp of those committed to political action in the background.

Blumhardt's ability to "represent God's cause in the world yet not wage war on the world, love the world and yet be completely faithful to God, ..." is predicated on his starting point:

> Blumhardt always begins right away with God's presence, might, and purpose: he starts out from God; he does not begin by climbing upwards to Him by means of contemplation and deliberation. God is the end, and because we already know Him as the beginning, we may await His consummating acts.[94]

Blumhardt begins with the promise and reality of the living God, i.e., that "God is God," and therefore he is able to take seriously the problems of the war, but not so seriously that he loses hope. The war is a judgment, but not for humanity's destruction. Rather, through it, God still works to bring his kingdom more fully into this world. What is it that gives Blumhardt this confidence? According to Barth, it is Blumhardt's belief that "—and here lies the key to everything—with *Jesus* the good actually began already, the good to which mankind and nature alike are called, which towers right into our own time also and goes forward toward a revelation and a consummation. Blumhardt takes his bearings untiringly from this point again and again, using it as his point of

---

93. Ibid., 22. In the German Barth's actual phrase is "Hausandachten" or "family devotions" by which was meant the simple reading of Scripture in a faithful and worshipful way.

94. Ibid., 22–23.

departure in ever new ways."[95] A new reality has entered into the old world, and the new reality is to be taken more seriously than the old. This was an insight Christoph's father had received in his struggles at Möttlingen, and Barth would refashion for his own use in "The Strange New World Within the Bible."[96]

This new reality moves forward through history because of the action of God, but also because of the movement of humanity, which is faithful "calling upon God." In an attempt to explain his own position and to persuade others in the Religious Socialist movement that this was the way forward, Barth argued that Blumhardt's waiting was revolutionary:

> It would be very good not to pass lightly over the fearful depth of what he means by this, because here and there a comfortable sort of nonsense is made out of this concept. Blumhardt's meaning, as far as I can understand it from the book of devotions, is that this waiting, although turned inward at first, is in its essence revolutionary: 'Lord God, make new! Make us new! Make new everyone who calls to Thee, for otherwise all is in vain!' To act [to 'wait'] means just the opposite of sitting comfortably and going along with the old order of things.[97]

If one reads "The Strange New World Within the Bible" in light of "Action in Waiting for the Kingdom of God" and vice versa, it becomes clear that for Barth, Blumhardt's "waiting" is nothing less than taking seriously the biblical witness in order to proclaim and await the coming new world of God. "When we 'hasten and wait' toward God like this, the consummation is prepared, coming from God himself."[98] The new world presses in on us, and this is the transformation of all things. This is a call to hope for a far more radical change than socialist revolutionary action could ever accomplish. The latter could only ever be a reform or emendation of the world, rather than its wholesale change. To take seriously the reality of "the strange new world of the Bible" would be to dare, "in faith what grace can offer us!"[99] The implication of this would mean that political engagement and action were secondary concerns to

95. Ibid., 32.

96. See Karl Barth, "The Strange New World Within the Bible," 37.

97. Karl Barth, "Action in Waiting for the Kingdom of God," 40.

98. Ibid., 42.

99. Karl Barth, "The Strange New World Within the Bible," 50.

hearing and proclaiming the Word of God. It would only be through taking seriously that to which the prophets and apostles pointed (i.e., the kingdom of God) that the real solution to all problems, let alone the problems of the war, would be found. In light of this, Barth's turn to Paul's *Epistle to the Romans* in July 1916 should be seen as his attempt to emulate Blumhardt and listen among the words of Paul for the echoes of the kingdom of God.

Barth's Interpretation of the Blumhardts and the Split with Religious Socialism: Initiating the Split with Ragaz and Religious Socialism

Markus Mattmüller has argued that chief among the reasons for Barth's withdrawal from Religious Socialism was an argument about his interpretation of Blumhardt.[100] Mattmüller also argues that not only the material theological differences between Barth and Ragaz, but also an inter-personal dimension was to play a role in Barth's turn from Ragaz's position and more broadly, from the Religious Socialist movement. Analysis of the correspondence between Ragaz and Barth bears out Mattmüller's contention.

That Barth did not mean for his new position to lead to total political disengagement is evident both in the ending of "The Strange New World Within the Bible," and in the fact that he submitted his first draft of "Action in Waiting for the Kingdom of God" to Leonhard Ragaz for publication in the *Neue Wege*. It was not that political action and struggle were unimportant, but they were of relative importance. Ragaz, however, did not see it that way.

His first letter to Barth, on July 18, 1916, was measured and friendly, though it bears a suspicion that Kutter had unduly influenced Barth's reading of Blumhardt. "I read your review with the feeling that you understood Blumhardt better than most people. Still, I felt certain sub-currents which gave me some concern."[101] In this first letter, Ragaz is somewhat muddled as to why he wanted Barth to re-write the essay. The primary point was that Barth made Blumhardt too much of a judge of others, such that he is identified with one position over against another, whereas Ragaz believed that Blumhardt should be the door-

---

100. Mattmüller, *Eine Biographie*, vol. 2, 218.

101. Leonhard Ragaz, *Leonhard Ragaz in seinen Briefen*, 2:85.

way through which anyone from any persuasion could come to receive something from God. This was not a minor point in Ragaz's thinking, because Barth's essay would be first time that Blumhardt was being publicly introduced to the larger reading public of the *Neue Wege*. Some interpretation is necessary here.

It is clear that the positions and conflicts that Ragaz had in mind was the brewing split within the Religious Socialist movement. He did not believe that Blumhardt should be brought down into the argument between the conflicting options of Kutter and himself. Rather, Blumhardt "should remain on his solitary height of nearness to Jesus. All kinds of people, injured in the daily conflict, are able to come to him, without receiving new wounds."[102] Mattmüller spells out Ragaz's intentions well, observing, "Obviously he did not want to monopolize Blumhardt for his own conception of things: . . . But he did not want to see him chosen as chief witness against him either."[103]

Furthermore, Ragaz, in a fairly diplomatic manner, indicates that Barth's reading reflects more of Kutter's position than his own. His suggestion: "It seems to me that a more indicative, entirely non-polemical, simple manner leading to the matter, may be the most suitable form."[104] Translation: re-write the piece so that the different interpretations of Blumhardt, both the activist (i.e., Ragaz) and the more contemplative (i.e., Kutter), can be recognized and embraced.

Ragaz also made the fateful mistake of expressing his observation and concern that some "very young men," take up the insights of Blumhardt, won through hard struggles, and make "theologumena" of them, which leads to a kind of spiritual laziness and conceit. Mattmüller argues that these comments were not aimed specifically at Barth, but at the followers of Kutter.[105] That Ragaz would not have recognized Barth as such is possible, but Barth's position had indeed come close to Kutter and he took the comments personally. In Barth's reply letter of July 19, Barth argued that he "wanted to say to these friends now, what I saw with Blumhardt and to explain what may be offensive to some—as well as I

---

102. Ibid., 85.

103. Mattmüller, *Leonhard Ragaz und der religiöse Sozialismus*, 223.

104. Ragaz, *Leonhard Ragaz in seinen Briefen*, 2:85.

105. Mattmüller, *Leonhard Ragaz und der religiöse Sozialismus*, 221.

could. I simply *gave* what I *had*, not more and not less."[106] Barth went on to criticize Ragaz's appeal to an outside reader who had confirmed his criticisms of Barth's perspective. He would not submit to the censure of an outside reader. Even still, Barth sent along a slightly amended form of the essay on July 24.

In his letter of July 28, Ragaz clarified that he did not mean to offend or hurt Barth either with his comments about "very young people," who become "couch-potatoes" nor in his appeal to an outside reader. Ragaz explained that the outside reader he had appealed to was Bertha Imhoff, a woman with intimate and deep connections to Bad Boll and Christoph Blumhardt. His motives in showing the piece to her had to do with the fact that Barth's essay would have introduced Blumhardt to the wider readership of the *Neue Wege*, many of whom were not aligned with either Kutter or Ragaz. Thus, it was important that Blumhardt be as accessible as possible to as many people as possible.

Finally, Ragaz turns from the tactical consideration to the material differences between Barth and himself regarding Blumhardt. What is ironic is that Ragaz acknowledges that Barth's interpretation of Blumhardt is "masterful." The issue, however, is not whether or not Barth has understood Blumhardt, nor even whether his interpretation is legitimate, but whether the current position of Blumhardt, i.e., the Blumhardt of the fourth phase that was exhibited in the *Hausandachten*, ought now to become a "doctrine." That is, Ragaz is asking if the Blumhardt who is committed to "waiting" in the form of prayer and biblical study should now really become *the* model for *all*:

> He [Blumhardt] knows that there also have to be people who give lectures and write essays. He knows that there has to be conflict and the chips have to fly. He himself did this also and even now!—occasionally he still does it. Recently I heard of a typical illustration of this. As he has now become old and more subdued, at least externally, should we, especially very young people, copy him?[107]

Ragaz acknowledged that part of the reason for this question is not just the tactical mode of Blumhardt's current actions, but also the understanding between divine and human action for the kingdom of God.

---

106. Ragaz, *Leonhard Ragaz in seinen Briefen*, 2:86.
107. Ibid., 89.

For Mattmüller, this was the central theological issue at stake between Ragaz and Barth, and between Ragaz and Blumhardt.

According to Mattmüller, Ragaz conceived of the progress of the kingdom of God as leaving "clearly recognizable lines,"[108] which referred to the ultimate goal of the kingdom of God on earth, but also to penultimate goals in the realm of politics, economics, etc. The penultimate goals, though rooted in God's action for the kingdom, were historical and the result of human cooperation. These goals had been identified with and consolidated in the forms of socialism and later pacifism. The implication was that in fighting for socialism or socialist ideals, one was fighting for the kingdom of God. Socialism was a "natural" or "human" development of the divine struggle for the kingdom of God.

But in light of the war, the identification of socialism with the kingdom of God was far more problematic for Barth and his friends. What was needed now was a clarification, a re-examination and reconnection of these ideas with their origin. This meant they needed to "hear" the Word of God afresh. In light of this concern, Mattmüller correctly interprets Barth's essay as recommending that "A reconstruction has to come from a direct comprehension of the Scriptures which is to be in the style of Blumhardt."[109] Ragaz was not prepared to go this direction, not because it was an illegitimate interpretation of Blumhardt, but because there had to be freedom to "constantly press on to the ever greater."[110] Blumhardt had inspired Ragaz, but he did not have the last word over Ragaz's endeavors.

Barth decided not to publish the essay in *Neue Wege*, turning instead to the *Der freie Schweizer Arbeiter*, a paper more closely associated with those around Hermann Kutter. This event marked the beginning of the end of Barth's association with Swiss Religious Socialism. Reflecting on this period, Barth commented that, "Ragaz and I roared past one another like two express trains: he went out of the church, I went in."[111]

---

108. Mattmüller, *Leonhard Ragaz und der religiöse Sozialismus*, 223.

109. Ibid., 222.

110. Ragaz, *Leonhard Ragaz in seinen Briefen*, 2:89.

111. Busch, *Karl Barth*, 92.

Consummating the Split with Ragaz and Religious Socialism

In the wake of this exchange, Thurneysen arranged a meeting between Barth and Ragaz in November of 1916 in which the differences between the two were smoothed over. But their correspondence virtually ceased after this time.[112] When the first *Römerbrief* was published in December of 1918, Ragaz immediately saw himself as one of its targets. As he noted in his diary on January 1, 1919:

> Barth, *Römerbrief*: This is possibly the strongest assault against me so far, since it hits the center. Inspired by Kutter, misusing Blumhardt, full of poison, spiteful and arrogant. But thereby much of significance and depth. It is my tragedy that I always seem to be too late with my best. But still, I was in the service of GOD, he knows, and will not permit that I will take revenge. It was a strong blow to my heart, but I am recovering already.[113]

McCormack describes the whole of Barth's interpretation of Romans 13:1–7 as an *Auseinandersetzung* ("sharp debate or clash") with Ragaz and Religious Socialism.[114] Religious Socialism was "not the kingdom of God, but the old kingdom of man in new forms."[115] The issue for Barth was to clarify that God's kingdom was in fact *God's* kingdom. Only as such could real help come for humanity.

To this end, Barth employed the Blumhardts' eschatology to great effect. A detailed analysis of the Blumhardts' influence on the first *Römerbrief* has yet to be undertaken and will not be attempted here. But numerous commentators have noted their influence on it, especially their eschatology.[116] The Blumhardts' presence can also be detected in the key document that marked the end of his association with Religious

---

112. Ibid., 92.

113. Mattmüller, *Leonhard Ragaz und der religiöse Sozialismus*, 251.

114. McCormack, *Critically Realistic Dialectical Theology*, 173–80.

115. Karl Barth, *Der Römerbrief*, 1st ed., 24; as quoted in Mattmüller, *Leonhard Ragaz und der religiöse Sozialismus*, 248.

116. For example, see Gorringe, *Against Hegemony*, 37–47; Gollwitzer, "Kingdom of God and Socialism," in Hunsinger, *Karl Barth and Radical Politics*, 77–120; Dorrien, *Theology Without Weapons*, 61–62; Busch, *Karl Barth and the Pietists*, 30–35, 54. Though mentioned nowhere explicitly, the eschatology that McCormack outlines in *Romans I* bears the marks of the Blumhardts. See his *Karl Barth's Critically Realistic Dialectical Theology*, 141–55.

Socialism, the 1919 Tambach lecture, "The Christian's Place in Society."[117] This becomes especially evident if this document is read in conjunction with "Past and Future: Friedrich Naumann and Christoph Blumhardt,"[118] the memorial that Barth wrote to honor Christoph Blumhardt after his death on August 2, 1919. To these we now turn.

"PAST AND FUTURE: FRIEDRICH NAUMANN AND CHRISTOPH BLUMHARDT"

With the publication of the *Römerbrief*, Barth had broadened and deepened the new theological standpoint that he had begun to imagine in 1915. Even with this publication, Barth's theological endeavors did not cease. Both Busch and McCormack note that during the spring of 1919, Barth's radicalism was sharpened by his engagement with the thought of his brother, Heinrich. He wrote to Thurneysen that, "Heiner's lecture has become for me an impetus to keep much more powerfully in view the *totaliter aliter* of the Kingdom of God."[119] Barth's theological investigations would also continue in other directions over the summer. In June he wrote to Thurneysen of the many new discoveries he was making: "Overbeck's realism, Mencken's resistance to the Zeitgeist, Kierkegaard's protest against the reality of the world, and Blumhardt's thoughts on the second coming and the Spirit."[120] The source referred to here is not named explicitly, but it probably refers to Christoph Blumhardt's *Gedanken aus dem Reich Gottes*, written and published in 1895.[121] In our discussion of this source in chapter 3, we noted that Christoph subjected his father's hopes and thoughts to criticism in order to get at that which was of abiding significance in them for himself and the new direction he was going. Barth's reading of this material means that he was now familiar with the theological positions of the second and fourth phases of Blumhardt, though he would never have thought in such terms. Of great significance, however, is that during these two

---

117. In Karl Barth, *Word of God and the Word of Man*, 272–327.

118. In *Beginnings of Dialectical Theology*, 35–45.

119. Thurneysen, *Karl Barth—Eduard Thurneysen: Briefwechsel*, vol. 1, 325; as quoted in McCormack, *Critically Realistic Dialectical Theology*, 223. See idem, 218–26, for a comprehensive discussion of Heinrich's influence on Barth.

120. Thurneysen, *Karl Barth—Eduard Thurneysen: Briefwechsel*, vol. 1, 336.

121. Barth evidences knowledge and use of this work as early as April 1918. See ibid., 272–73.

periods Christoph gave his most pointed critique and emphasized most strongly the distinction between God and the world.

During this same period, Barth was also embroiled in controversy over his identification with Social Democracy. Many in the parish of Safenwil had been wary of Barth's engagement with socialism since his earliest lecture, "Jesus and the Movement for Social Justice."[122] But now, with the Russian Revolution of 1917, the end of the war and rise of the Sparticist movement in Germany, and the general strike in Switzerland in November 1918, Barth's identification with the workers had led many to leave the church. In August, an attempt was made to block a needed pay raise for Barth in the hopes of dissuading him from continuing as pastor. But Barth stood his ground, disavowing Bolshevism and Sparticism, while adamantly refusing to desert the cause of the working class in the village.[123] Undoubtedly, he was steeled in his resolve by word that Christoph Blumhardt had passed away on August 2.

Barth closed his August 10 sermon—the very same day that he defended his identification with the workers—with a postscript on Blumhardt. For Barth, "the only importance of this man was in this, that he had only one concern in his life: the coming of the Kingdom of God. He based his entire salvation and hope on it, that God will once more do something great toward man and his entire world, if we asked Him for it and when the time for it is at hand."[124] But this hope was not the mere idiosyncratic hope of Blumhardt, rather, "the goal remains unchanged, no, it comes closer and closer that Jesus is Victor and in the radiance of this coming victory we are standing today, blessed with a hope, in the midst of dark times."[125] His involvement in Social Democracy was merely a way "to put himself deeper and more sincerely into the movement of that Kingdom which is not of this world."[126] For Barth, Blumhardt's life and hope were a beacon and example, and if others wanted to know the reality to which he pointed, if they wanted to be caught up into the kingdom of God as it progressed through history in its hidden and

122. See the pointed exchange between Barth and a local factory owner over his 1911 lecture, "Jesus Christ and the Movement for Social Justice," in Hunsinger, *Karl Barth and Radical Politics*, 37–45.

123. See Busch, *Karl Barth*, 107.

124. Karl Barth, *Predigten 1919*, 290.

125. Ibid., 290.

126. Ibid., 292.

open manifestations, then "the reality [die Sache] of the Kingdom of God has to appear and become great again before our mind. For this we must again step into the light of the resurrection and the future of the Savior—rather, we must become aware that we are standing in this light. May God give us the eyes which are needed for this."[127]

Barth later re-wrote and expanded this in his essay, "Past and Future: Friedrich Naumann and Christoph Blumhardt." The essay should be seen both as a memorial to Blumhardt and as an attempt to set forth in simple terms how one could identify with the questions raised by Social Democracy and the workers movement, while simultaneously not allowing the gospel to become instrumental to party politics. From the first he makes it clear that he speaks of Naumann and Blumhardt, not as a disinterested observer, but as "a partisan," arguing for Blumhardt and against Naumann.[128] With this, continuity is established with his earlier "Action in Waiting for the Kingdom of God" in which he identified Blumhardt as one not merely to be heard, but to be emulated.

Naumann represents one who came close to the flame, only to pass it by.

> He found in it [the New Testament] a message so radical, so revolutionary, directed so precisely to a *transformation* of the world, that as a result the church's petty balance between God and world seemed to him to threaten to fly apart. He was then very near to the sacred fire, very near to understanding the God whom the church does not understand. He had an inkling of the transience of the present world, and that behind all its appearances a new world was striving to be born.[129]

In Barth's view, Naumann had discovered "the strange new world of the Bible," the coming and transforming kingdom of God. This discovery had pushed Naumann out into the world and into involvement with the social Christianity of Adolph Stöcker and the Evangelical Social Congress. But this involvement counter-intuitively robbed Naumann of his original insight. No longer was the world longing for transformation in the here and now, but merely amelioration through religion and social progress, and eventually only through the latter. With Naumann,

127. Ibid., 295.

128. Karl Barth, "Past and Future: Friedrich Naumann and Christoph Blumhardt," 35.

129. Ibid., 36.

it was no longer the pressing through of the great transformation of the kingdom of God that might be experienced in parable in the here and now, but the transformation of the here and now through the potentialities latent in creation and history.

Naumann abandoned the radical God of the New Testament who brings the kingdom, which "means the conversion of not only a few, but of all things, the renewal of the whole world, a transformation of life, in which not one stone can remain on another," for the god who "binds man with necessity to his nature and to the general laws of nature, which throws him into the struggle for existence, which, although not without religious and moral by-products, supplies the drive for self-preservation and racial instinct and teaches him to use them."[130] For Barth, Naumann represented the tragic greatness of the whole age, because he chose to grasp the possible and real, and thereby lost hold of the *real* reality.

Blumhardt, in contrast, believed and hoped in the God who comes to transform all things. "To believe in 'God' meant, for the two Blumhardts, to take this comprehensive hope seriously, more seriously than all other considerations; to regard and deal with everything on the basis of this hope; to place one's self and one's life in all particulars in the great light of this hope."[131] Christoph remained in the hope of his father, but expressed it in his day and for his generation.[132] The one thing that this hope meant for Christoph was that "a comprehensive attack on the bases of present-day society, culture, and church," was necessary.[133] There could be no compromise with "reality." Rather, hope for the kingdom of God meant a hope that the whole of human life would be transformed. But this led him in the counter-intuitive direction of affirming all of human life as the sight of God's coming kingdom. "Because he believed in God, he also believed in man, and because he believed in man, he also believed in the renewal of the world." All things became for him possible parables of the kingdom of God. Though not the thing itself,

130. Ibid., 38.

131. Ibid., 42.

132. This essay further confirms that Barth was by this time familiar with Christoph Blumhardt's 1895, *Gedenken aus dem Reich Gottes*, in which Christoph critiqued his father's hope. See chapter 3 for a discussion of this work.

133. Karl Barth, "Past and Future: Friedrich Naumann and Christoph Blumhardt," 42.

they were still to be affirmed. "'All that is perishable is but a parable,' but still a parable of the *imperishable*."[134]

Barth interprets Blumhardt's connection to Social Democracy not as primarily a commitment to the practical amelioration of working class ills, though such was not to be ruled out entirely, but rather as a commitment to the radical utopian hope of socialism. For "in the radicalism and the teleological thought of the socialists the parable of the Kingdom of God for our time," was to be discerned. As such—and this would also be a critical point in the Tambach lecture—it did not need to be "Christianized." Ordinary human endeavor and longing can be a parable of the kingdom of God, since no human work, not even Christian work, can bring the kingdom into being. It is, or rather becomes, a parable, because God appropriates it. There is no need to give it religious justification or grounding. As he had said it in the *Römerbrief*:

> Fulfill your duties without illusion, but no compromising of God! Payment of tax, but no incense to Caesar! Citizens initiatives and obedience but no combination of throne and altar, no Christian Patriotism, no democratic crusading. Strike and general strike, and streetfighting if needs be, but *no* religious justification and glorification of it! Military service as soldier or officer if needs be but under *no* circumstances army chaplain! Socialdemocratic but *not* religious socialist! The betrayal of the gospel is *not* part of your political duty![135]

The socialist hope is an instance of, "the sighing for redemption which runs through all of creation and mankind," and insofar as it bears correspondence in its hope for a new world, it comes near to the hope for the kingdom of God and deserves our attention and respect, but no further.[136] It goes without saying that such correspondence calls Christians to join the socialist cause, not to allow socialism to become the gospel, but to highlight those elements of hope and praxis that correspond to the coming kingdom of God. One cannot preach the gospel of socialism, only the gospel of the kingdom of God.

In the light of Blumhardt, engagement with socialism begins with the conviction that, just as in the New Testament, God is at work in the world engaged in "a victorious struggle, which must end with the

---

134. Ibid., 43.

135. *Römerbrief*, 390; as quoted in Gorringe, *Against Hegemony*, 46.

136. "Past and Future: Friedrich Naumann and Christoph Blumhardt," 42.

renewal of all things. The cheap assertion by all the churches, so often in contradiction to the facts, of the omnipotence and dominion of God *is* not true, but it *becomes* true through the victory of Jesus on earth."[137] Socialism was a sign of this and therefore a parable of the kingdom, not because of anything inherent in socialism or the socialists, but because it was God who sowed the longing in those who did not know him. It was Blumhardt's genius to recognize this movement of the living God and to follow it freely. "Blumhardt's secret was his endless movement between hurrying and waiting, between lively participation in the fullness of what is and astonished inner waiting for that which seeks to be through the power from on high. In his relation to God, he achieved also a vital relation to his own time."[138] The Tambach lecture, written in the same month as "Past and Future," can be read as Barth's attempt to give a more theoretical account of the way "in which the hurrying and the waiting, the worldly and the divine, the present and the coming, again and again met, were united, supplemented one another, sought and found one another," in Blumhardt's life and message.[139]

"The Christian's Place in Society" The 1919 Tambach Lecture

As devastating as the *Römerbrief* was for Ragaz, it was Barth's lecture at the Tambach conference in September 1919 that finalized his split with Religious Socialism. Though Blumhardt is mentioned only once in the lecture, his presence can be felt throughout. Following the witness of Scripture and the example of Blumhardt, Barth begins with the assumption that God *is* in the world, for the "Christian" who is in society is none other than the "Christ." The presence of Christ, of the kingdom of God, however, cannot be straightforwardly identified with human movements for righteousness. For,

> The divine is something whole, complete in itself, a kind of new and different something in contrast to the world. It does not permit of being applied, stuck on, and fitted in. It does not permit of being divided and distributed, for the very reason that it is more than religion. It does not passively permit itself to be

137. Ibid., 41.
138. Ibid., 44.
139. Ibid., 45.

used: it overthrows and builds up as it wills. It is complete or it is nothing.[140]

In face of the "wholly otherness of the kingdom of God," we must resist the temptation to secularize Christ by attaching "religious-" or "Christian-" in front of the various movements for social change. We must also resist the desire to "clericalize society" through merely re-conceiving the church as socialist in orientation, for this is still an attempt to change the world by recourse to possibilities within the world. In Barth's estimation, this way will eventually mean giving a vacuous Yes to the world as it is, which "certainly ends in the liberalism of Naumann."[141] What is needed is for Christians to be reminded again, and thereby to remind the world, of the way in which God has and is moving into the world. For only in this movement are the world and God brought together, only by divine action is the "Christian" in society.

What is this movement? Nothing other than the objective movement of the kingdom of God actualized in the life, death and resurrection of Jesus Christ:

> By "movement," to be sure, I do not mean either the socialistic movement, the social movement in religion, or the general, somewhat problematical, movement of so-called Christianity. I mean the movement from above, a movement from a third dimension, so to speak, which transcends and yet penetrates all these movements and gives them their inner meaning and motive; a movement which has neither its origin nor its aim in space, in time, or in the contingency of things, and yet is not a movement apart from others: I mean the movement of God in history or, otherwise expressed, the movement of God in consciousness, the movement whose power and import are revealed in the resurrection of Jesus Christ from the dead.[142]

The resurrection of the dead is not an idea, nor is it the "new inner life" of the pious Christian and therefore possibly a "figment of thought." Rather, "The *resurrection* of Jesus Christ from the dead is the power which moves both the world and us, *because* it is the appearance in our corporeality of a *totaliter aliter* constituted corporeality."[143] As such, it is

---

140. Barth, "The Christian's Place in Society," 277.

141. Ibid., 281.

142. Ibid., 283.

143. Ibid., 323.

a judgment on our world, on "society" as it is. But it is a judgment that reveals the true meaning of the "world" by recreating it, and therefore it infuses this world and our actions in it with relative value.

By associating the kingdom of God with the resurrection of Jesus Christ from the dead, Barth does three things. First, he definitively qualifies human work for the "kingdom of God." The "kingdom of God" had been a central motif or goal towards which Christian movements of various stripes believed they were moving, especially Religious Socialism. But to identify the "kingdom of God" with the "resurrection of the dead," was to seriously call into question the aspirations of such enterprises, because there is no imaginable way in which one could realistically describe practical political, social, or ethical, let alone religious work, as being capable of "raising the dead." Thus, Barth placed an insurmountable problem before such movements: was their work capable of bringing about the "resurrection of the dead?"

Second, by linking the resurrection of the dead and the kingdom of God, Barth does not leave all human action as bereft of meaning or purpose. Rather, he rooted both in the promise of God that had already received a historical confirmation in the resurrection of Jesus Christ. Barth takes the resurrection utterly seriously.[144] "God in history is *a priori* victory in history. This is the banner under which we march. This is the presupposition of our being here."[145] This was the great positive that outweighed the question mark placed against all human action. We are not capable of bringing the kingdom, but God is, is intent on doing so, *and* has already begun to do so.

This was not meant to be a mere triumphalist assertion. It should not be taken to mean that we can or should turn away from the seriousness of our predicament. Rather, "*we* live more deeply in the No than in the Yes, more deeply in criticism and protest than in naiveté, more deeply in longing for the future than in participation in the present."[146] In fact, the divine invasion of the world is sobering because it unmasks the "world as it is," both as a judgment and a promise. It reveals that the world's purported autonomy is really the power of death, because absolute autonomy assumes that things can exist "in and for themselves,"

144. It is this author's belief that if there is a center to Barth's theology then it is the resurrection of Jesus Christ.

145. Ibid., 297.

146. Ibid., 311–12.

and thus the "world as it is" must be resisted. But resistance is not futile, because the resurrection of the dead, the reclamation of creation for God's kingdom, also reveals that the true Origin of the individual and society are found in God. Thus, both the "whence and whither" of our existence find their coordinates in God's love, which means that even in the midst of the sober reality of death, God's life is triumphing.

Third, Barth comes into close proximity again with Blumhardt. As Blumhardt expressed it: "And yet, dear friends, what is the focal point, the real center of gravity in the kingdom of God? Resurrection—God revealing himself through resurrection."[147] For Blumhardt as for Barth, this meant that our only real hope was to come from God, not our efforts to bring His kingdom into the world. For, "Only the Risen One, coming from on high, will take the whole world in his hands and shake it until finally man can do naught else but submit and give honor to the Father in heaven!"[148] Our calling was first to let our "gaze penetrate so deeply into his being that you come to see in him the life and victory that is able to renew not only you but also the whole world." This doesn't rule out action in the world, for

> this costs a struggle in this world, and we still have to face all manner of toil and tribulation that may cause the outer man a little trouble. But all that is as nothing compared to the effects made by this truth: *Jesus lives!* If this stays *with* us the nations will yet come to this Jesus. The Spirit of God will so prepare everything that the whole creation will shout with joy as it shares in the life of the Risen One. Let your gaze penetrate so deeply into his being that you come to see in him the life and victory that is able to renew not only you but also the whole world.[149]

The same dialectical tension between judgment and hope produced by Barth's alignment of the kingdom of God with the resurrection of the dead is also evident in Blumhardt, though Barth has employed it in a different context and with more conceptual clarity than Blumhardt strove for.

---

147. Christoph Blumhardt, *Auswahl*, II:349 (unpublished translation by the Brüderhof and Plough Publishing).

148. Ibid., 349.

149. Christoph Blumhardt, *Auswahl*, II:350–51 (unpublished translation by the Brüderhof and Plough Publishing).

According to Barth, the restlessness exhibited by the various movements and revolutions was nothing other than a desire for the world no longer to exist in and for itself, but to be "brought into the glorious freedom of the children of God" (Rom 8:21, NIV). They were a "parable of the *imperishable*."[150] Thus, we can and must enter into these movements, but,

> We shall have to remember that the relation between God and the world is so thoroughly affected by the resurrection, and the place we have taken in Christ over against life is so unique and preeminent, that we cannot limit our conception of the kingdom to reform movements and social revolutions in the usual narrow sense. A protest against a particular social order, to be sure, is an integral moment in the kingdom of God, and there have been dark, blundering, godless times when this moment of protest was suppressed and hidden. But it is also a blundering and godless time when Christ is thought of as a Savior, or rather Judge, who up to that hour for some incomprehensible reason has kept himself concealed, and is now emerging into this sin-stricken world for the first time. The kingdom of God does not begin with our movements of protest. It is the revolution which is before all revolutions, as it is before the whole prevailing order of things.... Insight into the true transcendence of the divine origin of all things permits, or rather commands, us to understand particular social orders as being caused by God, by their connection with God. Naturally, we shall be led first not to a denial but to an *affirmation* of the world as it is.[151]

In the light of the world to come, the world as it is is reminded of its meaning and the goal of its life. For Barth this is particularly evident in the Synoptic parables, wherein the simple realities of life are left to stand as they are and are simultaneously illumined from within as parables of the kingdom of God. In the light of this our restlessness and No to the world as it is, cannot be absolute, but must always be seen as resonating with a deeper Yes, which both precedes and encapsulates the No. It precedes the No because the world is still the good creation of God, in all of the cultural, political, artistic, and other endeavors that we pursue. Thus with Blumhardt, one may welcome, "joyfully and hopefully, as signs and harbingers of the coming victory of Jesus Christ, everything

---

150. Barth, "Past and Future: Friedrich Naumann and Christoph Blumhardt," 43.

151. Barth, "The Christian's Place in Society," 299.

that seemed . . . to point toward the renewal of the world which was in preparation."[152] But our No must also be raised forcefully because, "*we live more deeply in the No than in the Yes, more deeply in criticism and protest than in naiveté, more deeply in longing for the future than in participation in the present.*"[153]

The reality of the resurrection, calls us to place ourselves within the same dialectical tension that it exhibits—affirmation, negation, and finally transformation—in hopeful longing. This means that in our social engagement,

> Simple cooperation within the framework of existing society is followed by radical and absolute opposition to that society. But as we had to guard ourselves against thinking that we could set up our overturned idols again by confining ourselves objectively to the world as it is, we must now fortify ourselves against expecting that our criticizing, protesting, reforming, organizing, democratizing, socializing, and revolutionizing—*however fundamental and thoroughgoing these may be*—will satisfy the ideal of the kingdom of God.[154]

We place ourselves in this tension—we work, we hasten, in the conviction that true action and work, true transformation, comes only from God. And that the same has already begun:

> We throw our energies into the most humdrum tasks, into the business nearest to hand, and also into the making of a new Switzerland and a new Germany, *for the reason* that we look forward to the New Jerusalem. We have the courage in this age both to endure limitations, chains, and imperfections and also to do away with them, *for the reason* that, enduring or not enduring, we are thinking of the new age in which the last enemy, death, the limitation *par excellence*, shall be destroyed. We enjoy the liberty of living naively with God or critically with God *for the reason* that in either case our eyes are open to the day of Jesus Christ, when God shall be all in all.[155]

It is the movement of God towards the world, God's own revolution, that should really have our attention, for if we are caught up in this move-

---

152. Barth, "Past and Future: Friedrich Naumann and Christoph Blumhardt," 43.
153. Barth, "The Christian's Place in Society," 311–12.
154. Ibid., 320.
155. Ibid., 323–24.

ment then our actions will correspond in radical obedience to God's action, which will lead us to a freedom to say both Yes and No. Again, one is reminded here of Barth's description of Blumhardt: "Blumhardt's secret was his endless movement between hurrying and waiting, between lively participation in the fullness of what is and astonished inner waiting for that which seeks to be through the power from on high."[156]

The practical result of this stance, this movement into which we must step, was that it radically disavowed all ideologies in favor of looking for God's work of revolution in order that we might participate in it. But looking for God's revolution was no simple matter; it required a careful attentiveness to the Scriptures and to the newspaper, to hear God speak. For, "What else can the Christian in society do but follow attentively the deeds of *God*?"[157] For Barth, to follow attentively the deeds of *God* meant learning to hear the Word of God in a new way. Thereby the primacy of theological and exegetical work was assured and the path into a "theology of the Word" shaped by the thought-form of a dialectical methodology, a path that Barth had been moving down since 1915, was reinforced and increased in momentum.

Ragaz, among others, understood Barth's Tambach lecture as undermining the revolutionary potential of Religious Socialism.[158] Barth's position, however, was not meant to undermine the revolutionary potential of Religious Socialism, but to problematize its very existence and the naïve attempt to identify one's political and social work directly with the work of *God*. Whether the latter was a fair interpretation of Ragaz is debatable,[159] but what should be evident is that Barth was seeking to carve out a position that he believed was faithful to the kingdom of God as he understood it and that resonated deeply with his interpretation of Christoph Blumhardt, an interpretation that was dominated by the themes of the second and fourth phases. This means that Barth's split from Religious Socialism did not mean a split from the Blumhardts. Rather, the splits with both Protestant Liberalism and Religious Socialism were made possible in large measure under the guidance of the theological themes and living examples of the two Blumhardts.

156. Barth, "Past and Future: Friedrich Naumann and Christoph Blumhardt," 44.

157. Karl Barth, "Der Christ in der Gesellschaft," in idem, *Das Wort Gottes und Die Theologie*, 37.

158. Mattmüller, *Leonhard Ragaz und der religiöse Sozialismus*, 255–56.

159. Ibid., 249–51.

Conclusion

In his study, *Revelation and Theology: An Analysis of the Barth-Harnack Correspondence of 1923*, H. Martin Rumscheidt gives an excellent and succinct description of what Barth found so appealing in the Blumhardts which is confirmed by our exposition of the essays we have discussed:

> What are the characteristic features in the thought of the Blumhardts that influenced Barth? These men were witnesses for God in so far as they wanted above all to call man's attention to God. Exactly for this reason they saw themselves compelled to attack the Christianity of their day. The tools, so to speak, of their witness to God were faithfulness to the message of the Bible and objectivity towards the 'object' of their proclamation: God as revealed in Christ and testified to us in the biblical witness. Thus, we see them involved in an eschatological dialectic which speaks of God in the flesh, of God present in the world and in history, of God who is to come, who is radically different from the world, who nevertheless entered into the world in an earthly form. It is a dialectic which states that God is understood and even found only through himself; his revelation in fact creates the ears and eyes with which he is heard and seen.[160]

Rumscheidt goes on to argue that, "it would be false to assume that Barth discovered eschatology and dialectic in the Blumhardts. Rather he saw in them kindred spirits, who in their confrontation with the Scriptures preached that the kingdom was coming and that we can only wait for it."[161] This is true. Barth did not discover eschatology or dialectic in the Blumhardts. However, Barth's approach to Scripture, new commitment to theological realism, understanding of eschatology and the kingdom of God, and even his understanding of the relationship between theology and political action after 1915 and at least up to the 1921 *Römerbrief* were all construed and deployed in terms that are so saturated with the images and themes of the Blumhardts, that the two Blumhardts have to be seen as far more than simply kindred spirits. They were indeed fellow pilgrims, but they were also forerunners and guides in showing Barth how to think about the living God who breaks into history to bring the kingdom to its fulfillment. What our analysis reveals is that Barth had internalized the Blumhardts' concerns and made them his own.

160. Rumscheidt, *Revelation and Theology*, 12–13.
161. Ibid., 13.

The Blumhardts' conviction that *die Sache*—i.e., "the content of the contents"—of Scripture was the living and active God who has invaded his world in a decisive fashion in Jesus Christ, through whose resurrection the kingdom of God is now present in the world working its way towards the final *telos* of the redemption of humanity and the whole cosmos, became Barth's own inner theological standpoint and presupposition after April 1915. As Barth moved forward, deepening and extending his theological and biblical investigations, his conviction that this standpoint was in fact the standpoint of the New Testament would be confirmed and a host of other theological interlocutors would join the chorus in affirming the original conviction bequeathed to him by the Blumhardts.[162]

This conviction, however, was no mere standpoint. Rather, it was a starting point that was always already in motion and one of the key endeavors that Barth can be seen attempting to do during this period is to give an account of the movement of the living God—*die Sache* of Scripture—in relation to theological, kerygmatic, and political work. Here again, as in the basic conviction of *what die Sache* of Scripture was, the Blumhardts, especially Christoph, can be seen to have played a pivotal role in seeking to show *how die Sache* of the kingdom of God moved in Scripture and the world. Whether in trying to get at the thought form of the New Testament and the reality to which it points as well as the way of knowing presupposed in it—as can be seen in "The Strange New World Within the Bible"—or in trying to get at the way in which the reality of the kingdom of God both delimits but also founds our social and political engagement—as can be seen in "The Christian in Society"—the Blumhardts' life and thought were the pattern and guides and were certainly the most critical of the many interlocutors that Barth was in dialogue with during this period.

We now come full circle to the claim of Emil Brunner with which we began our chapter: "The real origin of the Dialectic Theology is to be

---

162. An example of this can be seen in Barth's brief engagement with the thought of J. T. Beck. I agree with Eberhard Busch's assessment, over against Claudia Hake and Tjarko Stadtland, that what Barth found appealing in Beck was only that which resonated with the Blumhardts' thought. For Busch see his *Karl Barth and the Pietists*, 34. For Hake, see *Der Bedeutung der Theologie Johann Tobias Beck*, 217. For Stadtland, see *Eschatologie und Geschichte*, 43–51. This is confirmed by the fact that when Barth moved away from Beck, he did not move away from Blumhardt. This is particularly evident in Barth's 1920 essay, "Unsettled Questions for Theology Today," 55–73.

traced, however, not to Kierkegaard, but to a more unexpected source, to a place still farther removed from the main theological thorough-fare—to the quiet Boll of the two Blumhardts."[163] Notwithstanding the role of Religious Socialism, especially Kutter, our investigation supports the truth of this claim as it relates to the early development of Barth's theology. The Blumhardts' realistic eschatology and concrete hope for the kingdom of God that had already entered into history through the resurrection of Jesus Christ from the dead and was moving forward in history, became a dominant motif of Barth's theology during this early period.

No less important was their ability to both "wait and hasten" to-wards the subject matter that they found in Scripture: (*die Sache des Reiches Gottes*). This mode of "waiting and hastening" became the start-ing point for the kind of faithful "following after" of the thought-form of the New Testament that Barth became convinced theology should seek to emulate.

Not to be forgotten is Christoph's critical clarification that only "God is God," which contained both a word of judgment against our religious and political attempts to grasp at God and bring the kingdom into the world, but also a word of promise that in fact though the way is barred from here to there, it is not barred from there to here. That "God is God" means resurrection from the dead, the kingdom of God, and therefore a relative affirmation of our work and witness in the here and now and the promise that in spite of darkness, the day is not far off.

Thus, the Blumhardts hope for the kingdom of God was a major source for Barth as he sought out a new direction for his theology. He made their concerns his own because he viewed their concerns as syn-onymous with the concerns of the New Testament witness. But was the influence of the Blumhardts' merely episodic? Did Barth finally discard it as he later moved forward into what is sometimes referred to as his "dogmatic phase"? We will seek an answer to that question in our next chapter.

---

163. Brunner, "Continental European Theology," 141.

The Significance of the Blumhardts for Barth's Dogmatic Theology

Introduction

"He will reign." These words of Christoph Blumhardt were the last comments that Barth spoke to his faithful friend and theological compatriot, Eduard Thurneysen, on the night of December 9, 1968.[1] Later that night, Barth would slip away peacefully, dying in his sleep. It seems fitting that Barth's life-long friendship with Thurneysen would end with a quotation from the prophet of Bad Boll, with which both had initially begun their theological journey. After their 1915 meeting, Barth and Thurneysen launched on a journey of discovery that was fueled in large measure by the kerygmatic witness of both Blumhardts. As our last chapter showed, from 1916 to 1919 the themes and insights of the Blumhardts were of central concern to Barth as he sought to re-imagine his theological and political commitments. After his 1921 appointment as Honorary Professor of Reformed Theology at the University of Göttingen, a vast field of theological enquiry was opened to Barth that would lead him in new directions. Eventually Barth would grow to become the most important and influential Protestant theologian since F. D. E. Schleiermacher (1768–1834). His *Church Dogmatics* would be hailed as one of the greatest theological achievements of the twentieth century.

It is only natural that the concerns of the Blumhardts that he had adopted as his own after 1915 would be modified, clarified, extended, and corrected by other theological interlocutors as Barth grew into his own.

1. Eberhard Busch, *Karl Barth*, 498.

His work at Göttingen (1921–1925) and later at Münster (1925–1930), Bonn (1930–1935), and Basel (1935–1962) was comprised of extensive engagement with the history of theology (especially Reformation theology), continuing work in New Testament exegesis, and especially the development of his own creative dogmatic theology, which came to mature expression in the great *Church Dogmatics*, published in 13 volumes from 1932 to 1967. Concurrent with this work was Barth's continual and lively engagement with contemporary theological, political, and cultural debates of all kinds. Anyone familiar with the course and development of his life is bound to be astonished at the wealth and breadth of Barth's interests and interlocutors, both contemporary and historical.

What is just as surprising is that the Blumhardts, whose theology and concerns might appear on the surface to be naïve and provincial, especially when compared with the likes of a Calvin or Luther, would have remained of any great interest to someone like Barth. In distinction with some of the key interlocutors Barth had engaged during his early theological development (like, for instance, J. T. Beck), however, the presence of the theological themes of the Blumhardts would remain more or less intact throughout his long career even if they were placed into a larger theological context.[2] Their influence can be detected in various contexts with different modifications throughout Barth's *oeuvre*.[3] Barth's final remark to Thurneysen, therefore, was no mere homage to those with whom they had begun their theological journey. In fact, he had revisited the key themes of both Blumhardts' in *Church Dogmatics* IV/3 and in the unpublished lecture fragment *The Christian Life*, both of which Barth had worked on during the late 1950s and early 1960s.

In the former, Barth concludes his exposition of the doctrine of reconciliation under the Blumhardts' watchword "Jesus is Victor!", while in the latter, Barth expounds the ethics of reconciliation under the other key Blumhardtian watchword, "Thy Kingdom Come!" In both sections,

---

2. For discussion of the waning significance of J. T. Beck, see Claudia Hake, *Der Bedeutung der Theologie Johann Tobias Beck*, 277–80.

3. Key texts where the Blumhardts' influence on Barth can be detected, which will need further examination, include but may not be limited to the following: Karl Barth, "Unsettled Questions for Theology Today," 55–73; *The Epistle to the Romans*, 1st and 2nd editions; *The Resurrection of the Dead*; and, '*Unterricht in der christlichen Religion*', vol. 3.

Barth explicitly acknowledges that his own independent position has been substantially shaped by the Blumhardts' witness and theology:

> What has been presented here rests on personal exegetical reflection and theological deliberation. If something is now being said about the Blumhardts, it is not with the intention of summoning them as subsequent star witnesses for what has been developed. In fact, it could not have been stated and developed as it has without the impulse they gave and their influence through other mediations and modifications.[4]

It is also evident, however, that in this late material the Blumhardts' kerygmatic witness has been placed into a larger theological context and idiom. Thus, as will be seen, Barth integrates their insights into the larger matrix of his theological vision and does so through the very different idiom and structure of dogmatic theology. These factors led to some distinctions between Barth's understanding and exposition of the Blumhardtian themes and the original meaning of the same.

It is the overwhelming similarity and continuity between Barth and the Blumhardts, however, that is so striking. A reading of these documents, especially *CD* IV/3, reveals multiple Blumhardtian themes. Not only is the "Jesus is Victor!" motif present, with its identification of Jesus Christ with the kingdom of God and the resurrection of Jesus as the first advent and revelation of the kingdom that is present in history pressing towards the *telos* of God's universally present kingdom, but so also is the elder Blumhardt's hope for the outpouring of the Holy Spirit, which is the form of the presence and struggle of the advent of the crucified and victorious Christ during the interim time before the final and cosmic advent (*CD* IV/3.1, 274–367). The vocation of humanity and the church are both expounded under the concept of witness and hope in such a way that the elder Blumhardt becomes an example of the vocation of witness and hope that is not, because it cannot be, aimed merely at individual or even ecclesial blessedness, but which points beyond to the witness and hope for the coming of the cosmic kingdom of God that will transform the whole earth (*CD* IV/3.2, 554–614, 762–795, esp. 570, 598–99, 792–93). Thus, the liberation enacted by the living Jesus

---

4. Karl Barth, *The Christian Life: Church Dogmatics IV/4, Lecture Fragments*, 256–57. Hereafter abbreviated as *CL*. Though written and developed as a part of the *Church Dogmatics*, these lectures were never revised, expanded, and prepared by Barth for publication, but were only published posthumously in 1976.

Christ which confronts the Christian in the form of a summons draws the Christian out into the world to struggle for the kingdom of God, which does and will one day encompass the whole inhabited earth. At the same time, following both the elder and the younger Blumhardt, the hope for that which comes from beyond cannot and should not diminish hope for penultimate signs of the imminent coming kingdom (*CD* IV/3.2, 935–39). Furthermore, seen under the rubric of "vocation," the Christian life and the witness of the community are rendered as personal and communal participation in the dynamic and historical reality that "Jesus is Victor!" (*CD* IV/3.1, 216; *CD* IV/3.2, 647–80, esp. 663), and the witness of the community includes practical diaconal service that moves in the direction of holistic ministry, just as the elder and younger Blumhardt had imagined and developed (*CD* IV/3.2, 892–93).

A few commentators have noted the palpable presence of the Blumhardts in the final volumes of the *Church Dogmatics*.[5] Even though many of the themes mentioned above are modified by Barth, none of them is substantially changed, such that the later volumes could be said to be saturated by the themes and concerns of the Blumhardts. In view of their ubiquitous presence in this later material, we will concern ourselves primarily with an exposition of the key sections related to "Jesus is Victor!" and "Thy Kingdom Come!" in an attempt to show that Barth was influenced substantially by the Blumhardts' witness even into his so-called "dogmatic phase."

Before we turn to these sections in the late *Church Dogmatics*, we will pause to consider the critical independence that Barth showed vis-à-vis the Blumhardts. The insights gained from their theology early on were a catalyst for Barth in his move away from Protestant Liberal theology in search of a new theological direction. Their insights had given to Barth a certain freedom vis-à-vis the many theological traditions that he had known during his early education. This critical freedom would remain as Barth engaged broader circles of contemporaries, but also as he delved more deeply into the rich history of Christian theology. Barth was always able to maintain a certain critical independence vis-à-vis his most cherished interlocutors, whether contemporary or historical. This was no less true in the case of the Blumhardts. Barth also exercised the same loyal freedom in relation to the Blumhardts themselves as he

5. See, for example, Gorringe, *Against Hegemony*, 224, 238–43.

did toward others, such that at key points he was able to subject their thought to critique and emendation.

In what follows, we will explore one such episode. Our primary goal is to highlight that Barth's loyalty to the Blumhardts thought was always under the proviso that they could be followed only where their thought was able to get at the subject matter at hand. When their thought did not adequately address the subject matter, it could be critiqued, combined with other insights, or even rejected. Our secondary goal, however, is to show that this critical freedom was in fact inspired by the example of the Blumhardts' themselves, as seen especially in the attitude of Christoph towards his father's legacy.

Barth's Critical Independence vis-à-vis the Blumhardts

Preliminary Remarks

As we noted in chapter 4, Barth early on appropriated the Blumhardts' conviction that the Scriptures point to the living God breaking into this world to bring to completion the renewal, renovation, and recreation of the world that was definitively inaugurated in the death and resurrection of Jesus Christ. "The Strange New World Within the Bible," is nothing other than the new world present in the old as evidenced by the acts of the living God *there* and *then*, which are extending themselves into the *here* and *now*, and moving forward to their final cosmic dénouement, the kingdom of God.

What we want to highlight here is that the Blumhardts were and remained important to Barth for no other reason than that he believed that their position and movement of thought represented an authentic recovery of the central dynamic of the New Testament. That the kingdom of God, embodied in Jesus Christ, was, is, and will be present in history as it moves towards its final end, the definitive extension and revelation of the transformation of the cosmos; that this reality cannot be controlled by human action, thought, or theological construction, but can only be hoped for within the same; and that the kingdom of God is *God's* kingdom, present, on the move, sometimes hidden, other times in the open, and yet never the *result* of human action, precisely because the ultimate *sign* and *power* of the kingdom was the resurrection of Jesus Christ. All of these insights could be affirmed by Barth, because he believed they were and could be confirmed by an authentic and careful reading of Scripture and reflection on "die Sache" (i.e., "the reality") found therein.

The Blumhardts' insight that "Jesus is Victor" can be affirmed, because "in content, far from having the character of a new revelation, it merely sums up and succinctly formulates many New Testament sayings behind which there may be seen either directly or indirectly the central witness of the whole of the New Testament."[6] Barth believed that the Blumhardts' experiences and witness threw light on an element of the New Testament that had receded to great extent as a theme for Christian reflection and practice. At the same time, their witness was not authenticated by their own persons or even their personal history, but rather, received authentication in the light of the living Jesus Christ to which Scripture pointed.

Thus, though the personal magnetism and courage of the younger Blumhardt and the extraordinary gentleness and tenacity of the elder Blumhardt were important, they could not be decisive for Barth. They spoke "with authority and not as the scribes," because "both of them constantly pointed beyond themselves and beyond everything connected with Möttlingen and Boll, which from the very first stood under some threat in this regard."[7] Likewise, what Barth believed about the events that had purportedly occurred at Möttlingen and Bad Boll—and there is reason to believe that he viewed them as a form of *Sage*, much like the New Testament accounts of Jesus's miracles[8]—is beside the

6. *CD* IV/3.1, 168.

7. *CL*, 258.

8. There is no single instance or textual reference that one can point to that would substantiate this claim. It can be partially substantiated, however, if one takes all of Barth's reflections on the Blumhardtian stories together. For Barth's reflections and comments on the events at Möttlingen see his, "Past and Future: Friedrich Naumann and Christoph Blumhardt," in *The Beginnings of Dialectical Theology*, 40–41; "Blumhardt," in *Protestant Theology in the Nineteenth Century*, 644–53; *CD* IV/3.1, 168–71; *CL*, 256–60.

There are at least 3 reasons to believe that Barth did approach the Blumhardt stories in a realistic and matter-of-fact way: 1) in none of the discussions does Barth ever question the historical reality of the purported events at Möttlingen and later at Bad Boll. It is true that in his reflections he allows for legitimate psychosomatic, and even mythological interpretation of these events, but these forms of interpretation are never pursued by Barth nor would they be decisive for him if he held to them. What is decisive in every context is the spiritual meaning of the events; 2) in every case Barth is carepoint. It was rather the truth and reality to which these events pointed, or perhaps put more carefully, it was the interpretation given to these events in the light of the New Testament and the subsequent reflection on the New Testament itself in the light of these events that proved their authenticity for Barth.

When Barth exercised a critical glance towards the Blumhardts themselves, he was affirming that his primary allegiance was not to a specific theological tradition, but to the living Christ who was, is and will be the kingdom of God. What Barth's later theological reflection on the Blumhardts reveals is that from the very beginning their insights were situated in a larger theological context and matrix that was oriented fundamentally towards the reality of the living Jesus Christ who is authoritatively attested in Holy Scripture. That Barth had come to the conviction that theology should be guided by the presence of the risen Christ under the influence of the Blumhardts' was important, but it did not exempt their thought from being corrected by the reality to which they pointed. Thus, their theological insights could be subjected

---

ful, with the sole exception of the early reflection on Christoph Blumhardt, to recount the stories and events in detail. As Barth notes in his lecture on the elder Blumhardt, "The life of Blumhardt must partially be regarded also as a portrayal of the theological matter with which we are concerned here" (*Protestant Theology in the New Testament*, 644). It is highly questionable that Barth, the "critical realist," would have referred to and invested these stories with any deep theological meaning if they were not rooted in some sort of realistic "historicality." That is, it may be put forth as entirely plausible that Barth would have allowed the category of "saga" to be applied to these events. Barth highlights Blumhardt's own reticence at naming the case of Gottliebin Dittus as a case of demonic possession to emphasize that this interpretation is almost forced on Blumhardt by the phenomenon itself, further adding to the plausibility that the events portrayed in the stories deserve to be taken seriously; 3) the real point of these events though, is their spiritual and theological meaning. Barth continues to recount the stories precisely because they throw light on the dynamics within the New Testament. As experiences, they represent a recovery of the insight that "Jesus is Victor," that the living Jesus is in fact at war with the powers and principalities which are both human and spiritual. The implication is that the portrayal of Jesus' miracles in the New Testament are not in need of de-mythologization, but of re-interpretation. Their significance lies in the fact that God cares for the real needs of humanity. That salvation is not for the soul only, but for the whole person and likewise for the whole cosmos. These insights and the realistic theological force that they carried for Barth and the Blumhardts would hardly stand if the events that inspired them were merely "fables."

For a masterful discussion of Barth's conception of the nature of what might called theological history (i.e., the historical nature of the resurrection, etc.), see MacDonald, *Strange New World within the Bible*.

to critique, change, and emendation in the light of the living presence of the kingdom of God, Jesus Christ, whose fundamental form is attested in the New Testament. At the same time, Christian discourse from other theological traditions could also be subjected to critique from this vantage point. One example of this critical independence can be seen in Barth's reflections on the eternity of God in *Church Dogmatics* II/1.

Barth's Critical Glance towards the Blumhardts' in CD II/1

In his closing comments on the four-hundredth anniversary of the death of John Calvin, Barth remarked about the great Swiss Reformer:

> If today, after the experience we have had of his life's work in its historical shape, and after a renewed return to the sources and origins to which he pointed so insistently, one can think and speak with him only by going beyond him in important areas, then one can fruitfully go *beyond* him only by thinking and speaking *with him* in the direction in which he pointed and do so looking back to the days of his work, his struggles and sufferings, in great reverence and great gratitude.[9]

The loyal freedom expressed here towards Calvin, one of the most important influences on his theology, is similar to that which Barth displayed towards the Blumhardts. To highlight this fact, we will explore the critical comments that Barth directed at the Blumhardts' in the context of his discussion of God's eternity in *Church Dogmatics* II/1. What will be evident is that Barth's free relationship to the Blumhardts was in certain respects grounded in the pattern that the Blumhardts themselves exhibited towards their own thought, as we have highlighted above regarding Christoph Blumhardt's *Gedanken aus dem Reich Gottes*.

THE CONTEXT: GOD'S TRIUNE ETERNITY

The context of Barth's critical comments is his discussion of God's eternity in *Church Dogmatics* II/1. In paragraph 31 on "The Perfections of the Divine Freedom," Barth argues for a three-fold conception of God's eternity, which, though qualitatively different from time, is not barred from taking time into itself. In the characteristic Christocentric style of

---

9. Barth, "Thoughts on the Anniversary of Calvin's Death," in *Fragments Grave and Gay* by Karl Barth, 110.

the *Church Dogmatics*, Barth argues that God can and does take time into himself in his own personal self-defining act, Jesus Christ:

> In Jesus Christ it comes about that God takes time to Himself, that He Himself, the eternal One, becomes temporal, that He is present for us in the form of our own existence and our own world, not simply embracing our time and ruling it, but submitting Himself to it, and permitting created time to become and be the form of His eternity.[10]

In the Incarnation God takes time into himself allowing it to, "become and be the form of His eternity." God's eternity, therefore, is not a place or container in which God exists, it is not the pure duration that knows no beginning, middle, and end, a duration that God must endure. Rather it is the mode of God's existence in which origin, movement, and goal are not in conflict but are known and exist in simultaneity. It is pure duration, but not to the exclusion of origin, movement, and end. Eternity is not, therefore, strictly speaking, non-temporality. Rather, eternity is God's temporality in which the contradiction of created time does not exist, the contradiction between our beginning, middle, and end. This divine temporality is the triune God.

God's ability to take time into himself as actualized in the Incarnation of Jesus Christ is rooted in his own prior triune existence as Father, Son, and Holy Spirit. In his eternal life as Father, Son, and Holy Spirit, origin, movement, and goal are eternally one, and yet "there is a before and an after. God is once and again and a third time, without dissolving the once-for-allness, without destroying the persons or their special relations to one another, without anything arbitrary in this relationship or the possibility of its reversal."[11] Eternity as the mode of existence of the triune God, has its own temporality, its own before and after, only these are not in conflict. In the wake of this christological- and trinitarian-structured understanding of eternity, Barth can describe God's eternity in the three-fold form of pre-temporality, supra-temporality, and post-temporality. Through this description, eternity can be seen as the primordial form of time, or rather, time can be seen as the form of eternity that lacks the simultaneity and harmony of the eternal triune God.

10. *CD* II/1, 616.
11. *CD* II/1, 615.

Of importance to our discussion is Barth's expressed desire to do justice to all three forms of the divine eternity. His exposition of these three forms of time is accompanied by an historical excurses on the recent Protestant theologies that have highlighted one or another of the three-fold forms of eternity at the expense of the others.

THE HISTORICAL EXCURSES

According to Barth, during the Reformation justice was done to the dimension of pre-temporality in the form of the Reformers' (especially Calvin) preoccupation with the doctrine of election and divine providence. This led to a healthy affirmation of the God who existed before all time, and who as such determined the creature's life in an objective fashion quite apart from any co-operation on its part. This fashioning indicates that history does in fact move in a certain direction, a direction that in its most decisive sense is determined by its origin, the eternal and living God.

Though, in Barth's estimation, this was a good and positive affirmation that should be made on the basis of the witness of Scripture, it failed to say all that was necessary, and was therefore too one-sided. And this one-sidedness was not without its problems: "But in this theology time itself in its duration, and human life in time with its responsibilities, problems and possibilities, came to have the position of a kind of appendix, though one that was expressed with force."[12] In other words, Barth affirms that the Reformation preoccupation with God's pre-temporality tended to construe remaining history in the shadow of Stoic fate, in which a real and dynamic relationship between God and humanity in the here and now was made deeply problematic. God's ongoing supra-temporal relationship to the world and history was lost sight of in favor of a relationship that could only be understood from the perspective of a primeval and—from a creaturely vantage—obscure decision. Furthermore, Barth notes that because of their interest in the pre-temporal dimension of God's eternity, the Reformers showed little or no interest in God's post-temporality or eschatology, relegating it to the end of the appendix of the human experience of time.

In contrast, the theology of the eighteenth and nineteenth century was concerned above all with God's supra-temporality, almost to the to-

---

12. *CD* II/1, 632.

tal exclusion of pre-temporal and post-temporal eternity. "Too much attention was now paid to man in time, his needs and problems, but above all his positive possibilities."[13] This was a reaction to the former way of conceiving the relationship between time and eternity and therefore of understanding the nature of God's eternity. No longer was speculation about the pre-temporal "divine decrees" of election considered legitimate. One could only affirm that the eternal God was now present in time in the human soul. In this case, the preoccupation was with God's actual presence in the here and now, to the exclusion of God's eternal constancy from the beginning and towards a final end. To Barth, the result of this was to open the door to conceiving of God's eternity merely as an infinite and therefore unending form of the experience of creaturely time, which led to the cul-de-sac of Feuerbach and the anthropologizing of theology.

Finally, with the end of the nineteenth-century interest in God's post-temporality reemerged in response to the preceding generations. Barth identifies the Blumhardts and the work of Johannes Weiss and Albert Schweitzer with this more recent emphasis. The Blumhardts' hope in the coming Christ placed God's post-temporality back into the center, and was polemically aimed at Pietism's so-called concern for the individual soul's experience of God in the here and now. The present Christ is the Christ who is *coming*, and he is coming for the *whole cosmos*, which includes all of creation and all of humanity and not just the individual soul.

In Barth's view, however, this new emphasis on God's post-temporality was not sufficiently sharp because the elder Blumhardt had concentrated less on the final coming of Christ—in which he really did place his hope—and more on the "time before the end" during which the Holy Spirit would be poured out and signs of the kingdom would reemerge in the form of the miraculous. Thus, in Barth's view, the Blumhardtian hope was more about "signs of the kingdom" in the here and now that were harbingers of the future world, rather than a concern about the future world itself.[14] This required, in Barth's view, a further intensifica-

---

13. *CD* II/1, 632.

14. Though questionable, this is not an entirely unfair critique of the elder Blumhardt's approach. Blumhardt's hope for real irruptions in the here and now, however, was predicated on the real longing for the final coming of the kingdom of God, which had already invaded the world in the person of Jesus Christ. Though Blumhardt

tion in the direction of post-temporality. Therefore, in the 1920s Barth took up the Blumhardts' emphasis on God's post-temporality and "tried to make a fresh start at what we saw to be the original point of departure of the elder Blumhardt. . . . We felt compelled to press beyond all temporal expectations whether individual, cultural or political; even beyond what necessarily seemed to us to be the foreground view of the elder Blumhardt—to the view of a pure and absolute futurity of God and Jesus Christ as the limit and fulfillment of all time."[15]

The fruit of this new consideration of the relationship between time and eternity, between our time and God's post-temporality was, in Barth's view, embodied in the eschatology of the second *Römerbrief*, which, though it had a great deal to say about the crisis that time is plunged into by the presence of the End in time, could not speak about the end of time and the coming of the kingdom as such.

> The result was that we could not speak about the post-temporality of God in such a way as to make it clear that we actually meant to speak of God and not of a general idea of limit and crisis. That we had only an uncertain grip of the matter became apparent, strangely enough, in those passages of the exposition in which I had to speak positively about the divine future and hope as such. It emerged in the fact that although I was confident to treat the far-sidedness of the coming kingdom of God with absolute seriousness, I had no such confidence in relation to its coming as such. . . . The 'last' hour, the time of eternity, was not an hour which followed time. Rather at every moment in time we stood before the frontier of all time, the frontier of 'qualified time.'[16]

This perspective was and remained true but it was not and could not be the whole truth. In Barth's view, it resulted in the loss of the teleological

---

himself was concerned with the foreground of the final *parousia*, that concern was ultimately linked to and rooted in the real conviction that the final appearing of Jesus was assured. As I noted in fn. 125 of chapter 2, Blumhardt's reticence of speaking about the final appearing had more to with his own context within the Württemberg tradition, which, shaped by J. A. Bengel, had tended to over-describe and thereby over-emphasize the final coming, thus emptying the present of real hope and transformation. It could be argued, therefore, that the elder Blumhardt sought to do justice to the past, present and future dimensions of time and eternity, but that his context and experiences limited his ability to express the same.

15. *CD* II/1, 634.
16. *CD* II/1, 635.

movement of time towards a real end and therefore, any real hope in history was emptied of its power because it was no longer based on the real coming of a real end. Ironically for Barth, his conception had managed to reinstate the supra-temporality of God as the crisis of creaturely time and thus threatened to reduce God's eternity to the human experience of an existential crisis.

The Basis of Barth's Self-Criticism

In brief, the self-critical assessment that Barth offers here is funded by his conviction that the reality to which Scripture points is not a principle, but the living and active God who is known in Jesus Christ:

> The above-mentioned over-emphases and omissions in relation to this three-fold form are perhaps connected with the fact that it was thought possible to advance and maintain the idea of a pre-temporal, supra-temporal or post-temporal as such. Involuntarily, then, thinkers became slaves of a systematization and finally a secularization, forgetting that under all these conceptions they were really dealing with the living God, and with the person of God, which cannot be tied to concepts of this kind or exhausted by them. The unity of the three forms of eternity is guaranteed if here too the knowledge of God is the knowledge of the personal God.[17]

The task of the theologian is to follow the movement and thought-form of God's own self-disclosure, which finds its definitive attestation in the New Testament and is identified with the present and living Jesus Christ.[18] As we noted at the beginning of this section, Barth's re-conceptualization of eternity as pre-temporality, supra-temporality, and post-temporality sought to do justice to this reality by taking seriously the Trinitarian being and act of God and the reality of God's invasion of the world as the Son of God become Son of Man. Thus, his reflections on God's eternity attempted to follow the movement of the biblical witness regarding the constancy of the life of God which the Trinitarian dogma expressed as including a non-contradictory and harmonious

---

17. *CD* II/1, 639.

18. "Throughout his life, Barth wanted to be led not by a methodological principle but only by the theological 'material in motion'" (Sauter, "Shifts in Karl Barth's Thought," 123).

beginning, middle, and end. God can and does take to himself time in the Incarnation because he has and is temporality within himself.

Barth ends his self-critical reflections by noting, "it was most fortunate that in part at least a new consciousness of the theology of Luther and Calvin was successfully linked, before it was too late, with the awakening to eschatology which proceeded from Blumhardt and the exegesis of the New Testament. Without detriment, then, to the necessary recognition of God's post-temporality, His pre-temporality was again perceived, though it had been neglected in the 18th and nineteenth centuries no less than His post-temporality."[19] If one reads between the lines, it becomes evident that Barth's realization of possible one-sidedness occurred because the different forms of God's eternity as they are rendered in the different theological traditions were not able to do justice to the one reality of Jesus Christ, who is the same yesterday, today and forever. However true they were in themselves, they were not adequate expressions of the fullness of the eternity of the living God to which Scripture points. Therefore, they must be modified through combination with other perspectives. In this case Barth understood himself as having combined the Blumhardts' conceptions and understanding of the post-temporality of God with the Reformers emphasis on God's pre-temporality and the nineteenth century's understanding of God's supra-temporality. By so doing, these perspectives were situated in a larger context than the individual theological traditions out of which they arose and were made to witness to the one living reality that is not static because alive. Barth believed that this new combination was able to render an understanding of God's eternity that was dynamic, and yet included a sense that there was real direction and real movement towards a real end even in the eternity of God.

Reading With—in Order to Go Beyond—the Blumhardts

What this has to do with the Blumhardtian influence on Barth is that their influence and insights remained important only insofar as they served to get at "die Sache" to which Scripture pointed. When it failed to do so, as all human words and actions inevitably do, it could be corrected, emended, or even rejected. Barth turned this same critical lens on other theologians and theological traditions that were important

19. *CD* II/1, 637.

interlocutors for him, like, for instance, the Reformers. But by so doing, Barth was reading the Blumhardts, and others, in a way that was consistent with the Blumhardts' understanding of themselves. Barth was certainly attuned to this aspect of the Blumhardts.

In his 1895 *Gedanken aus dem Reich Gottes*20—which we discussed in chapter 3 and which Barth read sometime in 1918–1919[21]—Christoph Blumhardt sought to explain the new developments in his thought that had begun to raise concerns among his friends during the early 1890s. These new developments would bear substantial fruit by the late 1890s, including his move into Social Democracy.

In the *Gedanken*, Christoph's aim was to show that his new orientation was deeply consonant with the innermost concerns of his father, even if he did not express it in the same fashion that his father had. To accomplish this, Christoph critiqued his father's hope in the light of the reality of the kingdom of God to which his father had pointed. His critique was aimed primarily at the thought structures by which his father sought to explain and express the new insights gained through the Möttlingen *Kampf* and awakening to the wider audience of the extended Bad Boll community.

Christoph believed that by doing so his father had filled an old wineskin (i.e., traditional Church doctrine) with new wine (i.e., the recovered hope for the kingdom of God). Such was bound to cause the progress of the kingdom of God to be hampered. Thus, Christoph's aim was to retain the central and basic insights of his father [i.e., 1) that the kingdom of God had entered into history in a decisive fashion with the death and resurrection of Jesus; 2) that it was progressing through history sometimes in a hidden and sometimes in an evident fashion; 3) that the vocation of humanity was to struggle alongside of the God who was at war with the powers of darkness, bringing His kingdom into fruition], but to drop certain traditional elements [i.e., 1) like traditional forms of Christian worship and ecclesial organization; 2) and some traditional doctrines like belief in a literal eternal hell which contradicted God's eternal love and the universal hope for the kingdom of God] so that the cosmic reality of the kingdom of God would progress through the world and witness to the same would not be hampered. He would

---

20. Recently republished in facsimile form under the title, *Damit Gott Kommt: 'Gedanken aus dem Reich Gottes'*.

21. See Thurneysen, *Karl Barth—Eduard Thurneysen: Briefwechsel*, 1:336.

not allow the insights his father had gained through the Möttlingen events to become a new orthodoxy. Rather, the kingdom moves forward, and so our witness and action—and for Barth by extension, our thought—must also be on the move with the reality that we seek to be faithful to.

Barth commented on Christoph's loyal freedom to his father after his death in 1919:

> What was original in the younger Blumhardt was precisely that he did not feel that he had to be original, as is usually the way of sons in relation to their fathers. He merely continued to be true to the insights of his father concerning God and the world, which were indeed those of the Bible. He represented and expressed them in *his* day; that means, however, in *our* day, the period of the end of the nineteenth century and the beginning of the twentieth. Thus it was natural that in time much that his father had placed great hope in assumed less importance for him; for example, the visible church with its forms, experiments, and successes; theology with its points of doctrine and its historical erudition; foreign missions and the activities of Christian societies with their rather doubtful self-assurance and busy-work.[22]

Christoph sought to be faithful to the insights that his father had gained, but sought to do so in his time and from his vantage, thus some of the forms and concerns that had claimed his father's attention were allowed to fade away. Barth's own loyal freedom vis-à-vis the Blumhardts can be read, therefore, as working within a pattern or orientation that was already exhibited by the Blumhardts' themselves.

Their fundamental insight—that our obligation is to follow after the living Jesus Christ—who periodically breaks into the world in the form "Jesus is Victor"—in our Christian practice and hope, has been transferred into the realm of Christian dogmatics by Barth as the axiom that we must follow after the living God who is attested in Scripture, but who is also really present in and through the words of Scripture, and by extension, the church's faithful proclamation (i.e., Christian theology). "If there is any Christian and theological axiom, it is that Jesus Christ

---

22. Karl Barth, "Past and Future: Friedrich Naumann and Christoph Blumhardt," 35–45.

is risen, that He is truly risen."[23] But this axiom is neither invented, nor controllable, and implies a serious critique to all Christian knowledge:

> The statement that Jesus Christ is the one Word of God has really nothing whatever to do with the arbitrary exaltation and self-glorification of the Christian in relation to other men, of the Church in relation to other institutions, or of Christianity in relation to other conceptions. . . . It cannot, then, be legitimately advanced and stated except as the men who live in this sphere submit themselves first, with all their Christian views and concepts, dogmas and institutions, customs, traditions and innovations, to the relativisation and criticism which come through Jesus Christ as the one light of life. The judgment on the world indicated in this statement begins 'in the house of God' (1 Pet. 4:17), and it is from there that it spreads to embrace the world around.[24]

In the case of his discussion of the eternity of God, Barth has submitted the Blumhardts' conceptions as well as his own to the judgment outlined here. It is important to also underline, however, that though he could critique them in their limitations and move beyond them— which he inevitably did in many respects—he could still say that despite their limitations, they raised questions that must be heard, because they get at the heart of the matter. This was not because the forms of their questions or expressions were timeless, or had to be slavishly repeated, but because their questions and expressions pointed beyond themselves to the living reality with which all theology should be concerned.[25]

Summary

Barth was able to exhibit a certain critical distance and independence vis-à-vis the Blumhardts thought because his ultimate concern was not with staying true to them, but to the One to whom they pointed. But this critical distance was already exemplified in the Blumhardts' themselves. Christoph assumed the essential insights and content of his

---

23. *CD* IV/3.1, 44.

24. *CD* IV/3.1, 91.

25. Barth exercises the same critical distance in his lecture on the elder Blumhardt given in 1932–1933. See his, *Protestant Theology in the Nineteenth Century*, 643–53. Importantly, this criticism of Blumhardt disappears when we get to the 1956–1957 *CD* IV/3.1. See idem, 168–71.

father's hopes, but he also saw a need to break free of those elements in his father's thought which he believed hampered a full understanding and therefore the final coming of the kingdom of God. Likewise, Barth assumed the insights of the Blumhardts in his theological thinking, but found that they were limited in many respects and in need of correction and emendation. But what Blumhardtian insights was it that Barth assumed and how did this shape his mature theology? To answer these questions we will now turn to consider Barth's reflections on the Blumhardt themes "Jesus is Victor" and "Thy Kingdom Come."

An Argument between Friends: "What is Christological Thinking?"

Preliminary Remarks

The key insights that Barth took from the Blumhardts which remained with him into the late *Church Dogmatics* are found in the sections "Jesus is Victor" and "Thy Kingdom Come." But of what do these consist? Both of these sections are embedded in the larger context of the doctrine of reconciliation, which comprises some 3,639 pages in the original text. As with all of Barth's thought, the embedding of these insights into the larger context of the doctrine of reconciliation means that commentary on any one section impinges on all the others. Therefore, a point of entry is needed that will allow us to get at the content and function of the evident Blumhardtian insights that Barth has retained without becoming bogged down in a general exposition of every relevant aspect of Barth's thought which these sections necessarily touch upon.

Fortunately, just such a point of entry is presented to us in *Church Dogmatics* IV/3.1 in Barth's response to G. C. Berkouwer's study, *The Triumph of Grace in the Theology of Karl Barth*. As we showed in chapter 4, Barth had conceived of theological discourse in relation to its object and content (i.e., "die Sache" of Scripture) as a "movement of thought," and he looked to the Blumhardts as examples of how to progress along that way. In his response to Berkouwer's work, as found in *Church Dogmatics* IV/3.1, Barth unfolds the methodological insights recounted in chapter 4 and in the section above, but in the context of and as belonging to the Blumhardts' watchword, "Jesus is Victor!" His response, therefore, assumes the material content that is developed and elaborated throughout *Church Dogmatics* IV/3.1, but especially the material found in those sections that bear the imprint of the Blumhardts' influence.

Berkouwer's Critique as Expressed in CD IV/3.1

As we noted in chapter 1, G. C. Berkouwer's *The Triumph of Grace in the Theology of Karl Barth*, received well-deserved praise from Barth because of "its wide range of knowledge and reading, is perspicuous and penetrating mode of exposition, and the sharpness and balance of its criticisms."[26] Despite this praise, however, Barth remained unconvinced that Berkouwer had truly understood him. He expresses his doubts as follows:

> I must admit, however, that I was taken aback when I saw the title given to his book. If I am in a sense understood by its clever and faithful author, yet in the last resort cannot think that I am genuinely understood for all his care and honesty, this is connected with the fact that he tries to understand me under this title. If my guess is right, it was an incidental remark of H. U. von Balthasar, to the effect that Christianity is for me an absolutely 'triumphant affair,' which inclined Berkouwer to adopt this title. This is something which can be said, though I should prefer not to say it of Christianity. . . . Yet understood thematically, and in connection with the concept of grace, it does not seem to me to say with sufficient acuteness what should be said at this point.[27]

Though Barth had already conveyed these same thoughts to Berkouwer in a letter on December 30, 1954, and had given public praise to Berkouwer's book in the preface to *Church Dogmatics* IV/2, he clearly felt that the points and objections raised by Berkouwer were of such importance that they needed to be, in his words, "weighed and answered" in the context of the section entitled "Jesus is Victor."[28]

Berkouwer's primary objection was that Barth's descriptions of evil as "nothingness," "impossible possibility," and "ontological impossibility" led to an all too easy and unbiblical triumph of the principle of grace. In Berkouwer's view, these descriptions removed the sense of

26. *CD* IV/3.1, 173.

27. *CD* IV/3.1, 173–74.

28. *CD* IV/3.1, 174. For discussion of the contents of the letter to Berkouwer, see Busch, *Karl Barth*, 381; for Barth's previously published comments on Berkouwer's study, see *CD* IV/2, xii.

a real conflict between God and evil as seen in the cross and thereby emptied ongoing history itself of real meaning, reducing history to the site of the process wherein God's grace triumphs, rather than the sphere and time in which genuine encounter between God and humanity and our continuing struggle with sin and evil occurs.

Barth's answer to Berkouwer reveals that the question of the reality and existence of evil was merely a jumping off point for a much deeper and more fundamental issue, which Barth had been wrestling with from early in his theological career. Though Barth's response to Berkouwer is developed under four points, it revolves around a single question: "What is Christological thinking?"

"What is Christological Thinking?"

The objection that Berkouwer raised against Barth was not new, and has continued to live on into the present.[29] Barth's answer, however, is revealing not only of what he thinks about the nature and reality of evil or about the charge of "Christian triumphalism," but is also revealing of the central methodological insight that Barth sought to hold to, both successfully and unsuccessfully, throughout his theological career. It could be argued that the question, "what is Christological thinking?" was at the heart of all of Barth's theological concerns, especially as the *Church Dogmatics* progressed and moved in a more and more Christocentric direction.

Distinguishing between "Christological thinking," on the one hand, and "Christology" on the other is not easily done. Barth himself had struggled to distinguish between these two "methods" for theology. The progression of thought on this question is illustrated when one compares the following passages on the proper method or direction for theology that come from the earlier and later periods of his life.

The first from his famous essay, "Fate and Idea in Theology" (1929):

> Even for theology there is no other justification than justification by faith. Or, to put it another way, theology is justified only by obedience. For even obedience can be obedience only when

---

29. See my discussion in chapter 1 of McDowell, *Hope in Barth's Eschatology*. Though this work is one of the best and most balanced assessments of Barth's eschatology, it still ends with the qualified accusation that Barth remains too "triumphalistic."

it understands itself as faith—as the human affirmation of God's free, unearned, unowed and uncompelled grace. Theology, too, must do its work in appropriate humility. And we say nothing different if we remember in conclusion that Luther put the decisive contradiction in all *speculatio majestitas* like this: '...begin where Christ began—in the Virgin's womb, in the manger, and at his mother's breasts.' Begin, in other words, where God's Word has and does concretely come to us: In truth, because it is God's Word. In reality, because it was made flesh. True God and real humanity—in just that way, the one, the divine, the binding, the justifying and sanctifying Word. Theology will really be theology—of Word, election, faith—when from beginning to end it is Christology.[30]

Put succinctly: theology only really speaks truly of *God*, and not about idols or figments of our imagination, when God, so to speak, shows up and speaks through it. This audaciously conceived theology, which Barth outlined as early as 1920, puts the theologian in a genuine predicament, because he or she cannot force God to speak.[31] They can only sigh for God to come and reveal himself.

In 1925, Eduard Thurneysen had voiced a similar conviction when he asked his troubled pastoral and theological mentor Hermann Kutter:

Do you not recognize the *sighing* for the real, the living *God*, that resides also in our theology, in fact is its deepest root? I believe I may say myself that I have never had any pleasure in an empty play of concepts; moreover, such things, especially things that have to do with ideas, come too hard for me. This sighing, ever since it was awakened in me by Blumhardt and you, has been the most essential part of me—certainly often obscured and denied, yet never quite lost, and in the last analysis it has been from that source that I have written not only my sermons but also my few theological works. For Karl Barth I am not able to offer any explanations here, I can only say for myself in truth the one thing, that I have never felt even his *Letter to the Romans* to be anything other than one great *sigh* for what you call *God himself*, especially in the impetuousness of its dialectical movement.

30. Karl Barth, "Fate and Idea in Theology," 60.

31. The outline of which I am referring can be found in Barth's essay, "Unsettled Questions for Theology Today," in *Theology and Church* by Karl Barth, 55–73. For an excellent exposition of this essay, see Eberhard Jüngel, *Karl Barth, a Theological Legacy*, 54–70.

> ... That he is really in earnest about it is evident to me in the fact
> that no lecture hour passes for him without his laying down all
> the concepts with which he works, and in laying them down and
> expressing them he makes clear that no one can attain to God
> with his concepts, that when God speaks he can do it only in his
> own Word, and that he does it in his Word. ... Barth's theological
> work consists in the self-surrender of all concepts and in that
> he, too, *bears witness* truly to—God.[32]

One can deduce from these passages that conceptual idolatry is to be
avoided at all costs when one is engaged in the labor of theological
description. For both Barth and Thurneysen, the ultimate goal of the
theologian is to construct a theology that does not hamper, but rather is
transparent, so that when God speaks nothing obfuscates. This means
that our use of conceptual categories and schema as well as our allegiance to certain biblically derived principles (in the case of Berkouwer
it was the principle of grace), are all secondary and thus cannot be the
primary object of theological discourse or exposition.

In 1929, Barth's counsel is that if we are to avoid confusing our
own intellectual or even biblically derived principles with the one true
object who is also the speaking subject of theology (i.e., the living God),
the theologian would do well to elaborate his or her theology by following the contours of God's own revelation, i.e., in Jesus Christ and the
history in which He is known. In the 1929 essay, Barth explicitly labels
this path "Christology."

In the following years, Barth would come to believe that though
his basic insights were sound, they needed to be sharpened and expanded such that a different kind of confusion could be avoided. This
new confusion was really a version of the old one that he had warned
against back in 1929. In the wake of Barth's own constructive and dogmatic work, many had come to believe that he was only engaged in—
and was therefore recommending to others—building a comprehensive
Christology. But this procedure would have been just as illegitimate to
Barth, as our second passage shows.

Though written in 1960, our second passage, from his essay
"Philosophy and Theology," retains the same basic insights found in
the 1929 essay, but it exhibits the sharpening and expansion that was
needed to further clarify his earlier insight. In contrast to the philoso-

---

32. Barth and Thurneysen, *Revolutionary Theology in the Making*, 212–14.

pher, the theologian does not begin with principles or general truths but with the history of the living Jesus Christ as portrayed in all of its scandalous particularity:

> Jesus Christ is the one whole Truth . . . Not a Christ-idea, but the Jesus of Nazareth, who lived under Augustus and Tiberius, has died and been raised from the dead, in order to die no more—and this not as a distinguished (perhaps as the most distinguished) 'vehicle' or symbol, as the preferred cipher of the Truth, but the later one as true God and true human being—he Himself the Truth illuminating the whole world and thus also the philosopher and the theologian![33]

The distinction that Barth wants to get at is the same as that pointed to in 1929. If what we have to say, even about Jesus Christ, is going to be a true word, then the living and present Jesus Christ must speak it. Thus, the obligation of the theologian is to construct their theology as if in motion, following along the history of the Son of God become Son of Man, which is in some measure different from simply building a comprehensive Christology.

As Phil Butin and others have shown, Barth sought to follow his own advice, and constructed the primary Christological volume of the *Church Dogmatics*, IV/1–3 *The Doctrine of Reconciliation*, as a "Christology in motion."[34] Briefly stated, Barth draws on the many traditional categories of Christ's person and work, as well as the states of exaltation and humiliation, bringing them all together into a coherent whole through the ordering of the *munus triplex* ("Three-fold office of Christ"), but in such a way that his explication retains a profound attention and openness to narrative explication and thereby is able to integrate lengthy passages of the Synoptics with reflections from the Pauline literature. However, given Barth's pointed comments to his friend Hans Iwand, even this comprehensive and integrated construction of Christology cannot be the primary aim of theology:

---

33. Karl Barth, "Philosophy and Theology," 89. One can hear in these comments a sharp barb aimed at his friend and theological opponent, Paul Tillich. For Tillich's alternative approach see his *Systematic Theology*, vol. 2, 88–180.

34. See Butin, "Two Early Reformed Catechisms," 206–9. For a more comprehensive account of Barth's Christology, see Mueller, *Foundation of Karl Barth's Doctrine of Reconciliation*.

I was asked my opinion, so I said, 'Sometimes I don't like the word Christology very much. It's not a matter of Christology, nor even of christocentricity and a Christological orientation, but of *Christ himself.* Any preoccupation with Christology— and I have been preoccupied a little with that—can only be a critical help towards coming to the point where we may have the experience of the disciples on the Mount of Transfiguration: "They saw no one, but Jesus alone."'[35]

The real aim has to be to let the living Jesus speak, such that all principles, conceptual categories and constructs, and even traditional doctrinal formulas can only be secondary and useful in so far as they help to clarify rather than obfuscate the living, present, speaking Christ.

"Christological thinking," therefore, should not be confused with merely expounding the categories of Chalcedon, or of the *munus triplex*, or of the "two states" of Christ, or of any of the other formal Christological categories that have been developed in the history of doctrine. These can be helpful for ordering our thought and even reminding us of what *must* be said about Jesus Christ, the Son of God become Son of Man, but, in Barth's mind, a genuine danger arises when "Christological thinking" becomes confused with mere "Christology." The *former* requires a hopeful intellectual and spiritual submission and obedience that issues forth in the constant petitions "Thy kingdom come!" and "Come Holy Spirit," as well as a genuine flexibility in the concepts and categories that we use and in our willingness or reticence to deploy them. It is undertaken in the hope that in fact Jesus lives, and that because Jesus lives, he will speak. While the *latter* procedure, according to Barth, will necessarily lead to conceptual and categorical ossification, lacking the flexibility and thus distorting the living voice of the one who wishes to speak through our presentation. It can also very easily exist as a form of arrogant scholarly gymnastics which is dependent not on the living voice of Jesus, but on our intellectual virtuosity and thus become nothing more than the figment of human imagination.

In view of these comments, then, "Christological thinking" can be described as necessarily dynamic and "historical" in character, with a definite shape and direction. It favors narrative form, rather than static ontological and metaphysical categories, but it cannot be reduced to

35. Busch, *Karl Barth*, 411.

the same, for it presupposes the real existence of a living history whose locus is not found in a textual narrative construction, even those of the Bible (!), but in the life-act of one who though given a place among the dead is there no longer, but is making himself present in the *here* and *now* as the very same one he was *there* and *then*.

The Blumhardts and "Christological thinking"

Questioning Berkouwer

For Barth, in the argument with Berkouwer, "the question is whether he and I mean the same thing by 'christological' thinking and the related investigations, definitions, conclusions and foundations."[36] To be sure, Barth believed that he and Berkouwer shared a certain level of understanding of what "Christological thinking" was comprised and the obligation that the same put upon the theologian. Barth noted, that when formally conceived, "thinking is Christological only when it consists in the perception, comprehension, understanding and estimation of the reality of the living person of Jesus Christ as attested by Holy Scripture, in attentiveness to the range and significance of His existence, in openness to His self-disclosure, in consistency in following Him as is demanded."[37] In view of this formal definition, "Christological thinking" means to derive one's theological knowledge strictly in the light of Jesus Christ, such that our knowledge of God, our knowledge of ourselves as God's creatures, and our knowledge of sin and evil, are all to be sought and found in the uncontrollable yet promised speaking of Jesus Christ, the True Witness.

In his debate with Berkouwer, Barth was especially concerned to emphasize that this way of thinking is very different from thought-forms that unfold themselves from a given principle and he underlines, "that we are not dealing with a Christ-principle, but with Jesus Christ Himself as attested by Holy Scripture."[38] As we noted above, "Christological thinking" consists not in the unfolding of a principle, doctrine, or any intellectual construct, but rather in following after the living Jesus Christ who is attested in Holy Scripture.

36. *CD* IV/3.1, 174.
37. Ibid.
38. Ibid..

According to Barth, if one thinks in this way, or rather, if one progresses along the path that this type of thinking indicates, one will in fact end up traversing the story of the One who presents Himself, for to say the name Jesus, or rather to have it uttered by the Spirit, is in fact to be caught up into the history that is enacted under that name. Though Barth felt that Berkouwer could affirm his formal definition of "Christological thinking," he was very doubtful that Berkouwer knew how to put it into practice. Berkouwer's description and attendant objection that Barth's theology was far too triumphalistic revealed as much.

In Barth's eyes, Berkouwer's interpretation of his description of evil as qualitatively inferior to God and as eternally doomed to lose in its contest and conflict with God, was not predicated on the close following after the living Jesus Christ who presents and reveals Himself *here* and *now* as the One who was *there* and *then* grappling with evil in real conflict and combat, but whose ending was, though difficult and filled with suffering and pain, secure. Rather, Berkouwer's interpretation could only issue in his accusation of "triumphalism" if he was interpreting Barth as, "ensnared in the unilateral and one-sided manipulation and development of a principle."[39] In Barth's eyes, his intentions to take "with unconditional seriousness the fact that, 'Jesus is Victor'" was wholly incomprehensible to Berkouwer for two possible reasons.

The first was that Berkouwer was too "deeply rooted" in the Reformed tradition, in whose doctrine of election the principle of the divine decision did, in Barth's view, take precedence over the reality of Jesus Christ, who is the living God in the form of his electing will. In view of this, "Berkouwer can explain my conception of the relationship between God and evil only thinking that I, too, proceed on the basis of a prior decision, and am thus ensnared in the unilateral and one-sided manipulation and development of a principle." Barth rejects this approach as "quite illegitimate," arguing instead for "Christological thinking" of the type outlined above, in which "we should take with unconditional seriousness the fact that 'Jesus is Victor.'"[40]

The second reason that Barth gives for Berkouwer's inability to think in the direction that Barth is recommending, was that "it may

39. *CD* IV/3.1, 175.
40. Ibid.

be that he cannot do so because, so far as I can see, the story and influence of the Blumhardts have not yet penetrated effectively the very Calvinistic environment to which he owes his development."[41] What does this reference to the Blumhardts mean in this context?

The Blumhardtian Root

For Barth, the Blumhardt story, in a compact and accessible manner, reminds one that if the reality of God—and therefore a true conception of the reality of the evil that resists God—is to be known and powerfully present, then "God Himself must come and speak."[42] That is, the living presence of the living reality of Jesus Christ is necessary for our witness to be both true and effective witness. If this person comes into view, if this person peers through the words of Scripture, tradition, proclamation, communal action, or theology as one is engaged on their particular path then true knowledge of God can also be present.[43] In the present case, if the living reality of Jesus Christ is before us in our deliberations on the reality and existence of evil—that is, if Jesus Christ is really present and therefore really known, he will be known only in the form of the history of His crucifixion and resurrection, and therefore—there can really be no doubt of the absolute superiority of this person vis-à-vis his opponent.

To expound this point, Barth employed Blumhardt's experience in the Möttlingen *Kampf*:

---

41. Ibid.

42. *CD* IV/3.1, 98.

43. "No Christology can reproduce either the Easter event in which He has come forth alive from the dead both to be and to be revealed and knowable as the One He is, nor Himself as the living One who attests Himself authentically in His being and action for and among and in us. It can be Easter Christology in preaching, teaching, worship, pastoral care and dogmatics only if it does not attempt such reproduction and if its declarations leave place, and indeed finish up by yielding place, *to His self-declaration*, just as the resurrection accounts of the Evangelists and Paul never narrate the event as such but always record and bear witness to the appearances of the Resurrected. . . . If our christological assertions are sustained and determined and filled by this respect and anticipation, then they are reliable as theological statements, and we need not be mortally concerned about the elements of incompleteness and incorrectness which even at best will cling to them, since they can be valid and helpful as a positive answer to our question concerning this exit, transition and entry" (*CD* IV/3.1, 286 [italics mine]).

Blumhardt never even dreamed that He could control Jesus. He did something which is very different, and which is the only thing possible in relation to this person. He called upon Him for two years. He did so with absolute confidence. But he still called upon Him. It is thus a matter of confidence in this person, of His free act, of calling upon Him. Yet the counter-question has to be put to those who are concerned about this matter whether confidence in Jesus can be limited or assurance in calling upon Him restricted. Do we not forget or deny that we are dealing with this person in this character if we regard with caution or a limited confidence as the better part? Yet if we do not forget or deny this, we must agree with Blumhardt that it is 'eternally settled' that, no matter what may be thought of His opponent, this Partner is in any case absolutely superior to him, that the action between them can end only in His triumph, and that we have thus to say that the issue of this action is in fact decided from its very commencement in view of the fact that the One who is the First will also be the Last. . . . Where does the Bible teach the contrary?[44]

If we go the way of "Christological thinking" then we are necessarily led down a path that leads through Good Friday and Holy Saturday, to Easter, in the light of which we will know in faith, hope and love, the absolute superiority of the One to whom we are looking. But this path is a real path, a real history, in which there is call and response, give and take. For Barth, accordingly, victory over evil cannot be described as conceptually guaranteed in every penultimate historical instance. The knowledge of God's victory and the corresponding intellectual path cannot be a path that is either predicated on or leads to a formulaic certitude. Rather, it is a path that requires our participation, our hope, and our calling upon God, even in our theological deliberations.[45]

Thus to Barth, Blumhardt was confident in God's Lordship, but this did not exempt him from the conflict. Blumhardt had to enter into

---

44. *CD* IV/3.1, 176.

45. ". . . the epistemological model of theological knowledge true to this personal co-presence of the risen Christ with us is not knowledge by description but knowledge by participation, not propositional knowledge based on the authority of the Church's teaching but personal participation in God's self-communication which precedes and grounds all human testimony and teaching" (Dalferth, "Karl Barth's Eschatological Realism," 21).

the conflict embodied in the case of Gottliebin Dittus in order to participate in, and therefore really know, that "Jesus is the Victor."

> This emerges in the sense of dread yet also the daring resolution with which he undertook the struggle. 'Lord Jesus, help me. We have seen long enough what the devil can do. We now desire the power of Jesus.' This was from the very first his prayer with and for the sufferer. Nor did he meet with anything new—except the new thing of the New Testament—at the crisis of the battle. *Yet the fact remains that this well-known truth was then much more to him than the confirmation of an existing conviction or the success of his pastoral venture in the strength of his conviction.* It came as a new thing and in an unexpected way when he heard that simple statement: 'Jesus is Victor,' at the beginning of the healing of the afflicted in demonstration of the power of Jesus. . . . For Blumhardt the new and surprising thing in the issue of the conflict, which necessarily found immediate expression in new insights and impulses and directives, was the fact that the victory of Jesus is 'eternally settled,' as it is put in a later hymn, that it is objectively decided even in the darkest darkness of the world, and that it is now manifested, known and declared.[46]

By entering into the conflict Blumhardt was given new light on an old truth which he had hoped and believed in, but could not be said to have thought was somehow conceptually guaranteed. He still had to traverse that history, and in so doing he *experienced* a form or dimension of the same conflict and tension that Jesus himself experienced. Thus, Blumhardt came to know existentially that Jesus' victory was "eternally settled." Put differently, through entering into the history of the conflict—which was a penultimate instance of the one history of Jesus the Victor—the truth that he had already believed broke over him afresh, giving him new insight, not because it was conceptually guaranteed, but because he had gone down the path of Jesus the Victor and had thereby entered into a history of struggle, whose ultimate end was known, even if the penultimate end as seen in the case of Dittus may not have been.

The account of the events at Möttlingen given by Zündel in his biography of the elder Blumhardt, which Barth had first read back in 1915, is filled with a tension that leaves the reader with the impression that Blumhardt was not entirely sure as to the outcome of the struggle

---

46. *CD* IV/3.1, 170 (italics mine).

that he was engaged in.[47] At the same time though, the cognitive dissonance that Blumhardt experienced was never whether or not Jesus was really the Lord, but whether or not he (i.e., Blumhardt) would stay the course and enter into the struggle that Jesus was calling him to engage in. As Blumhardt recounted:

> My desire to end the whole thing became even stronger. . . . I felt myself in a net out of which I could not possibly extricate myself by merely retreating without danger to myself and others. In addition, I felt ashamed before myself and my Savior, to Whom I prayed so much, and in Whom I trusted so much and Who had given me so many proofs of His help—I confess it openly—to give in to the devil. 'Who is the Lord?' I had to ask myself many times. And with faith in Him, Who is the Lord, the words were formed in me again and again, 'Forward! Forward! It has to lead to a good end, even though it will lead into the deepest depths, unless it were not true that Jesus had crushed the head of the serpent.'[48]

Barth's interpretation of the presupposition of Blumhardt is consonant with the portrayal given in Zündel's biography: "the fact" of Jesus's Lordship in relationship to the powers of darkness; the fact that Jesus was, in reality, the living Lord, and therefore Victor, was never in doubt for Blumhardt. What was in doubt, was whether Blumhardt would really stay the course, would really progress along the path, would really enter into the history in which Jesus the Victor could be known as the one who conquers death and darkness. The fact that he did enter this way, that he did progress along this path, was predicated on his belief in the crucified and living Jesus, not on a principle.

Furthermore, for Barth, the Blumhardts' embodied the kind of thinking and witness that was distinct from the form of thinking that Berkouwer was interpreting Barth in the light of:

> Their true theme—and for those who know them there is no doubt about this—was the world to come, which they did not just perceive in those reflections but saw in faith and hope as an action and event at the beginning and end of the whole of this world. But what is this world to come? When the two Blumhardts did not speak of the kingdom of God indirectly, in

47. See Zündel, *Johann Christoph Blumhardt, ein Lebensbild*, 117–60.
48. Johann Christoph Blumhardt, *A Conflict with Satan*, 21–22.

experiments, or with only penultimate seriousness, but directly, thetically, and with ultimate seriousness, then with astounding simplicity and directness they pronounced the name of Jesus which illumines and infinitely outshines all the miracles at Möttlingen and the experiences at Boll, all the expected new outpouring of the Spirit, all the later possibilities which may be noted in science or religion or accepted in politics. Without being polemical in this regard, what they had in view was neither the God-man of early Christology nor the so-called historical Jesus for whom their age already had such a lively concern. Very naively, but with axiomatic certainty, they were thinking of the reality of the risen and living Jesus himself, acting and speaking as a distinctive factor no less actual today than yesterday: the Jesus who is self-evidently, as in the primitive church, both the beginning and also the end [Rev 21:6; 22:13]; the Jesus who has already come and will come again, and who is thus present to his people and—unknown to it—the world.[49]

What this passage indicates is that the Blumhardts, in all of their naiveté, modeled and were concerned above all with "Christological thinking" and the object that it sought to follow. Again, "Christological thinking" is the attempt to follow after the movement of the living Christ who presents Himself in the here and now, as the One He was. This kind of thinking is not primarily concerned with expounding, as Barth says, "the God-man of early Christology nor the so-called historical Jesus," but with narrative description, conceptual flexibility, and ultimately giving way to speaking of the living Christ. In light of his remarks, it is both legitimate and necessary to say that, at least for Barth, the Blumhardts' life and witness embodied in rudimentary form the dynamic and distinctiveness of the kind of "Christological thinking" that he sought to emulate and to recommend to Berkouwer and others.

The Blumhardts' "Jesus is Victor" and It's Implications for "Christological thinking"

Returning again to Barth's argument with Berkouwer, in light of the genuine and real conflict of God with the powers of sin, death, and the devil, Barth asks how else the reality of evil should be described. In his mind, the only option is to acknowledge it as that which God, "never did

---

49. *CL*, 259.

nor could will, nor ever will nor can."[50] If one takes seriously that this is a real conflict between two genuine opponents and not a sham fight then evil cannot be attributed to the will of God but can only be seen as that which God does not will. Furthermore, Barth makes clear that to name evil as an "ontological impossibility" is not to deny that it really exists, but to highlight that its existence is baffling and that the cognitive dissonance created by the presence of evil in God's good creation cannot be conceptually diffused. Rather, it can be known only as that which in Jesus, God has confronted, overcome, and vanquished, and as such has had a limit and end set to its existence.

Barth lends an ear in the direction of Berkouwer, hoping that he might hear from his Dutch Reformed friend some less cumbersome description of the reality denoted by "nothingness," "impossible possibility" and "ontological impossibility." But, whatever suggestion may come from Berkouwer, it is clear that in Barth's mind it will not be able to have any other meaning than what is, in his view, ascribed to the nature of evil in the light of Jesus the Victor.

Barth closes his argument by taking up the question of whether or not his definition and delimitation of evil as "nothingness," "impossible possibility" and "ontological impossibility" do in fact empty out the teleological and historical character of the conflict between God and this opponent and therefore reduce history and our participation in it to a mere footnote. Again, he appeals to what he means by "Christological thinking."

If we are in fact going to know about the confrontation between God and evil in the light of the living Jesus, and are therefore going to go the way and direction of "Christological thinking" as Barth envisioned it, then we are necessarily going to be led into a history, whose end we may know, but along whose difficult way we must still go.

> To say 'Jesus' is necessarily to say 'history,' His history, the history in which He is what He is and does what He does. In His history we know God, and we also know evil and their relationship the one to the other–but only from this source and in this way. *But at this point a way is trodden.* A question is raised and answered. A sentence is pronounced and judgment is executed and suffered. A faith and obedience are demanded and displayed. Prayer is offered. A cross is borne, on this cross suffering

50. *CD* IV/3.1, 177.

is endured. From the deepest depths a cry is raised to heaven. *Nothing is self-evident, obvious or matter-of-course.* The day must be carried against the fiercest opposition. A war is waged against sin, death, and the devil. It is in this war that Jesus is Victor, even though He is the almighty Mediator between God and man, and the eternal will of God fulfilled in His faith and obedience is absolutely superior to the contradiction and opposition which are only contemptible nothingness in face of this towering opponent, and the issue is thus certain at the commencement and therefore 'from the very outset.'[51]

For Barth, in the *there* and *then* occurrence, as depicted in the New Testament witness, there can be no question that we have really to do with "encounter and struggle, and therefore with history."[52] The Gospels are written from the perspective of the resurrection, but they do not empty out the real struggle and difficulty, the physical and spiritual agony, separation and death that Jesus experienced and encountered in His passion and cross. They traverse this way in all seriousness, but in the hope and view of an end that is never in doubt.

Can knowledge still be considered "historical" in the sense that Berkouwer wants to affirm, in the sense of our knowledge being partial and possibly even wrong, when the end of the story is already known? Or put differently, does this conception of knowledge and history really leave room for anything new, either in the form of the progress of history or in the final revelation of the kingdom of God? For Barth, in light of the Scriptures, the answer to this question is and has to be yes.

In one sense, the history of Jesus has ended. In his life, death and resurrection the end has come, the kingdom of God has drawn nigh. Reconciliation has occurred and been accomplished for all of humanity. In another sense, however, this history continues to move forward, not amending or adding to the original form and event, but occurring in another dimension, the dimension of ongoing history. In this latter sphere, though Jesus does in fact move through it towards a known end, this is still a historical movement. "If from the very first there can be no doubt as the issue of the action, there can also be no doubt that there is an action, and that it is taking place, and can thus be described only in

51. *CD* IV/3.1, 179 (emphasis mine).
52. *CD* IV/3.1, 180.

the form of narration."[53] In this sense, this history and our knowledge of it can be said to be "historical" even if the ultimate end is known.

Furthermore, because in this history Jesus really confronts the powers of evil, because He really subdues them through the cross, the history of Jesus is the inner meaning of all history:

> As reconciliation is reconciliation of the world, of all men, it applies to the whole world, to all men, whether in terms of its self-declaration to all in Jesus Christ, or in terms of its hindering and questioning by the opposition and obstruction offered to Him as the Word of God. That it applies to all in this twofold sense means that as the light of life *shines* in the darkness, the world and all men come within the reach of its beams, but as it shines in the *darkness*, the world and all men are still in the sphere of darkness.[54]

This history, the history of the salvation of the whole world, the coming of the kingdom of God, is the inner meaning and shape of all history and thus impinges on all history. As such, it not only gives a definite direction to our history, but it also gives form to the history that we experience when we begin to enter into the knowledge of God.

Therefore, the history of Jesus Christ, as the inner meaning of world history, does not as such exclude or exempt our experience of history from the anxiety, dynamism and tension that is presupposed in real conflict and historical development. It does not do this, since the same are not excluded in Jesus' own history. Our own experience of history and knowledge of God are authentically Christian, and therefore true, insofar as they are marked by the same difficulty, angst and confrontation that marked Jesus.

> Indeed, we may note at this point that the disciple is not above the Master. We, too, must enter into this history and therefore this conflict of His. We have clear confidence concerning its issue. Only victory is to be expected in view of its commencement, in view of Jesus, who has already fought the battle. Yet we have this confidence with the last and bitter seriousness enjoined and demanded by this commencement, by Jesus. Neither hesitant qualifications nor rash or slothful assurance are possible at this point. The only possibility is perfect confidence in

53. *CD* IV/3.1, 168.
54. *CD* IV/3.1, 191.

the perfect, yearning, yet resolute expectation of that on which it is grounded.[55]

Barth will go on to describe the whole history of "Christian knowledge" as a confrontation between the "True Witness" Jesus Christ and the falsehood of humanity. Thus, Christian knowledge—not only our knowledge of the reality of sin and evil, but our knowledge of God, and of ourselves—shares in the form of the history of Jesus Christ who in his proclamation of the kingdom of God encountered deadly resistance, but who was ultimately victorious. The form and experience of our knowledge, therefore, correspond to the event which they seek to know. We are not excused from the difficulties and deadly penultimate ends and fates that await us, but we encounter and even embrace them under the proviso that the ultimate end is in fact secure.

This dynamic parallels the Blumhardts' conviction that the struggle for the kingdom of God enjoined on them through the events at Möttlingen meant a following after the living Lord who was at work in the world, but at work in the very same way that His work had inaugurated itself, i.e., in the history of His life that had culminated in the cross and resurrection. As Christoph Blumhardt stated it, "the history of Jesus's life, is the history of the kingdom of God then and now."[56] Though the end of this history is known in hope, we participate in it only by entering into it. Thus Christoph's saying, "Die, that Jesus may live," was not meant to be a form of moralistic introspection, but of allowing one's flesh to begin to experience the judgment of Golgotha in the here and now so that the resurrection power of the kingdom of God could come into the every day. The problem, in their estimation, was that the church had turned its back on this struggle, had forgotten what it meant to pray, "Thy kingdom come" and thereby had become unfaithful.

Barth's point was that this insight of the Blumhardts' about Christian discipleship belonged in the realm of theological reflection and discourse, which was but another form of discipleship. Christian knowledge of God must be shaped by a spiritual and cognitive follow-

---

55. *CD* IV/3.1, 180.

56. Christoph Blumhardt, *Action in Waiting*, 3. "He lives among men and he is the kingdom of God. He does not make it; He *is* the kingdom!" (Christoph Blumhardt, *Auswahl*, III:61, unpublished translation by the Brüderhof and Plough Publishing).

ing after, and not merely the following after of intellectual constructs, but quite literally following the risen and present Lord.[57] Thus, prayer was the central act of the theologian, because what one desired to follow was the present and living Lord, whom one must call on.[58] The only real difference between Barth and the Blumhardts' here is the context and idiom in which Barth has made his very Blumhardtian point: it was not a pastoral, but a dogmatic context and idiom.

"Christological thinking" vs. "Christology": A Distinction without a Difference?

It is difficult to put one's finger on the real difference between "Christological thinking" in the form that Blumhardt represents and the kind of "Christology" that Barth believed was behind Berkouwer's accusation of conceptual arrogance. It almost seems like a distinction without a difference. What Barth is up to in his appeal to the Blumhardts and the description of "Jesus is Victor" in the wider context of *Church Dogmatics* IV/3.1, becomes clearer if we see that the real question for him is whether or not we will allow the living Jesus to speak into our situation and thinking. The need and predicament of the Christian disciple, and the theologian no less, is always to call upon the living God to come.[59] But this coming is always in a certain form, which is itself a path or history that moves in a certain direction.

To know that it is "eternally settled" that Jesus is Victor is in one sense no different from assuming an easy "triumph of grace." But in another sense, it is very different, because it takes seriously the form, content, and final issue of God's speaking to us in Jesus Christ, behind whom we need not look. And it becomes *the* central challenge and sum-

---

57. See Gorringe, *Against Hegemony*, 188–90.

58. "The first and basic act of theological work is *prayer*. . . . Properly understood, this act is still only a single one, the very one which we called to mind at the end of our fifth lecture: *Veni, Creator Spiritus!* In his movements from below to above and from above to below, the one Holy Spirit achieves the opening of God for man and the opening of man for God. Theological work, therefore, lives by and in the petition for his coming. All its questions, inquiries, reflections, and declarations can only be forms of this petition. And only in God's hearing of this entreaty is theological work at any time a successful and useful work. . . . The certainty that this petition will be heard is consequently also the certainty in which theological work may and should be courageously started and performed" (Karl Barth, *Evangelical Theology*, 160, 169–70).

59. "The first and basic act of theological work is *prayer*" (ibid., 160).

mons to the theologian because we, in our thinking, acting, and witness, are caught up into this same history of conflict. It is, thus, "a drama which can only be followed, or rather experienced and recounted."[60] Furthermore, the form of this knowledge and history is not triumphant, but is quite literally the form of the crucified:

> It is naturally to be expected, indeed, it is inevitable, that the revelation of this action should correspond to its content, and therefore that in practice the prophetic work of Jesus Christ should have the form of passion. It is the work of Jesus Christ the Victor, i.e., of the One who definitively in His own person bore for all men the sin which separates man from God, who robbed the devil of his right to them and death of his power over them, who introduced the new and free man. . . . But He is the Victor of Gethsemane and Golgotha. Hence in all its moments His coming again is His manifestation as this Victor, as the strange, unlikely, inconspicuous *Imperator* and *Triumphator* who enters, rules and triumphs in this form: elected by God as rejected of Him; judging the world as judged by it; superior to all men as despised by all; free as bound; mighty as impotent; eternally living as dead and buried; completely victorious in complete defeat. He not only was, but here and now in His ongoing prophetic work He still is the suffering Servant of God, the King crowned with thorns. How else could He be that on which everything hinges–the same today as yesterday? How else could He bear witness here and now to the reconciliation effected in Him, to Himself as the One who accomplishes, brings and guarantees salvation, and therefore to the name and kingdom and will of God? . . . In this form He is at the core not only of the kerygmatic theology of Paul but also of the kerygmatic accounts of the Gospels. In this form—'unto the Jews a stumblingblock, and unto the Greeks foolishness' (1 Cor. 1:23)—He has addressed His own, His community, and through this the world, from the time of His resurrection onwards and therefore from the very first. He has continually proffered Himself to the Church and the world in this form. He encounters us in this form or not at all. To look past it is not to see Him. *To miss the Word of the cross is not to hear Him.* . . . The Jesus who lives and is among us in our time is the One who is still harassed and forsaken, accused and condemned, despised and smitten. He has already fought and won as such, but He still does so as the true Witness, unmasking the falsehood of our time and therefore of

60. *CD* IV/3.1, 166.

us all. It would not be our time, this strange era *post Christum*, if
He could be present in it otherwise than as the Man of Sorrows.
. . . In correspondence with present world as the setting of His
prophetic work, Jesus Christ is thus not merely the One who
suffers, but, as in Gethsemane and on Golgotha, He is the One
who is smitten and afflicted by God, and it is in this way alone
that He is the true Witness.[61]

The implication of the form of the revelation of Jesus the Victor is that
our own knowledge and experience of God will be marked by this.

In one sense, Barth is trying to press on the theologian that even
in their theological deliberations and constructions they must take seriously the command of Jesus: "If anyone would come after me, he must
deny himself and take up his cross daily and follow me" (Luke 9:23,
NIV). In another sense, Barth is seeking to avoid the danger that he sees
evident in *aprioric* theological thinking.

If we assume a "triumph of grace" or the triumph of a cognitive
construct or conceptual principle of grace, then questions immediately
arise as to whether or not these are simply a figment of our imagination.
The abstract principle of grace could simply be a cipher into which we
put any conceptual content. But the living history of Jesus the Victor,
as attested in Scripture, and as experienced anew by the Blumhardts,
is rooted in the narratives of Scripture that points beyond itself to an
actual concrete occurrence. To be sure, this too remains open to the
charge that it could be nothing more than a figment of our imagination.
But here, at least, because our construction seeks to follow as closely as
possible that which it purports to point to, it is not so easily opened to
the charge. Rather, it is placed in the very same tension that seems to
haunt the Scriptures, i.e., that the one spoken about is not actually dead,
but in fact living and present. And it is the presence of this one that
secures the authority and effective power of these depictions, rather
than the credibility of those who wrote about or attest to the events
depicted.

Furthermore, this way of thinking leads one forward into the
thought-form of the very history that we are trying to recount as we
are forced to call upon God to speak His truth through our narrative

61. *CD* IV/3.1, 389–94 (italics mine).

description.[62] We are personally drawn into the history of conflict, becoming a part of the ongoing history of the revelation of God's victory over evil as it moves in the starts and fits of a drama, but nevertheless inexorably to its final end. Because of the nature of the object, our knowledge is necessarily personal.

~

We have reached a point where it is worthwhile to stop and consider in more detail exactly what "Jesus is Victor" meant for Barth. For even the most cursory reading of the section "Jesus is Victor" in *Church Dogmatics* IV/3.1 will reveal that though Barth assumed the Blumhardt stories as the background and form of what he was trying to get at by using their phrase, his elaboration of the inner-logic and implications of this insight is far more rigorous, coherent, and theologically intricate than any of the written reflections produced by either Blumhardt on this theme. We should therefore examine Barth's multi-dimensional elaboration of the Blumhardtian insight that "Jesus is Victor." By so doing we will also be able to understand the central thrust of Barth's response to the objections of Berkouwer and others.

"Jesus is Victor": The Form, Content, and Direction of the History of Reconciliation

For Barth, the Blumhardts' watchword, "Jesus is Victor" is a multifaceted *theologumenon* whose elaboration is dense and complex and whose presuppositions and implications impinge on a vast terrain of the *Church Dogmatics*. In an attempt to unpack Barth's understanding of this central insight of the Blumhardts, we will give a summary description under the following four interrelated points: 1) "Jesus is Victor" = The Form, Content, and Direction of the "There and Then" History; 2) "Jesus is Victor" = Resurrection: Crossing Over from the "There and Then" into the "Here and Now"; 3) "Jesus is Victor" = The Inner-Meaning of

---

62. "Here, too, nothing is self-evident, given or necessary. . . . Its occurrence is the prophecy of Jesus Christ. That He Himself, and in Him the life, covenant and reconciliation, shine out and are disclosed and made known, is an event, and can only be understood as such. It is a drama which can only be followed, or rather experienced and recounted" (*CD* IV/3.1, 166).

Ongoing History; and 4) "Jesus is Victor" = The Goal of History, the Cosmos and the Ways of God.

"Jesus is Victor" = *The Form, Content, and Direction of the "There and Then" History*

The first and most basic point is that "Jesus is Victor" refers to and sums up the form, content and issue of the *there* and *then* history of Jesus Christ, in which "He is the Lord humbled for communion with man and likewise the Servant exalted to communion with God."[63] He is Victor, because He was the eschatological event of the kingdom of God which issued in God's triumph, whose provisional sign is the resurrection. As Barth describes in *The Christian Life*:

> *He* is the total and definitive limitation of human unrighteous-ness and disorder, of the interim demonic world of unchained powers: the conqueror of this world, the victorious enemy of all the enmity of men against God, one another, and themselves. *He* at that time was in his history, on the path that he trod to the end in his time, the imminent kingdom of God.[64]

"Jesus is Victor," sums up the content of the there and then history. But it is especially the historical or dynamic character of this occurrence that Barth is concerned to emphasize.

Just as God is not a static idea or principle, neither is the history in which God is known and humanity is reconciled. "In the 'is' which links the life with the light, the covenant with the Word of God, the recon-ciliation with the revelation, Jesus Christ the High-priest and King with Jesus Christ the Prophet, there is concealed a drama. The 'is' is thus to be understood in a dynamic rather than static terms."[65]

> That the Son of God humiliated Himself to be with us and for us in order that He could uncover the pride of man and positively accomplish his justification, the gathering of His community in the world and the awakening of faith in Him; and again, that the Son of Man should be exalted to fellowship with God in order that He should uncover the sloth of man, and positively accomplish his sanctification, the upbuilding of the commu-

63. Karl Barth, *The Humanity of God*, 46.

64. *CL*, 252.

65. *CD* IV/3.1, 165.

nity of God on earth, and the awakening of love, all this was worked out on the dramatic way of conflict from Bethlehem to Golgotha, and was and is therefore history.[66]

In fact, God's being and the history in which he reconciles creation to himself are one and the same, as Bruce McCormack and Eberhard Jüngel have shown.[67] For Barth, Jesus Christ is the actualizing of the being of God, and as Jesus has a history or can be described as a historical event, this move constitutes the historicizing of the being of God. Thus, "as Jesus Christ lives, there takes place in Him both creative actualization of being, yet also in and with it creaturely actualization; creative and creaturely life together, without the transformation of the one into the other, the admixture of one with the other, or separation or division between them."[68]

From this vantage then, "Jesus is Victor" could be described as the Christological iteration or elaboration of the being and act of the living God, who has chosen not to be without us. Or, put another way, "Jesus is Victor" describes the inner dramatic content and the objective intra-historical actualization of the one electing decision in which God determines Himself and creation, His life and ours as a life that will be lived in covenant. Or, put succinctly, "Jesus is Victor" summarizes in dramatic form God's decision that "I will be their God, and they will be my people" (Jer 31:33, NIV).

"Jesus is Victor" = Resurrection: Crossing Over from the "There and Then" into the "Here and Now"

Our first point could be described as a summary statement of the material content of the doctrine of reconciliation as Barth developed them in *Church Dogmatics* IV/1 and IV/2. In those volumes Barth describes the event of reconciliation as disclosed in the history of Jesus Christ in His cross and resurrection. As Barth himself summarizes it: "As the one Jesus Christ is both true Son of God and true Son of Man, so there take place in His one history both the humiliation of God and the exaltation of man, the conflict and victory of God for man, and therewith

66. *CD* IV/3.1, 181.

67. See McCormack, "Grace and Being," 92–110; Eberhard Jüngel, *God's Being is in Becoming*.

68. *CD* IV/3.1, 40.

and thereby the achievement of covenant faithfulness on both sides, the establishment of peace in this twofold form."[69] What *Church Dogmatics* IV/3 is meant to take seriously is the fact that "revelation takes place in and with reconciliation. As God acts in it, He also speaks. Reconciliation is not a dark or dumb event, but a perspicuous and vocal."[70] Thus, it deals with the revelation of reconciliation, seeking to delve into the Christological basis and form of the same in order to uphold the axiom that "God is only known through God."[71] In this frame, "Jesus is Victor" refers to the "there and then" history enacted in Jesus Christ, but as that history bursts the bounds of normal history, as it becomes a living history, confronting humanity in order to reconcile it.

"Jesus is Victor" refers not only to the "there and then" history in which God has reconciled the world to himself, but also to the illumination of that event such that it becomes real of itself in the here and now. For Barth, the illuminative power of this history rests primarily on the fact that it is God's life with humanity that is being enacted in the history of Jesus Christ, and

69. *CD* IV/3.1, 4.

70. *CD* IV/3.1, 8.

71. "This objectivity of even its revelatory character must be emphasized so expressly because misunderstanding can so easily creep in, as if the problem of the knowledge, understanding and explanation of reconciliation, or more generally of the doctrine of reconciliation as such, of the question how there can possibly be even the most rudimentary theology and proclamation of reconciliation, were really a problem of the theory of human knowledge and its spheres and limitations, its capacities and competencies, its possible or impossible approximation to this object. Only too easily the reference to the enlightening work of the Holy Spirit can be understood as the final and then, like a *Deus ex machina*, the very doubtful word of such a theory of knowledge. But this reference is the last word of the doctrine of reconciliation itself. It is only as such that it can be meaningful, namely as a reference to the fact that in the power of reconciliation itself, i.e., of its character as revelation, in virtue of the self-attestation of Jesus Christ, there are world phenomena which have their basis in it. If this reference is not to be left hanging in the air, it is necessary to hold fast not only to the objectivity of reconciliation as such and its occurrence in the world, but also to the objectivity of its character as revelation to the *a priori* nature of its light in fact of all human illumination and knowledge. There is human knowledge, and a theology of reconciliation, because reconciliation in itself and as such is not only real but true, proving itself true in the enlightening work of the Holy Spirit, but first true as well as real in itself, as disclosure, declaration and impartation. This is the basis of certainty and clarity when it is a matter of the knowledge of Jesus Christ and His work through the work of the Holy Spirit" (*CD* IV/3.1, 10–11).

> Where God is present as active Subject; where He lives, as is the case in the life of Jesus Christ, life is not just possibly or secondarily but definitely and primarily declaration, and therefore light, truth, Word and glory. A mute and obscure God would be an idol. The true and living God is eloquent and radiant. If He is in large measure mute and obscure to us, this is another matter. In Himself, whether we perceive it and accept it or not, He is eloquent and radiant.[72]

The radiance of God's being is rooted in the eternal generation of the Son or Word of God, whose movement and essence are one with the Father. Thus, because God's life is the real subject of Jesus Christ, this history and the life lived in it is also light. But this basis is deduced from a particular concrete event: *the resurrection of Jesus Christ from the dead*. Our knowledge that this Jesus is also the self-speaking and eloquent God becomes evident in the fact that in his resurrection the history that Jesus lived—i.e., the history of the reconciliation of the world, the history of the kingdom of God come in our midst—is irradiated from within so that we come to know that this is in fact the living God reconciling the world to himself.

Thus, the resurrection is God's speech and the vindication of the life that Jesus lived as the Victor. But it is also an aspect of that life. As you will recall, because the subject of the life of Jesus is God, this life presses to be known. If "Jesus is Victor" describes the form, content and direction of the life of God, then it also describes its proclamation as such. The transition out of past history into the present is not something that is somehow to be added to the work of Christ, but rather belongs to the same. Thus, the overcoming of the limitation of death placed before all history, or the transition from the "there and then" into the "here and now" as realized in the resurrection, is also indicated in the watchword "Jesus is Victor."[73]

In an early sermon, Barth had already identified the resurrection with "Jesus is Victor," much as the Blumhardts had done before: "What is Easter? The Bible answers: resurrection, resurrection of Jesus from the dead; and this means: the living God, forgiveness of sins, the empty

---

72. *CD* IV/3.1, 79.

73. "*Resurrexit* means—*Jesus* is conqueror" (Karl Barth, *Credo*, 98).

tomb, conquered death—in a word, Jesus is victor."[74] The history of Jesus's overcoming of the powers of death, sin and the devil, i.e., the history of the atonement, is not sealed off from the event of his eloquent irradiation of that same event, but is one and the same.

The illumination and publication of the truth of the life and death of Jesus are also to be included in the work of Christ. Thus, Barth conceives the resurrection as the commencement of the Prophetic Office of Jesus. It is Jesus who speaks about the truth of His own life, and He does so because He himself is present to all of world history. In this way, the resurrection is the living Christ's doorway into ongoing history itself. The bursting of the banks, in which the there and then history of Jesus Christ overcomes the barrier of death that confronts all history, is for Barth the eschatological *parousia* or "coming again" of Jesus Christ, whose three-fold form finds its inauguration in the resurrection, but which is continued in the outpouring of the Holy Spirit and moves towards the definitive goal of the cosmic dénouement of the kingdom of God.

For Barth, the three-fold *parousia* is the resurrection, the outpouring of the Holy Spirit and the final cosmic transformation of the world. This is a perichoretically conceived three-fold event of the single eschatological reality of the kingdom of God, already come in Jesus the Victor.[75] In the three-fold *parousia* the history of Jesus the Victor—the history of the there and then life of Jesus Christ—shows that though it was like all other history, it was in fact radically unlike it, for in it the inner meaning of the history of the world was enacted, and in such a way that this inner-meaning impinges upon all other history, a confrontation that occurs in the different dimensions and forms of the three-fold *parousia.*

The second reason that this history presses to make itself known, which is implied as the *telos* of the first, is that in it the reconciliation of the world occurs, which means that since it occurs for the sake of the world, its intent is that the world will know about and come to share in the alteration of its predicament. In this event God's grace towards

---

74. Karl Barth and Eduard Thurneysen, *Come Holy Spirit*, 146. For a discussion of the Blumhardts' connection of "Jesus is Victor!" and the resurrection see, infra, chapter 2, "Blumhardt's Hope" and chapter 3, "Eschatological Christology."

75. See *CD* IV/3.1, 295–96.

humanity is known and enacted, not above history, but in and for it.[76] If in this history the reconciliation of world is effected, then as such it presses to be known. Jesus lives, but he lives as the one he was, in which took place the reconciliation of the whole world. The history of Jesus constitutes God's address to humanity and therefore has everything to do with the course of human history.

"Jesus is Victor" = The Inner-Meaning of Ongoing History, Pt. 1

In the eschatological event of the resurrection, the living Christ, as the One he was, crosses over the barrier of death that confronts all of history, and thereby enters into the flow of ongoing history. As such, his history takes all of history up into itself. "The determination given the world and man by this event is a total one. The reconciling work of Jesus Christ is not just accomplished, but has gone out into the reconciled world as a shining light comparable with the leaven hid among three measures of meal (Matt 13:33). This means that the leavening of the whole, the determination and alteration of the world and humanity by the kingdom of heaven in all its power and glory, is not merely possible but actual and in process of fulfillment."[77] The confrontation between the living risen Jesus and the rest of history is the extension of the ontological transformation of the world begun and fulfilled in the life of Jesus and irradiated by the resurrection. It moves in a teleological direction to a final and cosmic end at which "every knee should bow . . . and every tongue confess that Jesus Christ is Lord to the glory of God the Father" (Phil 2:10–11, NIV).

---

76. "As the life of God and His grace, it is not lived in a distant height and therefore in mute obscurity; it is concrete event in the sphere in which this is true of our own lives. It is placed in this sphere, opposed to us in all its singularity and strangeness, yet also set alongside. To be sure, it is new as compared with the accustomed realities of this sphere. It stands in marked contrast with our own life, or what we regard as such. It radically questions all our positions. Yet it is unmistakably real because, for all its difference from ours, it is the life of a man like us: the name which is hallowed in our situation, time and history; the kingdom which has drawn near and impinged as it were upon us; the will of God which is done not merely in heaven but on earth. This happening has as such a voice. It is a declaration. And as it comes to us, it is an address, promise and demand, a question and answer" (CD IV/3.1, 83).

77. CD IV/3.1, 301.

Therefore, in this life-act, the inner meaning of all history is unfolded, but now in a new dimension. It is unfolded in the once-for-all event of the resurrection which irradiates the "there and then" life. In that event we know the true intention that God has for humanity and the creation. But this inner-meaning is also unfolded in on-going history as the illumined history and life of Jesus and his conflict with the powers of darkness on the cross, comes into contact with the history of all humanity. In his self-declaration, in the ongoing discharge of his Prophetic Office, Jesus's work of reconciliation not only was, but continues to be "historical" as Jesus, the "True Witness," mediates and establishes knowledge of himself within the flow of history.

Barth envisioned the confrontation in which Jesus's life-act encountered humanity as necessarily involving a real change in the individual and their history.

> As the event of salvation it thus takes place, not just primarily there and then in Him, but also secondarily and no less really in the knowledge of salvation created by Him. It is thus the case that the one who participates in this knowledge participates in the event of salvation itself. The event becomes the living seed and therefore the fruitful element in the events of his own life. Conversely, the events of his human life become the fruit-bearing field and therefore the confirmation and authentication of the event of salvation which comes to him.[78]

The change that Barth imagined was gradual, in which the believer and the community were always moving in the direction out of darkness into light.[79] This movement from darkness to light, however, was in no sense smooth, but filled with conflict.

Mimicking the dramatic conflict seen in the "there and then" history of Jesus, the history of the interim period between Christ's resurrection and his final appearing is also filled with conflict. For as the risen Jesus whose life is the inner-meaning of all of history enters into the world, this gives rise to resistance. "As the prophetic work of Jesus

---

78. *CD* IV/3.1, 217.

79. "Within and among us men there is no such thing as either an angelic and therefore exclusive knowledge or a devilish and therefore exclusive ignorance. As those who know, we always exist in face of the abnormal and sinister possibility of ignorance, and as those who do not, in face of the normal and bright, yet not completely lacking, but present possibility of knowledge. We exist under the threat of the one possibility and the promise of the other" (*CD* IV/3.1, 193).

Christ takes place, and the atonement is thus revealed and known, there also emerges the opposition of the world and man towards it."[80] Here, in history, we resist the implications of the knowledge of God that is addressed to us in the presence of the risen Christ because the word of grace spoken to us in the cross is also a word of judgment. In the living Jesus, sinful humanity meets God's verdict, which speaks of the definitive limitation and end that has been set on it in the judgment poured out on Jesus. For Barth, therefore, it is this sinful humanity, this element both within us and the world, which rises up in resistance.

Barth wants to take seriously that the progress of the extension and transformation of the world implied and realized in the fact that Jesus really is the Victor, is hampered and resisted by real chaotic forces and genuine and deadly darkness.

> Again, as the world is told, not merely what is resolved concerning it, but what has already been done for it, for its total renewal and transformation; as it is thus given news concerning itself, it has to decide whether it will accept this information or not. But how could it be the unredeemed world on this side of the final coming of Jesus Christ if it did not seriously reject this information which is so diametrically opposed to its own understanding of itself? Again, as there begins this process of knowledge of the true and living God in His acts; as that which, or rather the One whom man would like to regard as a distant object to be regarded, studied and contemplated only at a distance, now threatens to come to him and even into him, overpowering him and subjecting him to a total alteration and renewal, it must be shown whether or not he will accept the proffered liberty of the children of God. Will he allow the process of knowledge which begins on this basis, and therefore his own alteration and renewal, to take its course? . . . How could he be the being which continually thinks that by saying 'I' it places itself on the basic rock of all reality, if in this situation he did not find himself incited and summoned to resolute opposition?[81]

---

80. *CD* IV/3.1, 185.
81. *CD* IV/3.1, 186–87.

Barth highlights, in broad terms, the various strategies employed by humanity to resist the knowledge of God as resistance, competition, and compromise.[82] All three are found both within and outside the church.

It is in the dynamic confrontation between these two factors in the interim period that "Jesus is Victor" takes on a new a different meaning. For "Jesus is Victor" does not just summarize the "there and then" history, nor the overcoming of the limitation of the grave through the resurrection, but it also indicates the confrontation within history between the knowledge of God's reconciliation of the world in Jesus Christ—the will of God done on earth as it is in heaven—and the ongoing resistance to this truth and reality among humanity in history.

The dramatic conflict between God and the chthonic forces of evil that have had a limit set to their existence, becomes a kind of non-identical repetition of the original battle won in the cross. In this way, the ongoing history of conflict between God and the forces of darkness can be described as the inner-meaning of the history of the world. "Jesus is Victor" indicates not merely the actual event of God's overcoming, but it also subsumes and indicates the human community's reception and resistance to the alteration of the world actualized in Jesus Christ.

Barth is careful to emphasize that the conflict between Jesus' self-attestation and the powers of darkness that continue to resist Him is a real and tension-filled conflict. Even if ongoing history, the history of the church and of the whole world, can be subsumed under the watchword "Jesus is Victor" this does not mean that history is emptied of its real and deadly tension and conflict. In the narrative depictions in the Gospels Jesus is portrayed as filled with a resolution of purpose and confidence in the outcome, but he is also portrayed as filled with apprehension, tension, and even fear in the face of the conflict that awaits him in his passion. For Barth, the interim period between Jesus's resurrection and second-coming, whose inner-meaning and course moves under the form of the history of the crucified (i.e., Jesus is Victor), is filled with the same tension. "It may well be 'eternally settled' that the Sower should not go forth to sow in vain, that Jesus should be Victor. Yet in face of this threat to His work, this is by no means self-evident. It

---

82. See *CD* IV/3.1, 250-261. Barth gives a fuller consideration to the forms of humanities resistance in his discussion of the "Falsehood of Man," (434–61), and later in his consideration of "The Lordless Powers," in *CL* (213–33).

has to take place that He conquers."[83] The enemy who arises to resist the living Christ is a real enemy who must be taken seriously.

"Jesus is Victor" = The Inner-Meaning of Ongoing History, Pt. 2

"Jesus is Victor" indicates the inner-meaning of all history, because it indicates the confrontation between the Word of God's reconciliation of the world and the powers of darkness that would resist it. "The proclamation of Jesus Christ and its dreadful limitation are together the history which embraces and comprises, and thus controls and determines, the history of the world and the history of each and every man."[84] In this sense, the ongoing history of the church and the world is enclosed in the history of reconciliation.

Barth is here, working out in a concrete sense and from a different direction the claim that: "Revelation is not a predicate of history, but history is a predicate of revelation."[85] In its primary sense, this theological dictum refers to the fact that revelation is not to be subjected to the vagaries or the limitations of history or historical investigation, the point being that though revelation happens *in* history, it is not *of* history. In Barth's move to subsume world history into the history of reconciliation in the form of the ongoing history of reconciliation, the Prophetic Work of Christ, this point takes on a new meaning. That is, history is real and existent insofar as it exists in the tension of the conflict between Jesus the Victor and the forces of darkness, as it continues to exist in the shadow of revelation. "As the prophecy of Jesus Christ is historical in this concrete sense, so is human existence in the same concrete sense."[86] This implies an ontological and epistemological reversal.

That which is "historical" in its proper sense is not the every day experience of history that we have. Rather, that which can be said to be "historical" in its most proper sense is that which has occurred in the "there and then" history of Jesus, and by the extension of the Prophetic Work of Christ, that which occurs in our lives in the flow of history

---

83. *CD* IV/3.1, 190–91.

84. *CD* IV/3.1, 191.

85. *CD* I/2, 58.

86. *CD* IV/3.1, 193.

as we are encountered and confronted by the living Christ.[87] All are addressed by that event as it traverses the barrier of death revealing the intention and goal of God and as it moves forward through history, "Its fulfillment as the *shining* of light in the darkness, but also its limitation as the light shining in the *darkness*, is the law under which our history, the history of the world and of each and every man, necessarily stands and which it has no choice but to follow."[88] Furthermore, now our history and our lives—i.e., the history that we participate in and help to shape and lives that we live within that history—can and should be read in light of the ongoing history of revelation, rather than vice versa.[89] Truly, revelation is not a predicate of history, but history is a predicate of revelation, or rather, true history is the history of revelation.

It in this sense that Barth can describe the whole history of Christian knowledge, which is the history of the community that believes as well as the history of those who do not know or believe as yet, under the watchword "Jesus is Victor." The history of Christian knowledge is rooted in the living history of Jesus Christ, as Jesus the victor moves to overcome the darkness that still resists him. As this history happens or unfolds, salvation happens, because in it *we* are encountered by the living Christ. "He thus presents Himself to this man. He appears to him. To be sure, He does so in a secondary form. Yet He does so *realiter* and not just *nominaliter*. It is He Himself who appears."[90] My existential experience of salvation consists in my being caught up into the "there and then" history of Jesus Christ as it breaks in upon me in the "here and now," not as a recollection, but as a living reality. At the same time, in keeping with his dialectically conceived doctrine of revelation, the in-breaking is not a straightforward direct presence, but rather a

87. "He does not exist without belonging to Jesus Christ, and therefore without having to do with His adversary; without sharing in the knowledge established by His Word, but also without being bound to the ignorance established in this limitation of His Word" (*CD* IV/3.1, 192). Barth acknowledges (see pp. 192–93) that there is an important difference within history between people, but that the difference is only the relative difference between those who have heard and those who have not, or those who are relatively moving more in the direction of light, and those still engulfed in the darkness.

88. *CD* IV/3.1, 193.

89. For an excellent explanation of this reversal and the kind of theological realism that it produces, see Dalferth, "Karl Barth's Eschatological Realism," 14–45, esp. 20–30.

90. *CD* IV/3.1, 217.

"veiled unveiling" of the living history of Jesus. The living history of Christ inhabits the creaturely medium (i.e., Scripture, proclamation, etc.), simultaneously appropriating it, making it fit to bear witness to the living God, and rendering it translucent. By so doing, the living God really can and does speak through these media and a real encounter between God and humanity occurs, all the while God's loving freedom is secured and the distinction between *God* and *words and concepts about God* is acknowledged and kept.[91]

The result of this confrontation, which Barth describes as an attack,[92] is not simply the conveyance of knowledge, but is literally the beginning of humanity's and history's transformation:

> In Christian knowledge, Jesus Christ comes to be and is really present to him. What He does for him He also does to and in him. He gives him the freedom, permission and command to be the man he is in Him, the new creature, the justified and sanctified sinner, His brother, the child of God, the responsible witness of the atonement which has taken place in Him.[93]

The reconciliation actualized in the cross of Christ comes upon humanity and in that event, in the history of Jesus the Victor, salvation occurs, and the human person is changed. The mode of this encounter in the here and now is pneumatological, in that the outpouring of the Spirit is a form of the *parousia* of the living Lord, whose first actualization was in the resurrection.[94] Furthermore, because this change is only beginning

91. See *CD* IV/3.1, 44.

92. See *CD* IV/3.1, 237–49.

93. *CD* IV/3.1, 220. "We can and should say even more emphatically that knowledge in the biblical sense is the process in which the distant 'object' dissolves as it were, overcoming both its distance and its objectivity and coming to man as acting Subject, entering into the man who knows and subjecting him to this transformation . . . So radical is the transformation which comes on man in this knowledge, so full of content is his own history in it, and so far is this *intelligere* from a merely ratiocinative, argumentative, or even contemplative process which might be described as intellectualistic and the results of which might be attacked and denounced as empty *gnosis*! Paul was well aware what he was about when among the various things for which he gives thanks or prays in relation to his churches he almost always gives pride of place to *gnosis* (*pasa gnosis*, which is included in the one), and when he says that for his own part he counts everything loss compared with the *huperchon* of the one knowledge which includes all others, the knowledge of Jesus Christ His Lord (Phil 3:8)" (184–85).

94. "The return of Jesus Christ in this middle form, in which it takes place here and now, is His coming in the promise of the Spirit. This is His direct and immediate pres-

in the individual and the world, moving towards the final and definitive form of the revelation of "the sons and daughters of God" in Christ's cosmic *parousia*, Christian knowledge of Jesus the victor is especially oriented towards hope.[95]

"Jesus is Victor" = *The Goal of History, the Cosmos and the Ways of God*

"Jesus is Victor" refers to the tension filled history in which the "there and then" history of Jesus Christ breaks into the "here and now" of every individual, confronting the darkness that remains resistant to His work and word of reconciliation. The event of revelation—the prophetic work of the living Jesus Christ as extended into history in the outpouring of the Holy Spirit—is a real tension-filled confrontation that is only real as it happens, as it unfolds in history. Thus, all of history, whether secular or sacred, stands under the sign of the work of Jesus the Victor, whose work of reconciliation addresses because it has altered and therefore affects the whole world.

In the last of our interrelated points, we encounter the most straight-forward meaning of "Jesus is Victor": in relation to the final issue or outcome of the real and deadly conflict in which we all stand in relative light and darkness, the fact that "Jesus is Victor" stands as the

---

ence and action among and with and in us. In it He is the hope of us all" (*CD* IV/3.1, 350); "To put it again in a single sentence: In the work of the Holy Spirit the history manifested to all men in the resurrection of Jesus Christ is manifest and present to a specific man as his own salvation history" (Karl Barth, *CD* IV/4, 27).

95. "What does the Christian really expect as he hopes? . . . It means even for him, too, glory and reward and gain. It means pardon in the final and strictest sense. It means his departing to be with Christ. It means his translation out of the darkness around into the great coming light. It means his transformation, his investiture with a new being which is neither exposed to corruption nor subject to death, his restoration and the beginning of his eternal salvation and life. But it means all these things only in the comprehensive context of the final redeeming act of God in full manifestation of the reconciliation of the world accomplished in Jesus Christ, of the conclusion of peace between the Creator and the creature established in Him, of the kingdom or establishment of the rule of God over all men and all things enacted in Him, of the alteration of the whole of human and cosmic reality effected in Him. . . . Not to him alone, therefore, but to the whole community of which he is a member, and indeed to all men and all creation, there will then come the great change of the overthrow of all the contradiction in which they now exist and the necessary bending of every knee to Jesus Christ and the confessing of Him as Lord by every tongue. This, then, is what the Christian expects" (*CD* IV/3.2, 931–32).

ultimate truth of the end of this conflict. That is, though the disciple is not greater than her master and therefore must trod the road that Jesus trod, which is an experience and knowledge marked with suffering, distress, and even God-forsakenness, the end of this road does not, because it cannot, end in the triumph of death, sin or the devil. Rather, it ends in the final cosmic victory of Jesus Christ. Though the penultimate ends towards which our histories unfold are open to relative success or relative failure, their ultimate end can only be God's triumph.

Barth describes this insight gleaned from Blumhardt and encapsulated in the phrase "Jesus is Victor," as follows:

> In relation to the issue of the conflict, as it is unforgettably brought before us in the Blumhardt story, and even at its very commencement, He is characterized as the One who is greatly superior in relation to His greatly inferior adversary. In some degree the saying analyzes the name of Jesus, and it gathers up this analysis in the simple equation: Jesus=Victor. This tells us that from the very outset, and come what may, the dynamic and teleology of the prophetic ministry and rule of Jesus Christ are unshakeably stamped by the fact that He is this One, Jesus. . . . The equation made in this saying thus forbids us to take with equal seriousness both light and darkness, both Jesus and the contradiction and opposition which He meets. It certainly forbids us to take the contradiction and opposition even more seriously than Jesus. It commands us simply yet resolutely to count on it that, although the contradiction and opposition are to be taken seriously, yet we are to take infinitely more seriously the One whom it encounters, or rather who encounters, contradicts and opposes it, i.e., Jesus, and the dignity and power with which He does this as the One against whom the adversary can bring nothing corresponding, equivalent, or even similar.[96]

For Barth, the conflict between God and evil, between the word of forgiveness and our continued rebellion, and the attendant collateral agonistic and tragic events and aspects in our history and experience, cannot and should not be undervalued or overlooked. But even if we give suffering, struggle and sin the serious attention they deserve, this cannot be the last word, for ultimately, they will not stand before the One who conquers through suffering. Though it is still dark, and there is only a modicum of light, nonetheless we know that we can believe that

96. *CD* IV/3.1, 172.

the light is not simply going to fade away because Jesus's victory will in fact cover the face of the earth.[97]

Again, none of this is self-evident. It is not self-evident that the victory won at Golgotha presses to be actualized throughout the cosmos. And just as it is not self-evident that the resurrection of Jesus happened, neither is it self-evident that His resurrection constitutes a sign that God is in process of fulfilling His promise to restore the whole cosmos. These things are known only in faith, love, and above all, hope. Hope is the human orientation created by the One who breaks into the world in his "there and then" history, beginning our transformation in the here and now. Though Jesus is really present, he is not present in his fullness, nor does his presence eradicate the sinful humanity we know only too well, this will only be removed in his final appearing.[98]

Thus, in our faith, love and hope in Jesus the Victor, though knowledge of the *telos* of history is known, that knowledge does not become a stopping point. Rather, it creates longing for the full truth of Jesus's triumph to be revealed and actualized in history and us and thereby puts us in motion to hope and move towards the final manifestation of the kingdom of God, the history of Jesus the Victor.[99] Furthermore

97. "In the history of Jesus Christ as the New Testament bears witness to it we really do have the already effected and completed victory of light over darkness in the unique and definitive act whereby God himself hallows his name. This was and is already the end of all God's ways, the eschaton" (*CL*, 163).

98. "Even the best of Christians can hardly boast of an absolutely clear vision of Easter Day, of wholly lucid thought on the basis of it, of a comprehensive knowledge of Jesus Christ free from every form of defect or distortion. . . . Every great or small, qualitative or quantitative deficiency in his knowledge of Jesus Christ, his ensuing self-knowledge and his demonstration of his given freedom in consistent following of the way to which he is directed, signifies a tarrying in or regression to the situation and mode of existence of the non-Christian. In this deficiency he must recognize, if he is sincere, that he is not merely a poor or weak Christian but a decided non-Christian. In it he himself is blind and deaf; he himself is a prisoner; he himself is under the dominion of conditions which are simply the conditions of fate and bondage. . . . We cannot be Christians and non-Christians. But we are. What has to be said basically and materially concerning our being as Christians in these circumstances is thus valid only in the light of this very dangerous contradiction which is never resolved in our historical existence and situation as Christians" (*CD* IV/3.1, 341–42).

99. Barth continued to understand Christian faith within this dynamic tension, as is illustrated in the short piece he was working on the night before he died: "The church does not turn back to primitive Christianity but to the new which is, of course, primarily, directly, and normatively attested for all times in its first records. Paul did not proclaim himself but the crucified and risen Jesus Christ. So, too, in their own ways did

for Barth, our hope for this final manifestation is not a hope for *our* troubles and suffering to cease, but hope for the whole world and all of humanity to be changed. Thus, our knowledge that "Jesus is Victor" and the hope that it sets in motion within us, moves in a decidedly universalistic direction. Though Barth will not endorse a systematically conceived doctrine of *apokatastasis ton panton* ("restoration of all things"), neither does he rule it out. Rather,

> If we are certainly forbidden to count on this as though we had a claim to it, as though it were not supremely the work of God to which man can have no possible claim, we are surely commanded the more definitely to hope and pray for it as we may do already on this side of this final possibility, i.e., to hope and pray cautiously and yet distinctly that, in spite of everything which may seem quite conclusively to proclaim the opposite, His compassion should not fail, and that in accordance with His mercy which is 'new every morning' He 'will not cast off for ever' (La. 3:33f., 31).[100]

Thus, our the hope and confidence that is encountered and conveyed in the event of Christian knowledge, which is actualistically conceived as an ongoing history both within the life of the individual, the history of the community and of the larger human community, presses the Christian and the Christian community into solidarity with the rest of humanity, rather than away from it. That Jesus *is* Victor means the liberation of all of humanity and the entire cosmos, rather than some small segment within creation.

"Thy Kingdom Come!" Faithful Human Response in the Interim

Barth's elaboration of the historical and conflictual nature of Christian existence and knowledge in the interim even in the light of the fact that "Jesus is Victor" is developed in conversation with the other central emphasis of the Blumhardts' theology: "Thy kingdom come!" The knowledge that Jesus is Victor—i.e., that there is a real end towards which

---

Peter and John and also the Evangelists. He, Jesus Christ, is the old and is also new. He it is who comes [to the church] and to whom the church goes, but goes to him as him who was. It is to him that it turns in its conversion" (Karl Barth, "Starting Out, Turning Round, Confessing," in *Final Testimonies*, 59).

100. *CD* IV/3.1, 478.

history is moving—does not create complacency, rather it gives rise to a hopeful calling out for Jesus to definitively consummate and fulfill the promise of our reconciliation with God. That is, the knowledge and confession that "Jesus is Victor" grounds and presupposes its human correlate: "Thy kingdom come!"

Here, on the pivot between the divine in-breaking signified by "Jesus is Victor" and the human sigh "Thy kingdom come" which happens in the present of the Christian, the orientation of Christian knowledge turns the disciple away from the past towards the future unveiling of the kingdom of God. Christology and Pneumatology show that they are internally and teleologically related to and fulfilled in eschatology.

Barth's elaboration of the theme "Thy Kingdom Come," occurs within the context of the ethics of reconciliation. Its placement is instructive, for it is located at the center of the center of his discussion of the primary characteristic of the Christian life: prayer. The Christian life, lived in the shadow of "Jesus is Victor" is enacted through the multifaceted act of invocation.[101]

The Importance of the Blumhardts' Understanding

Though Barth was only able to expound the first two petitions of the Lord's Prayer, "Hallowed be thy Name," and "Thy Kingdom Come", he was quite straightforward that in the exposition of the second petition, his deliberations and concerns were shaped and inspired almost exclusively by the Blumhardts:

> The present view of the kingdom of God and its coming may sound new, but it can and will lay no claim to complete originality. We could not have spoken or tried to speak as we did if, quite apart from the academic theology of their days, the two Württembergers J. C. Blumhardt (1805–1880) and his son, C. Blumhardt (1842–1919) of Möttlingen, and then Bad Boll, had not in sermons and devotional and edificatory utterances, not only taught the reality denoted by the term the 'kingdom of God,' but with much greater theological relevance attested and proclaimed it. What has been presented here rests on personal exegetical reflection and theological deliberation. If something

---

101. Because he assumes that the Christian life is essentially invocation for the kingdom of God to come, Barth also develops his theology of baptism within this same logic. See *CD* IV/4, 75–85.

is now being said about the Blumhardts, it is not with the intention of summoning them as subsequent star witnesses for what has been developed. In fact, it could not have been stated and developed as it has without the impulse they gave and their influence through other mediations and modifications.[102]

Barth emphasizes the originality of their understanding, noting that it was distinct in the history of Christian thought. In general, Patristic, Medieval, Reformation, nor post-Reformation theology had come to the understanding of the kingdom of God at which the Blumhardts' had arrived.

The exception for Barth was the New Testament scholarship of Albert Schweitzer and Johannes Weiss, and theological musings of the atheist church historian Franz Overbeck. The similarity between all these figures lay in their emphasis on the eschatological dimension of the New Testament. For Barth, the recovery made by Schweitzer and others, though cast primarily in critical terms, was similar to the rediscovery that the Blumhardts' had made.[103] What distinguished them from one another was that, while for Schweitzer and others the recovery of the eschatological dimension of the New Testament had been a basis for discrediting Jesus and subsequent Christian history, for the Blumhardts that recovery had meant a confrontation with the heart of the Christian faith which cast the New Testament in new light and reinvigorated the faith, hope and love of the community. In the differing assessments of the significance of the eschatological dimension of the New Testament, Barth clearly follows the Blumhardts.

We will briefly look at what the petition "Thy Kingdom Come" meant for Barth under the following two interrelated points: (1) What is the kingdom of God?; and (2) The Sigh for the Kingdom and Human Righteousness

---

102. *CL*, 256–57.

103. "They hardly knew each other, and if they had they would have been objects of considerable astonishment to one another. But I would still say, perhaps even more definitely, that what underlay a certain movement in academic theology at the end of the nineteenth century must be seen together with what was championed most unacademically but very positively by the two Blumhardts, father and son" (*CL*, 257).

What is the Kingdom of God? "Jesus is the victorious hero who has defeated all his foes"[104]

In his concluding remarks in the debate with G. C. Berkouwer recounted above, Barth asks: "How can we pray: 'Thy kingdom come', if we do not start with the sure and certain fact that in Jesus the kingdom has already drawn near in all its glory?"[105] For Barth, the kingdom of God is the "unthinkable thought."[106] It is an utterly new reality that cannot be deduced from present creaturely reality. It sets a limit to our existence in its present form and represents its total and absolute transformation. If this is the case, how can Christians pray "Thy kingdom come"? How do they know what they are praying for? Barth's answer to this question is Christological and harkens back to our discussion of "Jesus is Victor."

Christians can and do pray "Thy kingdom come" because the kingdom for which they sigh has already manifested itself in the history of Jesus the Victor:

> Only one satisfactory answer can be given to the obvious question: what is meant in the New Testament by the presence of the kingdom of God, by its coming as already an event? What is meant is the center, the whence and whither, the basis, theme, and content of all the New Testament sayings, namely, the history of Jesus Christ, the words and deeds and suffering and death of the one Son of the one God as the Messiah of Israel and the Savior of the Gentiles, as the One in giving whom God loved the world, in whom, given up for it, he loves and will love it, in whom he has reconciled it to himself. 'The kingdom of God is at hand' means 'the Word was made flesh and dwelt among us' (Jn. 1:14). In him the divine righteousness and order contest, defeat, overcome, and set aside human unrighteousness and disorder. The first disciples found themselves confronted already in their lifetime with the kingdom of God as God revealed and declared Christ to be the One he was in his resurrection from the dead, as he, the Crucified and Slain, appeared and met them as the Living One, and as they thus found themselves confronted with

104. *CL*, 260. This is the first stanza of the hymn, "Jesus ist der Siegesheld" written by Johann Christoph Blumhardt shortly after the events at Möttlingen. For a facsimile copy see Troebst & Ising, *Christoph Blumhardt*, 19; Also, for a discussion about when this hymn was actually written, see Ising, *Johann Christoph Blumhardt*, 222–23. Barth concludes his reflections on the second petition with a brief exegesis of this hymn.

105. *CD* IV/3.1, 180.

106. *CL*, 237.

Jesus. Similarly, people of all times find themselves confronted already with the mystery of the absolutely new and inconceivable and incomparable thing of the kingdom of God as in the power of his Holy Spirit they find themselves confronted with this Living One as their Lord, as the Lord of all lords [Rev. 17:14; 19:16].[107]

Jesus is the *autobasilea*, the kingdom itself. Jesus is not merely the king, nor the one who ushers in the reality of the kingdom, rather in his life and death and through his resurrection and the outpouring of the Holy Spirit he was and is the kingdom of God in history which is moving to its final cosmic end.[108]

It is here that Barth's Christology is illumined from within as not only dynamic, but also eschatological through and through. As Adrio König states it, "Since his [i.e., Jesus Christ] entire history is described in the same eschatological terms, he himself must be the *eschatos* (the last). The reverse if also true: since he himself is the *eschatos* and *telos* (end or goal), his whole history must be eschatology."[109] In Jesus, the *eschaton* ("last time") has come upon us for he is the *Eschatos* (the last One). However, this is not a static event, for it reveals and enacts itself as a living history that continues to break into ongoing history and moving to its final end. From this vantage then, the eschatological dimension of the history of Jesus Christ is highlighted, for the history of reconciliation both as "there and then" and "here and now" moves teleologically to a final end that, though it does not add anything new to the being and act of God actualized in the life and death of Jesus Christ,

---

107. *CL*, 248–49.

108. In his discussion of baptism, Barth notes that the difference between the time of John the Baptist and that of the community that lived after the event of Pentecost was the realization of this fact. What John had preached, had in fact come upon them in the history of the one with whom they had lived, whom they had seen crucified, and whom they had experienced as still very much alive: "In the meantime the One whom John spoke of as the coming One had in fact come. The kingdom, judgment and remission of sins could no longer be anonymous factors for those to whom He disclosed Himself in His coming and who saw Him therein. In fullness and as an act they now stood before their eyes in the whole enacted history of Jesus Christ up to its consummation on the cross of Golgotha, and also in His resurrection in which this history was made manifest to them" (*CD* IV/4, 74).

109. König, *The Eclipse of Christ in Eschatology*, 37.

will manifest its true depth in such a way that creation and history will be radically transformed.[110]

Likewise, the fusing of Christology and eschatology works in reverse fashion. Again, in the concise description of König, "Eschatology is teleological Christology—goal-directed Christology."[111] Thus, to pray for the kingdom of God to come is to pray for the fullness of the life and death of Jesus to be revealed and actualized in history and creation as the end and goal of both. It is not to pray for the arrival of the *eschaton* ("last time"), or for the occurrence of the *eschata* ("last things"), but only for these as they are indelibly marked by and rooted in the living *Eschatos* ("last One"). We are not praying for a thing or concept but for the final coming of this One:

> We must emphasize the 'he'—not, then, an it, however lofty or profound; not a transcendent world of light; not an original and finally binding moral law; not a self-resting and self-moved ground of being as the origin and goal of all being; not a new philosophy, pedagogy, or politics asserting itself as better or the best; not a quintessence of personal human life either exemplary in love, purity, humility, and so forth, or fascinating in its originality; and finally, not a Christian dogmatics triumphantly proclaiming the triumph of grace, not a doctrine about him, not a Christology, not a doctrine of the kingdom of God. Simply and solely *he himself*: accomplishing and completing God's work for the salvation of the world, that is, its reconciliation to God; speaking without reservation or subtraction God's Word to all people without exception; *he*, this man in the history of his life and word and work and passion and death.[112]

In the identification of the kingdom of God with Jesus, we see the coming together of the two Blumhardtian watchwords "Jesus is Victor" and "Thy Kingdom Come." For, "Whoever knew and loved and proclaimed him knew and loved and proclaimed the imminent kingdom of God. Speaking about God's kingdom could only mean telling his story."[113] In

---

110. "In this transition from the old aeon to the new literally nothing in His creation will be broken or extinguished or destroyed. His faithfulness will triumph in the fact that in form it must and will undergo a total and radical and universal transformation" (*CD* IV/3.1, 241).

111. König, *The Eclipse of Christ in Eschatology*, 38.

112. *CL*, 252–53. See also *Credo*, 166.

113. *CL*, 253.

Jesus, the powers of evil have been subdued, the judgment of God has been poured out on sinful humanity, sin itself has been eradicated and the new creation has dawned.[114] In the life, death and resurrection of Jesus, the kingdom of God has come.

The Sigh for the Kingdom and Human Righteousness

The kingdom of God has come. For Barth, however, this is not the end of the matter. Rather, the coming of the kingdom of God in Jesus and its initial and ongoing manifestation in the resurrection and the outpouring of the Holy Spirit become a catalyst and summons for all of creation and humanity to long for the final cosmic revelation and restoration of creation that has been provisionally manifested. This is because, "the kingdom of God did present itself to the first community as present but also future in the history of Jesus Christ . . ."[115] That is, the resurrection reveals that though the kingdom of God has come in history, is now present in the risen Christ, and will be present in the outpouring of the Holy Spirit, it is a presence and reality that is on the move to the final goal, the restoration of the world.[116] The Christian community, then, as those who know about the presence of the kingdom, are enjoined to sigh for it to come in all its fullness, to sigh for the final cosmic revelation of Jesus the victor which will be the transformation of all things.

Barth is very careful to distinguish between the human sigh for the kingdom and its eventual coming. It is God alone who brings the kingdom.

> As it is prayed for in the second petition, the kingdom is not a kind of continuing, prolonging, excelling, and completing of

114. "In the history of Jesus Christ as the New Testament bears witness to it we really do have the already effected and completed victory of light over darkness in the unique and definitive act whereby God himself hallows his name. This was and is already the end of all God's ways, the eschaton" (*CL*, 163).

115. *CL*, 254.

116. "After Easter the turning of 180 degrees had to be made. Looking back to his previous history, to the *then* of the coming of God's kingdom, had to become at once looking forward to his future. It was impossible to look back to the risen Jesus, the revealed Son and Lord, the kingdom known as universal and not just particular to them. One could only look and move forward to this Jesus. It had and has to be said of the Easter history—this is the self-evident presupposition of the whole of the New Testament—that he *comes* who came, Jesus the Lord, and that it *comes* that came, the kingdom of God" (*CL*, 255).

what people may, as commanded, attempt and undertake in a more or less right understanding of their relationship to it or in some other form of reflection on what is good. It is instead the new thing that precedes the beginning of all such action if the latter is to be well done. It is the new thing that crowns—crowns with grace and mercy (Ps. 103:4)—all such completed action if it is to remain well done. It is not a refining or strengthening or intensifying or qualifying of such action which supposedly gives to it the character of a quasi-divine action. It is instead God's own action, which does not merge into the best of human action, for example, that of Christian faith or the Christian church, which does not mingle with it, let alone identify itself with it, which remains free and independent over against it, and which in its purity and freedom is God's gracious, reconciling, and finally redeeming action. . . . Conversely, then, it is not a divine work for whose commencement, continuation, and completion some human cooperation has to be considered and postulated and which could no standing or being without the assistance of certain people. It is God's work alone, which as it is revealed to them can be known by people in faith, gratefully hailed and extolled by them, and then attested and proclaimed, but which cannot in any circumstances be made their own operation or promoted, augmented, or perhaps improved by their action.[117]

Because the kingdom is the "unthinkable thought," the resurrection from the dead, the new creation, the end and transformation of history, it cannot become the agenda of any human action, it can only be received as a gift from God.

At the same time, however, God does in fact bring about His kingdom in response to the human petition for its coming. The history of human longing is enfolded into the history of the coming of the kingdom. For "Salvation history is the history of the *totus Christus,* of the Head with the body and all the members. This *totus Christus* is *Christus victor.*"[118] We are given a part in the history of God's kingdom as we sigh for its coming. The time between the resurrection and the final appearing, interim time, is set aside for us so that we might have a

117. *CL,* 239–40.
118. *CD* IV/3.1, 216.

part in God's own work.[119] Though our actions and longing cannot in and of themselves be invested with a divine power or authority, they are enfolded by God's grace into the history of God's kingdom. Human action corresponds to the divine, and thus as a creaturely response, it anticipates and witnesses to the coming kingdom. A couple of items call for clarification here.

1. The first is that, for Barth, to pray the second petition is not to become quietistic, but to engage in radical, active, and hope-filled action. It is a struggle for human, as well as divine righteousness. "The time between that beginning and that end, our time as the time of the presence of Jesus Christ in the Holy Spirit, is for Christians the space for gratitude, hope, and prayer, and also the time of responsibility for the occurrence of human righteousness."[120] Our knowledge that the king-

119. "Why did He will to interpose between His own beginning and His own end this way and warfare and time with its 'still' and 'not yet'? ... The answer is quite simply that it is His good will because it has as its aim the granting to and procuring for the creation reconciled to God in Him both time and space, not merely to see, but actively to share in the harvest which follows from the sowing of reconciliation. In willing this and not something supposedly better, Jesus Christ confirms Himself and His whole being and action. From all eternity He is not alone, but He is the Elect of God in whom and with whom creation is also elect, not in order that it should vanish and dissolve in Him, nor to be merely the object of His work, but in Him and through Him to be free. ... And now the good will of Jesus Christ in the matter which here concerns us is that the world, His people and ourselves should not be merely the objects of His action but that we should be with Him as independently active and free subjects when it is a question of this harvest, of the redeeming and consummating declaration of His life as given for us, of the illumination and irradiation of the world by the reconciliation effected and revealed by Him" (CD IV/3.1, 331–32).

120. CL, 264. "Nevertheless, for those who in the power of the resurrection of Jesus Christ from the dead, enlightened by the Holy Spirit of the Father and the Son, look ahead from that beginning to this end, this cannot possibly mean that they are commanded or even permitted to be idle in the meantime; to acquiesce for the time being in human unrighteousness and disorder and their consequences, in the mortal imperiling of life, freedom, peace, and joy on earth under the lordship of the lordless powers; so far as possible to adjust themselves during the interim to the status quo; to establish themselves on this; and perhaps even with gloomy skeptical speculation to find comfort in the thought that until God's final and decisive intervention, the course of events will necessarily be not only as bad as previously but increasingly worse. No, they wait and hasten toward the day of God's day, the appearing of his righteousness, the parousia of Jesus Christ (2 Pet. 3:12). They not only wait but also hasten. They wait by hastening. Their waiting takes place in hastening. Aiming at God's kingdom, established on its coming and not on the status quo, they do not just look toward it but run toward it as fast as their feet will carry them. This is inevitable if in their hearts and on their lips the petition 'Thy kingdom come' is not an indolent and despondent prayer but one that is

dom has come in Jesus, or that "Jesus is Victor" cannot be an excuse to become lethargic, uninterested or smug in our attitude as to the ongoing course of history or its end. Rather, it is a knowledge that when heard aright, will necessarily lead the faithful Christian into the struggle for a human righteousness that anticipates, however modestly, the coming revelation of divine righteousness that is the kingdom of God.

For Barth, our attempts to concretize our prayer for the kingdom will necessarily lead us into conflict with the world. In this conflict, however, the Christian community always assumes the form of the crucified. Thus it does not conquer the world, nor dictate to the world, but suffers alongside and with it. When our course of action leads us into conflict with others, whether this is a conflict between good and evil, or more likely between relative goods and relative evils, it is never in an absolute sense that the Christian says no or yes to the world around and within, for the true aim of Christian witness and action is not principled consistency, but the freedom of humanity that only God can bring. "Their total and definitive decision is for man and not for any cause. They will never let themselves be addressed as prisoners of their own decisions or slaves of any sacrosanct consistency."[121] This leads us to our second point.

2. Our knowledge that the kingdom of God has come, that "Jesus is Victor," is not a cause for Christian triumphalism but for solidarity with the world. The reason for this is two-fold. On the one hand the knowledge given to the community in the presence of the risen Jesus and acted on in the sigh "Thy kingdom come" is not a knowledge that permits of schematic or conceptual control. We only have this knowledge as we follow the one who is in the process of bringing the fullness of His kingdom to its cosmic end. *When* this ending will come and *how* it will come in its final form, is not something that can be anticipated or produced by our sigh. In the end, only God brings the kingdom. Thus, our hope in the kingdom cannot be a hope in our knowledge of the same, but only hope in the living One on whom that knowledge is based. In other words, Christian knowledge, whose real content is the living and self-speaking God, is too dynamic to permit of conceptual control, thus it does not allow for an absolute epistemological distinc-

---

zealous and brave" (*CL*, 263).

121. *CL*, 268.

tion between the Christian and the non-Christian. Rather, both are on the same level and are constantly addressed and summoned to follow the living God.

On the other hand, the ultimate orientation towards which Jesus moves as He subdues the remaining forces of darkness is universal. In his exposition of the second stanza of the Blumhardts' hymn "Jesus ist der Siegesheld," Barth appeals to the dying words of the elder Blumhardt as an appropriate commentary on the goal of all Christian and human sighing: that, "the Lord will lay His gentle hand in mercy on all peoples."[122] Our knowledge that "Jesus is Victor" and the command to pray "Thy kingdom come" is not meant to arrogate a happy ending to ourselves, or to the Christian community. Rather, it is a prayer that places us in solidarity with the whole humanity community. For Jesus's victory and the kingdom of God realized in His being and act as both God and man, is addressed to every person and the whole creation.

To pray "Thy kingdom come," is to revolt against the cosmic and human powers of disorder for the liberation of the whole inhabited earth. Thus it is a prayer whose aim is the whole human community: "The task of little righteousness which Christians are given when they may pray for the coming of God's kingdom is to see and understand man in this plight from which he cannot rescue himself, but only God can rescue him, to turn to him openly and willingly, to meet him with mercy."[123] The hope embodied in the cry "Thy kingdom come" is a universal hope for the whole of humanity.

Though the "waiting and hastening" towards the kingdom of God that constitutes the human act of sighing "Thy kingdom come" is oriented towards the ultimate, it does not forget the penultimate. The hope of the Christian is not just for a possible *apokatastasis ton panton* ("restoration of all things") at the end of history, but also for forms of solidarity in the here and now. Because Christian action follows the path of its master, even in its penultimate forms it is oriented

---

122. *CL*, 260. For the historical setting of this saying see, Zündel, *Johann Christoph Blumhardt*, 532–37, esp. 536.

123. *CL*, 270. "As Christians, obedient to the command that they are given, busy themselves with this task, whose execution can begin only with the merciful seeing and understanding of man himself, they confess solidarity at every point with man himself, they show themselves to be his companions and friends without worrying about his garb or mask, and they make his cause their own" (*CL*, 270).

towards the whole of humanity. "Their invocation of God is as such a supremely social matter, publicly social, not to say political and even cosmic."[124] Therefore it will necessarily be more socialistic than not, and will undertake its political, social and practical endeavors in more experimental and *ad hoc* manner, rather than from a definite ideological commitment or stance.[125]

Concluding Observations

By way of conclusion of our consideration of the Blumhardts' influence on Barth's mature theology we will offer the following observations: 1) that the Blumhardts remained significant interlocutors for Barth's mature theology is undeniable; 2) that the influence exerted by the Blumhardts is multifaceted and substantive; and that 3) Barth's

124. *CL*, 95.

125. Barth develops the multifaceted contours of what Christian action as parable of the kingdom might look like in his considerations of the diaconal ministry of the community. See *CD* IV/3.2, 862–901. In this context he reconsiders the legitimacy of Christian socialism as a way to address systemic injustice and sin: "First, its distinctive task of giving help to the needy in the totality of their human existence cannot be undertaken in the long run unless the community realizes that the need of individuals is also and indeed decisively, though not exclusively, grounded in certain disorders of the whole of human life in society, so that at certain points a limit will be set to what it can do or try to do by prevailing social, economic and political conditions. . . . This recognition will not cause the diaconate to refrain from fulfilling its task at the frontier set by these relationships. But it cannot refrain from expressing this recognition, from imparting it to the community in order that the latter may raise its voice and with its proclamation of the Gospel summon the world to reflect on social injustice and its consequences and to alter the conditions and relationships in question. In this situation there is need for the open word of Christian social criticism in order that a new place may be found for Christian action and a new meaning given to it.

"The way must be trodden whose main direction (the helping of God, of the brethren and the state) was indicated in Germany in the latter part of the 19th century by the successive thinkers J. H. Wichern, F. v. Bodelschwingh, A. Stoeker, F. Naumann and C. Blumhardt Jr. Every step taken involved a host of difficulties, objections, genuine and spurious problems, differences of opinion and conflicts. These were all in some way connected with the fact that in this as in so many other matters the community had been too long asleep or inactive, and that it needed the competition of godless Marxist Socialism with its evangelization and diaconate, combined under the name of Home Missions, to set it moving in the necessary direction. The same difficulties will arise in the altered relationships of the present. But they should not prevent the Christian diaconate, even at the risk of being accused of singing a political and therefore an unwelcome tune, from reaching out in this direction, while not of course neglecting its proper task" (*CD* IV/3.2, 892–93).

appropriation of Blumhardtian metaphors and themes was not a re-prinstination, but was rather constructive and creative.

The Undeniable Influence of the Blumhardts on Barth's Mature Theology

The first and most basic observation that should be made in light of our deliberations is that the Blumhardts remained important theological interlocutors for Barth up into his mature theology as embodied in the *Church Dogmatics*. Our investigation concentrated primarily on the sections "Jesus is Victor" in *Church Dogmatics* IV/3.1 and "Thy Kingdom Come" in *The Christian Life* lecture fragments.

These sections constitute the most sustained and intensive theological engagement with the themes and concerns of the Blumhardts in the whole of Barth's literary *oeuvre*, overshadowing the important early essays "Action in Waiting for the Kingdom of God" and "Past and Future: Friedrich Naumann and Christoph Blumhardt" as well as the consideration of Johann Christoph Blumhardt in the lectures on nineteenth century theology.[126] In both sections Barth makes explicit that his concerns have been decidedly shaped by the thought and witness of the Blumhardts, such that he is not appropriating their provocative metaphors, while abandoning the meaning that these metaphors had for the Blumhardts.[127] Rather, he understood himself as attempting to

---

126. See "Action in Waiting for the Kingdom of God," in *Action in Waiting* by Karl Barth and Christoph Blumhardt, 19–45; see also, "Past and Future: Friedrich Naumann and Christoph Blumhardt," in *The Beginnings of Dialectical Theology*, 35–45; see also "Blumhardt," in *Protestant Theology in the Nineteenth Century*, 644–53.

127. "It would be ungrateful if we did not conclude this subsection with an historical statement. The present view of the kingdom of God and its coming may sound new, but it can and will lay no claim to complete originality. We could not have spoken or tried to speak as we did if, quite apart from the academic theology of their days, the two Württembergers J. C. Blumhardt (1805–1880) and his son, C. Blumhardt (1842–1919) of Möttlingen, and then Bad Boll, had not in sermons and devotional and edificatory utterances, not only taught the reality denoted by the term the 'kingdom of God,' but with much greater theological relevance attested and proclaimed it. What has been presented here rests on personal exegetical reflection and theological deliberation. If something is now being said about the Blumhardts, it is not with the intention of summoning them as subsequent star witnesses for what has been developed. In fact, it could not have been stated and developed as it has without the impulse they gave and their influence through other mediations and modifications. This is what must be expressly confirmed here in expansion of what has already been said in *CD* IV,3, pp. 168–71" (*CL*, 256–57).

think along with the Blumhardts such that it could be said that he was attempting to make their concerns, questions and issues his own, all the while expressing them in his own distinctive voice. Furthermore, as briefly noted at the beginning of this chapter, the concerns and themes of the Blumhardts are not confined to the sections that we have investigated, but are everywhere evident throughout *Church Dogmatics* IV/3 and in *The Christian Life* lecture fragment. The almost pervasive presence of the themes and concerns of the Blumhardts in these volumes—which, in over 1200 pages, constitutes the summation and crown of the doctrine of reconciliation, arguably the most important part of the *Church Dogmatics*[128]—is evidence that the creative and decisive impulse they had given to Barth in his theological beginnings, remained with him.

The Influence of the Blumhardts is Multi-faceted and Substantive

The influence of the Blumhardts is multifaceted and substantive. It can be found functioning on multiple levels.

In the methodological argument with G. C. Berkouwer, the Blumhardts functioned as exemplars for how to engage in the kind of "Christological thinking" that was the very heart of Barth's theological intentions. They were guides, albeit in outline form, for a theological orientation and methodology that can be described as dynamic, flexible, concerned with the narrative structure and flow of the witness of Scripture, and above all spiritually aware that the witness of the Christian community, and therefore of the theologian, is only true and vivifying if the living and risen Christ is present to speak through it. Barth's understanding of "Christological thinking" displays the same dynamic movement that he had attributed to the Blumhardts in the very beginning of his theological development. With an almost uncanny consis-

---

128. Though many different doctrines or themes within the *Church Dogmatics* have been held up as central, Barth himself certainly felt that the doctrine of reconciliation should be considered of the utmost importance: "I have been very conscious of the very special responsibility laid on the theologian at this centre of all Christian knowledge. To fail here is to fail everywhere. To be on the right track here makes it impossible to be completely mistaken in the whole. Week by week and even day by day I have had, and will have (in the continuation), to exercise constant vigilance to find that right track and not to lose it" (*CD* IV/1, ix).

tency, Barth can be seen in his debate with Berkouwer to be emulating and recommending the very same form and way of thinking—though undoubtedly in a more complex and rigorous form—that he had commended to his compatriots during the 1910s.[129]

On the level of content, the theological complex denoted by the watchword "Jesus is Victor" gives form and orientation to the whole of Barth's considerations of the presence of the risen Christ in the interim period. "Jesus is Victor" sums up the history of reconciliation both in its "there and then" form and in its status as a history that lives in the "here and now" through the three-fold *parousia* of Jesus Christ inaugurated in the resurrection and experienced now in the power of the Holy Spirit. It is also the decisive word to be said about the interim time, the time of ongoing history. Our own ongoing and constant struggle to both receive and reject the word of reconciliation announced in Christ is enfolded into the one history of Jesus the Victor, and thus we become not merely objects, but active subjects in the work of God's redemption of the world in Christ.

In the Blumhardts' watchword "Thy Kingdom Come" Barth finds a concise indicator and description of the primary action that is enjoined on the Christian community and the individual Christian during the interim period that still labors under the shadow of the deadly conflict between the Crucified and the chthonic forces of darkness and evil. In his appeal to this theme, Barth shows that Christology, Pneumatology and eschatology belong together, for Jesus the Victor *is* the kingdom of God that has come, comes in the Spirit, and will come as the final *Eschatos* whose life and light will liberate and transform the cosmos, humanity and history itself.

---

129. Dalferth also highlights this consistency, and obliquely connects it to the Blumhardts: "'Jesus is victor'—this motto of the Blumhardts he accepted to be the starting-point and guiding principle of all Christian existence and theology. Accordingly, the reality with which theology must deal, is 'the reality of the risen and living Jesus himself, acting and speaking as a distinctive factor no less actual today than yesterday.' It is the reality of the resurrection in which the eschatological kingdom of God became manifest and which, in the proclamation of the gospel, continually represents itself by the power of the Spirit.... From the publication of his *Epistle to the Romans* in 1919 to the very end of his life, Barth did not waver on this fundamental point: the reality to which theology refers is the eschatological reality of the risen Christ and the new life into which we are drawn by the Spirit" ("Karl Barth's Eschatological Realism," 20–21).

Barth's appeal to these two watchwords and the theological themes for which they stand bears a striking similarity to the Blumhardts' own more fragmentary thoughts on the same. As we noted in the close of chapter 3, "Jesus is Victor" and "Thy kingdom come" are the two conceptual poles of the Blumhardts' theology. The former representing the in-breaking kingdom of God which is directly identified with Jesus Christ, and the latter pointing to the task enjoined on the community to "wait and hasten" towards the coming kingdom of God which desires a human corollary to freely welcome the final universal manifestation of God's rule. In commenting on Blumhardt, Gerhard Sauter has noted that, "With Blumhardt the confession of 'Jesus is Victor!' and the cry '—Our Lord, come!' (1 Cor. 16:22, cf. Rev. 22:20) penetrate each other: the certainty of the presence of Christ and the imminent expectation of the coming Christ, with whom the creation will be redeemed in the consummation of the kingdom of God. The victory of Jesus does not bring the battle to an end, but rather leads it creatively forward."[130] Likewise for Barth, the presence of the kingdom of God as realized in the "there and then" history of Jesus the Victor, which through the Holy Spirit is present in the "here and now" is what empowers and calls the community to sigh for its future and final coming. The history of the interim period, the time between the resurrection and revelation of Jesus the Victor and the final cosmic revelation of the same, is a period of struggle in which the living Christ is actively seeking out a faithful community that will pray and act in light of his victory, "Thy kingdom come!"

We should note that, in many ways, Barth's construal of these two themes bears more of the influence of Christoph Blumhardt than has often been acknowledged. Gerhard Sauter has noticed that as the *Church Dogmatics* progressed references to the elder Blumhardt increased while, "In contrast, the references to Christoph, the younger Blumhardt (1842–1919), become increasingly sparse, even though Barth had come to know him personally and, since 1915, had received orientation form Blumhardt in his search within the charged context of theology and politics. Apparently Barth later understood the influence of the younger Blumhardt as part of a trail that did not lead further; and thus he came

---

130. Sauter, " Barth's Understanding of Eschatology," 417.

to see it, at least in part, as a wrong path."[131] It may be the case that Barth felt himself to have turned away from the approach of Christoph, but the Christocentric orientation of both Barth and Christoph is difficult to deny.

Consider the following:

1. Though the elder Blumhardt also identifies the kingdom of God with Jesus, it is Christoph who makes this explicit in the way that Barth will come to embrace in his discussion of this theme in *The Christian Life*.[132]

2. Though the elder Blumhardt understood "Jesus is Victor" to refer to the ongoing history of struggle that Jesus wages in the here and now in extension of his there and then life, it was Christoph who came closest to the formulation that Barth would later describe. As Christoph put it: "Behind the veil of world-history, as it were, stands the Cross of Christ; now and then the veil parts and this history of the Crucified presses through into our world."[133] As we elaborated in chapter 3, "The history of the Crucified," refers to a self-enclosed living reality that continues to invade ongoing history in order to change it.

3. Finally, just as Christoph had done, Barth has set aside the elder Blumhardt's loosely periodized theology of history. Barth's construction allows for ongoing irruptions of the kingdom of God or Jesus the Victor to be detected in the form of parables, but he does not go out of his way to give an account of past events in which that has happened. His concern is to avoid over-identification of the kingdom with any event in ongoing history, while continuing to allow that every event and period can be used as a doorway through which the living God might come.

At the same time, however, the elder Blumhardt's influence should not be downplayed or overlooked. The experiences of the elder Blumhardt during the Möttlingen *Kampf* and Johann

---

131. Ibid., 418.

132. "He lives among men and he is the kingdom of God. He does not make it; He *is* the kingdom!" (Christoph Blumhardt, *Auswahl*, III, 61, unpublished translation by the Brüderhof and Plough Publishing).

133. Christoph Blumhardt, *Vom Reich Gottes*, 66 (unpublished translation by the Brüderhof and Plough Publishing).

Christoph's subsequent reflections on it continue to be of genuine importance in Barth's theological reflections on "Jesus is Victor" and "Thy Kingdom Come." One can also detect in Barth's elaboration of the three-fold *parousia* Christ, the influence of the fragmentary reflections of Johann Christoph on the same.[134]

Finally, the placement of the two watchwords and their attendant themes in the *Church Dogmatics* also indicates that Barth understood their inter-relationship in a way similar to the Blumhardts themselves. "Jesus is Victor" refers to the divine action of God's ongoing struggle to liberate creation, while "Thy kingdom come" refers to the task enjoined on the community to seek, ask, and knock, to "wait and hasten" towards the same. They are ordered as an asymmetrical dialectical pair. "Jesus is Victor" is primary, and "Thy kingdom come" is secondary. The first precedes, grounds and creates the second, while the existence of the second is presupposed in the action of the former.

Thinking With, in Order to Go Beyond the Blumhardts

Our final observation is quite simple, though in its simplicity it is the most difficult to elaborate. Though Barth was working with the themes of the Blumhardts, he was also moving beyond them. While there is great concern to listen carefully and thereby to hear fully what the Blumhardts' witness has to say, there is no concern whatsoever in Barth's considerations to slavishly repeat them.

There are two reasons for this. The first we have highlighted in our discussion of Barth's critical independence from the Blumhardts. Insofar as their reflections, aphorisms and kerygmatic witness were able to do justice to *die Sache* of Scripture, it could be followed wholeheartedly, even if contextual and theological modifications were needed. When, in Barth's estimation, it failed to do so, their witness could be emended, modified or even jettisoned.

The second reason that Barth did not slavishly repeat the Blumhardts is that the primary context of his own creative theological thinking and labors prohibited such a repristination. Barth was a dogmatic theologian whose aim was to rigorously investigate the internal

---

134. See above, chapter 2, under the section heading "Blumhardts Hope" for our discussion of this.

logic of the Christian faith and to expound the same within the context of the living conversation of the Church which is not able to cast aside its history anymore than it can cast aside the contexts that confront the Church in any age. Thus, Barth's reflections on the themes of the Blumhardts were far more rigorous, with more attention to the dogmatic presuppositions, implications and structure of the claim that "Jesus is Victor" and the task for the community to pray "Thy kingdom come" than either of the Blumhardts' could be described as undertaking.

For some, the dogmatic context of Barth's reflections may represent a bastardization of the Blumhardts' thought and witness. While for others Barth's construal might represent the needed sharpening and clarification lacking in the *ad hoc* and fragmentary form that the Blumhardts' thought comes to us in. Whatever the case may be, it is clear that Barth gathered up the essential though fragmentary insights that the Blumhardts had developed and sought to live in, and incorporated them into a more elaborate theological mosaic that, in its intentions, sought to keep faith with the Blumhardts' witness.[135] If one allows that this larger mosaic does in fact do justice to the Blumhardts' life and witness, then one can say that Barth has indeed thought with the Blumhardts, in order to go beyond them.

135. I owe the image of a mosaic to conversations with my friend Peter G. Heltzel.

Conclusion

THE BASIC THESIS AND BURDEN OF THIS DISSERTATION HAS BEEN TO demonstrate that the life and thought of the Blumhardts was of decisive importance for the theology of Karl Barth. Our study has shown that not only were the Blumhardts of great importance for Barth's break from the Protestant Liberal theology that he had been trained in as a student, but that these two men—both simultaneously unassuming and charismatic—and the powerful theological vision that animated their lives and thought remained of great importance to Barth, even into his mature theology.

With the failure of German Protestant Liberal theology and the international and Religious Socialist movements to prophetically resist the beginning of the First World War, Barth had lost confidence in the theological and political orientations that had guided his ministry. In the midst of this confusion he was reintroduced to the kerygmatic theology of the Blumhardts' through his friend Eduard Thurneysen. The Blumhardts' life and witness, as succinctly summed up in the two watchwords "Jesus is Victor!" and "Thy kingdom come!", pointed to the living and active God who was invading His world in order to bring it to its final *telos*, the kingdom of God on earth.

After the personal meeting with Christoph Blumhardt in April 1915 and subsequent reading of Blumhardt texts, Barth's theological trajectory had changed and was moving in a direction that was deeply influenced by their concrete hope for the kingdom of God that had broken into the world in the resurrection of Jesus Christ from the dead. Their conviction that *die Sache*—i.e., "the content of the contents"—of Scripture was the living and active God who has invaded His world in a decisive fashion in Jesus Christ became Barth's own inner theological standpoint and presupposition after April 1915. Barth's subsequent work, at least up to 1919, bears this out.

This new inner theological standpoint and presupposition pushed Barth to reconsider not merely the thematics, but the direction that theological thought moves in. From 1916 to 1919, Barth can be seen attempting and presenting to friends and colleagues theologically "necessary and promising experiments for the hour,"[1] that were deeply influenced by the movement of thought represented by the Blumhardts. Inspired by the example of the Blumhardts', Barth was particularly keen to reflect on and attempt to follow the movement of *die Sache* of Scripture, a process he described as "tracing a bird in flight."[2] The attempt to follow the movement of thought exemplified by the Blumhardts became central to Barth's reflections on theology and political engagement during this period.

Our study has also shown that the influence of the Blumhardts did not wane over the course of Barth's own theological pilgrimage. Our analysis of the late published and unpublished volumes of the *Church Dogmatics* has shown that their continued multifaceted and substantive influence on Barth's theology, both in terms of thematics and in methodology, is simply undeniable. Methodologically, Barth's description of "Christological thinking" evidences continuity with his early attempts to "trace a bird in flight," which had been inspired by the Blumhardts' own witness. "If there is any Christian and theological axiom, it is that Jesus Christ is risen, that He is truly risen."[3] Though his thought has clearly deepened and matured, taking on a more clearly Christocentric coloring, he remains committed to the idea that if theological thinking is going to be consonant with its purported subject matter, it will have to follow the movement of its object, the living risen Christ.

Our study has also shown that the use of the watchwords "Jesus is Victor!" and "Thy kingdom come!" in Barth's mature theology does not constitute a mere homage to the early influence of the Blumhardts. Nor does Barth appropriate the form of their thought while jettisoning its content. Rather, he appropriates, internalizes, and reconstructs their thought from within. Though definite differences can be detected, they have to do far more with the different contexts in which Barth and the Blumhardts' thought and lived. The Blumhardts' pastoral context pushed their thought in a pastoral direction that was less systematic and rigor-

---

1. *CL*, 258.

2. "For our position is really an instant in a *movement*, and any view of it is comparable to the momentary view of a bird in flight" (Karl Barth, "The Christian's Place in Society," 283).

3. *CD* IV/3.1, 44.

ous, but in some ways more concrete, while the dogmatic context into which Barth sought to integrate the Blumhardts' insights pushed him to give more systematic rigor, internal consistency and theological depth to the conviction their common conviction that "Jesus is Victor!." At the same time, we have noted that if one allows that Barth's appropriation of the theologically dense though systematically fragmented insights of the Blumhardts' was consonant with their meaning, then Barth's integration of these insights into a larger and more rigorous theological mosaic could be described as advancing, and advancing beyond, the Blumhardts' own theological intentions and kerygmatic witness.

The influence of the Blumhardts on Barth, and Barth's own independent construal of their thought opens up a possibility for the heirs of Barth's own theology. Contrary to common misconception, Barth's loyal independence vis-à-vis the Blumhardts was precisely what Barth had hoped would be extended towards his thought by those who came after him. As he had noted, "I have never understood the whole *Church Dogmatics* as a house but as the introduction to a way which must be followed, as the description of the movement of something that can only be described in dynamic, not static, concepts."[4]

For Barth, the way that must be followed in theological thought began and ended with the living Jesus Christ, but that did not mean that he believed that his approach to theology was the only one. Rather,

> Christian truth is a living whole. I do not like the term 'architecture' too much, for it connotes 'building or system.' Christian truth is like a globe, where every point points to the centre. We must hold out the possibility of beginning a dogmatics with any doctrine, for instance, with the doctrine of the Church, or with the topic in Calvin's Book III: sanctification, or even a universal doctrine of the Holy Spirit. Indeed, we might even begin with the Christian man! The Christian and the Christian theologian must be a *free* man.[5]

Barth's commitment to following after, to "tracing the bird in flight," frees up those who would follow after him, for it calls the theologian to listen attentively to Barth's witness to the living God, but all the while to allow for freedom to deviate, to correct, to alter, and even to reject where necessary.

4. Busch, *Karl Barth*, 375.
5. Godsey, *Karl Barth's Table Talk*, 13.

Barth was never interested in portraying himself as having arrived or in having his theological endeavors ossified through theological re-pristination. To be sure, he wanted the next generation of theologians to give him an ear, to listen carefully, to allow his central concern to become their own. But his hope was that, rather than simply repeating what he had said, they might learn to give a faithful witness in a new idiom, to a new generation, with new concerns. As Barth understood his relation-ship to his own theological forbearers, including the Blumhardts, so we should understand our relationship to Barth. Perhaps by learning to think along with Barth, we will go beyond him, following after the One who lives, crying out "Even so, come, Lord Jesus!"

Bibliography

Primary Sources

Karl Barth

Eugen Jäckh to Karl Barth, October 31, 1945. Original in Landeskirchliche-Archiv, Stuttgart, Germany.

Barth, Karl. *Anselm, Fides Quaerens Intellectum: Anselm's Proof for the Existence of God in the Context of his Theological Scheme*. 2nd ed. Translated by Ian W. Robertson. London: SCM, 1960.

———. *Call For God*. New York: Harper & Row, 1967.

———. *The Christian Life: Church Dogmatics IV.4, Lecture Fragments*. Translated by G. W. Bromiley. Grand Rapids: Eerdmans, 1981.

———. *Die christliche Dogmatik im Entwurf*. München: Kaiser, 1927.

———. *Church Dogmatics*. Translated by G. W. Bromiley. 14 vols. Edinburgh: T. & T. Clark, 1956–1975. German, *Kirchliche Dogmatik*. Zürich: Evangelischer, 1932–1967.

———. *Credo*. New York: Scribner's, 1962.

———. *The Epistle to the Romans*. 6th ed. Translated by Edwyn C. Hoskyns. Oxford: Oxford University Press, 1968. German, *Römerbrief*. 1st ed. Zürich: EVZ, 1963; 2nd ed. Zürich: EVZ, 1940.

———. *Evangelical Theology: An Introduction*. Translated by G. Foley. Grand Rapids: Eerdmans, 1963.

———. *Final Testimonies*. Edited by Eberhard Busch. Translated by G. W. Bromiley. Grand Rapids: Eerdmans, 1977.

———. *Fragments Grave and Gay*. Translated by E. Mosbacher. London: Fontana, 1971.

———. *Gespräche: 1959–1962*. Edited by E. Busch. Zürich: Theologischer, 1995.

———. *The Göttingen Dogmatics: Instruction in the Christian Religion*. Vol. 1, translated by G. W. Bromiley. Grand Rapids: Eerdmans, 1990.

———. *The Holy Spirit and the Christian Life*. Translated by R. B. Hoyle. Louisville: Westminster John Knox, 1993.

———. *The Humanity of God*. Atlanta: John Knox, 1982.

———. *How I Changed My Mind*. Richmond: John Knox, 1966.

———. *Karl Barth Letters, 1961–1968*. Translated and edited by G. W. Bromiley. Grand Rapids: Eerdmans, 1981.

———. *Karl Barth's Table Talk*. Edited by John D. Godsey. Richmond: John Knox, 1963.

————. *Prayer According to the Catechisms of the Reformation.* Translated by Sara F. Terrien. Philadelphia: Westminster, 1952.

————. *Predigten 1915.* Edited by Heinrich Schmidt. Zürich: Theologischer, 1996.

————. *Predigten 1916.* Edited by Heinrich Schmidt. Zürich: Theologischer, 1998.

————. *Predigten 1919.* Edited by Hermann Schmidt. Zürich: Theologischer, 2003.

————. *Protestant Theology in the Nineteenth Century.* Valley Forge: Judson, 1973.

————. *The Resurrection of the Dead.* Translated by H. J. Stenning. New York: Fleming H. Revell, 1933. German, *Die Auferstehung der Toten.* Zurich: Theologischer, 1933.

————. *The Theology of John Calvin.* Translated by G. W. Bromiley. Grand Rapids: Eerdmans, 1995.

————. *The Theology of the Reformed Confessions.* Translated by Darrell L. Guder and Judith J. Guder. Louisville: Westminster John Knox, 2002.

————. *The Theology of Schleiermacher.* Edited by Dietrich Ritschl. Translated by Geoffrey W. Bromiley. Grand Rapids: Eerdmans, 1982.

————. *'Unterricht in der christlichen Religion.'* Vol. 3, *Die Lehre von der Versöhnung —die Lehre von der Erlösung, 1925–1926.* Zurich: Theologischer, 2003.

————. "Action in Waiting for the Kingdom of God." In *Action in Waiting*, by Karl Barth and Christoph Blumhardt, 19–48. Rifton: Plough, 1969.

————. "Biblical Questions, Insights, and Vistas." In *The Word of God and the Word of Man*, 51–96. Translated by Douglas Horton. New York: Harper & Row, 1957.

————. "Church and Theology." In *Theology and Church: Shorter Writings, 1920–1928*, 286–306. Translated by Louise Pettibone Smith. New York: Harper & Row, 1962.

————. "Extra Nos—Pro Nobis—In Nobis." Translated by G. Hunsinger, 50 (1986) *The Thomist*, 497–511.

————. "Fate and Idea in Theology." In *The Way of Theology in Karl Barth*, edited by H. Martin Rumscheidt, 25–62. Allison Park: Pickwick, 1986.

————. "Gospel and Law." In *Community, State and Church: Three Essays*, 71–101. Gloucester: Peter Smith, 1968.

————. "Immer Noch Unerledigte Anfrangen." In *Vorträge und Kleinere Arbeiten, 1922–1925*, edited by H. Finze, 58–64. Zürich: Theologischer, 1990.

————. "Jesus Christ and the Movement for Social Justice." In *Karl Barth and Radical Politics*, edited by G. Hunsinger, 19–45. Philadelphia: Westminster, 1976.

————. Karl Barth to Eugen Jäckh, 22 July 1932. Unpublished typescript letter. Original in Landeskirchliche-Archiv, Stuttgart, Germany.

————. "Liberal Theology—An Interview." In *Final Testimonies*, 33–40. Grand Rapids: Eerdmans, 1977.

————. "Ludwig Feuerbach." In *Theology and Church*, 217–37. Translated by Louise Pettibone Smith. New York: Harper & Row, 1962.

————. "Nachwort einer Predigt von Pfarrer Barth, Eph 6: 1–4," 14 August 1919. Transcript in the hand of Karl Barth. Original in Landeskirchliche-Archiv, Stuttgart, Germany.

————. "Past and Future: Friedrich Naumann and Christoph Blumhardt." In *The Beginnings of Dialectical Theology*, vol. 1, edited by James M. Robinson, 35–45. Richmond: John Knox, 1968.

————. "Philosophy and Theology." In *The Way of Theology in Karl Barth*, 79–95. Edited by H. Martin Rumscheidt. Allison Park: Pickwick, 1986.

————. "Revelation." In *Revelation*, edited by J. Baillie and H. Martin, 41–81. London: Faber and Faber, 1937.

————. "Testimony to Jesus Christ." In *Final Testimonies*, 13–15. Grand Rapids: Eerdmans, 1977.

————. "The Christian Community and the Civil Community." In *Community, State and Church: Three Essays*, by Karl Barth, 149–89. Gloucester: Peter Smith, 1968.

————. "The Christian Message and the New Humanism." In *Against The Stream: Shorter Post-War Writings, 1946–1952*, 181–92. London: SCM, 1954.

————. "The Christian Understanding of Revelation." In *Against The Stream: Shorter Post-War Writings, 1946–1952*, 203–40. London: SCM, 1954.

————. "The Christian's Place in Society." In *The Word of God and the Word of Man*, 272–327. Translated by Douglas Horton. New York: Harper & Row, 1957.

————. "The Desirability and Possibility of a Universal Reformed Creed." In *Theology and Church*, 112–35. Translated by Louise Pettibone Smith. New York: Harper & Row, 1962.

————. "The Doctrinal Task of the Reformed Churches." In *The Word of God and the Word of Man*, 281–71. Translated by Douglas Horton. New York: Harper & Row, 1957.

————. "The First Commandment as an Axiom of Theology." In *The Way of Theology in Karl Barth*, edited by H. Martin Rumscheidt, 63–78. Allison Park: Pickwick, 1986.

————. "The Principles of Dogmatics according to Wilhelm Herrmann." In *Theology and Church*, 238–71. Translated by Louise Pettibone Smith. New York: Harper & Row, 1962.

————. "The Problem of Ethics Today." In *The Word of God and the Word of Man*, 136–82. Translated by Douglas Horton. New York: Harper & Row, 1957.

————. "The Righteousness of God." In *The Word of God and the Word of Man*, 9–27. Translated by Douglas Horton. New York: Harper & Row, 1957.

————. "The Strange New World Within the Bible." In *The Word of God and the Word of Man*, 28–50. Translated by Douglas Horton. New York: Harper & Row, 1957.

————. "The Word in Theology from Schleiermacher to Ritschl." In *Theology and Church*, by Karl Barth, 200–216. Translated by Louise Pettibone Smith. New York: Harper & Row, 1962.

————. "The Word of God and the Task of the Ministry." In *The Word of God and the Word of Man*, by Karl Barth, 183–217. Translated by Douglas Horton. New York: Harper & Row, 1957.

————. "Unsettled Questions for Theology Today." In *Theology and Church*, by Karl Barth, 55–73. Translated by Louise Pettibone Smith. New York: Harper & Row, 1962.

————, and Eduard Thurneysen. *Come Holy Spirit*. New York: Round Table, 1933.

————. *Karl Barth-Eduard Thurneysen: Briefwechsel*, Vol. 1, *1913–1921*, edited by Eduard Thurneysen. Zürich: Theologischer Zürich, 1973.

————. *Karl Barth-Eduard Thurneysen Briefwechsel*, Vol. 3, *1930–1935*, edited by Caren Algner. Zürich: Theologischer Zürich, 2000.

———. *Revolutionary Theology in the Making: Barth-Thurneysen Correspondence, 1914–1925.* Translated by James D. Smart. Richmond: John Knox, 1964.

———, and Eduard Thurneysen. *Suchet Gott, so werdet ihr Leben!* 2nd ed. München: Kaiser, 1928.

———, and Rudolph Bultmann. *Karl Barth/Rudolph Bultmann: Letters, 1922–1966.* Edited and translated by G. W. Bromiley. Grand Rapids: Eerdmans, 1981.

Jäckh, Eugen. Eugen Jäckh to Karl Barth, October 31, 1945. Unpublished typescript letter. Original in Landeskirchliche-Archiv, Stuttgart, Germany.

Johann Christoph and Christoph Friedrich Blumhardt

Blumhardt, Christoph. *Action in Waiting.* Farmington: Plough, 1998.

———. *Ansprachen, Predigten, Reden, Briefe: 1865-1917.* 3 vols. Edited by J. Harder. Neukirchen-Vluyn: Neukirchen, 1978–1980.

———. *Christus in der Welt.* Zürich: Zwingli, 1958.

———. *Damit Gott Kommt: "Gedanken aus dem Reich Gottes."* Edited by W. J. Bittner. Giessen: Brunnen, 1992.

———. *Eine Auswahl aus seinen Predigten, Andachten und Schriften.* 4 vols. Edited by R. Lejeune. Zurich: Rotapfel, 1925–1937.

———. *Haus-Andachten nach Losungen und Lehrtexten der Brüdergemeinde.* Stuttgart: von Holland und Josenhaus; Basel: Helbing und Lichtenbahn, 1916.

———. *Politik aus der Nachfolge, Der Briefwechsel zwischen Howard Eugster-Züst und Christoph Blumhardt 1886-1919.* Zurich: TVZ, 1984.

———. *Schöpfung und Erlösung.* Edited by E. Jäckh. Stuttgart: Evangelisch Missionverlag, 1935.

———. *Vom Reich Gottes.* Edited by E. Jäckh. Berlin: Erschienen im Furche, 1923.

Blumhardt, Johann Christoph. *Besprechung wichtiger Glaubensfragen.* Vol. III of *Gesammelte Werke von Johann Christoph Blumhardt,* edited by C. F. Blumhardt. Karlsruhe: Evangelischer Schriftenverein für Baden, 1886–1888.

———. *Blätter aus Bad Boll.* Vol. II of *Gesammelte Werke von Johann Christoph Blumhardt 1968–2001,* edited by Paul Ernst. Göttingen: Vandenhoeck & Ruprecht, 1968–1974.

———. *Blumhardt's Battle: A Conflict with Satan.* Translated by Frank S. Boshold. New York: Thomas E. Lowe, 1970.

———. *Der Kampf in Möttlingen.* Vol. I/1 and I/2 of *Gesammelte Werke von Johann Christoph Blumhardt 1968–2001,* edited G. Schärfer with P. Ernst and D. Ising. Göttingen: Vandenhoeck & Ruprecht, 1979.

———. *Die Verkündigung.* Vol. II of *Ausgewählte Schriften in drei Bänden,* edited by B. Otto. Zurich: Gotthelf, 1947–1949.

———. *Evangelienpredigten auf alle Sonn- und Festtage des Kirchenjarhres.* Vol. II of *Gesammelte Werke von Johann Christoph Blumhardt,* edited by C. F. Blumhardt. Karlsruhe: Evangelischer Schriftenverein für Baden, 1887.

———. *Handbüchlein der Missiongeschichte und Missiongeographie.* Calw and Stuttgart: Steinkopf, 1844.

Eller, Vernard, editor. *Thy Kingdom Come: A Blumhardt Reader.* Grand Rapids: Eerdmans, 1980.

Ising, Dieter, editor. *J. Chr. Blumhardt: Ein Brevier*. Göttingen: Vandenhoeck & Ruprecht, 1991.

Lejeune, R., editor. *Christoph Blumhardt and His Message*. Rifton: Plough, 1963.

Other Sources

Arndt, Johann. *True Christianity*. New York: Paulist, 1979.

Arnold, Hardy. "A Letter Concerning the Blumhardts." *Brethren Life and Thought* 13, no. 3 (1968) 184–89.

Aulén, Gustav. *Christus Victor*. New York, MacMillian, 1931.

Balthasar, Hans Urs von. *The Theology of Karl Barth: Exposition and Interpretation*. Translated by Edward T. Oakes, S. J. San Francisco: Communion; Ignatius, 1992.

Barter, Jane A. "A Theology of Liberation in Barth's *Church Dogmatics* IV/3." *Scottish Journal of Theology* 53:2 (2000) 154–77.

Barth, Markus. "Current Discussions on the Political Character of Karl Barth's Theology." In *Footnotes to a Theology—The Karl Barth Colloquium of 1972*, edited by H. Martin Rumscheidt, 77–94. Waterloo, Ontario: Sciences Religieuses, 1974.

Bauckham, Richard. "Eschatology in *The Coming of God*." In *God Will Be All in All: The Eschatology of Jürgen Moltmann*, edited by Richard Bauckham, 1–34. Edinburgh: T&T Clark, 1999.

Beintker, Michael. *Die Dialektik in der 'dialektischen Theologie' Karl Barths*. München: Kaiser, 1987.

Bengel, "Toward an Apocalyptic Chronology." In *Pietists—Selected Writings*, edited by Peter C. Erb, 272–73. Mahwah: Paulist, 1983.

Bentley, James. *Between Marx and Christ: The Dialogue in German Speaking Europe 1870–1970*. London: Verso, 1982.

———. "Christoph Blumhardt: Preacher of Hope." *Theology* 78, no. 665 (1975) 577–82.

———. "Karl Barth as a Christian Socialist." *Theology* 76, no. 3 (1973) 349–56.

Berger, Joachim. "Die Verwurzelung des theologische Denkens Karl Barths in dem Kerygma der beiden Blumhardts von Reich Gottes." PhD diss., University of Berlin, 1956.

Berkhof, Hendrikus. *Christ and the Powers*. Translated by J. H. Yoder. Scottdale: Herald, 1977.

———. *Two Hundred Years of Theology: Report of a Personal Journey*. Translated by John Vriend. Grand Rapids: Eerdmans, 1989.

Berkouwer, G. C. *The Triumph of Grace in the Theology of Karl Barth: An Introduction and Critical Appraisal*. Grand Rapids: Eerdmans, 1956.

Bettis, Joseph D. "Is Karl Barth a Universalist?" *SJT* 20 (1967) 424–36.

Biggar, Nigel. *The Hastening that Waits: Karl Barth's Ethics*. Oxford: Clarendon, 1995.

Bisanz, Rudolf. "Jesus is Victor! Karl Barth and Pietism, the Blumhardts and Politics." *Journal for Christian Theological Research* 6:4 (2001). Online: http://www.luthersem.edu/ctrf/JCTR/Vol06/Bisanz.html.

Bloesch, Donald G. *Jesus is Victor: Karl Barth's Doctrine of Salvation*. Nashville: Abingdon, 1976.

Bock, Paul, ed. *Signs of the Kingdom: A Ragaz Reader*. Translated by Paul Bock. Grand Rapids: Eerdmans, 1984.

Bodamer, W. G. "The Life and Work of Johann Christoph Blumhardt." ThD diss., Princeton Theological Seminary, 1966.

Bohren, Rudolf. *Preaching and Community*. Translated by David E. Green. Richmond: John Knox, 1965.

Bolich, Gregory G. *Karl Barth and Evangelicalism*. Downers Grove: InterVarsity, 1980.

Bradfield, Margaret, ed. *The Good Samaritan: The Life Story of "Father" Bodelschwingh*. London: Marshall, Morgan & Scott, 1961.

Brown, Dale W. *Understanding Pietism*. Rev. ed. Nappanee: Evangel, 1996.

Brunner, Emil. "Continental European Theology." In *The Church Through Half a Century, essays in honor of William Adams Brown*, edited by S. M. Cavert and H. Van Dusen, 133–44. New York: Scribner's, 1936.

Buess, Eduard, and Markus Mattmüller. *Prophetischer Sozialismus: Blumhardt—Ragaz—Barth*. Fribourg: Exodus, 1986.

Bultmann, Rudolf. "Karl Barth, *The Resurrection of the Dead*." In *Faith and Understanding*, by Rudolf Bultmann, 66–94. Translated by L. P. Smith. Philadelphia: Fortress, 1969.

Burrow, J. W. *The Crisis of Reason: European Thought, 1848–1914*. New Haven: Yale University Press, 2000.

Busch, Eberhard. *Karl Barth: His Life from Letters and Autobiographical Texts*. Grand Rapids: Eerdmans, 1994.

———. *Karl Barth and the Pietists: The Young Karl Barth's Critique of Pietism & Its Response*. Translated by Daniel Bloesch (Downers Grove: InterVarsity, 2004).

———. "God is God: The Meaning of a Controversial Formula and the Fundamental Problem of Speaking about God." *The Princeton Seminary Bulletin* 7 (1986) 101–13.

Butin, Phil. "Two Early Reformed Catechisms, The Threefold Office, and the Shape of Karl Barth's Christology." *Scottish Journal of Theology* 44 (1991) 195–214.

Calvin, John. *Institutes of the Christian Religion*. Edited by J. T. McNeill. Translated by F. L. Battles. 2 vols. Philadelphia: Westminster, 1960.

de Certeau, Michel. *The Mystic Fable*. Vol. 1, *The Sixteenth and Seventeenth Centuries*, translated by M. B. Smith. Chicago: University of Chicago Press, 1992.

Chapman, Mark D. *Ernst Troeltsch and Liberal Theology: Religion and Cultural Synthesis in Wilhelmlmine Germany*. Oxford: Oxford University Press, 2001.

Cox, James C. *Johann Christoph Blumhardt and The Work of the Holy Spirit*. Assen: Van Gorcum, 1959.

Crowner, David, and Gerald Christianson, eds. *The Spirituality of the German Awakening*. Translated by D. Crowner and G. Christianson. New York: Paulist, 2003.

Dalferth, Ingolf U. "Karl Barth's Eschatological Realism." In *Karl Barth: Centenary Essays*, edited by S. W. Sykes, 14–45. Cambridge: Cambridge University Press, 1989.

Danneman, Ulrich. *Theologie und Politik im Denken Karl Barths*. München: Kaiser, 1977.

———. "'Den Gefangenen Befreiung!' Impulse der religiös-sozialistischen Bewegung in der Theologie Karl Barths." *Zeitschrift für Evangelische Ethik* 27 (1983) 156–82.

———. "Karl Barth und der religiöse Sozialismus." *Evangelische Theologie* 37 (1977) 127–48.

Dayton, Donald W. "Karl Barth and Evangelicalism: The Varieties of a Sibling Rivalry." *TSF Bulletin* 8, no. 5 (1985) 18–23.

———. "The Radical Message of Evangelical Christianity." In *Churches in Struggle: Liberation Theologies and Social Change in North America*, edited by W. K. Tabb, 211–22. New York: Monthly Review, 1986.

Diephouse, David J. *Pastors and Pluralism in Württemberg, 1918–1933.* Princeton: Princeton University Press, 1987.

Dorrien, Gary. *The Barthian Revolt in Modern Theology.* Louisville: Westminster John Knox, 2000.

Eller, Vernard. "Who are These Blumhardt Characters Anyhow?" *Christian Century* 86, no. 41 (1969) 1274–78.

Erb, Peter C., ed. *Pietists: Selected Writings.* Mahwah: Paulist, 1983.

Feuerbach, Ludwig. *The Essence of Christianity.* Translated by George Eliot. Amherst: Prometheus, 1989.

Finke, Anne-Kathrin. *Karl Barth in Großbritannien: Rezeption und Wirkungsgeschichte.* Neukirchen-Vluyn: Neukirchener, 1995.

Fisher, Simon. *Revelatory Positivism? Barth's Earliest Theology and the Marburg School.* Oxford: Oxford University Press, 1988.

Frei, Hans. "The Doctrine of Revelation in the Thought of Karl Barth, 1909 to 1922: The Nature of Barth's Break with Liberalism." PhD diss., Yale University, 1956.

———. *The Eclipse of Biblical Narrative: A Study in Eighteenth and Nineteenth Century Hermeneutics.* New Haven: Yale University Press, 1974.

———. *The Identity of Jesus Christ: The Hermeneutical Bases of Dogmatic Theology.* 1975. Reprint, Eugene, OR: Wipf & Stock, 1997.

Fulbrook, Mary. *Piety and Politics: Religion and the Rise of Absolutism in England, Württemberg and Prussia.* Cambridge: Cambridge University Press, 1983.

Gay, Peter. *Weimar Culture: The Outsider as Insider.* 2nd ed. New York: Norton, 2001.

Gerdes, Egon W. "Theological Tenets of Pietism." In *Contemporary Perspectives on Pietism: A Symposium*, edited by D. W. Dayton, 25–60. Chicago: Covenant, 1976.

Gollwitzer, Helmut. "Christoph Blumhardt: Neu Sichtbar." *Evangelische Theologie* 41, no. 3 (1981) 259–75.

Gorringe, Timothy J. *Karl Barth: Against Hegemony.* Oxford: Oxford University Press, 1999.

———. "Eschatology and Political Radicalism: The Example of Karl Barth and Jürgen Moltmann." In *God Will Be All in All: The Eschatology of Jürgen Moltmann*, edited by Richard Bauckham, 87–114. Edinburgh: T&T Clark, 1999.

Groth, Friedhelm. *Die 'Wiederbringung Aller Dinge' Im Württembergischen Pietismus, Theologiegeschichtliche Studien Zum Eschatologischen Heiluniversalismus Württembergischer Pietisten Des 18. Jahrhunderts.* Göttingen: Vandenhoeck & Ruprecht, 1984.

————. "Chiliasmus und Apokatastasishoffnung in der Reich-Gottes-Verkündigung der beiden Blumhardts." *Pietismus und Neuzeit* 9 (1983) 56–116.

Grünzweig, Fritz. *Die evangelische Brüdergemeinde Korntal: Weg, Wesen u. Werk.* Metzingen, Württermberg: Franz, 1958.

Hake, Claudia. *Der Bedeutung der Theologie Johann Tobias Beck für die Entwicklung der Theologie Karl Barths.* Frankfurt am Main: Peter Lang, 1999.

Hammer, Karl. *Deutsche Kriegstheologie (1870–1918).* Munich: Koesel, 1971.

Harnack, Adolf von. *What is Christianity?* Translated by T. B. Saunders. New York: Harper & Brothers, 1957.

Hart, John W. *Karl Barth vs. Emil Brunner: The Formation and Dissolution of a Theological Alliance, 1916–1936.* New York: Peter Lang, 2001.

Haug, Richard. *Johann Christoph Blumhardt: Gestalt und Botschaft.* Metzingen: Ernst Franz, 1984.

————. *Reich Gottes im Schwabenland: Linien im württembergischen Pietismus.* Metzingen: Ernst Franz, 1981.

Hegel, G W. F. *Lectures on the Philosophy of Religion: The Lectures of 1827.* Single-volume ed. Edited by Peter C. Hodgson. Translated by R. F. Brown, P. C. Hodgson, and J. M. Stewart. Berkley: University of California Press, 1988.

Henry, Martin. *Franz Overbeck: Theologian?* Frankfurt am Main: Peter Lang, 1995.

Heppe, Heinrich. *Reformed Dogmatics: Set out and illustrated from the sources.* Translated by G. T. Thomson. Grand Rapids: Baker, 1950.

Hermann, Wilhelm. *The Communion of the Christian with God.* Edited by Robert T. Voelkel. Philadelphia: Fortress, 1971.

Herzog, Fredrick. "Diakonia in Modern Times, Eighteenth–Twentieth Centuries." In *Service in Christ: Essays presented to* Karl Barth *on his 80ᵗʰ birthday,* edited by J. I. McCord and T. H. L. Parker, 135–150. Grand Rapids: Eerdmans, 1966.

Hood, Robert E. *Contemporary Political Orders and Christ: Karl Barth's Christology and Political Praxis.* Allison Park, PA: Pickwick, 1985.

Hunsinger, George. *Disruptive Grace: Studies in the Theology of Karl Barth.* Grand Rapids: Eerdmans, 2000.

————. *How to Read Karl Barth: The Shape of His Theology.* Oxford: Oxford University Press, 1991.

Hunsinger, George, editor. *Karl Barth and Radical Politics.* Philadelphia: Westminster, 1976.

Hütter, Reinhard. "Between McCormack and von Balthasar: A Dialectic." *Pro Ecclesia* 8 (1999) 105–9.

Ising, Dieter. *Johann Christoph Blumhardt. Leben und Werk.* Göttingen: Vandenhoeck & Ruprecht, 2002.

————. "Der politische Blumhardt: Vom der 1848er Revolution bis zum Deutsch-Französichen Krieg 1870–1871." *Blätter für württembergische Kirchengeschichte* 106 (2006) 39–52.

————. "Eine 'Weckstimme durch alle Völker'. Die Revolution von 1848/1849 und die Anfänge der Inneren Mission in der Sicht Johann Christoph Blumhardts." *Pietismus und Neuzeit* 24 (1998) 286–308.

Jäckh, Eugen. *Blumhardt Vater und Sohn und ihre Botschaft.* Berlin: Furche, 1925.

Jehle, Frank. *Ever Against the Stream: The Politics of Karl Barth, 1906–1968.* Translated by Richard and Martha Burnett. Grand Rapids: Eerdmans, 2002.

Jüngel, Eberhard. *Barth–Studien*. Zürich and Cologne: Benzinger; Gütersloh: Gütersloher Verlagshaus, 1982.

———. *God's Being is in Becoming: The Trinitarian Being of God in the Theology of Karl Barth*. Edinburgh: T&T Clark, 2001.

———. *Karl Barth: A Theological Legacy*. Philadelphia: Westminster, 1986.

———. *Theological Essays*. Edited by J. Webster. Edinburgh: T&T Clark, 1989.

Kant, Immanuel. "Religion Within the Boundaries of Mere Reason." In *Religion and Rational Theology*, edited and translated by Allen W. Wood and George Di Giovanni, 39–216. Cambridge: Cambridge University Press, 2001.

Kähler, Martin. *The So-Called Historical Jesus and the Historic Biblical Christ*. Translated by C. Braaten. Philadelphia: Fortress, 1964.

Kierkegaard, Søren. *The Moment and Late Writings*. Edited and translated by H. Hong and E. Hong. Princeton: Princeton University Press, 1998.

König, Adrio. *The Eclipse of Christ in Eschatology: Toward a Christ-Centered Approach*. London: Marshall Morgan & Scott, 1989.

Krüger, Günter. "Johann Christoph Blumhardt: A Man for the Kingdom." *Covenant Quarterly* 54, no. 4 (1996) 3–26.

Kümmel, Werner G. *Promise and Fulfillment: The Eschatological Message of Jesus*. Naperville, IL: Alec R. Allenson, 1957.

Kutter, Hermann. *Hermann Kutter in seinen Briefen, 1883–1931*. Edited by M. Geiger and A. Lindt. München: Kaiser, 1983.

———. *They Must, or God and the Social Democracy*. Chicago: Cooperative, 1909. German, *Sie Müssen! Ein offenes Wort an die christliche Gesellschaft*. Berlin: Hermann Walthersbuchhandlung, 1904.

La Montagne, D. Paul. "Critical Realism as a Context for Barth's Dialectical Theology." *Zeitschrift für Dialektische Theologie* 15, no. 1 (1999) 45–63.

Lamirande, Emilien. "The Impact of Karl Barth on the Catholic Church in the last half Century." In *Footnotes to a Theology—The Karl Barth Colloquium of 1972*, edited by H. Martin Rumscheidt, 112–41. Waterloo, Ontario: Sciences Religieuses, 1974.

Lang, U. M. "Anhypostasis-Enhypostasis: Church Fathers, Protestant Orthodoxy and Karl Barth." *Journal of Theological Studies* 49, no. 2 (1998) 630–57.

Lehmann, Hartmut. *Pietsimus und weltliche Ordnung in Württemberg, vom 17. bis zum 20. Jahrhundert*. Stuttgart: W. Kohlhammer, 1969.

———. "'Community' and 'Work' as Concepts of Religious Thought in Eighteenth-Century Württemberg Pietism." In *Protestant Evangelicalism: Britain, Ireland, Germany and America, c. 1750–1950*, edited by Keith Robbins, 79–98. Oxford: Basil Blackwell.

Lehmann, Paul. "Karl Barth, Theologian of Permanent Revolution." *Union Seminary Quarterly Review* 28 (1972) 67–81.

Lejune, R. "Christoph Blumhardt, 1842–1919." In *Christoph Blumhardt and His Message*, edited by R. Lejune, 5–92. Rifton: Plough, 1963.

Lewis, Alan. *Between Cross and Resurrection: A Theology of Holy Saturday*. Grand Rapids: Eerdmans, 2001.

Lim, Hee-Kuk. *'Jesus ist Sieger!' bei Christoph Friedrich Blumhardt: Keim einer kosmischen Christologie*. Bern: Lang, 1996.

Lohmeyer, Ernst. *The Lord's Prayer.* Translated by John Bowden. London: Collins, 1965.

Lovin, Robin W. *Reinhold Niebuhr and Christian Realism.* Cambridge: Cambridge University Press, 1995.

Lowe, Walter. "Barth as the Critic of Dualism: Re-reading the *Römerbrief.*" *Scottish Journal of Theology* 41 (1988) 377–95.

Lundström, Gösta. *The Kingdom of God in the Teaching of Jesus: A History of Interpretation from the Last Decades of the Nineteenth Century to the Present Day.* Translated by Joan Bulman. Richmond: John Knox, 1963.

Luther, Martin. *A Short Explanation of Dr. Martin Luther's Small Catechism: A Handbook of Christian Doctrine.* St. Louis: Concordia, 1943.

McCormack, Bruce. *Karl Barth's Critically Realistic Dialectical Theology: Its Genesis and Development 1909–1936.* Oxford: Clarendon, 1995.

———. "Article Review: Graham Ward's *Barth, Derrida and the Language of Theology.*" *SJT* 49, no. 1 (1996) 97–109.

———. "Beyond Nonfoundationl and Postmodern Readings of Barth: Critically Realistic Dialectical Theology, part 1." *Zeitschrift für Dialektische Theologie* 13, no. 1 (1997) 67–95.

———. "Beyond Nonfoundationl and Postmodern Readings of Barth: Critically Realistic Dialectical Theology, part 2." *Zeitschrift für Dialektische Theologie* 13, no. 2 (1997) 170–94.

———. "Grace and Being: The role of God's gracious election in Karl Barth's theological ontology." In *The Cambridge Companion to Karl Barth*, edited by John Webster, 92–110. Cambridge: Cambridge University Press, 2000.

———. "Revelation and History in Transfoundationalist Perspective: Karl Barth's Theological Epistemology in Conversation with a Schleiermacherian Tradition." *Journal of Religion* 78 (1998) 18–37.

———. "Review of *Karl Barth: Against Hegemony*, by Timothy Gorringe." *Scottish Journal of Theology* 55, no. 2 (2002) 236–39.

———. "Significance of Karl Barth's Theological Exegesis of *Philippians.*" In *Epistle to the Philippians, 40th Anniversary Edition*, by Karl Barth, v–xxv. Louisville: Westminster John Knox, 2002.

———. "The Limits of the Knowledge of God." *Zeitschrift für Dialektische Theologie* 15, no. 1, (1999) 75–86.

———. "The Sum of the Gospel: The Doctrine of Election in the Theologies of Alexander Schweizer and Karl Barth." In *Toward the Future of Reformed Theology*, edited by David Willis and Michael Welker, 470–93. Grand Rapids: Eerdmans, 1999.

McDowell, John C. *Hope in Barth's Eschatology: Interrogations and Transformations Beyond Tragedy.* Aldershot: Ashgate, 2000.

———. "Learning Where to Place One's Hope: The Eschatological Significance of Election In Barth." *SJT* 53, no. 3 (2000) 316–38.

———. "Theology as Conversational Event: Karl Barth, the Ending of 'Dialogue' and the Beginning of 'Conversation.'" *Modern Theology* 19, no. 4 (2003) 483–509.

McGinn, Bernard, ed. *Apocalyptic Spirituality.* Mahwah, NJ: Paulist, 1979.

Macchia, Frank. *Spirituality and Social Liberation: The Message of the Blumhardts in the Light of Württemberg Pietism.* Metuchen: Scarecrow, 1993.

————. "The Secular and the Religious Under the Shadow of the Cross: Implications in Christoph Blumhardt's Kingdom Spirituality for a Christian Response to World Religions." In *Religion in a Secular City: Essays in Honor of Harvey Cox*, edited by Arvind Sharma, 59–77. Harrisburg: Trinity, 2001, 59–77.

MacDonald, Neil B. *Karl Barth and the Strange New World within the Bible: Barth, Wittgenstein, and the Metadilemmas of the Enlightenment.* Carlisle: Paternoster, 2000.

Macken, John. *The Autonomy Theme in the 'Church Dogmatics': Karl Barth and His Critics.* Cambridge: Cambridge University Press, 1990.

Mackintosh, H. R. *Types of Modern Theology: Schleiermacher to Barth.* London: Nisbet, 1952.

Marquardt, Friedrich-Wilhelm. *Theologie und Sozialismus: Das Beispiel Karl Barths.* Müchen: Kaiser, 1972.

————. "Socialism in the Theology of Karl Barth." In *Karl Barth and Radical Politics*, edited by G. Hunsinger. Philadelphia: Westminster, 1976.

Massanari, Roland L. "Christian Socialism: Adolf Stoecker's Formulation of a Christian Perspective for Social Change for the Protestant Church in Nineteenth Century Germany." *Lutheran Quarterly* 22, no. 2 (1970) 185–98.

————. "Christian Socialism in Nineteenth-Century Germany: A Case Study of a Shift in Anthropological Perspective." *Union Seminary Quarterly Review* 29 (1973) 17–25.

————. "True or False Socialism: Adolf Stoecker's Critique of Marxism from a Christian Socialist Perspective." *Church History* 41, no. 4 (1972) 487–96.

Massy, Marilyn Chapin. *Christ Unmasked: the Meaning of 'The Life of Jesus' in German Politics.* Chapel Hill: University of North Carolina Press, 1983.

Matheny, P. D. *Dogmatics and Ethics: The Theological Realism and Ethics of Karl Barth's Ethics.* Oxford: Oxford University Press, 1990.

Mattmüller, Markus. *Leonhard Ragaz und der religiöse Sozialismus: Eine Biographie.* 2 vols. Zürich: EVZ, 1968.

————. "Der Einfluss Christoph Blumhardts auf schweizerische Theologen des 20 Jahrhunderts." *Zeitschrift für Evangelische Ethik*, 12 (1968) 233–46.

Marx, Karl. "Theses on Feuerbach." In *The German Ideology*, by Karl Marx, 569–75. New York: Prometheus, 1998.

Maury, Pierre. *Predestination and Other Papers.* Richmond: John Knox, 1960.

Meier, Klaus-Jürgen. *Christoph Blumhardt: Christ, Sozialist, Theologe.* Bern: Peter Lang, 1979.

Merz, George. "Christoph Blumhardt unter der Kritik der dialecktischen Theologie." *Zwischen den Zeiten* 10 (1932) 541–50.

Metzger, Paul Lewis. *The Word of Christ and the World of Culture: Sacred and Secular through the Theology of Karl Barth.* Grand Rapids: Eerdmans, 2003.

Molnar, Paul D. "Some Dogmatic Implications of Barth's Understanding of Ebionite and Docetic Christology." *International Journal of Systematic Theology* 2, no. 2 (2000) 151–72.

Moltmann, Jürgen. *On Human Dignity: Political Theology and Ethics.* Edited and translated by D. M. Meeks. London: SCM, 1984.

————. *The Coming of God: Christian Eschatology.* Translated by Margaret Kohl. Minneapolis: Fortress, 1996.

———. *Theology of Hope*. Translated by John W. Leitch. Minneapolis: Fortress, 1993.

———. "Barth's Doctrine of the Lordship of Jesus Christ and the Experience of the Confessing Church." In *On Human Dignity: Political Theology and Ethics*, translation by D. M. Meeks, 79–96. Philadelphia: Fortress, 1984.

———. "Christoph Blumhardt—ein Theologe der Hoffnung." In *Warten und Pressieren—150 Jahre Blumhardt in Bad Boll*, edited by Albrecht Esche, 57–72. Bad Boll: Evangelische Akademie Bad Boll, 2002.

———. "The Hope for the Kingdom of God and Signs of Hope in the World: The Relevance of Blumhardt's Theology Today." *Pneuma* 26, no. 1 (2004) 4–16.

———. "The Logic of Hell." In *God Will Be All in All: The Eschatology of Jürgen Moltmann*, edited by Richard Bauckham, 43–47. Edinburgh: T&T Clark, 1999.

———. "The World in God or God in the World? *Response to Richard Bauckham*." In *God Will Be All in All: The Eschatology of Jürgen Moltmann*, edited by Richard Bauckham, 35–41. Edinburgh: T&T Clark, 1999.

———. "What Has Happened to Our Utopias? *1968 and 1989*." In *God Will Be All in All: The Eschatology of Jürgen Moltmann*, edited by Richard Bauckham, 115–21. Edinburgh: T&T Clark, 1999.

Morgan, Robert. "Ernst Troeltsch and the Dialectical Theology." In *Ernst Troeltsch and the Future of Theology*, edited by J. P. Clayton, 33–77. Cambridge: Cambridge University Press, 1976.

Muddiman, John. "The Resurrection of Jesus as the Coming of the Kingdom—the Basis of Hope for the Transformation of the World." In *The Kingdom of God and Human Society*, edited by R. S. Barbour, 208–23. Edinburgh: T&T Clark, 1993.

Mueller, David L. *Foundation of Karl Barth's Doctrine of Reconciliation: Jesus Christ Crucified and Risen*. Lewiston: Mellen, 1990.

Muller, Richard A. "Directions in the Study of Barth's Christology." *WTJ* 48, no. 1 (1986) 119–34.

Neuer, Werner. *Adolf Schlatter: A Biography of Germany's Premier Biblical Theologian*. Translated by R. Yarbrough. Grand Rapids: Baker, 1995.

O'Malley, Stephen J. "Pietist Influences in the Eschatological Thought of John Wesley and Jürgen Moltmann." *WTJ* 29 (1994) 127–39.

———. "The Role of Pietism in the Theology of Jürgen Moltmann." *Asbury Theological Journal* 48 (1993) 121–27.

Overbeck, Franz. "On The Christian Character of Our Theology Today." Translated by J. M. A. Cunningham. PhD diss., University of Toronto, 2000.

Pasztor, Janos. "Hermann Kutter: Pioneer Social Theologian, 1863–1931." *Princeton Seminary Bulletin* 65 (1972) 80–87.

———. "Leonard Ragaz: Pioneer Social Theologian." *Union Seminary Quarterly Review* 29 (1973) 27–33.

Pentz, Wolfhart. "The Meaning of Religion in the Politics of Friedrich Naumann." *Zeitschrift für Neuere Theologiegeschichte* 9, no. 1 (2002) 70–97.

Petersen, Robin. "Theology and Socialism." In *On Reading Karl Barth in South Africa*, edited by Charles Villa-Vicencio, 59–74. Grand Rapids: Eerdmans, 1988.

Pinson, Koppel S. *Pietism as a Factor in the Rise of German Nationalism*. New York: Columbia University Press, 1934.

Pressel, Wilhelm. *Die Kriegspredigt 1914–1918 in der evangelischen Kirche Deutschlands*. Göttingen: Vandehoeck & Ruprecht, 1967.

Pugh, Jeffrey Carter. "Tracking the Influence: An Examination of Anselm's Influence Upon Karl Barth's Christological Formulation." PhD diss., Drew University, 1985.

Ragaz, Leonhard. *Der Kampf um das Reich Gottes in Blumhardt Vater und Sohn—und weiter*. Erlenbach-Zürich: Rotapfel, 1925.

———. *Israel, Judaism and Christianity*. London: Victor Gollancz, 1947.

———. *Leonhard Ragaz in seinen Briefen*. Vol. 2, *1914–1932*, edited by C. Ragaz, M. Mattmüller, and A. Rich. Zürich: Theologischer Zürich, 1982.

———. *Leonhard Ragaz in seinen Briefen*. Vol. 3, *1933–1945*, edited by H. U. Jäger, M. Mattmüller, and A. Rich. Zürich: Theologischer Zürich, 1992.

———. "Gottesreich und Politik. Gespräch zwischen Quidam und einem Pietisten." In vol. 1 of *Weltreich, Religion und Gottesherrschaft*, by Leonard Ragaz, 80–104. Erlenbach-Zürich: Rotapfel, 1922.

———. "Wir harren eines neuen Himmels und einer neuen Erde." In vol. 2 of *Weltreich, Religion und Gottesherrschaft*, by Leonhard Ragaz, 404–25. Erlenbach-Zürich: Rotapfel, 1922.

Redeker, Martin. *Schleiermacher: Life and Thought*. Translated by John Wallhausser. Philadelphia: Fortress, 1973.

Reeves, Marjorie. *Joachim of Fiore & The Prophetic Future: A Medieval Study in Historical Thought*. Rev. ed. Gloucestershire: Sutton, 1999.

Regehr, John. "The Preaching of Christoph Blumhardt." ThD diss., Southern Baptist Seminary, 1970.

Reist, John S. Jr. "Commencement, Continuation, Consummation: Karl Barth's Theology of Hope." *Evangelical Quarterly* 87 (1987) 195–218.

Ritschl, Albrecht. "Instruction in the Christian Religion." In *Three Essays*, by Albrecht Ritschl, 219–91. Translated by P. Hefner. Philadelphia: Fortress, 1972.

———. "'Prolegomena' to *The History of Pietism*." In *Three Essays*, by Albrecht Ritschl, 51–148. Translated by P. Hefner. Philadelphia: Fortress, 1972.

Roberts, Richard H. *A Theology on Its Way? Essays on Karl Barth*. Edinburgh: T&T Clark, 1991.

Roessle, Julius. *Vom Bengel bis Blumhardt, Gestalten und Bilder aus der Geschichte des schwäbischen Pietismus*. Metzinger: Ernst Franz, 1959.

Rosato, Philip. *The Spirit as Lord: The Pneumatology of Karl Barth*. Edinburgh: T&T Clark, 1981.

Rumscheidt, H. Martin. *Revelation and Theology: An Analysis of the Barth-Harnak Correspondence of 1923*. Cambridge: Cambridge University Press, 1972.

———. "The First Commandment as Axiom for Theology: A Model for the Unity of Dogmatics and Ethics." In *Theology Beyond Christendom: Essays on the Centenary of the Birth of Karl Barth May 10, 1886*, edited by John Thompson, 143–64. Allison Park: Pickwick, 1986.

Rüsch, Ernst Gerhard. *Die Erlösung der Kreatur. Die Geschichtstheologie Johann Christoph Blumhardts*. Zürich: Zwingli, 1956.

Rupp, George. *Culture-Protestantism: German Liberal Theology at the Turn of the Twentieth Century*. Missoula: Scholars, 1977.

Sabean, David Warren. *Power in the Blood: Popular Culture & Village Discourse in Early Modern Germany*. Cambridge: Cambridge University Press, 1984.

Sauter, Gerhard. *Die Theologie des Reiches Gottes beim älteren und jüngeren Blumhardt*. Zürich: Zwingli Zürich, 1962.

————. *What Dare We Hope? Reconsidering Eschatology*. Harrisburg: Trinity, 1999.

————. "Current Issues in German Theology." In *Eschatological Rationality*, by Gerhard Sauter, 154–61. Grand Rapids: Baker, 1996.

————. "Eschatological Rationality." In *Eschatological Rationality*, by Gerhard Sauter, 171–200. Grand Rapids: Baker, 1996.

————. "Johann Christoph Blumhardt als Theologe der Hoffnung: Seine Erwartung des Reiches Gottes und seine Zuversicht für den Weg der Christenheit." *Blätter für württembergische Kirchengeschichte* 106 (2006) 77–102.

————. "Shift's in Karl Barth's Thought." In *Eschatological Rationality: Theological Issues in Focus*, by Gerhard Sauter, 111–35. Grand Rapids: Baker, 1996.

————. "The Concept and Task of Eschatology." In *Eschatological Rationality*, by Gerhard Sauter, 136–54. Grand Rapids: Baker, 1996.

————. "Was hat Johann Christoph Blumhardt der Kirche und Theologie heute zu sagen?" In *Johann Christoph Blumhardt, leuchtende Liebe zu den Menschen: Beiträge zu Leben und Werk*, edited by W. Günter and G Schäfer, 92. Stuttgart: Steinkopf, 1981.

————. "Why is Karl Barth's *Church Dogmatics* Not a 'Theology of Hope? Some Observations on Barth's Understanding of Eschatology." *SJT* 52 (1999) 407–29.

Schleiermacher, F. D. E. *Brief Outline of Theology as a Field of Study*. Translated by Terrence N. Tice. Lewiston: Mellen, 1988.

————. *On Religion: Speeches to its Cultured Despisers*. Translated by John Owen. New York: Harper Torchbooks, 1958.

————. *The Christian Faith*. Edited by H. R. Mackintosh and J. S. Stewart. Edinburgh: T&T Clark, 1956.

Schmid, Heinrich. *The Doctrinal Theology of the Evangelical Lutheran Church*. Translated by C. H. Hay and H. E. Jacobs. Philadelphia: United Lutheran, 1899.

Scholder, Klaus. *A Requiem for Hitler*. London: SCM, 1989.

————. *The Churches and the Third Reich: Volume One: 1918–1934*. Philadelphia: Fortress, 1988.

————. *The Churches and the Third Reich: Volume Two: The Year of Disillusionment: 1934, Barmen and Rome*. Philadelphia: Fortress, 1988.

Schorske, Carl E. *German Social Democracy, 1905–1917: The Development of the Great Schism*. Cambridge: Harvard University Press, 1955.

Schwarz, Hans. *Eschatology*. Grand Rapids: Eerdmans, 2000.

Schweitzer, Albert. *The Quest of the Historical Jesus: A Critical Study of Its Progress from Reimarus to Wrede*. New York: MacMillian, 1968. German, *Von Remarius zu Wrede*. Tübingen: J. C. B. Mohr, 1906.

Schwöbel, Christoph. "Theology." In *The Cambridge Companion to Karl Barth*, edited by John Webster, 17–36. Cambridge: Cambridge University Press, 2000.

Selinger, Suzanne. "Review of *Karl Barth: Against Hegemony*, by Timothy Gorringe." *Theology Today* 58, no. 1 (2001) 110–13.

Shanahan, William O. *German Protestants Face the Social Question*. Vol. 1, *The Conservative Phase 1815-1871*. Notre Dame: University of Notre Dame Press, 1954.

———. "Friedrich Naumann: A Mirror of Wilhelmian Germany." *The Review of Politics* 13, no. 3 (1951) 267-301.

Smart, James D. *The Divided Mind of Modern Theology: Karl Barth and Rudolf Bultmann, 1908-1933*. Philadelphia: Westminster, 1967.

———. "Eduard Thurneysen: Pastor-Theologian." *Theology Today* 16 (1959 74–89.

Spieckermann, Ingrid. *Gotteserkenntnis: Ein Beitrag zur Grundfrage der neuen Theologie Karl Barths*. München: Kaiser, 1985.

Stadtland, Tjarko. *Eschatologie und Geschichte in der Theologie des jungen Karl Barth*. Neukirchen-Vluyn: Neukirchener des Erziehungsvereins, 1966.

Stayer, James M. *Martin Luther, German Savior: German Evangelical Theological Factions and the Interpretation of Luther, 1917-1933*. Montreal & Kingston: McGill-Queen's University Press, 2000.

Stober, Martin. *Christoph Friedrich Blumhardt d.J. zwischen Pietismus und Sozialismus*. Giessen: Brunnen Giessen, 1998.

Stoeffler, Ernest F. *German Pietism During the Eighteenth Century*. Leiden: Brill, 1973.

———. *The Rise of Evangelical Pietism*. Leiden: E. J. Brill, 1965.

———. "Pietism: Its Message, Early Manifestation, and Significance." In *Contemporary Perspectives on Pietism: A Symposium*, edited by D. W. Dayton, 3-24. Chicago: Covenant, 1976, 3-24.

Sutherland, Arthur Marvin. "Christology and Discipleship in the Sermons of Karl Barth: 1913-1916." PhD diss., Princeton University, 2000.

Swedenborg, Emanuel. *The Four Leading Doctrines of the New Church, Signified by the New Jerusalem in the Revelation: Being Those Concerning the Lord, the Sacred Scripture, Faith, and Life*. New York: AMS, 1971.

Sykes, Stephen W., ed. *Karl Barth: Studies of His Theological Method*. Oxford: Oxford University Press, 1979.

Taylor, Anne. *Visions of Harmony: A Study in Nineteenth-Century Millenarianism*. Oxford: Oxford University Press, 1987.

Thorne, Phillip R. *Evangelicalism and Karl Barth: His reception and influence in North American Evangelical Theology*. Allison Park, PA: Pickwick, 1995.

Thurneysen, Eduard. *Christoph Blumhardt*. Munich: Kaiser, 1926.

———. "Hermann Kutter." *Zwischen den Zeiten* 1 (1923) 3-13.

———. "Zum religiös-sozialen Problem." *Zwischen den Zeiten* 5 (1927) 513-22.

Tillich, Paul. *A History of Christian Thought: From its Judaic and Hellenistic Origins to Existentialism*. Edited by C. Braaten. New York: Simon & Schuster, 1968.

———. *The Socialist Decision*. Translated by F. Sherman. New York: Harper & Row, 1977.

———. *Systematic Theology*. Vol. 2, *Existence and the Christ*. Chicago: University of Chicago Press, 1957.

Torrance, Thomas F. *Karl Barth: An Introduction to His Early Theology 1910-1931*. Edinburgh: T&T Clark, 2000.

———. *Karl Barth: Biblical and Evangelical Theologian*. Edinburgh: T&T Clark, 1990.

———. "Universalism or Election?" *Scottish Journal of Theology* 2 (1949) 310–18.

Troebst, Christian & Dieter Ising. *Christoph Blumhardt 1842–1919: Mahner zwischen den Fronten.* Weißerhorn: Anton H. Konrad, 1992.

Troeltsch, Ernst. "Eschatology." In *Religion in History*, by Ernst Troeltsch, 146–58. Edinburgh: T&T Clark, 1991.

———. "Historical and Dogmatic Method in Theology." In *Religion in History*, by Ernst Troeltsch, 11–32. Edinburgh: T&T Clark, 1991.

———. "Political Ethics and Christianity." In *Religion in History*, by Ernst Troeltsch, 173–209. Edinburgh: T&T Clark, 1991.

Van Asselt, Willem J. *The Federal Theology of Johannes Cocceius (1603–1669).* Translated by R. A. Blacketer. Leiden: Brill, 2001.

Victoria-Vangerud, Nancy. "The Counterpart of Others: Some Questions for Barth's Doctrine of Reconciliation." In *Karl Barth: A Future for Postmodern Theology?* edited by G. Thompson and C. Mostert, 171–90. Hindmarsh: Australian Theological Forum, 2000.

Villa-Vicencio, Charles. "Karl Barth's 'Revolution of God': Quietism or Anarchy?" In *On Reading Karl Barth in South Africa*, edited by Charles Villa-Vicencio, 45–58. Grand Rapids: Eerdmans, 1988.

Ward, Graham. *Barth, Derrida, and the Language of Theology.* Cambridge: Cambridge University Press, 1995.

Ward, W. R. *Christianity under the Ancien Régime, 1648–1789.* Cambridge: Cambridge University Press, 1999.

———. *The Protestant Evangelical Awakening.* Cambridge: Cambridge University Press, 1992.

———. *Theology, Sociology and Politics: The German Protestant Social Conscience, 1890– 1933.* Bern: Peter Lang, 1979.

Webb, Stephen H. *Re-figuring Theology: The Rhetoric of Karl Barth.* Albany: State University of New York Press, 1991.

Weborg, John C. "Eschatological Ethics of Johann Albrecht Bengel." *Covenant Quarterly* 36 (1978) 31–43.

Webster, John. *Barth's Ethics of Reconciliation.* Cambridge: Cambridge University Press, 1995.

———. "'Assured and Patient and Cheerful Expectation': Barth on Christian Hope as the Church's Task." In *Barth's Moral Theology*, by John Webster, 77–98. Grand Rapids: Eerdmans, 1998.

———. "'Eloquent and Radiant': The Prophetic Office of Christ and the Mission of the Church." In *Barth's Moral Theology*, by John Webster, 125–50. Grand Rapids: Eerdmans, 1998.

———. "The Grand Narrative of Jesus Christ: Barth's Christology." In *Karl Barth: A Future for Postmodern Theology?* edited by G. Thompson and C. Mostert, 29–48. Hindmarsh: Australian Theological Forum, 2000.

Weiss, Johannes. *Jesus' Proclamation of the Kingdom of God.* Translated by R. H. Hier and D. L. Holland. Philadelphia: Fortress, 1971. German, *Die Predigt Jesu vom Reiche Gottes.* Göttingen: Vandenhoeck & Ruprecht, 1892.

Werpehowski, William. "Karl Barth and Politics." In *The Cambridge Companion to Karl Barth*, edited by John Webster, 228–42. Cambridge: Cambridge University Press, 2000.

West, Philip. "Re-reading Schweitzer's *Quest*." In *The Kingdom of God and Human Society*. edited by R. S. Barbour, 164–72. Edinburgh: T&T Clark, 1993.

Willis, Robert E. *The Ethics of Karl Barth*. Leiden: Brill, 1979.

Willis, Wendell, ed. *The Kingdom of God in 20th Century Interpretation*. Peabody: Hendrickson, 1987.

Winzeler, Peter. *Widerstehende Theologie: Karl Barth 1920–1935*. Stuttgart: Alektor, 1982.

———. "Der Sozialismus Karl Barths in der neusten Kritik." *Evangelische Theologie* 48, no. 3 (1988) 262–72.

Yeide, Harry Jr. "A Vision of the Kingdom: The Social Ethic of Friedrich Christoph Oetinger." PhD diss., Harvard University, 1965.

———. *Studies in Classical Pietism: The Flowering of the* Ecclesiola. New York: Peter Lang, 1997.

Zahl, Simeon. "'… dieses Kreigsgeistes, dieses Satans': Christoph Blumhardt's Theological Critique of World War I War Enthusiasm." Unpublished Paper Presented to the Society for the Study of Theology, Cambridge University, 2007.

Zündel, Friedrich. *Johann Christoph Blumhardt, ein Lebensbild*. 4th ed. Zurich: S. Hohr, 1883.

———. *The Awakening: One Man's Battle with Darkness*. Farmington, PA: Plough, 1999.

Index